FALL 2001
Spring 2002

BLOND'S®
CONTRACTS

S&G

Sulzburger & Graham Publishing, Ltd.

New York

BLOND'S®
CONTRACTS

Fifth Edition

by
Neil C. Blond
Louis Petrillo

Fifth Edition
revised and edited
by
Kevin L. Kite
Adam Rappaport
Craig A. Sperling

How To Use This Book
"You teach yourself the law, we teach you how to think"
— Professor Kingsfield, The Paper Chase

Law school is very different from your previous educational experiences. In the past, course material was presented in a straightforward manner both in lectures and texts. You did well by memorizing and regurgitating. In law school, your fat casebooks are stuffed with material, most of which will be useless when finals arrive. Your professors ask a lot of questions but don't seem to be teaching you either the law or how to think. Sifting through voluminous material seeking out the important concepts is a hard, time-consuming chore. We've done that job for you. This book will help you study effectively. We hope to teach you the law and how to think.

Preparing for class
Most students start their first year by reading and briefing all their cases. They spend too much time copying unimportant details. After finals they realize they wasted time on facts that were useless on the exam.

Case Clips
Case Clips help you focus on what your professor wants you to get out of your cases. Facts, Issues, and Rules are carefully and succinctly stated. Left out are details irrelevant to what you need to learn from the case. In general, we skip procedural matters in lower courts. We don't care which party is the appellant or petitioner because the trivia is not relevant to the law. Case Clips should be read before you read the actual case. You will have a good idea what to look for in the case, and appreciate the significance of what you are reading. Inevitably you will not have time to read all your cases before class. Case Clips allow you to prepare for class in about five minutes. You will be able to follow the discussion and listen without fear of being called upon.

This book contains a case clip of every major case covered in your casebook. Each case clip is followed by a code identifying the casebook(s) in which it appears as a principal case. Since we accommodate all the major casebooks, the case clips may not follow the same sequence as they do in your text. The easiest way to study is to leaf through your text and find the corresponding case in this book by checking the table of cases.

"Should I read all the cases even if they aren't from my casebook?"

Yes, if you feel you have the time. Most major cases from other texts will be covered at least as a note case in your book. The principles of these cases are universal and the fact patterns should help your understanding. The Case Clips are written in a way that should provide a tremendous amount of understanding in a relatively short period of time.

Hanau Charts

When asked how he managed to graduate in the top ten percent of his class at one of the ten most prestigious law schools in the land, Paul Hanau introduced his system of flow charts now known as Hanau Charts.

A very common complaint among first year students is that they "can't put it all together." When you are reading 400 pages a week it is difficult to remember how the last case relates to the first and how November's readings relate to September's. It's hard to understand the relationship between different torts topics when you have read cases for three or four other classes in between. Hanau Charts will help you put the whole course together. They are designed to help you memorize fundamentals. They reinforce your learning by showing you the material from another perspective.

Outlines

More than one hundred lawyers and law students were interviewed as part of the development of this series. Most complained that their casebooks did not teach them the law and were far too voluminous to be useful before an exam. They also told us that the commercial outlines they purchased were excellent when used as hornbooks to explain the law, but were too wordy and redundant to be effective during the weeks before finals. Few students can read four 500-page outlines during the last month of classes. It is virtually impossible to memorize that much material and even harder to decide what is important. Almost every student interviewed said he or she studied from homemade outlines. We've written the outline you should use to study.

"But writing my own outline will be a learning experience."

True, but unfortunately many students spend so much time outlining they don't leave time to learn and memorize. Many students told us they spent six weeks outlining, and only one day studying before each final!

Mnemonics

Most law students spend too much time reading, and not enough time memorizing. Mnemonics are included to help you organize your essays and spot issues. They highlight what is important and which areas deserve your time.

Text Correlation

Blond's Contracts	DHH	KGK	FE	MS	CPB	KC	R
Chapter 2	1-212	1061-1328	192-325	1010-1278	588-687	334-519	891-1136
Chapter 3	213-327 569-583	418-551 705-752	2-189	97-251	146-277	202-334	135-228
Chapter 4	328-457	111-418	328-490	252-511	1-145	520-616	229-350
Chapter 5	457-510	821-860	491-627	747-803	757-801	48-83	413-584
Chapter 6	510-658	553-705 861-910	628-695	512-683 987-1009	313-378 802-846	11-48 83-201	585-728
Chapter 7	658-726	910-971	696-742	924-986	538-587	635-687	729-808
Chapter 8	727-876	973-1060	848-1027	804-923	379-537	617-635 743-779	809-890
Chapter 9	877-905	1329-1440	744-794	1279-1334	688-721	780-802	1197-1230
Chapter 10	921-956	1441-1559	795-846	1334-1390	722-756	802-827	1231-1260
Chapter 11	95-98	753-819	B1-B39	683-746	278-312	163-175 293-334	351-412

Abbreviations used in this book

S.Ct. - United States Supreme Court

DHH - Dawson, Harvey & Henderson, Contracts, Cases and Comment (Sixth Edition, 1993)

KGK - Kessler, Gilmore & Kronman, Cases and Materials (Third Edition, 1986)

FE - Fuller & Eisenberg, Basic Contract Law (Fifth Edition, 1990)

MS - Murphy & Speidel, Studies in Contract Law (Fourth Edition, 1991)

CPB - Calamari, Perillo & Bender, Cases and Problems on Contracts (Second Edition, 1989)

KC - Knapp & Crystal, Problems in Contract Law, Cases and Material (Third Edition, 1993)

R - Rosett, Contract Law and its Application (Fifth Edition, 1994)

TABLE OF CONTENTS

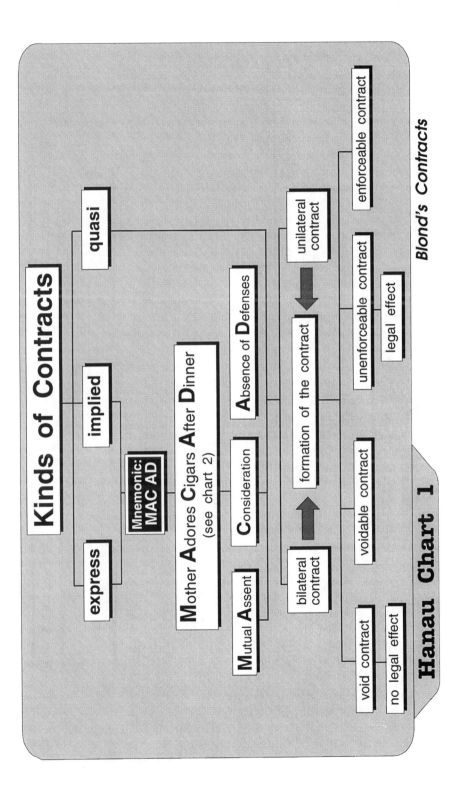

Kinds of Contracts

express   implied   quasi

Mnemonic: MAC AD

Mother **A**dores **C**igars **A**fter **D**inner
(see chart 2)

Mutual **A**ssent   **C**onsideration   **A**bsence of **D**efenses

bilateral contract → formation of the contract ← unilateral contract

void contract   voidable contract   unenforceable contract   enforceable contract

no legal effect   legal effect

Blond's Contracts

Hanau Chart 1

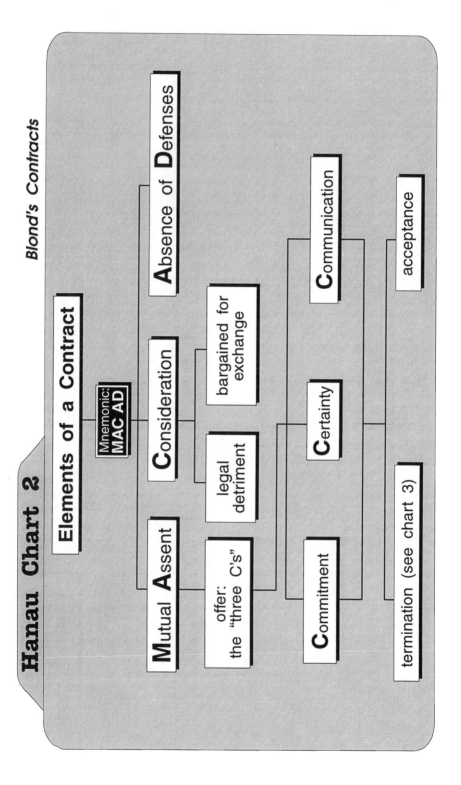

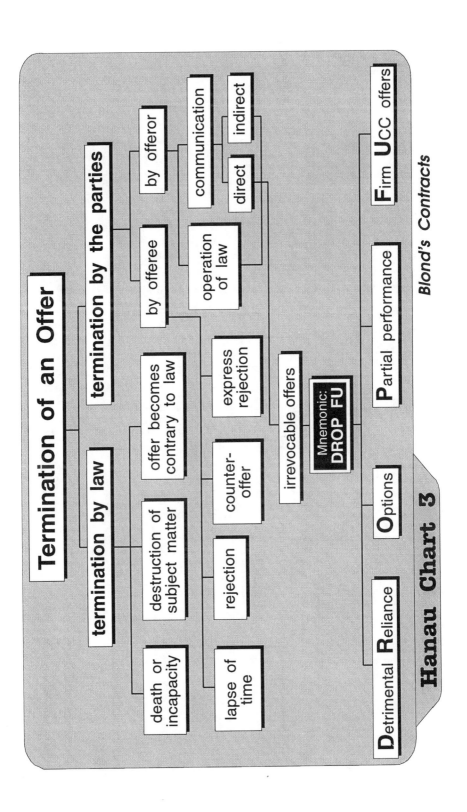

Termination of an Offer

termination by law
- death or incapacity
- destruction of subject matter
- offer becomes contrary to law

termination by the parties

by offeree
- rejection
  - lapse of time
  - counter-offer
  - express rejection

by offeror
- communication
  - direct
  - indirect
- operation of law

irrevocable offers

Mnemonic: **DROP FU**

- **D**etrimental Reliance
- **O**ptions
- **P**artial performance
- **F**irm UCC offers

Blond's Contracts

Hanau Chart 3

Statute of Frauds

Mnemonic:
MAD GLO

Marriage

Administrator or executor

Debt of another

sale of Goods > $500

interest in Land

performance >One year

elements of a written agreement

parties

terms

price

consideration

signature

satisfies statute

voided by the statute

remedies

unjust enrichment

promissory estoppel

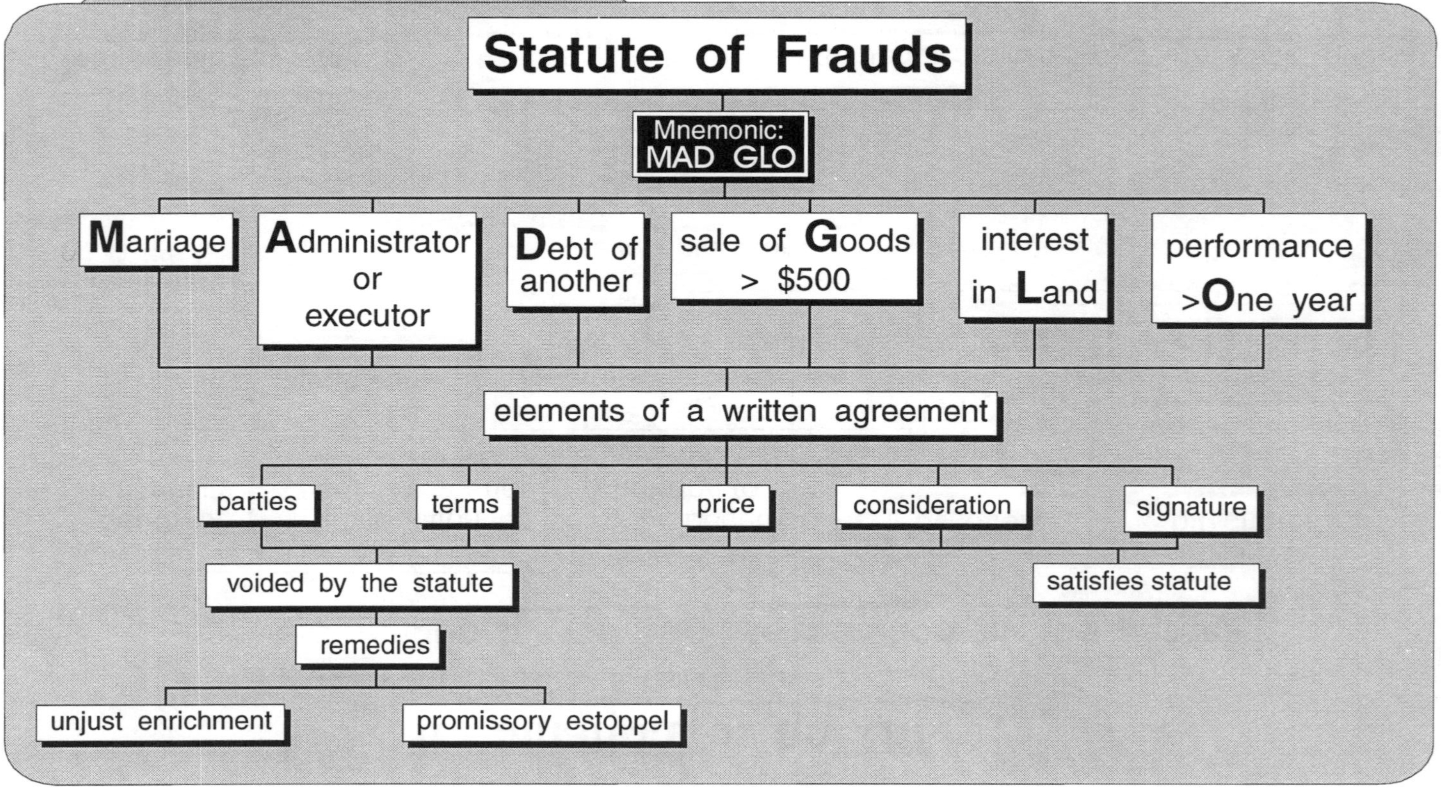

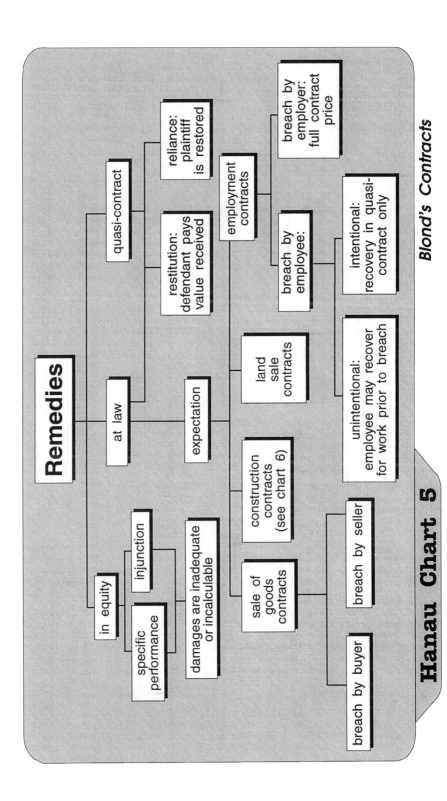

Remedies

in equity
- specific performance
- injunction
- damages are inadequate or incalculable

at law

expectation
- sale of goods contracts
  - breach by buyer
  - breach by seller
- construction contracts (see chart 6)
- land sale contracts
- employment contracts
  - breach by employee:
    - unintentional: employee may recover for work prior to breach
    - intentional: recovery in quasi-contract only
  - breach by employer: full contract price

restitution: defendant pays value received

quasi-contract
- reliance: plaintiff is restored

Blond's Contracts

Hanau Chart 5

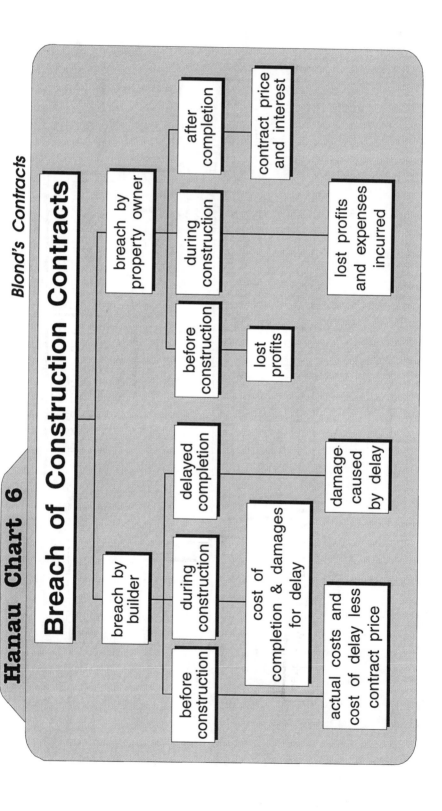

Breach of Construction Contracts

- **breach by builder**
  - before construction
    - during construction
      - cost of completion & damages for delay
        - actual costs and cost of delay less contract price
    - delayed completion
      - damage caused by delay
- **breach by property owner**
  - before construction
    - lost profits
  - during construction
    - lost profits and expenses incurred
  - after completion
    - contract price and interest

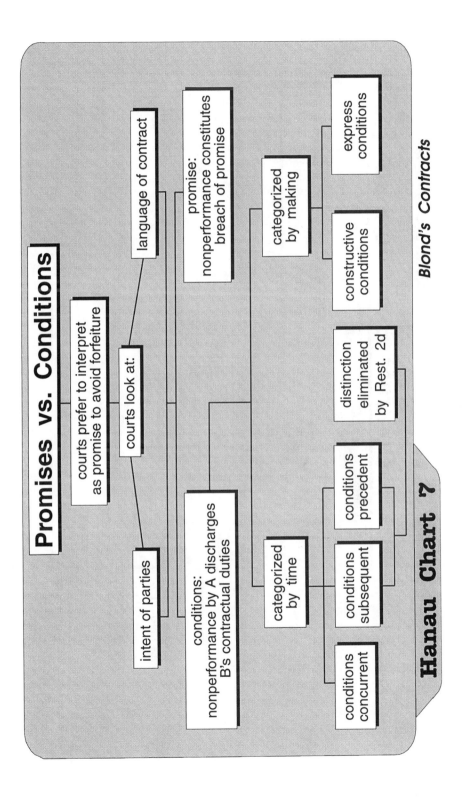

Promises vs. Conditions

courts prefer to interpret
as promise to avoid forfeiture

courts look at:

intent of parties

language of contract

conditions:
nonperformance by A discharges
B's contractual duties

promise:
nonperformance constitutes
breach of promise

categorized
by time

categorized
by making

conditions
concurrent

conditions
subsequent

conditions
precedent

distinction
eliminated
by Rest. 2d

constructive
conditions

express
conditions

Hanau Chart 7

Blond's Contracts

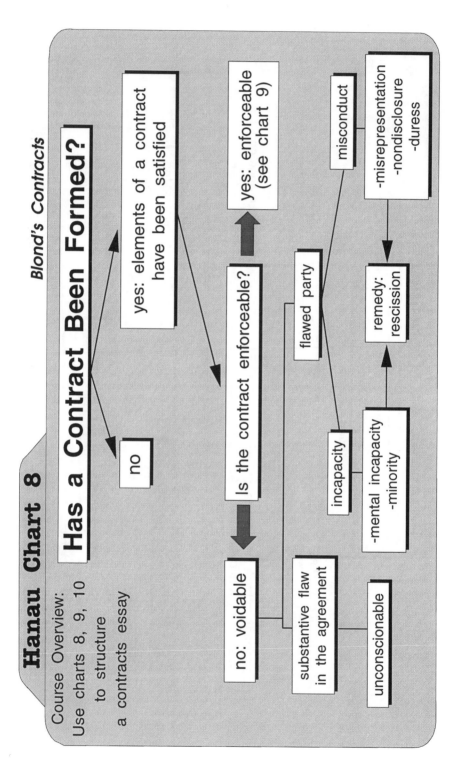

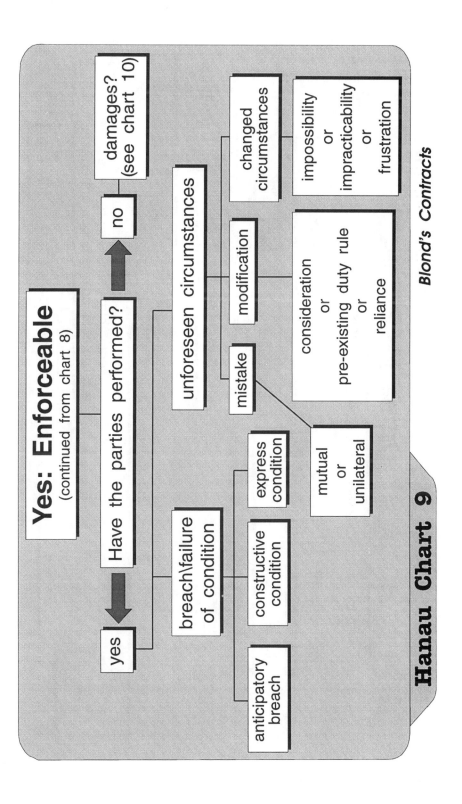

Hanau Chart 9

Blond's Contracts

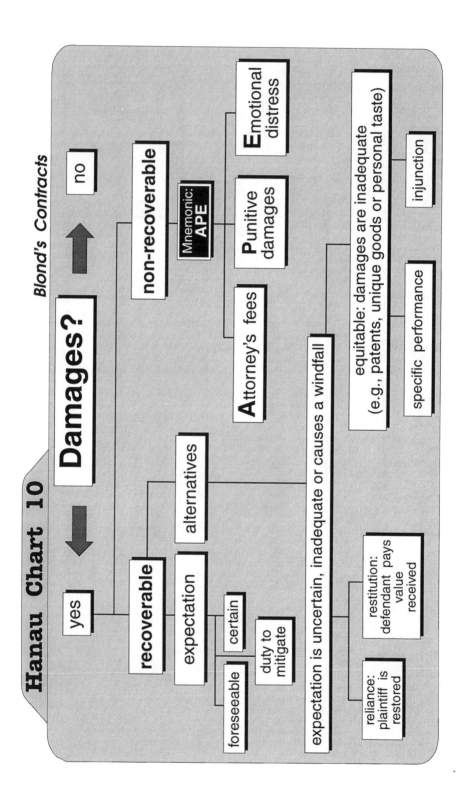

Blond's Contracts

Hanau Chart 10

Damages?

yes → **recoverable**

no → **non-recoverable**

Mnemonic: **APE**

non-recoverable (APE):
- **A**ttorney's fees
- **P**unitive damages
- **E**motional distress

recoverable:
- expectation
  - foreseeable
  - certain
  - duty to mitigate
- alternatives

expectation is uncertain, inadequate or causes a windfall
- reliance: plaintiff is restored
- restitution: defendant pays value received

equitable: damages are inadequate (e.g., patents, unique goods or personal taste)
- specific performance
- injunction

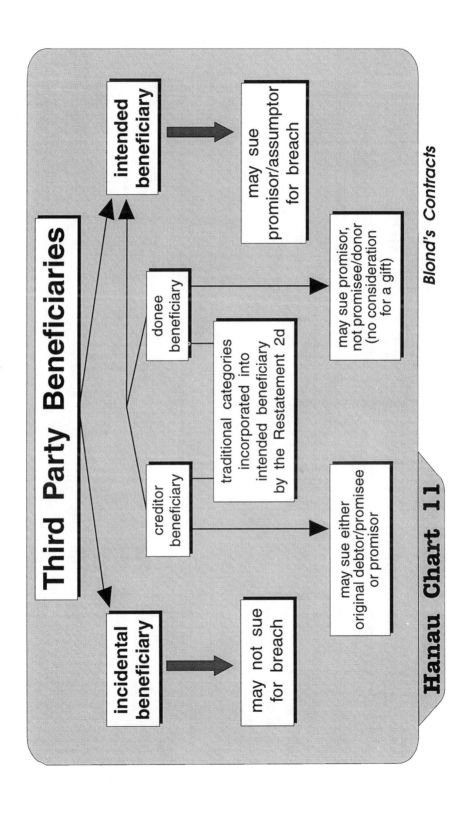

Third Party Beneficiaries

intended beneficiary

→ may sue promisor/assumptor for breach

donee beneficiary

→ may sue promisor, not promisee/donor (no consideration for a gift)

traditional categories incorporated into intended beneficiary by the Restatement 2d

creditor beneficiary

→ may sue either original debtor/promisee or promisor

incidental beneficiary

→ may not sue for breach

Blond's Contracts

Hanau Chart 11

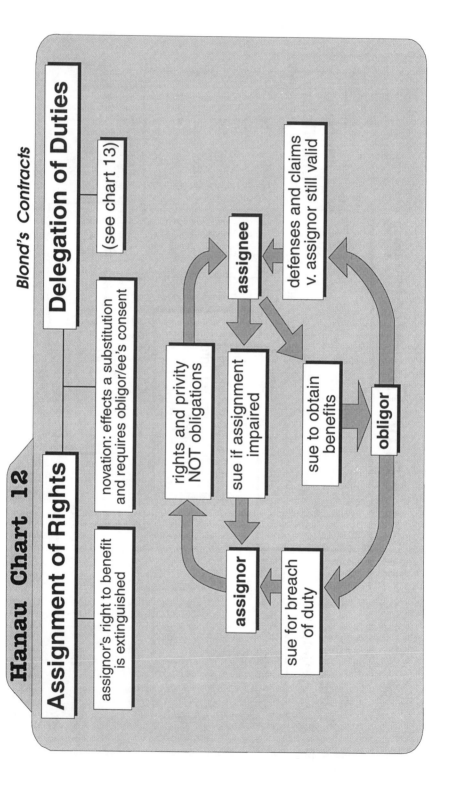

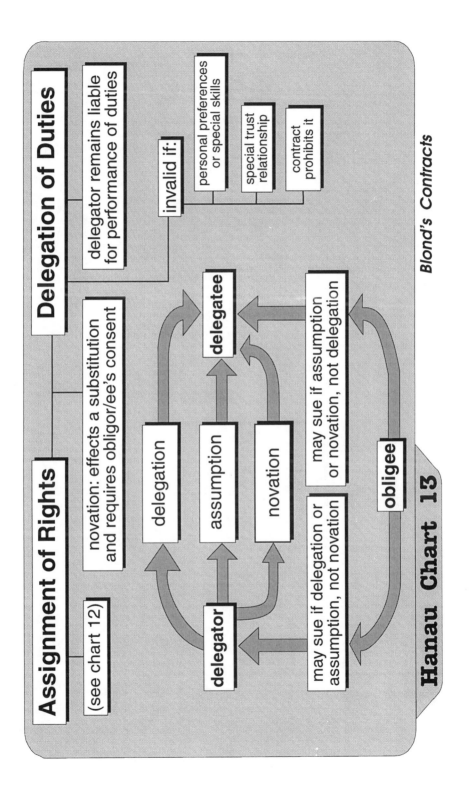

Assignment of Rights

(see chart 12)

Delegation of Duties

novation: effects a substitution and requires obligor/ee's consent

delegator remains liable for performance of duties

invalid if:

- personal preferences or special skills
- special trust relationship
- contract prohibits it

delegation

assumption

novation

delegatee

delegator

obligee

may sue if assumption or novation, not delegation

may sue if delegation or assumption, not novation

Hanau Chart 13

Blond's Contracts

Chapter 1

INTRODUCTION TO CONTRACTS

I.   CONTRACT DEFINED

There is no universally accepted definition of a contract, but in general a contract is a promissory agreement that is legally enforceable. However, some contracts are unenforceable or voidable under certain circumstances, and others can be formed without an actual agreement (e.g., quasi-contracts).

II.   KINDS OF CONTRACTS

A.   Express
An express contract is formed by written or oral language.

B.   Implied in Fact
An implied-in-fact contract is manifested by the actions of the parties, although it is not explicitly written or stated. Example: plunking down 50 cents at a newsstand and taking a paper.

C.   Implied in Law (quasi-contract)
A quasi-contract is a recovery or obligation that is not created by an actual agreement, but by the law for "reasons of justice." It is not an actual contract negotiated by the parties. Example: A plumber walks by a home and fixes a burst pipe that was flooding the basement while the homeowner was absent. The plumber may be able to recover in quasi-contract, notwithstanding the absence of an actual agreement with the owner to perform the service and receive compensation.

D.   Unilateral-Bilateral Distinction

     1. Bilateral Contract
         A bilateral contract is formed by mutual exchange of promises by the contracting parties. Example: A promises B that he will sell B ten baseball cards, and B promises to pay A one dollar.

     2. Unilateral Contract
         A unilateral contract is one in which a promise is made in

exchange for actual performance, as opposed to a promise to perform. Example: A promises to pay B $100 if B paints A's home. A has not asked B for a promise to paint, but rather to actually paint.

3. Distinction Between Unilateral and Bilateral Contracts
   The difference between unilateral and bilateral contracts is not as important today as in the past. However, one significant difference is the extent of the obligations they impose. Once parties exchange promises in bilateral contracts, they are obligated to perform their promises. In a unilateral contract, the nonpromising party is not obligated to perform and the promisor's obligation does not arise until the requested act is completed.

III.   VALIDITY OF CONTRACTS

A.   Enforceable
      An enforceable contract is a normal contract that has legal effect.

B.   Void
      A void contract has no legal effect. Example: a contract to commit crime.

C.   Voidable
      A voidable contract has legal effect unless one party (e.g., a minor) chooses to void it.

D.   Unenforceable
      An unenforceable contract is one that has some legal status but no conventional means for a party to assert his rights. Example: The statute of limitations precludes a party from bringing an action in court after a specified time period has elapsed. While corrective measures cannot make a void contract enforceable, an unenforceable contract can sometimes be validated by corrective action of the parties (e.g., memorializing an agreement in writing to satisfy the Statute of Frauds).

IV. SOURCES OF LAW

A. Common Law
Contract law has traditionally been governed by common law (case law), although many important areas have been superseded by statute in recent years.

B. Uniform Commercial Code
All states except Louisiana have largely adopted the provisions of the Uniform Commercial Code (UCC), which governs many aspects of various commercial transactions. Article 2, which governs sales, is the section of primary importance to basic contracts courses.

C. Restatements
A persuasive but not binding source of contract law is the Second Restatement of Contracts of 1980, which replaced the 1932 Restatement of Contracts. It is an annotated summary of common law by the American Law Institute. However, the law in a given jurisdiction is not necessarily that propounded by the Restatement.

Chapter 2

REMEDIES

Once a contract has been made, the parties are obligated to perform their duties under the contract. However one party may refuse to perform for some reason and will thus breach the contract. The nonbreaching party can sue to recover the damages it incurred. Relief is available at law and in equity in a variety of forms. (Note: A party can recover in restitution the value of benefits conferred where no valid contract exists between the parties.)

I.   EQUITABLE REMEDIES

Although the standard relief for breach of contract is monetary damages, they may be inappropriate in certain situations, such as where the amount of damages is too speculative, or the contract was for unique goods. In such cases, courts will grant primarily two forms of equitable relief: injunctions and specific performance. Originally, there were two court systems, law and equity. Today, the distinction has been abolished and all courts can grant either form of remedy. A primary consideration in granting equitable relief is the issue of justice and fairness (treated in more detail in Chapter 11).

A.   Specific Performance (Rest. 2d. § 359; UCC § 2-716)
Instead of giving monetary damages, a court can force the breaching party to perform as promised in the contract. Specific performance is usually granted where a contract involves a unique good, such as land. Before granting this remedy a court will consider several issues:

1. Indefiniteness (Rest. 2d. § 362)
The agreement between the parties must be sufficiently definite and certain to be specifically performed, all material terms included.

2. Extensive Supervision (Rest. 2d. § 366)
If specific performance of the agreement requires extensive supervision by the court to ensure that each party is fulfilling its duties properly, the court will avoid awarding this measure of

damages. Judicial time is scarce enough without such additional burdens. Building contracts generally involve much supervision.

3. Adequacy of Alternative Remedies (Rest. 2d. § 360)
   Specific performance is an attractive remedy if other remedies do not appear adequate. Relevant considerations include:

   a. The difficulty of proving monetary damages,

   b. The availability of satisfactory substitute goods, and

   c. The likelihood the plaintiff will be able to collect a monetary judgment from the defendant.

4. "Do equity to get equity" (Rest. 2d. § 364)
   A court may refuse to grant equitable relief if the party requesting such relief did not act fairly in forming the contract or if denial of equitable relief would cause great hardship to the breaching party.

5. Land
   Traditionally, courts have had a strong preference for requiring specific performance in land contracts because each parcel of land is unique.

6. Personal Service Contract (Rest. 2d. § 367)
   Contracts made for the personal services of a party are rarely specifically enforced because courts dislike the idea of forcing people to work in places not of their choosing. However, injunctions are used to prohibit the breaching employee from working for his employer's competitors for the duration of the contract.

B. Injunctions (Rest. 2d. § 361)
   As another alternative to monetary damages (and to specific performance), a court may prohibit the breaching party from rendering the contracted-for performance to anyone but the nonbreaching part. Courts will grant an injunction if:

   1. A noncompetition clause is in the contract.

2. The contract is for unique services.

The employer must prove that the employee's services or abilities are special or unique. This relates to the issue of availability of alternate remedies.

3. The employee's livelihood is not threatened.

A court will not grant an injunction if doing so would leave the employee with no other reasonable means of making a living.

II.   REMEDIES AT LAW

At law, the nonbreaching party is awarded monetary damages to compensate for the loss incurred. Courts seek to protect three interests when awarding monetary damages:
- Expectation
- Reliance
- Restitution

III.   EXPECTATION

Courts have a strong preference for awarding damages measured by the expected value of the promise/contract. The object is to put the party in the same position he would be in if the contract was performed as expected. This includes both the value of expenses incurred and expected profits.

A.   Computing the Value of Expectations (Rest. 2d. § 347)

Professor Farnsworth's formula for calculating expectation damages is

General damages = Loss in value + other loss - cost avoided - loss avoided

1. Loss in Value

a. The difference between the *value to the injured party* of the performance he should have received and that of any performance he did receive. Example: If the defendant paid the plaintiff $100 of a $1,000 debt, the loss in value is $900.

b. If defective service was rendered, then loss in value is value of flawless service less value of the defective service. This is a subjective standard (the value is the value to the plaintiff).

2. Other Loss
Other loss involves two types of damages, incidental and consequential.

   a. Incidental
Costs incurred in a reasonable attempt to avoid loss, even if unsuccessful.

   b. Consequential
Costs or injury to persons or property resulting from breach.

3. Cost Avoided
Savings to the plaintiff from not having to perform further.

4. Loss Avoided
Any loss avoided by the salvaging or reallocation of resources that would have been devoted to performance.

5. Example
A contracts to build B a home for $100,000, payable as work progresses. A's cost would be $60,000. A does half the work ($50,000 due) incurring $30,000 in expenses. B refuses to pay. A uses the unused lumber and materials, worth $10,000, on another job. A's loss in value is $100,000 (what is due to him overall less what he has actually received). He has incurred no other loss. By stopping work midway, A avoids spending an additional $30,000. Therefore, A's expectation damages award is $100,000 - 30,000 - 10,000 = $60,000.

B. Promised Performance (Nonmonetary) (Rest. 2d. § 348)
There is difficulty in measuring loss in value when the performance not rendered involves services, e.g., builder refuses to complete work, seller does not deliver goods, etc. In such cases, courts utilize one of two measures of damages:

1. Cost of Completing Performance
Damages are awarded in the amount it would cost plaintiff to properly complete the work that the breaching party began.

2. Diminution in Value/"Benefit of the Bargain"
Damages are calculated as the difference between the value of a complete performance and the value of defendant's defective performance.

a. This measure in damages is favored when the cost of completing performance is clearly disproportionate to the probable loss in value resulting from the incomplete or defective work. Example: A builds a pool but erroneously uses blue tile instead of green tile. The diminution in the pool's market value is $1, but the cost of properly completing the work is $1,000. It would be economically wasteful to force A to expend $1,000.

b. However, willful breach or public policy may induce a court to award cost of completion damages; such considerations may override economic waste. Example: A knows the pool was supposed to have green tile, but he installs blue tile anyhow because he has too much of it lying around. A may be required to remedy the defective performance or pay for someone else to do it.

C.   Specific Examples of Expectation Damages

1. Sale of Goods Contracts

a. Breach by Buyer (remedies of seller) (UCC § 2-703) Mnemonic: **ROW SCRAP**

i. **R**ecover **O**rdinary contract damages, i.e., contract price less market price plus incidental damages (without reselling the goods).

    ii.   **W**ithhold delivery of goods.

    iii.   **S**top delivery by bailee or carrier.

    iv.   **C**ancel entire contract.

    v.   **R**esell **A**ll goods and recover any loss from the contract price.

    vi.   Recover **P**rice of goods that were actually accepted by the buyer.

  b. Breach by Seller (remedies of buyer) (UCC § 2-711)
      Mnemonic: **MSG Causes Cancer**

    i.   Recover **M**onetary Damages (market price at breach less contract price plus incidental and consequential damages).

    ii.   Obtain **S**pecific performance.

    iii.   Recover contracted for **G**oods (if total or partial payment was made).

    iv.   **C**ancel the contract.

    v.   **C**over – buy substitute goods and recover the difference between the contract price and market price.

2. Sale of Land Contracts
   Damages are awarded based on the difference between the contract price and the fair market value of the real property at the time of breach.

3. Employment Contracts
   In equity, an injunction may be granted. At law:

  a. Employer Breaches
     Employee recovers full contract price for the remainder of the employment term.

b. Employee Breaches
Employer recovers cost of obtaining a substitute if it is above the contract price. Two types of breaches by employee:

    i. Intentional
Employee is barred from recovering expectation damages but may recover restitution in quantum meruit for substantial performance.

    ii. Unintentional
Employee is allowed to recover in quasi-contract the value of work done prior to unintentional breach.

4. Construction Contracts

    a. Breach by Builder

        i. Before Construction Commenced
Owner of the premises can recover excess cost of building above the contract price and the reasonable cost of delays.

        ii. During Construction
Cost of completion and reasonable damages for delay.

        iii. Late Performance
Subjects builder to liability for damages caused by delay.

        iv. A builder can recover in quasi-contract for the value of work done if the breach was unintentional.

    b. Breach by Property Owner

        i. Before Construction Began
Builder recovers lost profits.

        ii. During Construction
Builder recovers lost profits and expenses incurred.

iii. After Construction is Completed
Builder recovers contract price plus interest.

D. Limitations on Recovery of Expectation Damages

1. Foreseeability (Rest. 2d. § 351; UCC § 2-715)
Generally applies to consequential and incidental losses. The damages must be foreseeable to the breaching party at the time the contract was made, not at the time of breach. A loss is foreseeable if it naturally follows from the breach or if the breaching party had actual notice that such a loss would result from a breach. (See *Hadley v. Baxendale*.)

2. Certainty (Rest. 2d. § 352)
A party must establish with reasonable certainty the amount of its loss and the fact that it would have avoided the loss but for the breach. Some types of damages are generally considered to be uncertain, such as lost profits or lost publicity.

3. New-business Rule
Courts are not very receptive to claims for lost profits made by new businesses that have no prior history of profitability, but a court will consider such claims in light of the plaintiff's experience in the industry and the diligence of his efforts in running the business.

4. Mitigation (Rest. 2d. § 350)
The injured party is not compensated for damages resulting from a breach that the nonbreaching party could have reasonably avoided. Compensation will be granted if an unsuccessful, but reasonable, effort to avoid the loss was made.

a. Comparable Alternatives
If a comparable opportunity exists, the plaintiff must accept it and use it to mitigate damages caused by the defendant's breach. If the plaintiff fails to accept a comparable alternative, the court will not award him the damages that could have been avoided. Criteria for comparability includes location, type of services, hours of work, status, etc.

b. Incomparable Alternatives

The existence of incomparable alternatives will not reduce damages unless they are actually accepted by the plaintiff. Money earned at a new opportunity will be used to mitigate the damage award if the party in breach proves that the plaintiff would not have accepted this opportunity but for the breach. (This is more likely to occur if the contract was for the personal services of the plaintiff). However, if the plaintiff shows that he could have accepted both opportunities, there will be no reduction of damages.

c. The breaching party has the burden of proving that the plaintiff failed to mitigate and that a comparable opportunity existed.

d. UCC: If a seller breaches a sales contract, the buyer must try to "cover" by buying substitute goods. If the buyer breaches, the seller does not have a duty to mitigate. He may choose from a number of remedies.

IV.   RELIANCE

There are two types of reliance damages that a party can incur. The first type involves actions done in reliance upon a valid and binding contract that is subsequently breached. In either case, the goal of the court is to put the nonbreaching party in as favorable a position as he enjoyed prior to the contract. Reliance damages are usually awarded if expectation damages are too uncertain. The second type involves the doctrine of promissory estoppel and results when there is no valid contract, but a party detrimentally relied on another's promise, and it is unfair not to enforce the promise (Rest. 2d. § 90).

A. Requirements
    Mnemonic: **Robin hood Finds Danger Inviting**
    To recover for reliance a party must show:

    1. That there was actual **R**eliance on the contract or promise,

    2. That the reliance was **F**oreseeable to the breaching party,

    3. That it was clearly **D**etrimental, and

    4. That **I**njustice can only be avoided by enforcement.

B. Reliance upon a Contract (Rest. 2d. § 349)

    1. Types of Reliance Damages

        a. Expenses Incurred in Preparation of Performance
            These are not part of the contract but are necessary to perform
            it.

        b. Expenditures Made in Performance Prior to Breach

        c. Foregone Opportunities
            Sometimes a court will grant the value of wages a party would
            have received had he remained at a prior job and not entered
            into the contract.

    2. Limitations on reliance damages:

        a. Net Loss
            If full performance by the breaching party would have resulted
            in a net loss to the nonbreaching party, the amount of the loss
            is deducted from the reliance damages award.

        b. Foreseeability and Certainty
            Reliance damages must be foreseeable to the breaching party
            and must be proved with certainty.

c. Mitigation
The nonbreaching party has an obligation to mitigate his damages if possible.

d. Cost to Plaintiff
The amount of reliance damages is determined by the costs incurred, regardless of the value of the benefit the breaching party received.

e. Essential v. Incidental Reliance Damages
Under the classical view, reliance damages were limited to a maximum of the full contract price. In such cases, a party could recover only essential reliance damages, i.e., expenses made in preparation for or in actual performance of the contract. The modern view allows recovery beyond the contract price in cases where incidental reliance naturally and foreseeably follows from the contract. Incidental expenses are those made in reliance upon having a contract, although they are not actually incurred in preparation or performance of the contract. Example: A rents a store from B for $100 and buys inventory worth $500. B breaks the lease before A takes possession. A can recover (1) rent paid to date ($100) in performance of the contract and (2) unsold inventory purchased in reliance on the lease (incidental).

V.   RESTITUTION

A court may require the breaching party to disgorge the value of any benefits received from the nonbreaching party. Unlike reliance damages, restitution is based upon the value of the benefit to the defendant rather than the cost to plaintiff. Restitution is granted when expectation damages are uncertain and reliance damages do not properly reflect the value defendant has received. The main goal of such damages is to avoid unjust enrichment. (Rest. 2d. § 370.)

A.   Value of Benefit to Defendant (Rest. 2d. § 371)
The value of the benefit a party has received is measured in one of two ways:

1. The reasonable value of such a "benefit" as measured by the market value of obtaining it from another source (not the subjective value to the defendant).

2. The extent to which the party's property has increased in value or other interests have been advanced where the benefit is not readily obtainable from another source.

B.   Limits on Restitution

1. Restitution can exceed the contract price if defendant was actually "enriched" beyond that amount.

2. If plaintiff has completed performance, then expectation damages are given, and restitution is not available.

VI.   QUASI-CONTRACTS, AGREED REMEDIES AND NON-RECOVERABLE DAMAGES

A.   Recovery in Quasi-contract
Recovery in quasi-contract occurs in any one of three general situations: (1) if a contract never existed but justice requires that the plaintiff be compensated; (2) if there was an unenforceable contract (due to the Statute of Frauds, illegality, etc.); and (3) if the plaintiff has materially breached an existing, valid contract and has conferred a benefit on the other party. Courts generally award either restitution or reliance damages, depending on fairness and equity.

1. Requirements of Quasi-contract:

   a. One party provided a benefit to another.

   b. The benefit was provided with the "reasonable expectation" of compensation.

   c. There was an express or implied request for the benefit.

   d. Party receiving the benefit would be unjustly enriched if he was not forced to compensate the party providing the benefits.

2. The size of recovery in quasi-contract (also called *quantum meruit*) is determined by the degree of the plaintiff's detriment.

3. If a party willfully breaches a contract, it is less likely that a court will grant quasi-contractual recovery, although this restriction is somewhat eased in cases of employment contracts in which an employee intentionally breaches.

4. UCC § 2-718
   A breaching buyer may recover the value of payments made to the seller before the breach that exceed any liquidated damages clause or, if there is no such clause, the value of such payments in excess of 20 percent of the contract price or $500, whichever is less. The seller can offset such recovery by any damages suffered.

B.   Agreed Remedies/Liquidated Damages
In some cases, the parties have included a liquidated-damages clause in their contract. Such a clause provides a remedy, should either party breach the contract. Such agreements take the place of expectation, reliance, restitution, and quasi-contractual remedies.

1. Enforceable if:

   a. Actual damages caused by the breach were difficult to ascertain at the time the contract was executed, and the remedy clause represents a good faith attempt by the parties to provide for the case of breach.

   b. The amount of stipulated or liquidated damages is reasonable as judged either at the time the contract was made or in light of the actual damages incurred (Rest. 2d. § 356; UCC § 2-718). A reasonable clause at the time of contracting is valid even if actual damages turn out to be lower than expected. Some courts will enforce a reasonable clause even if no actual damages occur. Other courts and the Restatement take the opposite view.

2. Unenforceable

   a. Penalties
      Courts are adamantly opposed to any liquidated-damages clauses that are made to penalize a party for not performing. Such clauses typically compensate the nonbreaching party far in excess of any actual damages suffered. However, if a liquidated remedy clause is reasonable, courts will generally not examine the intent of the parties.

   b. Disclaimers
      Clauses limiting a party's liability will not be enforced if the amount of liability allowed is unreasonably small given the foreseeable consequences of a breach.

C.   Nonrecoverable Damages
Certain types of damages are generally nonrecoverable:
Mnemonic: **APE**

1. **A**ttorney's Fees
   Under the American rule, the value of attorney's fees expended as a result of the breach are generally not recoverable. There are a few exceptions:

   a. In certain situations involving class actions.

   b. "Private Attorney General Theory"
      Litigation that involves important public policies.

   c. Abusive Litigation Practices
      If either party maintained an "unfounded claim or defense in bad faith, or for oppressive reasons."

   d. Statutory Exception

2. **P**unitive Damages (Rest. 2d § 355)
   Generally, damages serve a compensatory purpose only. Punitive damages are awarded only in certain situations:

   a. The breaching party acted in a way that is a tort (i.e., gross negligence) for which punitive damages are available.

   b. An insurance company refuses to give any reason for not honoring an insurance claim (bad-faith breach).

   c. Breach of fiduciary duty.

   d. Fraudulent conduct.

3. Emotional Distress (Rest. 2d. § 353)
   Recovery for emotional distress is denied unless the breach causes serious bodily harm or if serious emotional disturbance is a particularly likely result of breaching such a contract. Contracts where emotional distress will be compensated in case of breach include:

   a. Breach of contract to marry.

   b. Loss of cherished object. Example: A film developer loses the plaintiff's film covering his life over many years.

   c. Failure to properly transmit a message concerned with death or illness.

4. Nominal Damages (Rest. 2d. § 346)
   When a contract is breached, but the plaintiff has not suffered actual damages, a court may grant nominal damages.

CASE CLIPS

Hawkins v. McGee (1929) DHH, FE
Facts: A surgeon guaranteed that the plaintiff's hand operation would be 100 percent successful. The plaintiff sued for breach of warranty when the operation was not successful.
Issue: How are damages calculated in a case of breach of contract?

Rule: The measure of damages in a breach of contract case is the difference between the plaintiff's actual position and the position he would have been in had the contract not been breached.

Groves v. John Wunder Co. (1939) DHH

Facts: John Wunder's contract to lease Groves' land permitted the removal of sand and gravel and required that the property be restored to a level grade. Wunder deliberately did not restore the land's grade.

Issue: How are damages assessed when a party's willful breach of contract damaged another's land, but the cost of completion is greater than the value of the land?

Rule: One who wrongfully and willfully breaches a construction contract is liable for the reasonable cost of completing the required work, rather than the value that completion would add to the land (as held in the lower court).

Acme Mills & Elevator Co. v. Johnson (1911) DHH, KGK

Facts: Johnson breached a contract by failing to deliver wheat to Acme Mills. Market prices for wheat were lower than the contractual price at the time of the breach.

Issue: What is the measure of damages to the buyer from a breach of a sales contract?

Rule: A buyer can recover the difference between the contract and market prices at the time the breach occurs.

Note: In this case, no damages were actually suffered as the market price was lower than the contract price.

Louise Caroline Nursing Home, Inc. v. Dix Constr. Co. DHH (1972) KGK, FE

Facts: Dix failed to complete construction of a nursing home within the agreed upon time.

Issue: What is the measure of damages against a builder who fails to complete construction?

Rule: Damages awarded for failure to complete a construction contract are based on the reasonable cost to complete the contract and repair any defective performance less the unpaid part of the contract price.

Rockingham County v. Luten Bridge Co.
(1929) DHH, FE, KC, R

Facts: Luten was in the process of building a bridge for Rockingham when it was told to cease construction because of public opposition to the bridge. Luten completed the bridge and sued for the entire contract price.

Issue: Once notified of repudiation, is the nonbreaching party required to cease performance?

Rule: Once a party is notified of repudiation of or refusal to perform a contract, that party may not continue to perform and recover damages based on full performance.

Parker v. Twentieth Century-Fox Film Corp.
(1970) DHH, FE, R

Facts: Shirley MacLaine contracted to star in a musical for Twentieth Century-Fox. Twentieth Century-Fox later canceled the movie and offered MacLaine a starring part in a western for the same amount of money, which she refused.

Issue: Must a party mitigate damages by accepting alternate employment?

Rule: A wrongfully discharged employee is entitled to recover the agreed upon compensation less any amount the employer proves the employee has earned or with reasonable effort might have earned from other employment. The employer must show that the other employment was comparable, or substantially similar, to that of which the employee has been deprived.

Note: A female lead in a western drama filmed in Australia is not comparable to a female lead in a song-and-dance production filmed in Los Angeles.

Missouri Furnace Co. v. Cochran (1881) DHH, KGK

Facts: Missouri Furnace contracted to buy coke (coal) from Cochran at $1.20 per ton. After delivering about one-tenth of the agreed upon quantity, Cochran breached the contract. Missouri was forced to "cover" by buying coke elsewhere for $4.00 per ton, which was higher than the market price.

Issue: What is the measure of the buyer's damages when the seller breaches a sales contract?

Rule: When a contract for the sale of chattels is breached by a vendor failing to deliver, the measure of damages is the difference between the contract price and the market value of the article at the time it should have been delivered, regardless of the actual costs to "cover."

Note: This case was decided prior to and differs from UCC § 2-712.

Neri v. Retail Marine Corp. (1972) DHH, KGK, FE, CPB, R
Facts: Neri wrongfully repudiated a contract to buy a boat. Retail Marine sold the boat to a third party at the same price, but refused to return Neri's deposit. Retail Marine claimed damages for the lost profits.
Issue: Can a seller recover lost profits from a breaching buyer if he later sells the item at the same price?
Rule: A seller can recover lost profits from a breaching buyer even though the item was later sold at the same price because the seller could have sold two of the items but for the breach. (UCC § 2-708(2).)

Hadley v. Baxendale (1854) DHH, KGK, FE, KC, MS, CPB R
Facts: A mill operator, forced to shut down after a shaft broke, hired a common carrier to deliver the broken shaft to an engineer for repairs. The carrier negligently delayed delivering the shaft, forcing the mill to shut down longer than expected.
Issue: Is a party liable for all consequences resulting from breach of contract?
Rule: The amount of damages that is awarded for a breach is limited to those which were fairly and reasonably contemplated by the parties at the time of contracting. Special circumstances must be communicated by the plaintiff to the defendant beforehand.
Note: This landmark case is accepted by all courts and jurisdictions. Although the case mentions that the carrier was notified that the mill was shut down, this fact seems to have been ignored by the court.

Valentine v. Gen. American Credit, Inc. (1984) DHH, FE
Facts: Valentine sued to recover for the mental distress she suffered as a result of being wrongfully fired by the defendant.
Issue: Is a wrongfully discharged employee entitled to damages for mental distress?
Rule: Mental distress damages are not recoverable for breach of an employment contract even if the distress was foreseeable.

Freund v. Washington Square Press (1974) DHH, KGK, FE, R
Facts: Washington Square Press breached its contract to publish Freund's manuscript. Freund sued for damages claiming lost royalties, a delay in his academic promotion and the costs to find a new publisher.
Issue: Are uncertain damages recoverable?

Rule: The law compensates an injured party only for injuries that were foreseeable consequences of a breach and that can be measured with a reasonable degree of certainty. Further, damages are not measured by what the defaulting party saved (e.g., publishing costs) but rather by what the nonbreaching party expected to receive (e.g., lost profits, royalties).

Note: In this case only nominal damage will be awarded because Freund failed to prove the amount of lost royalties with adequate certainty. The "cost to complete" is sometimes awarded in construction contracts.

Chicago Coliseum Club v. Dempsey (1932) DHH

Facts: Dempsey, a world champion boxer, contracted to fight in Chicago Coliseum. As part of the contract, the Coliseum was obligated to spend a lot of money to promote the fight. Dempsey repudiated the contract a month before the fight.

Issue: How are damages calculated for the breach of a performance contract?

Rule: When a performance contract is breached, lost anticipated profits are only recoverable if they can be proved with certainty, which is not the case where profits would be affected by multiple factors (i.e., weather, reputation of fighters, promotion, etc.). Attorney's fees and other costs incurred in negotiating and preparing the contract are also not recoverable. However, expenses made in preparation for performance are recoverable.

Boone v. Coe (1913) DHH

Facts: Coe agreed to provide a dwelling for the plaintiffs on the condition that the plaintiffs would move from Kentucky to Texas and cultivate his farm for one year. The agreement violated the Statute of Frauds because it could not be performed within one year from the date of its inception. The plaintiffs sued to recover their traveling expenses.

Issue: Can a party recover the value of expenses incurred in reliance on a contract that is unenforceable under the Statute of Frauds?

Rule: Damages may not be awarded for breach of a contract that is unenforceable under the Statute of Frauds.

Note: Today, such reliance damages would probably be awarded to avoid injustice.

United States ex rel. Coastal Steel Erectors v. Algernon Blair, Inc. (1973) DHH, FE, KC

Facts: After Blair breached by its failure to pay for part of Coastal Steel's (suing under the name of the US) operating costs, Coastal ceased work and sought restitution for the work performed. Coastal would have lost money if the contract was fully performed.

Issue: Is a party who justifiably stops work under a contract entitled to restitution for work done, if it would have lost money had the contract not been breached?

Rule: A party can recover in *quantum meruit* (what is deserved) for the value of labor and equipment furnished pursuant to a contract that it justifiably breached, irrespective of whether it would have lost money.

Note: A party suffering a loss under a contract will not recover damages in a suit on the contract, but may always forego a suit on the contract and claim only the reasonable value of the performance rendered.

Britton v. Turner (1834) DHH, R

Facts: The plaintiff contracted to be employed by the defendant for one year. He was supposed to be paid at the end of the year, but he quit during the tenth month, and the defendant refused to pay him at all.

Issue: Can an employee who breaches an employment contract before its term is over recover the value of work actually done?

Rule: An employee can recover a pro rata share of his compensation under the theory of *quantum meruit* if he breaches an employment contract that he partially performed.

Pinches v. Swedish Evangelical Lutheran Church (1987) DHH

Facts: Pinches inadvertently deviated from the plans for the defendant's church by building the ceiling two feet lower and the windows shorter and narrower and by making other omissions. Even though the defendant objected to the defects, the church was reasonably adapted to the defendant's needs, and the costs of correcting the problems was prohibitively high. The defendant withheld payment.

Issue: Is a party relieved of all payments if a builder breaches a construction contract?

Rule: A party must pay the contract price less an amount for the diminution in value of the building if the builder inadvertently deviates from plans, and the structure is still reasonably fit for its intended purpose.

Vines v. Orchard Hills, Inc. (1980) DHH

Facts: The defendant kept the Vines' down payment as liquidated damages for repudiation of a contract to purchase a condominium, as provided in the contract. The value of the property appreciated later.

Issue: Is a liquidated damages clause in a land-sale contract enforceable, even if no actual damages were incurred because the value of the property later appreciated?

Rule: A breaching buyer in a land-sale contract can recover his down payment on the theory that the seller has been unjustly enriched, if he can prove that the seller was not financially damaged by the breach.

Barrett Builders v. Miller (1990) DHH

Facts: Barrett, a contractor, entered into a written contract with Miller for assorted home construction work. Barrett failed to provide Miller with a written contract containing the entire agreement, as required by the Home Improvement Act. Miller stopped payment on an installment of the contract price due to dissatisfaction with the quality of work, and Barrett sued for the work already completed.

Issue: May a contractor recover in quasi-contract for damages arising from a contract that does not comply with the Home Improvement Act?

Rule: Failure to comply with the Home Improvement Act serves as a complete bar to recovery by a contractor, on or off the contract. In the absence of such a rule, a contractor could unilaterally expand a project without consent, and recover for the unwanted work.

City of Rye v. Public Service Mutual Ins. Co. (1974) DHH

Facts: Defendant developers contracted with the City of Rye to construct twelve apartment buildings. After six of the buildings were completed, the developers were required to post a bond with the city in the amount of $100,000, to ensure the completion of the remaining buildings. The developers further agreed to pay $200 for each day the buildings remained incomplete beyond the contract date, up to the amount of the bond. The buildings had still not been completed more than 500 days after the contract date had passed, and the City sued to recover the entire amount of the bond as damages.

Issue: May a court refuse to enforce a liquidated damages clause that bears no reasonable relationship to anticipated probable damages?

Rule: A provision fixing damages in advance will not be upheld if the amount fixed is grossly disproportionate to the anticipated probable harm.

This type of clause will be considered a penalty or forfeiture, and is unenforceable without statutory authority.

Wilt v. Waterfield (1954) DHH

Facts: The defendant contracted to sell his farm to the plaintiff but breached the contract by selling the farm to a third party. A liquidated damages clause provided that 10 percent of the purchase price ($1,900) would be paid in case of breach. The plaintiff proved damages of $7,000.

Issue: Is a liquidated damages clause invalid if it was arbitrary?

Rule: A liquidated damages clause is unenforceable as a penalty if it is arbitrarily made. The reasoning behind this rule is that a liquidated damages clause must be a reasonable forecast of likely damages.

Fretwell v. Protection Alarm Co. (1988) DHH

Facts: Defendant installed a burglary alarm system in the plaintiff's residence. The residence was burglarized of property totaling $91,379.93. The contract between the parties limited the liability of the defendant to $50, and indemnified the defendant from any claims arising against it by third parties.

Issue 1: May a court enforce a contractual clause which sets forth a limitation on liability for damages?

Rule 1: An agreement limiting the amount of damages recoverable for breach is not an agreement to pay either liquidated damages or a penalty, as long as it does not purport to make an estimate of possible harms caused by breach, or operate to induce performance through fear. Accordingly, a damage limitation clause is enforceable in a majority of jurisdictions.

Issue 2: May a court enforce a contractual clause which serves to indemnify one party against all future claims, and relieve it from liability for future acts.

Rule 2: A promise of indemnity for the performance of an act is valid, as long as the act is not illegal, immoral, or against public policy, and the intention to indemnify is clearly provided for in the contract.

Van Wagner Advertising Corp. v. S & M Enterprises (1986) DHH

Facts: Plaintiff rented space on a wall of a building in Manhattan from Michaels for the purpose of erecting a billboard. Plaintiff erected a billboard and subleased it to a third party. Michaels later sold the building to the defendant, S & M. Defendant breached the contract by canceling the lease.

Issue: Should a court award specific performance for breach of a real property lease, when the property is considered unique?

Rule: Specific performance of a contract to lease real property is unavailable when damages are an adequate remedy to compensate the tenant, and equitable relief would impose a disproportionate burden on the landlord. The fact that a given property is unique does not entitle a party to specific performance, unless the value of the property cannot be calculated with reasonable certainty.

Timko v. Useful Homes (1933) DHH

Facts: Timko paid in installments for two building lots. When the agreed upon amount had been paid, she demanded and was denied the deeds which had been fraudulently sold to another purchaser. When Timko sued, she demanded the money received from the second purchaser rather than the deed itself.

Issue: May a defrauded purchaser of land recover the amount for which the land was resold, or may she only recover the deed in question?

Rule: A defrauded purchaser may recover either the amount for which the land was resold or the deed itself. Where misconduct was not involved (e.g., an inadvertent resale of the land), the purchaser would recover the deed.

Fitzpatrick v. Michael (1939) DHH

Facts: Michael promised to give Fitzpatrick, a nurse, a salary, room, board and a significant part of his estate if she cared for him until his death. Michael fired Fitzpatrick without cause after she worked for a year.

Issue: Is specific performance of an employment contract allowed?

Rule: Specific performance of a personal services contract is generally denied, because it would require excessive and burdensome supervision by the court.

American Broadcasting Co., Inc. v. Wolf (1981) DHH, KC, MS, R

Facts: Warner Wolf, a sportscaster, breached his contract with ABC by negotiating with another network (CBS) during the 90-day period of contract negotiations and did not honor the right of first refusal clause in the existing contract.

Issue: What form of equitable relief is available for the breach of an employment contract, if specific performance is denied?

Rule: An injunction prohibiting the employee from working for his employer's competitor will be granted against a breaching employee for the duration of the original contract term. Where that term has expired, such an injunction will only be granted if there is an express agreement or if necessary to avoid unfair competition, e.g., if employee threatens to reveal trade secrets.

Northern Delaware Indus. Dev. Co. v. E.W. Bliss Co. (1986) DHH, R

Facts: A clause in Bliss' contract to refurbish Northern Delaware's steel plant provided that Bliss should hire additional workers on night shift during certain parts of the work. Northern Delaware sought enforcement of the clause after Bliss fell behind schedule.

Issue: Will a court grant specific performance of a complicated construction contract?

Rule: Specific enforcement of large and complicated construction contracts is generally denied on the grounds that it would be impracticable to effectively enforce such an order.

Congregation Kadimah Toras-Moshe v. DeLeo (1989) DHH

Facts: DeLeo, on several occasions, orally promised to give the Congregation a $25,000 gift. The Congregation unilaterally made plans to use the money for a library named after DeLeo, and included the money in its budget. The oral promise was never reduced to writing, and DeLeo died intestate. DeLeo's estate refused to honor the promise.

Issue: Should a court enforce oral gratuitous promises?

Rule: An oral gratuitous pledge which is devoid of consideration or reliance will not be upheld. There can no consideration where there is no legal benefit to the promisor, nor detriment to the promisee. Budgeting with the expectation of a gift does not amount to reliance for the purposes of enforcing an oral promise.

Note: The court did not decide whether it would enforce an oral gratuitous promise where there was consideration or reliance. A written gratuitous promise (charitable subscription) is enforceable without consideration in a majority of jurisdictions.

Lumley v. Wagner (1852) KGK

Facts: Wagner, an opera singer, breached an exclusive employment contract with Lumley and performed at a competing theater.

Issue: Can a court order specific performance of an employment contract, thereby forcing a breaching employee to provide the services in question?

Rule: Courts will rarely order specific performance of a personal services contract. However, they will issue an injunction preventing the breaching employee from performing for a competitor.

Stokes v. Moore (1955) KGK

Facts: Stokes' contract to be a manager of Moore's loan company provided that liquidated damages would be paid for any contractual violation and that Stokes would not compete with Moore in the same city for one year if he quit. Stokes quit and opened a rival company; Moore sued for an injunction.

Issue: Will an injunction be granted to enforce a covenant not to compete, despite the presence of a liquidated damages clause?

Rule: A covenant not to compete, sustained by adequate consideration, is valid if it is reasonably limited in time and geography. Such a covenant will be enforced by an injunction if legal remedies are inadequate because of uncertainty as to the extent of monetary damages caused by the breach. A liquidated damages clause will not prevent the granting of an injunction against a solvent party if it is clear that liquidated damages were not intended to be the exclusive remedy for breach.

Campbell Soup Co. v. Wentz (1948) KGK, MS

Facts: Campbell always used Chantenay red cored carrots in its soups because of their distinctive coloring and appearance. Wentz, a farmer, breached his contract to sell the carrots to Campbell at $30 per ton when their market price rose to $90 per ton. The contract strictly regulated delivery of carrots, allowed liquidated damages for Campbell only, and prohibited Wentz from selling carrots that were not accepted without Campbell's permission. Campbell sued in equity for specific performance because the carrots were virtually impossible to obtain elsewhere.

Issue: When are sales contracts specifically enforced?

Rule: Specific performance of a sales contract is allowed when it can be done without extensive supervision by the court, and monetary damages are inadequate because of the unavailability of substitute goods. If the bargain is too hard and one-sided, however, equitable relief is denied.

Note: "To get equity, you must do equity." The carrots were considered "unique" goods because the plaintiff's commercial reputation was affected by uniformity in the appearance of its soups, but the relief was denied due to the one-sided nature of the bargain.

Jacob & Youngs v. Kent (1921)
KGK, KC, MS, FE, CPB

Facts: Jacob & Youngs, a contractor hired to build a home for Kent, inadvertently installed a different brand of pipes than that specified in the contract. The pipes used were of comparable price and quality to those specified, but Kent refused to pay Jacob & Youngs unless the pipes were replaced.

Issue: What is the measure of damages against a party who inadvertently breaches a contract in a nonmaterial manner?

Rule: When a party inadvertently breaches a contract in a nonmaterial manner, the measure of damages will be the difference in value between the specified and the actual performances, rather than the cost to correct.

Peevyhouse v. Garland Coal & Mining Co.
(1962) KGK, FE

Facts: Garland's lease of the Peevyhouse's farm for strip-mining operations obligated Garland to restore the land to its previous condition. Garland refused to restore the land. Although restoration would cost $29,000, the actual value of the land would only rise by $300 after such work.

Issue: Is "cost of completion" or "diminution in value" used to measure damages for breach of a construction obligation in a contract?

Rule: The measure of damages for breach of a construction obligation is ordinarily the reasonable cost of completing the work properly, unless the obligation is only incidental to the main purpose of the contract, and the cost of performing is grossly disproportionate to any economic benefit it will yield. In the latter case, damages are limited to the diminution in value of the property as a result of the breach in order to avoid "unreasonable economic waste."

Gainsford v. Carroll (1828) KGK

Facts: This case involved the breach of three contracts for the sale of bacon.

Issue: In calculating damages for a breach by a seller should the court use the market price on the day delivery was to be made or the day judgment was entered against the seller?

Rule: When a seller breaches, damages should be calculated based on the difference between the contract price and the market price on the date of the agreed upon delivery.

Panhandle Agri-Service Inc. v. Becker (1982) KGK

Facts: Becker breached a contract to sell hay in Kansas for $45 per ton. Panhandle had contracted to resell the hay in Texas for $67 per ton. The market price at the time of breach was $62 per ton, and shipping costs to Texas would have been $7,371.

Issue: What is the ordinary measure of damages when the seller breaches a sales contract?

Rule: Under UCC § 2-713, a buyer is entitled to the difference between the market price at the time of breach ($62 per ton) and the contract price ($45 per ton) plus incidental and consequential damages, less expenses saved by the breach. Transportation costs are not deductible, because it is assumed the buyer will "cover" at the seller's shipping point. Lost profits are only recoverable if "cover" was attempted.

Globe Ref. Co. v. Landa Cotton Oil Co. (1903) KGK, R

Facts: Landa breached a contract to sell and deliver crude oil to Globe. Globe sued to recover the difference between the contract and market prices at the time of breach, the cost of sending tankers to pick up the oil, and damages for failure to supply its customers with oil. The contract stated that Globe's tankers would go to Landa's mill.

Issue: Is a party liable for all consequences of a breach of which it has knowledge?

Rule: Knowledge of possible special damages is not enough to invoke liability against a party, unless it is shown that the party reasonably believed the special condition was part of the contract.

Kerr S.S. Co., Inc. v. Radio Corp. of America (1927) KGK

Facts: Kerr gave Radio Corp. a telegram involving freight instructions to transmit to Manila. The cable was never sent, causing Kerr to lose freight.

Issue: Is one liable for damages beyond the price of providing the service, if its negligent performance of the service leads to unforeseeable losses?

Rule: A party is not liable for damages caused by its negligence if it had no reason to know the extent of the harm that would result.

The Heron II (Kaufos v. C. Czarnikow, Ltd) (1967) KGK

Facts: The defendant breached the contract when its ship delivered the plaintiff's sugar nine days after the contractual delivery date. The market price of sugar had fallen during that time. Although the defendant did not know the plaintiff's reason for needing the sugar, the defendant was aware that a sugar market existed in that city.

Issue: Are falling prices too remote a loss to impose on a breaching party who delayed performance?

Rule: Damages for breach caused by delay include lost profits caused by falling prices if they are a "not unlikely" result of such a breach. "Not unlikely" denotes a degree of probability considerably less than a 50 percent chance but nevertheless not very unusual and easily foreseeable.

United States v. Behan (1884) KGK

Facts: The U.S. broke its contract without cause to have Behan build an artificial mat to keep a river clear for navigation. Behan recovered the value of work done because he could not prove lost profits with certainty.

Issue: What is the measure of damages for a party who is wrongfully prevented from performing a contract?

Rule: A party who is wrongfully prevented from completing a construction contract is entitled to recover all incurred expenditures and lost profits if they can be proved with reasonable certainty.

Kehoe v. Rutherford (1893) KGK

Facts: The plaintiff was prevented from completing its contract to grade a road because part of the land was later discovered to be private property whose owner refused to allow the road work.

Issue: Is a party that is prevented from fulfilling its contractual obligation through no fault of its own entitled to recover the "reasonable value" of the work done regardless of the overall contract price?

Rule: A plaintiff who is unable to complete a contract through no fault of his own may only recover the proportion of the contractual price that corresponds to the value of the work he completed.

Note: This view does not reflect the modern approach, which adopts a reasonable value standard regardless of contract price.

Philadelphia v. Tripple (1911) KGK

Facts: Tripple, a subcontractor, was wrongfully discharged after spending more than $24,000 for labor and materials. Full performance by Tripple would have involved expenses exceeding the contract price.

Issue: Is a contractor that was wrongfully discharged entitled to restitution for labor and materials expended regardless of the contract price?

Rule: A plaintiff who was wrongfully prevented from completing his contractual obligations can recover expenses incurred, regardless of the price fixed by contract.

Security Stove & Mfg. Co. v. American Rys. Express Co.
(1932) KGK, FE

Facts: Security, a furnace manufacturer, contracted to have American ship its furnace to an exhibition, for promotional purposes. Security rented a booth, sent its president, and incurred other expenses in preparation for the exhibition. American, fully aware of Security's plans, had assured it that it could make delivery within four days. American failed to deliver a key part of the stove on time.

Issue: What is the measure of damages against a carrier who fails to deliver on time?

Rule: Ordinarily a carrier who fails to deliver within a reasonable time is liable for any drop in the market value of the goods between the time set for delivery and the actual time of delivery. However, where lost profits are too speculative, and a carrier has notice of a shipper's special needs, the carrier must pay for the actual expenses incurred in reliance upon timely delivery.

L. Albert & Son v. Armstrong Rubber Co. (1949) KGK, MS

Facts: Albert breached its contract by delaying shipment of two out of four machines. Armstrong rejected all four and sued for reliance costs incurred in building foundations for the machines. If Armstrong had used the machines to recondition old rubber, as planned, it would have lost money on the venture.

Issue: Is a buyer entitled to full compensation for expenses made in reliance upon the receipt of goods if it would have lost money had the contract been fully performed?

Rule: Normally, a promisee is entitled to the value of the promised performance less any outlays avoided because of breach. But, in circumstances where full performance would not cover the promisee's outlays, the promisor has a privilege to reduce recovery for the outlays by as much as he can prove the promisee would have lost if the contract were performed.

Nute v. Hamilton Mutual Insurance Co. (1856) KGK

Facts: Nute brought suit in the county of Suffolk despite a provision in his insurance policy that suit should be brought only in the county of Essex.

Issue: May a contractual provision validly limit litigation on the contract to a specified venue?

Rule: Contractual provisions limiting the venue where a suit on the contract can be brought are not enforceable.

Garrity v. Lyle Stuart, Inc. (1976) KGK, CPB, R

Facts: Garrity, an author, was awarded both compensatory and punitive damages by an arbitrator, after Lyle Stuart, a publisher, acted maliciously and fraudulently and underpaid her royalties.

Issue: Does an arbitrator have the power to award punitive damages?

Rule: An arbitrator has no power to award punitive damages, even if agreed upon by the parties. There is strong public policy reserving this sanction to the state.

Kemble v. Farren (1829) KGK

Facts: The defendant's contract to perform in the plaintiff's theater provided £1,000 in damages in case of any breach. The defendant breached, causing actual damages of £750.

Issue: Is a liquidated damages clause enforceable if it is broadly worded to apply to all breaches?

Rule: A liquidated damages clause that applies to all breaches, no matter how minor, is unenforceable, and actual damages will be awarded.

McCarthy v. Tally (1956) KGK

Facts: The Tallys, lessors, sued to recover liquidated damages after the McCarthys breached a ten-year lease of a summer resort. The Tallys suffered no actual damages from the breach.

Issue: Are liquidated damages awarded in the absence of actual damages?

Rule: A provision for liquidated damages is enforceable if, at the time the contract was made, damages in the event of a breach were difficult to ascertain, and the sum agreed upon represented a reasonable forecast of damages and was not intended to be a penalty.

Note: Although damages from nonpayment of rent were easily ascertainable, the plaintiff claimed that the defendant's breach harmed the "goodwill" of the business.

Klar v. H. & M. Parcel Room, Inc. (1947) KGK

Facts: Klar paid ten cents to check furs and received a ticket that had a liability limiting clause ($25) printed in fine print on the back. The furs were lost.

Issue: Can a bailee limit liability by use of an inconspicuous clause printed on its tickets?

Rule: To limit its liability, a bailee must establish a special contract of which the bailor received reasonable notice and to which he assented.

Fair v. Negley (1978) KGK

Facts: The Fairs leased a house from Negley that had a leaky roof, defective windows, falling plaster, no heating, defective electrical wiring, etc. The lease provided that the Fairs took the house "as is."

Issue: Is the implied warranty of habitability waivable by an express provision in a residential lease?

Rule: A waiver of the warranty of habitability in a residential lease is void as being completely contrary to public policy and unconscionable.

Note: Four factors motivated the court: disparity of bargaining positions, scarcity of housing, public health and safety, and inability of tenants to properly inspect and repair.

Daniels v. Newton (1874) KGK

Facts: The defendants breached an agreement to purchase land before the end of the 60 days allowed for performance.

Issue: Can suit be brought against a party who renounced a contract before the time for performance has arrived?

Rule: One can only recover for actual injuries. Therefore, a party cannot recover for anticipated injuries when the other party announces his intention not to render a future performance. Suit can only be brought after the time for performance has passed.

Roehm v. Horst (1900) KGK

Facts: Roehm signed ten successive six-month contracts to buy hops from Horst. Roehm renounced the remaining contracts after the end of the sixth one.

Issue: How are damages calculated when a contract has been renounced but not breached?

Rule: Absolute and unequivocal renunciation of a contract before the obligation to perform arrives is treated as a breach, and damages are measured as if a complete breach had occurred.

Note: See Chapter 8 for more on anticipatory repudiation.

Phelps v. Herro (1957) KGK

Facts: Herro contracted to transfer interests in real estate and stocks to Phelps in 1955 in exchange for Phelps' promissory note that would be due in 1961. After Herro conveyed his interests, Phelps refused to issue the note and claimed he could not be sued for breach before 1961.

Issue: Does the doctrine of anticipatory repudiation apply to situations where the payment of money is the only obligation still due?

Rule: The doctrine of anticipatory repudiation has no application to simple unilateral contracts (or bilateral contracts that have become unilateral by full performance on one side) for the payment of money in the future, without surety or other conditions involved. Suit can only be brought at the time set for performance.

Oloffson v. Coomer (1973) KGK, R

Facts: Oloffson contracted to buy corn from Coomer, a farmer, to be delivered in October and December at approximately $1.12 per bushel. In June, Coomer notified Oloffson that he would not be planting any corn that year. The market price of corn was $1.16 per bushel. The plaintiff waited until the dates on which delivery was due before buying corn elsewhere at prices of $1.35 and $1.49 a bushel.

Issue: Can a buyer recover the value of additional damages that accrued between the times of the anticipatory and actual breaches?

Rule: Under UCC § 2-610, a buyer is allowed to await a "commercially reasonable time" before taking action in response to an anticipatory breach. Where a repudiation is unequivocal and "cover" is easily and immediately available, however, no waiting period is reasonable.

Clark v. Marsiglia (1845) KGK

Facts: Marsiglia continued to clean and repair Clark's paintings after Clark had repudiated their agreement.

Issue: Can a party recover for services rendered after a contract has been repudiated?

Rule: One who repudiates a contract must only compensate the other party for the performance rendered prior to repudiation and anticipated loss in regard to the unexecuted portion (i.e., lost profits minus cost avoided) and not for actions that only served to increase the amount of damages.

Mount Pleasant Stable Co. v. Steinberg (1921) KGK

Facts: Mount Pleasant agreed to supply Steinberg with horses for trucking goods. Steinberg breached and claimed in response to Mount Pleasant's suit for lost profits that Mount Pleasant had a duty to mitigate its damages by securing another contract.

Issue: Is the nonbreaching party required to mitigate its damages?

Rule: The rule that one must use reasonable effort to obtain other employment and thereby mitigate damages has no application to a situation where a plaintiff could simultaneously perform as many contracts as it could sign.

Jameson v. Board of Education (1916) KGK

Facts: The Board of Education hired Jameson, a music teacher, for a nine month period. Although the Board refused to allow her to teach, Jameson reported for work every day for the nine months. Jameson sued for her wages for that period.

Issue: Must an employee be ready and willing to work in order to recover against the breaching employer?

Rule: An employee can recover for breach of contract without a showing that she was willing and ready to perform after the breach occurred. She is only entitled to damages from the breach, not wages for the term of the contract, because she did not actually perform.

Aiello Constr. Inc. v. Nationwide Tractor Trailor Training & Placement Corp. (1980) FE

Facts: Nationwide was to pay Aiello in installment payments for construction work. When Nationwide stopped making full payments, much of the work was already completed, and Aiello won a judgment for breach of contract.

Issue: How are damages assessed for breach of a construction contract by the property owner after a portion of the contract has been performed by the builder?

Rule: Damages for a job partially completed where the contracting party has breached are set at the cost to the promisee for the work done, plus the profit to be gained, minus the amount already paid in installments by the promisor.

Sullivan v. O'Connor (1973) FE, MS, CPB, R

Facts: Sullivan sued her surgeon for breach of contract after the plastic surgery performed on her nose failed to "enhance her beauty and improve her appearance" as expressly promised.

Issue: Does a doctor breach a contract if a medical procedure does not produce the desired results?

Rule: If a doctor expressly promises that a procedure will produce certain results, a patient may recover damages if that promise is not fulfilled. Restitution (e.g., doctor's fees) and reliance (loss of the value of the organ operated upon) will be given, but not expectation (increased value had the operation been successful).

Note: Because of the fear that patients will elevate a doctor's opinion to a promise, some courts require written proof of the promise. Other courts completely deny recovery in such cases.

Truck Rent-a-Center, Inc. v. Puritan Farms, 2nd, Inc. (1977) FE

Facts: Puritan leased a fleet of trucks from the plaintiff. Puritan agreed that if it were to terminate the lease early, it would pay the plaintiff 50 percent of the rental price for the rest of the term. The agreement cited that the parties had considered the lessor's substantial initial investment in the trucks and their need for reconditioning prior to subsequent leasing.

Issue: Is a provision in a lease agreement that requires the payment of a specified amount of money to the lessor in the event of the lessee's breach an enforceable liquidated damages clause or an unenforceable penalty?

Rule: If the amount stipulated by the parties bears a reasonable relation to the amount of probable actual harm, it is not a penalty and is enforceable as a liquidated damages provision.

Lake River Corp. v. Carborundum Co. (1985) FE, KC, CPB

Facts: Lake River contracted to bag and ship "Ferro Carbo" for Carborundum. Because it had to invest in new machinery, Lake River required Carborundum to supply it with at least 22,500 tons of Ferro or pay prevailing rates for the difference between the quantity bagged and the quantity guaranteed. Carborundum failed to ship Lake River the minimum because of falling demand for its product. Lake River sued for the promised money.

Issue: Is a clause requiring payment for a minimum guaranteed quantity a penalty and therefore unenforceable?

Rule: A contractual damages provision is a penalty and unenforceable as such, where it does not reflect an estimate of the actual damages incurred. A minimum guarantee clause penalizes the breaching party based on when the breach occurs rather than on the gravity of the breach. It reflects neither the operating costs saved nor the actual profit foregone by the nonbreaching party, but simply rewards the nonbreaching party with a windfall.

Note: The court held that Lake River was entitled to the money due on the contract if it had been completed, less operating costs saved.

London Bucket Co. v. Stewart (1951) FE

Facts: Stewart sought specific performance of a contract to install a heating system in his motel.

Issue: Is specific performance granted if it would require extensive judicial supervision?

Rule: Contracts for building construction are generally not specifically enforced, because ordinary damages are an adequate remedy and because courts are reluctant to expend resources on the extensive supervision of performance that is necessary.

Laclede Gas Co. v. Amoco Oil Co.
(1975) FE, MS, CPB

Facts: Amoco breached a long term contract to supply Laclede with propane. Although alternative suppliers of the gas were readily available, none were willing to enter into a long term contract because of uncertainty as to future energy supplies and prices.

Issue: Can a sales contract be specifically enforced if there is no adequate alternative remedy at law?

Rule: Specific performance is granted if a remedy at law is inadequate because such remedy is not as certain, prompt, complete and efficient to attain the ends of justice as specific performance.

Osteen v. Johnson (1970) FE

Facts: Johnson contracted to promote Osteen, a country singer in exchange for $2,500. Johnson breached the contract by failing to properly promote the singer's second record after her first was a success. Osteen sued, but recovered only nominal damages of $1. The court then decided that restitution would be appropriate, even though Osteen did not sue for it.

Issue: What is the required magnitude of a breach, for granting restitution?

Rule: Restitution is awarded for "substantial breaches" that go to the essence of a contract.

Hochster v. De La Tour (1853) MS

Facts: On May 11 the defendant informed the plaintiff that the plaintiff would not be hired on June 1, pursuant to their contract. The plaintiff sued on May 22.

Issue: Can a party sue for breach of contract before the date of performance (i.e., June 1) arrives?

Rule: A renunciation of a contract by one party may be treated as a breach of contract by the other party who is immediately relieved of his duty to perform and need not wait before filing suit.

Note: Currently one may suspend performance upon the other party's repudiation but may not bring suit until actual breach has occurred.

Taylor v. Johnston (1975) FE, MS, R

Facts: Taylor contracted to use Johnston's stallion as a breeding stud for two mares. The contract provided that if the encounter was unsuccessful, Taylor would be entitled to another chance the following year. Subsequently, Johnston sold his stallion and informed Taylor that the contract was canceled. Under threat of suit, Johnston agreed to let Taylor's mares breed, but the stallion was constantly "booked" by its new owners and thus unavailable for Taylor's mares. Taylor bred his mares with another stud before the year was up, but had to abort the foals.

Issue: What are the remedies available to a party who disregards a repudiation which is later retracted prior to the time of performance?

Rule: If a party disregards anticipatory repudiation, and it is later retracted prior to the time of performance, the repudiation is nullified, and the injured party is left with his remedies, if any, invocable at the time of performance.

AMF, Inc. v. McDonald's Corp. (1976) FE, MS

Facts: AMF agreed to sell 22 computerized cash registers to McDonald's. McDonald's canceled the contract after AMF's prototype performed unsatisfactorily, projected delivery of the units was extended, AMF's plant was incapable of assembling the units, and it failed to provide adequate performance standards.

Issue: Can a party repudiate a contract if it has "reasonable grounds for insecurity"?

Rule: A contract can be repudiated if a party has reasonable grounds to believe the other party will not perform, and adequate assurances of performance are not given. (UCC § 2-610.)

Plotnick v. Pennsylvania Smelting & Ref. Co. (1952) MS

Facts: Plotnick contracted to sell battery lead to the defendant in a series of installment contracts. During the term of the contract both parties delayed shipment or payment, but still fully performed. Plotnick refused to complete the shipments until the defendant fully paid for a prior shipment and canceled the contract after the defendant requested full delivery prior to final payment.

Issue: Is a delay in payment a sufficient breach to constitute a repudiation justifying rescission by the other party?

Rule: Failure to make installment payments may constitute a constructive breach of contract only if the buyer's actions make the contract unreasonably, financially burdensome or risky for the seller to perform because of fear of future default. Whether an unreasonable risk of default exists partly depends on the prior behavior of the parties.

Allen v. Jones (1980) MS

Facts: The plaintiff entered into an oral contract with the defendant for the cremation and shipping of her brother's remains. Due to the defendant's negligence, the package was empty when it arrived. The plaintiff sought punitive and emotional damages for intentional infliction of emotional distress.

Issue: Are damages awarded in a contract case for infliction of emotional distress?

Rule: Under certain circumstances punitive damages will be awarded for intentional infliction of emotional distress, but the action should be brought in tort rather than contract.

Note: Emotional distress without physical injury caused by mishandling of a corpse is a recognized instance for which damages are awarded.

F.D. Borkholder Co., Inc. v. Sandock (1980) MS

Facts: Borkholder was hired to build an addition to Sandock's building, which was to be used as a retail carpet showroom and warehouse. Borkholder intentionally deviated from the contract plans, creating a recurring moisture problem. Borkholder promised that it would remedy the situation, but never did so. Sandock won a judgment for compensatory and punitive damages.

Issue: Will punitive damages be awarded for breach of contract?

Rule: Punitive damages may be awarded for breach of contract if separate torts accompany the breach and the public interest is served by imposing punitive damages.

Note: In the instant case, the award of punitive damages was upheld because the plaintiff engaged in wrongful acts constituting fraud, misrepresentation, deceit, and gross negligence, and because people generally lack knowledge of the construction industry and must be able to rely on the expertise and trustworthiness of builders.

Boise Dodge, Inc. v. Clark (1969) MS

Facts: Boise Dodge, a car salesman, reset a car's odometer and sold it to Clark as "new." Boise Dodge sued after Clark stopped payments, but was forced to pay $350 in actual damages and $12,500 in punitive damages.

Issue: Are punitive damages awarded in a contract action?

Rule: Punitive damages are awarded for breach of contract if the defendant has committed fraud, and the punitive damages bear a "reasonable relation" to the amount of actual damages. In addition to the actual loss, a jury can consider the need for deterrence, the defendant's motives, degree of disregard of the rights of others, and the sophistication of the scheme.

John Hancock Mutual Life Ins. Co. v. Cohen (1958) MS

Facts: After making monthly payments for 15 years on a life insurance policy issued to Cohen's deceased, John Hancock claimed the policy was expired and that its 20-year duration was in error. The lower court ruled that John Hancock had anticipatorily breached the contract and that Cohen was immediately entitled to all future payments in one sum.

Issue: Is an attempted refusal to make future payments an anticipatory repudiation of a contract?

Rule: The doctrine of anticipatory breach is not applicable when the only remaining obligation is the payment of money. Future installments have to be paid when they fall due.

American Mechanical Corp. v. Union Mach. Co. (1985) MS

Facts: American, who was having trouble meeting its mortgage payments, contracted to sell property and equipment to Union for $135,000. When

then rented the jukebox to a third party. Although jukeboxes were easily available at the time, prospective renters were scarce.

Issue: Are damages for breach of a lease reduced by the amount the lessor could realize from reletting the article?

Rule: A lessor who agrees to lease an article that is of practically unlimited supply will not have his damages for breach reduced by the amount he actually did or could have realized on a reletting of the article, because he could make a second lease, irrespective of the breach.

R.E. Davis Chem. Corp. v. Diasonics, Inc.
(1987) MS

Facts: Davis breached a contract to buy medical equipment from Diasonics. Diasonics eventually sold the equipment to a third party at the same price. Diasonics claimed it was entitled to offset its lost profits against Davis's deposit and return the balance.

Issue: Are damages for lost profits awarded to a seller who later resells the goods to a third party?

Rule: A seller can recover lost profits against a breaching buyer even if the goods were resold at the same price if the seller can prove that, but for the breach, he would have made two profitable sales.

Reliance Cooperage Corp. v. Treat (1952) MS

Facts: Treat agreed to sell and deliver barrel staves to Reliance by December 31. In August, Treat notified Reliance that it would not make the sale because the market price had risen. Treat waited until Dec. 31, when the price rose even more, and sued for breach.

Issue: Is the measure of damages for breach of a sales contract affected by the fact that the seller gave the buyer notice of its intent to repudiate prior to the date set for performance?

Rule: A breaching seller is liable for the difference between market price and contract price on the date delivery was due; damages are not affected by a seller's anticipatory repudiation.

Note: UCC § 2-713 has changed this rule. Damages are now measured by the difference between contract price and market price at the time notice of the breach was given.

Prier v. Refrigeration Engineering Co. (1968) MS

Facts: The plaintiff hired the defendant to design and install an ice rink. The defendant did defective work, and the plaintiff was forced to tear out the rink and extensively rebuild.

Issue: What is the liability of a party who fails to properly complete a project for which it held itself as an expert?

Rule: Where a party holds itself as qualified to supervise a construction project, it impliedly warrants to properly perform its services; in case of improper performance, it is liable for the cost of completing the work correctly.

American Standard, Inc. v. Schectman (1981) KC, MS

Facts: Schectman contracted to remove all foundations and structures on American's property and to grade it. After intentionally refusing to complete performance, Schectman claimed that damages should be measured by the drop in the property's value ($3,000) rather than the cost of completion ($90,000).

Issue: Is diminution in value used to measure damages for breach of a construction contract if the cost of completion is disproportionately high?

Rule: The general rule of damages for defective performance of construction contracts, "cost of completion," is replaced by the "diminution in value" rule to avoid causing "economic waste" where the cost of completion is disproportionately higher than the benefit that would be derived. This exception is not applicable to an intentional breacher who has not substantially performed in good faith.

Chatlos Sys. Inc. v. Nat'l Cash Register Corp. (1982) MS

Facts: NCR sold Chatlos a defective computerized payroll system. Chatlos claimed its damages should be measured by the difference between the contract price and the actual fair market value of the computer.

Issue: Will contractual price solely ever be used to determine damages without reference to market price?

Rule: The measure of damages in case of breach of warranty is the difference between the fair market value of the goods accepted and their value had they been as warranted. Evidence of the contract price may be relevant to the fair market value, but it is not controlling.

Spang Indus., Inc. v. Aetna Cas. & Surety Co. (1975) MS

Facts: Spang's delay in delivering steel needed to build a bridge forced the contractor to incur additional expenses, because the concrete had to be poured in one day to avoid oncoming freezing temperatures. Spang sued the surety company when the contractor withheld payment of the entire contract as damages. It is common knowledge that construction has to be delayed once the temperature drops significantly.

Issue: Can knowledge of the consequences of a delay in performance be imputed to a breaching party if the consequences were not expressly communicated?

Rule: A party is liable for all direct damages that both parties to the contract, had they been fully informed and given the issue proper attention, would have anticipated as flowing from a breach at the time they made the contract.

Note: The contractor was awarded the value of the additional expenses it incurred.

El Fredo Pizza, Inc. v. Roto-Flex Oven Co. (1978) MS

Facts: After several years of success in the pizza industry, El Fredo bought a defective oven for a new parlor from Roto-Flex, which caused higher costs and lost sales. El Fredo sued for lost profits as part of its suit for breach.

Issue: Can the owner of a new business recover for lost profits?

Rule: The owner of a new business can recover for lost profits if they can be proved with a "reasonable degree of certainty." A party with successful past experience in an industry may introduce evidence concerning the industry, costs and profitability to meet the requirement of certainty.

Note: The court allowed recovery for profits lost due to higher costs but not for those due to lost sales, because they were too uncertain.

Blandford v. Andrews (1599) MS

Facts: The plaintiff promised to excuse a debt if the defendant succeeded in convincing one Bridget Palmer to marry the plaintiff. The plaintiff then called Palmer a whore and vilified her. The plaintiff sued to collect his debt after Palmer refused to marry him.

Issue: If one party interferes with another's performance of a contract, is the second party relieved of its obligations to the interfering party?

Rule: A party whose performance was interfered with by the other party to the contract is only relieved of its obligation to perform upon showing that it did all it could to complete performance.

Note: The defendant did not introduce such evidence. Today, the duty to act in good faith would bar the plaintiff's recovery.

Patterson v. Meyerhofer (1912) MS, FE

Facts: The plaintiff agreed to sell four houses to the defendant. Both were aware that the plaintiff did not own the homes but intended to buy them at a foreclosure sale. Before the foreclosure occurred, the defendant repudiated the contract and outbid the plaintiff for each house during the sale. The defendant also bought a fifth house which both parties had orally agreed the plaintiff would keep. In defense of the plaintiff's suit for damages, the defendant claimed the plaintiff breached the contract because he never conveyed the properties to her.

Issue: Can a party who causes the other party not to perform raise such nonperformance as a defense to damages?

Rule: Every contract contains an implied promise by each party not to intentionally and purposely prevent the other party from carrying out the agreement. One who causes the breach of an agreement is precluded from recovering damages for nonperformance or from interposing it as a defense to an action on the contract.

Iron Trade Prod. Co. v. Wilkoff Co. (1922) MS

Facts: The plaintiff contracted to buy rails from the defendant. Supply of the rails was limited to two sources, and the plaintiff's subsequent purchase of part of its needs from one of them drove market supply down and prices up. As a result, the defendant was unable to acquire rails for the plaintiff.

Issue: Is a party to a contract excused from performance because the other party made its obligation more difficult?

Rule: Conduct by one party to a contract that makes performance by the other more difficult, but not impossible, will not excuse performance.

Billman v. Hensel (1979) MS

Facts: The Billmans made a deposit on the Hensels' home and agreed to buy it provided they succeeded in getting a mortgage. The Billmans, unable to get a mortgage for the full amount, refused the Hensels' offer to lower the price so that the mortgage would suffice. The Billmans sued for the deposit, which was treated as liquidated damages.

Issue: If a contract is subject to a condition, must a party make a good faith effort to meet the condition?

Rule: When a contract is subject to a condition, a party has an implied obligation to make a reasonable and good faith effort to satisfy the condition.

Vanadium Corp. of America v. Fidelity & Deposit Co. of Maryland (1947) MS

Facts: Vanadium agreed to buy a lease for a mine from another defendant subject to the condition that the Secretary of the Interior approved the assignment. After running into some difficulties, Vanadium pulled out and sued to recover a surety bond held by Fidelity.

Issue: When the cooperation of one of the parties is necessary to obtain approval of the transaction, is there an implied condition of cooperation?

Rule: Whenever the cooperation of a promisee is necessary to performance of the contract, there is a condition implied in fact that the cooperation will be given.

Curtice Bros. Co. v. Catts (1907) MS

Facts: Curtice Bros., a cannery, contracted to buy Catts' tomato crop. When Catts repudiated the contract, Curtice Bros. was unable to find a substitute source of tomatoes.

Issue: Is specific performance granted when monetary damages are inadequate, and substitute goods are unavailable?

Rule: Specific performance is granted for breach of a sale of goods contract if the facts surrounding a breach indicate that an award of monetary damages would not do justice to the nonbreaching party, and substitute goods are unavailable.

Northern Indiana Pub. Serv. Co. v. Carbon County Coal Co. (1986) MS

Facts: NIPSCO, a public utility, entered into a long-term fixed-price contract to buy coal from Carbon County. New government regulations required that if NIPSCO could acquire electric power from other suppliers at lower costs, it must charge its customers accordingly, even if it paid higher prices for Carbon County coal. The contract contained a clause that provided that NIPSCO could stop taking delivery of coal for any cause beyond its control, including acts of civil authority, which wholly or partly prevented utilizing the coal. NIPSCO tried to escape the contract on grounds that it was commercially impracticable to perform.

Issue: Is a buyer relieved from performance on the grounds of impracticability if the risk has been allocated to it through a fixed-price contract term?

Rule: A party is not excused from performance on the grounds of impracticability if it accepted the risk of a fixed-price term.

City Stores Co. v. Ammerman (1967) KC, MS

Facts: Ammerman promised to grant City Stores a lease on equal terms to those of other tenants in its proposed shopping mall in exchange for City's letter of commitment to open a store in Ammerman's mall. Ammerman used City's letter, among others, to secure approval of the project from the county council, but later refused to give City a lease. City sued for specific performance.

Issue: May an option to lease a store be specifically enforced?

Rule: Where monetary damages are inadequate to compensate a party's loss, and the terms of a contract can be verified or reasonably implied, a court will enforce despite supervisory problems, because leases, like land, are unique.

Karpinski v. Ingrasci (1971) MS, CPB

Facts: An oral surgeon hired another oral surgeon and made him agree not to practice dentistry or oral surgery in five counties if he quit the plaintiff's employ. The defendant quit and opened his own business.

Issue: Does a covenant not to compete bind a professional?

Rule: An agreement of a professional not to compete with his employer is enforceable even if it is for an unlimited period of time if the geographical area is limited and reasonable. However, a prohibition of a type of work which is not in competition can be struck from the covenant.

Southwest Engineering Co. v. United States (1965) MS

Facts: Pursuant to the terms of a contract, the U.S. deducted "late charges" from payments for construction work by Southwest that was partially delayed. No actual harm was suffered because of the delay.

Issue: Is a liquidated damages clause enforceable if actual damages were not incurred?

Rule: A liquidated damages clause will be enforced even though actual damages were not incurred if the clause was reasonable at the time of contracting, and the harm is of a type that is difficult to prove.

United Airlines, Inc. v. Austin Travel Corp. (1989) MS

Facts: United brought suit to recover accrued rents receivable and damages for breach of leases entered into for a computerized reservation and accounting system. Austin counterclaimed, asserting that United violated federal antitrust laws and that liquidated damages are unenforceable penalties.

Issue: What factors will a court consider to determine whether a liquidated damages clause is enforceable?

Rule: A liquidated damages clause generally will be upheld unless the liquidated amount is considered to be a penalty because it is grossly disproportionate to the probable loss anticipated when the contract was executed. A court will often uphold liquidated damages if it is difficult or impossible to accurately estimate the amount of actual loss.

Leeber v. Deltona Corp. (1988) MS

Facts: Leeber invested in a condominium unit being constructed by Deltona. He put down $22,530 (15 percent) against the $150,200 purchase price, with the balance due at the closing date. After Leeber was given several extensions, he failed to close. Deltona canceled the agreement, retained the down payment and sold the property to another party for $167,000. Leeber sued to recover its deposit. The lower court awarded Leeber $15,000, which was the amount of the deposit reduced by expenses incurred by Deltona in connection with the transaction.

Issue: Are liquidated damages unenforceable if they are far in excess of the nondefaulting party's costs, and the nondefaulting party actually profits from the breach?

Rule: A seller may retain liquidated damages if the amount is reasonable, because liquidated damages are preferred to litigation as a mechanism for resolving conflicts. Reasonableness is determined at the time of the breach. The fact that a seller subsequently resells property for a greater amount does not convert otherwise reasonable damages to unreasonable damages. Damage sums in the range of 15 percent of the contract price are reasonable.

Lewis Refrigeration Co. v. Sawyer Fruit, Vegetable and Cold Storage Co. (1983) MS

Facts: Sawyer was awarded lost profits and excess costs caused by a defective freezer bought from Lewis. The contract provided that Lewis was only obligated to repair or replace a defective product. Rescission was also available.

Issue: Can consequential damages be limited by express agreement in a contract?

Rule: Consequential damages may be limited by contract as long as the limitation is not unconscionable.

Evra Corp., Formerly Hyman-Michaels Co. v. Swiss Bank Corp. (1982) CPB

Facts: Hyman-Michaels chartered a ship under the agreement that it advance semi-monthly installments to the ship-owner's Swiss Bank account. Hyman-Michaels' bank sent its payment by wire transfer to the Swiss Bank. For unknown reasons, the bank failed to comply with the payment order, and this eventually led to cancellation of the charter. Hyman-Michaels sued the Swiss Bank.

Issue: May one recover consequential damages for a harm unknown to the party being sued at the time of breach?

Rule: The costs of an unfortunate consequence of a course of dealings should be borne by that party who was able to avert the consequence at least cost and failed to do so. Consequential damages cannot be imposed upon a party who has no knowledge of the risks its behavior entails.

Note: Hyman-Michaels had the burden of avoiding the loss.

Mader v. Stephenson (1976) CPB

Facts: Mader won a judgment on a contract action against Stephenson, but he also sought damages for various expenses pertaining to the lawsuit.

Issue: May a party recover for attorney fees and other expenses in connection with a lawsuit?

Rule: Absent statutory authority or contractual agreement, neither attorney fees nor travel expenses are recoverable.

Guard v. P & R Enterprises, Inc. (1981) CPB

Facts: Guard contracted to sell the Edgewater lounge, restaurant and motel to P & R but was unable to acquire title to the property. Another party acquired title, and P & R sued Guard for damages.

Issue: When may lost profits be awarded as consequential damages?

Rule: Reasonably certain lost profits, which can be established by the profit history of the party's similar business at a different location or the business in question if it was successfully run by someone else, may be awarded as consequential damages.

Note: Lost profits were denied to P & R.

Gruber v. S-M News Co. (1954) CPB

Facts: Gruber contracted with S-M to produce 90,000 sets of Christmas cards. S-M was bound to exercise reasonable diligence to promote and sell the cards but claimed Gruber would have lost money on the venture if S-M had performed by exercising such diligence.

Issue: Under "essential reliance," may a party recover out-of-pocket expenses even if the party would have suffered a loss had the defendant fully performed on its promise?

Rule: A party's recovery for out-of-pocket expenses must be diminished by any loss that would have resulted from the defendant's full performance.

Note: The burden of proving this loss in event of performance rests on the defendant.

Ballard v. El Dorado Tire Co. (1975) CPB

Facts: Ballard had a five year employment contract with El Dorado to serve as Executive Vice President and General Manager of its Florida subsidiary. El Dorado breached by selling all of its stock in the subsidiary.

Issue: Must an employee's damages from an employer's breach be mitigated by the amount he might have earned in other similar employment?

Rule: The employee's damages will be mitigated only if the employer proves a similar employment opportunity was available.

Laredo Hides Co. v. H & H Meat Products Co. (1974) CPB

Facts: H & H breached a contract to sell cattle hides to Laredo. Laredo purchased hides on the open market and sued for the difference in prices.

Issue: If the seller breaches, is a buyer entitled to recover the difference between the cost of "cover" and the contract price?

Rule: When a seller wrongfully breaches a contract, the buyer can "cover" by purchasing the goods elsewhere in good faith and recover the difference between the price of the substituted goods and the contract price. (UCC § 2-712.)

Note: The buyer is also entitled to incidental and consequential damages.

City of Louisville v. Rockwell Mfg. Co. (1973) CPB

Facts: Rockwell contracted to supply Louisville with all the parking meters needed for a seven month period. The city repudiated the agreement after a new mayor took office.

Issue: How shall a court establish lost profits under a requirements contract?

Rule: In establishing the quantity requirement of a contract, the court shall look at a comparable time period in which the breaching party purchased the goods in good faith.

Note: The rule addresses the possibility that a breaching party may try to reduce the lost profit damages it will have to pay by purchasing less in the time frame governed by the contract.

Emery v. Caledonia Sand and Gravel Co., Inc. (1977) CPB

Facts: The Emerys, husband and wife farmers, sold Caledonia the right to remove earth from their land provided that Caledonia restored the land to its productive capacity at the completion of operations.

Issue: How are damages for breach of contract different from tort damages which simply try to undo the wrong committed?

Rule: In the case of breach of contract, the goal of compensation is to place the plaintiff in the position he would have been in if the contract had been performed.

Note: The court held the injury to the Emerys was foreseeable and not disproportionate to the compensation damages awarded.

Patton v. Mid-Continent Systems, Inc. (1988) CPB

Facts: Patton entered into a franchise agreement with Mid-Continent to operate truck stops. Mid-Continent violated the contract by franchising other truck stops within the exclusive territory granted to Patton.

Issue: When may punitive damages be awarded in a contract action?

Rule: Punitive damages may be awarded in suits when the breach is malicious, fraudulent, oppressive, grossly negligent or otherwise blameworthy. The breach is blameworthy if it was opportunistic, voluntary and inefficient in the sense that the loss suffered by the plaintiff was greater than the profits gained by the breaching party.

Seaman's Direct Buying Service, Inc. v. Standard Oil Co. of California (1984) CPB, KC, R

Facts: Seaman signed a contract with Standard but changes in the condition of the oil industry negatively affected Standard's view of the agreement. Standard subsequently denied there was a binding agreement between the parties.

Issue: May a party recover in tort for breach of an implied covenant of good faith and fair dealing in a noninsurance, commercial contract?

Rule: A party may incur tort liability when, in addition to breaching the contract, it sought to shield itself from liability by denying, in bad faith and without probable cause, that the contract existed.

Hibschman Pontiac, Inc. v. Batchelor (1977) CPB

Facts: Batchelor purchased his Pontiac GTO from the Hibschman dealership. The car was under warranty and Batchelor relied on assurances from three Hibschman employees regarding the high dependability of the service department. However, he had constant problems with his car which Hibschman's service department repeatedly failed to fix. Eventually, the warranty expired and Batchelor had many of the defects corrected at another garage.

Issue: Are there limits to an award of punitive damages?

Rule: The amount of punitive damages may be assessed by the jury within their sound discretion guided by proper instruction of the court. However, the "first blush rule" dictates that the amount may not be so high that at first blush it appears outrageous, excessive or improper.

Wedner v. Fidelity Security Systems, Inc. (1973) CPB

Facts: Wedner suffered a loss of over $46,000 due to Fidelity's wrongful failure to perform under a burglary service contract. The contract contained a provision allowing recovery only up to a sum equal to the yearly service charge, which was $312.

Issue: Is a contract provision valid when it exculpates or limits a party from liability for its own acts of negligence?

Rule: Consequential damages may be limited or excluded by contract except when the limitation or exclusion is unconscionable.

Note: Such provisions are prima facie unconscionable when they concern consumer goods.

United States v. Western Casualty and Surety Co. (1974) CPB

Facts: Pacific subcontracted a portion of its work on a hospital construction contract to Fritz. Pacific paid Fritz monthly according to the percentage of the job completed and also paid Fritz's supplier of materials out of this same amount. Later, Fritz demanded that Pacific pay it the entire amount but Pacific refused. Because of the failure to pay, Fritz rescinded the contract. The lower court held that Fritz was entitled to the reasonable value of all labor and materials that Pacific received in performance of the contract.

Issue 1: How should restitution damages be calculated?

Rule 1: Restitution damages should equal the reasonable value for which the labor and materials could have been purchased from one in the plaintiff's position at the time and place the services were rendered.

Issue 2: When are rescission and restitution available remedies?

Rule 2: When a party has created unreasonable delay, imposed new and overly burdensome conditions, refused to pay or repudiated the agreement, the aggrieved party may rescind the contract. To recover restitution damages, the breach must be so important and material that it goes to the "essence of the contract."

Note: The goal is the prevention of unjust enrichment.

United States v. Americo Constr. Co., Inc. (1958) CPB

Facts: A subcontractor ceased work on a contract after the contractor fell far behind in the progress payments. The subcontractor later completed its obligation under the contract after a further oral agreement that it would receive payment after completion. However, the contractor still did not pay.

Issue: May a party sue for restitution damages after completion of its contractual obligations?

Rule: A party may not seek a restitution remedy after it has completed its contractual obligation; abandonment of performance is a requirement.

Centex Homes Corp. v. Boag (1974) CPB

Facts: Centex sold a condominium to Boag, who paid a $525 deposit and wrote a check for $6,870. When Boag's employer transferred him out of state, he consequently canceled payment on the check and notified Centex "he would be unable to complete the purchase agreement." Centex sought to make Boag complete the agreement.

Issue: When is specific performance an available remedy?

Rule: Specific performance is confined to those special instances where a vendor will otherwise suffer an economic injury for which his damage remedy at law will not be adequate, or where other equitable considerations require that the relief be granted.

Note: The court rejected the contention that mutuality of remedy is an appropriate basis for granting specific performance.

American Brands, Inc. v. Playgirl, Inc. (1974) CPB

Facts: American, a tobacco manufacturer and distributor, had a contract with Playgirl to advertise its products on the back cover of each issue. A provision provided that American could buy the back cover space for as long as Playgirl would be published. After a year, Playgirl informed American that it planned to diversify the advertisers on its back cover. American sought an injunction claiming that Playgirl appealed to a unique market and that an injunction prohibiting Playgirl from denying American the back cover was necessary to avoid irreparable harm for which monetary damages would not be compensable.

Issue: When may a preliminary injunction be granted in a contract dispute?

Rule: Before a preliminary injunction may be granted, the moving party has the burden of demonstrating that its damages cannot be calculated and that consequently it cannot be made whole by monetary relief.

Schlegel v. Moorhead (1976) CPB

Facts: Moorhead owned the oil and gas lease to 120 acres in Montana where he maintained one oil well. As the well did not produce much revenue, he had previously attempted to sell the property lease. Schlegel, after studying public records, determined that Union Oil had been very active in the area and that the property could be very valuable. Schlegel entered into discussion with Moorhead and, when asked why he was interested in the property, told Moorhead that he had a general interest in the area. Schlegel signed an option to purchase the lease but Moorhead refused to carry it out.

Issue 1: Absent a finding of fraud, must a court grant specific performance where the party seeking the remedy has concealed information or circumvented questions?

Rule 1: A court may refuse to grant specific performance if it would be unjust and unreasonable.

Issue 2: When should a lower court's refusal to grant specific performance be overruled?

Rule 2: The application of specific performance is left to the sound legal discretion of the court and should be overruled only in the case of an abuse of discretion.

Meyer v. Benko (1976) CPB

Facts: Benko agreed to sell a residence to Meyer for $23,500 which was below the market value.

Issue: Should specific performance be denied because of inadequate consideration?

Rule: Adequacy of consideration should be examined when deciding whether a contract was formed rather than when deciding what remedy is appropriate for breach.

Duane Sales, Inc. v. Carmel (1977) CPB

Facts: A court granted specific performance of an option agreement for the purchase and sale of real property.

Issue: In awarding specific performance, should a court take into account the respective losses and gains during the period of litigation?

Rule: Equity requires that both the contract provisions to be enforced and the consequences of specific performance be just and equitable. Thus, the court may consider the parties' losses and gains during the litigation.

Howard Schultz & Associates v. Broniec (1977) CPB

Facts: Howard Schultz & Associates sought an injunction against Broniec to enforce a covenant not to compete contained in his employment agreement. The plaintiff also sought to restrain him from divulging confidential and privileged information received during employment.

Issue: When is a covenant not to compete contained in an employment contract enforceable?

Rule: A covenant not to compete is enforceable only where it is strictly limited in time and territorial effect and is otherwise reasonable considering the business interest of the employer and the effect on the employee. The territorial restriction generally may include only the area where the employee was employed. The activities prohibited must also be specified.

Kemp v. Gannett (1977) KC

Facts: Kemp is a contractor who agreed to list a house he built with Gannett, if Gannett promised to buy the home himself if it was not sold in ninety days. After ninety days, Gannett refused to purchase the land, and Kemp was not able to sell the house for almost a year.

Issue: What is the proper measure of damages for breach of a sales contract?

Rule: When a sales contract has been breached by the buyer, expectation damages should be awarded to put the seller in the position he would have been in had the contract been performed. Expectation damages are the difference between the contract price and the market price on the date of the breach, plus other costs incurred because of the breach. Resale price, if within a reasonable time and at the highest price obtainable after breach, is evidence of the market price on the date of the breach.

Handicapped Children's Education Board v. Lukaszewski
(1983) KC

Facts: Lukaszewski had a one year teaching contract with the Board. Lukaszewski quit her job mid-year, and the Board had to hire a replacement at a higher salary.

Issue: What is the proper measure of damages for breach of an employment contract by an employee?

Rule: Expectation damages should be awarded to put the employer in the same position he would have been in had the contract been performed. Expectation damages include the cost of obtaining other services equivalent to those promised but not performed, plus any foreseeable consequential damages. The employer can still recover the extra cost of a replacement even if the replacement gives the employer added benefits.

Native Alaskan Reclamation & Pest Control, Inc. v. United Bank
Alaska (1984) KC

Facts: Defendant breached a loan agreement to help finance Plaintiff's purchase of military aircraft. Plaintiff could not find replacement financing and his attempts to purchase the aircraft failed. Plaintiff argued that it should recover the money it would have earned had the Defendant performed.

Issue: What limits should be placed on expectation damages?

Rule: Damages must be foreseeable, proven with reasonable certainty, and be caused by the breach. Restatement (Second) § 352 defines foreseeability as being foreseeable as a probable result of the breach when the contract was made. This occurs if the loss follows from the breach in the ordinary course of events, or is a result of special circumstances beyond the ordinary course of events that the party in breach had reason to know.

Stewart v. Board of Educ. Of Ritenour Consol. School Dist.
(1982) KC

Facts: Stewart, a tenured teacher, was wrongfully discharged for excessive absence. Five years later, pursuant to a court order, she was reinstated and awarded money damages in the form of back pay plus interest. During the time she was unemployed, Stewart made no effort to attain a comparable teaching position, although there were some teaching positions available.

The school board appealed the damage award, claiming that Stewart had made no effort to mitigate damages, and was thus not entitled to the full amount of the award.

Issue 1: Which party bears the burden of proof as to failure to mitigate damages?

Rule 1: The breaching party bears the burden of proving that the opportunity to mitigate existed, as well the amount of damages which could have been avoided.

Issue 2: How should a court determine the feasibility of mitigation?

Rule 2: Feasibility of mitigation is proven when the breaching party can show that feasible alternatives (e.g., employment openings) were available and that the non-breaching party could have obtained one of those alternatives using reasonable effort.

Wired Music, Inc. v. Clark (1960) KC

Facts: Wired supplied recorded music to various locations via telephone wire. Wired contracted to supply music to Clark's business for three years. The contract contained an express provision prohibiting assignment without permission. After seventeen months, Clark moved his business and discontinued service. A new tenant rented the space formerly occupied by Clark, but Wired refused to consent to the assignment of Clark's contract. Instead, Wired and tenant entered into a new one-year contract, that called for a five percent increase over the defendant's contract. Wired sued to recover lost profits stemming from Clark's breach. Clark argued that the new contract, which would entitle the plaintiff to more money than the old contract, served to mitigate any damages claimed.

Issue: May a party in breach of a sales contract claim mitigation of damages, when the items to be sold are in unlimited supply?

Rule: The doctrine of mitigation of damages may not be applied to sales contracts that involve items in unlimited supply, because its application would serve to deprive the non-breaching party of the benefit of his bargain. Unlike the sale of fixed quantity items, it is impossible to know whether an additional sale would have been made in the absence of breach.

Bunnett v. Smallwood (1990) KC

Facts: Smallwood wished to sever his ties to a company he owned with Bunnett. Smallwood gave his share of the company's stock to Bunnett in exchange for a release from all future claims. Nevertheless, Bunnett sued Smallwood.

Issue: Can the prevailing party in a lawsuit recover attorney fees and costs for breach of an agreement not to sue?

Rule: Violation of an agreement not to sue does not entitle the non-breaching party to attorney fees and costs. This would violate the American rule requiring each party to pay its own legal expenses. Attorney fees can only be imposed by contractual agreement, statute, or court rule.

Gaglidari v. Denny's Restaurants, Inc. (1991) KC

Facts: Gaglidari was a bartender at Defendant's restaurant and was fired when she fought with a patron. Gaglidari claimed that Denny's breached her employment contract and caused her emotional distress.

Issue: Are emotional distress damages recoverable for breach of an employment contract?

Rule: Tort damages for emotional distress caused by breach of an employment contract are not recoverable because the primary purpose of employment contracts is economic, and adequate pecuniary compensation is available.

Dissent: Damages for emotional distress caused by breach of an employment contract should be recoverable if the employer's conduct is wanton or reckless.

Roth v. Speck (1956) KC

Facts: Roth, the owner of a beauty salon, hired Speck as a hairdresser. The contract was to run for one year, and Speck's salary was to be $75 per week or 50 percent of the gross receipts from his work, whichever was greater. Although Speck proved to be an exceptional hairdresser, he quit after 6 ½ months and was hired by another salon for $100 per week. Roth, in an attempt to mitigate damages, hired two replacements, both of whom lost money for Ross due to their lesser skills. Roth sued for damages stemming from breach of the employment contract.

Issue: What is the proper measure of damages for breach of an employment contract by an employee?

Rule: Damages for breach of an employment contract by an employee are measured by the cost to the employer of obtaining services comparable to the ones which were unperformed due to the breach. The fair value of the employee's services may by deduced from, among other things, the salary received in a similar position elsewhere.

Wartzman v. Hightower Productions, Ltd. (1983) KC

Facts: Plaintiffs concocted a promotional venture whereby an entertainer, "Woody Hightower," would set a Guinness World Record for the longest time spent on top of a flagpole. Woody was to live in a specially constructed mobile flagpole perch for nine months, have his own theme song, and be displayed throughout the country at state fairs and shopping centers. He was to descend the flagpole on New Years Eve in New York's Times Square. Plaintiffs hired the Defendant law firm to incorporate their flag pole venture. Defendants structured the corporation improperly and Plaintiff's investments were lost.

Issue: What are the damages when breach of contract prevents a highly speculative venture from being performed?

Rule: When expectation interests are not provable or cannot be ascertained because of the speculative nature of a venture, reliance damages should be awarded. Reliance damages may include expenditures made in preparation for performance, less any loss that the breaching party can prove with reasonable certainty the injured party would have suffered had the contract been performed.

Colonial at Lynnfield, Inc. v. Sloan (1989) KC

Facts: Defendant contracted to buy an interest in Plaintiff's hotel. Defendant breached the contract and Plaintiff sued to recover $200,000 in liquidated damages.

Issue: Are liquidated damages provisions enforceable?

Rule: Liquidated damages provisions are enforceable if the amount is a reasonable estimate of difficult-to-ascertain damages at the time of the agreement. If the actual damages turn out to be easily ascertainable, a court must consider whether the stipulated sum is unreasonably disproportionate to the real damages from the breach. If the liquidated damages are unreasonable based on the actual damages, the liquidated damages clause is unenforceable because it constitutes a penalty.

Woods v. Fifth-Third Union Trust Co. (1936) R

Facts: Wood sued the executor of his mother's will to collect for personal services Wood had rendered prior to his mother prior to her death.

Issue: Is a child entitled to compensation for rendering services to a parent?

Rule: No contract arises from the performance of personal services by a child for the benefit of a parent. Because the relationship between a parent and child is close, any service is presumed to be rendered without the expectation of compensation. An individual may obtain payment only by showing clear and convincing evidence that there was an express promise under circumstances that manifest an intention to contract.

Clausen & Sons, Inc. v. Theo Hamm Brewing Co. (1968) R

Facts: Clausen & Sons alleged that it orally contracted to become Hamm's exclusive beer distributor in a certain area. Clausen discontinued all competitor's products and made further expenditures in reliance on the contract. When Hamm terminated the agreement, Clausen brought this suit for breach of contract based on reliance. Hamm asserted that the contract was unenforceable due to a lack of mutuality of obligation.

Issue: Does an exclusive franchise dealer have a claim for breach of contract for an unreasonable termination of the contract?

Rule: Where an exclusive franchise dealer is under a contract that is terminable at will, and has at the manufacturer's or supplier's insistence invested substantial resources, the supplier may not unreasonably terminate the contract without giving the dealer the opportunity to recoup his investment. Termination without notice gives rise to an action in breach, based on reliance.

White v. Benkowski (1967) R

Facts: The Whites contracted to receive water from the well of their neighbors, the Benkowskis. The Benkowskis maliciously shut off the water supply for short periods of time after the initially friendly relationship of the parties deteriorated. The Whites sought compensatory and punitive damages.

Issue 1: May a court reduce a jury award for compensatory damages in the belief that such damages were not adequately proven?

Rule 1: Compensatory damages need not be proven with precision; evidence of damages shall be reviewed in the light most favorable to the plaintiff.

Issue 2: Are punitive damages awarded for a breach of contract?

Rule 2: Punitive damages are not available in breach of contract actions.

Thorne v. White (1954) R

Facts: Thorne contracted to make certain repairs to White's house, including the installation of a new roof. Thorne began the work, but stopped because of inclement weather and never returned. White hired a new roofer and the work was completed, but at a cost higher than Thorne was charging. White sued Thorne for the difference in cost alleging breach of contract.

Issue: What is the proper measure of damages for a breach of contract, when substitute performance is obtained which calls for performance above and beyond the original contract?

Rule: A party damaged by a breach may recover for losses which are the natural consequence and proximate result of that breach. The non-breaching party in a contract should only get damages up to the difference in the cost of obtaining identical substitute performance.

Anglia Television Ltd. v. Reed (1971) R

Facts: Anglia hired Robert Reed to star in a television film after it had incurred numerous other production expenses. Reed later repudiated the contract. Anglia, unable to find a substitute, was forced to abandon production. Anglia then sued Reed for damages.

Issue: May a non-breaching party obtain damages for expenses incurred before a contract with the breaching party was formed?

Rule: While a party may always recover damages for expenditures incurred after a contract is formed, they may also recover costs incurred before the contract, if it was within the reasonable contemplation of the parties at the time of the contract that prior expenditures would be wasted if the defendant breached.

Sutherland v. Wyer (1877) R

Facts: Wyer was hired with a stipulation in his contract that he could be fired for incompetency. Halfway through his contract term, Wyer was discharged, allegedly for incompetency. Wyer contended that the real reason for his termination was his refusal to take a pay cut.

Issue: What remedies are available to an employee who has been wrongfully terminated?

Rule: When an employee has been wrongfully discharged, he is entitled to the salary that he would have earned during the remainder of his contract, reduced by the income which he has earned or could have earned through reasonable diligence during that period of time.

R.B. Matthews, Inc. v. Transamerica Transportation Services, Inc. (1991) R

Facts: Matthew agreed to purchase 300 used trailers from Transamerica, which was supposed to use its "best efforts" to make the trailers available for each of two years. By the end of the second year, Transamerica had only delivered a portion of the required trailers, and although it continued to express its intention to comply, it failed to deliver the remaining goods. Matthews brought suit, alleging breach of contract, fraud, misrepresentation, and bad faith.

Issue: What remedies are available to a buyer if a seller breaches a contract?

Rule: When a seller breaches a contract, the buyer may either (a) attempt to "cover" and obtain substitute goods, after which time he may recover the difference between the cost of cover and the contract price, plus any incidental or consequential damages, or (b) recover the difference between the market price and the contract price. If a buyer chooses the second remedy but could have covered, he cannot receive consequential damages.

Center Chemical Co. v. Avril, Inc. (1968) R

Facts: Avril contracted to sell cleaning products to Center and granted Center exclusive rights to sell the products in Florida for twenty years. Center was to buy only from Avril. Center breached the contract and Avril sought damages for loss of future profits for the remaining years of its contract.

Issue: Do courts award damages for prospective profits?

Rule: Courts do not permit the recovery of damages when a jury would have to rely on speculation and conjecture in assessing damages.

Mooney v. York Iron Co. (1890) R

Facts: Mooney agreed to sink a mine for York, but was prevented from finishing the job through no fault of his own. Mooney sued in quantum meruit for the cost of the work.

Issue: Can a party without fault recover in quantum meruit if he is prevented from completing performance?

Rule: A party without fault who is prevented from performing a contract is entitled to recover the value of his work and labor.

United States for the Use of Palmer Construction v. Cal. State Electric, Inc. (1991) R

Facts: Cal. State contracted with the U.S. Army Corp of Engineers to construct a power plant. Palmer, hired as a subcontractor, breached its contract with Cal State. Cal State was forced to spend $6000 more than it had agreed to pay Palmer to find substitute performance.

Issue: What is the measure of damages when a breach causes the non-breaching party to incur extra costs to find substitute performance?

Rule: The non-breaching party may recover the extra costs incurred to find substitute performance. Recovery by the breaching party is precluded where it would cause the non-breaching party to pay more than the actual contract price.

Petropoulos v. Lubienski (1959) R

Facts: Petropoulos agreed to build a house for Lubienski. Lubienski refused to pay after requested changes to the house had not been made, and "extras" were added to the bill. Petropoulos sued for breach of contract.

Issue: What amount of damages is available to a contractor when there is a breach of contract?

Rule: There are three measures of damages for breach of building contracts. First, award the contractor the total price of the contract, less the amount saved by the breach. Second, award the contractor the actual expenditure to the date of breach, less the value of materials that can be re-used, plus the profit he can prove with reasonable certainty would have been realized given full performance. Third, award quantum meruit damages for the reasonable value of work, labor, and materials used in performance of the contract before breach. The court applied the third measure.

Watson v. Wood Dimension, Inc. (1989) R

Facts: WDI lost its main customer, Fisher, and hired Watson to help reacquire Fisher's business. WDI orally promised Watson a commission on all of the Fisher's orders if Watson succeeded. Fisher resumed ordering from WDI, and Watson continued to wine and dine Fisher's president. Watson received his commission until he was fired.

Issue: When an employee procures an ongoing business relationship for his employer, for how long is the employer obligated to compensate his employee?

Rule: Based on quantum meruit, an employee must be compensated for a reasonable period of time beyond his termination or alliance with the employer. The court determines a cutoff point for compensation based on what is reasonable under the circumstances.

Hargrave v. Oki Nursery, Inc. (1980) R

Facts: Hargrave, president of Long Island Vineyards, sued Oki, alleging that Oki had fraudulently represented the quality of vines which Long Island Vineyards had purchased.

Issue: Can a plaintiff convert a breach of contract into a claim for tortious liability?

Rule: Where a legal duty exists independent of a contractual obligation, a plaintiff may recover in tort. The court ruled that Hargrave could maintain a tort fraud action.

J'Aire Corp. v. Gregory (1979) R

Facts: The County of Sonoma hired Gregory, a general contractor, to work on property the County had leased to J'Aire. J'Aire sued Gregory for tort damages because Gregory failed to complete the work in a reasonable time.

Issue: Does a contractor owe a duty of care to a tenant of a building undergoing construction work, when the contract is with the landlord, not the tenant?

Rule: A contractor owes a duty of care to the tenant of a building undergoing construction work. The contractor must act in a reasonable and timely fashion so as not to cause reasonably foreseeable losses to business and profits which would occur if the project is not undertaken with due diligence.

Foley v. Interactive Data Corp. (1988) R

Facts: Foley was fired from Interactive. Foley alleged that he was wrongfully discharged because Interactive's "Termination Guidelines" stated that employees would only be discharged for good cause. Foley claimed tort damages because he refrained from pursuing other possible job opportunities in reliance on Interactive's "Termination Guidelines."

Issue 1: May an at will employment agreement be modified by evidence of implied terms?

Rule 1: The presumption of at will employment may be modified by express or implied terms in an employment agreement.

Issue 2: Can a party recover tort damages for breach of an implied covenant in an employment contract?

Rule 2: Since the nature of an employment contract is fundamentally contractual, relief for the breach of an implied covenant of good faith and fair dealing should be limited to contract remedies.

Jarvis v. Swans Tours Ltd. (1973) R

Facts: Jarvis booked a holiday based on representations in Swans' brochure. However, the contents of the brochure were false, and Jarvis was disappointed by his trip.

Issue: What is the proper measure of damages when a party suffers disappointment, frustration, or distress because the other party breached a contract to provide entertainment and enjoyment?

Rule: Where a party breaches a contract for entertainment or enjoyment, damages should compensate the plaintiff for the disappointment suffered and the loss of entertainment which should have been received. The court should take into account the mental distress suffered by the plaintiff.

California and Hawaiian Sugar Co. v. Sun Ship, Inc. (1986) R

Facts: California hired Sun Ship to build a barge. A liquidated damages clause was included in the contract, requiring payment if the barge was not completed by a specified date. Sun missed the deadline and began to pay the daily liquidated damages charges, but ultimately denied liability for any damages.

Issue: When will a court uphold a liquidated damages clause?

Rule: Liquidated damages are permitted when informed parties with equal bargaining power have agreed to pay a reasonable measure of damages, and the actual injury is difficult to ascertain at the time the contract was formed.

Lake River Corporation v. Carborundum Company (1985) R

Facts: Carborundum hired Lake to provide distribution services in Carborundum's warehouses. The contract included a minimum-quantity provision, and provided for liquidated damages if the minimum quantity was not met. Carborundum did not meet the minimum requirement.

Issue: When is a liquidated damages clause a penalty for breach instead of a valid effort to liquidate damages?

Rule: When a damage formula is designed to award the non-breaching party more than its actual damages, it is void as a penalty.

Board of Education of Niagara, Wheatfield, Lewiston and Cambria
v.
Niagara-Wheatfield Teachers Association (1979) R

Facts: The Teachers Association claimed that the district violated their collective bargaining agreement by hiring an outside guidance counselor instead of a counselor from the district. An arbitrator found that the district breached its agreement with the Association. The arbitrator granted damages without specifically detailing the manner he used in fixing the amount.

Issue: Are arbitration awards unenforceable as punitive damages if the arbitrator uses his discretion in computing damages?

Rule: Arbitration awards are enforceable even if the arbitrator uses his discretion in computing damages. Awards are not punitive merely because they are not specifically articulated.

Oliver v. Campbell (1955) R

Facts: Oliver represented Campbell in a divorce action. After the trial was concluded, but before a final judgment was entered, Campbell fired Oliver. Oliver sought to recover the reasonable value of the services he had rendered to Campbell.

Issue: May an attorney recover the reasonable value of his services under quantum meruit when he is replaced after trial but before judgment?

Rule: When a contract has in effect been fully performed, an attorney may recover only upon the contract, not under quantum meruit. His recovery is limited to the amount specified in the contract.

Fracasse v. Brent (1972) R

Facts: Brent retained Fracasse to represent her in a personal injury suit, based upon a contingency fee agreement. Before any recovery was obtained, Brent discharged Fracasse. Fracasse filed this action alleging discharge without cause.

Issue: May an attorney who has been discharged without cause recover the full fee specified in the employment contract, regardless of the reasonable value of the services performed at the time of his termination?

Rule: A client may discharge his attorney at any time, with or without cause. Upon being discharged without cause, an attorney's recovery is limited to the reasonable value of his services under quantum meruit. The recovery, however, is contingent upon the success of a client's suit.

Rosenberg v. Levin (1982) R

Facts: Levin hired Rosenberg to render legal services for a fixed fee of $10,000, plus a contingent fee equal to 50 percent of all amounts recovered in excess of $600,000. Levin discharged Rosenberg without cause and subsequently settled the matter for $500,000. Rosenberg sued for compensation.

Issue: What is the proper basis for compensating an attorney discharged without cause by a client after substantial legal services have been rendered?
Rule: An attorney discharged without cause is entitled to the reasonable value of his services on the basis of quantum meruit. The recovery is limited to the maximum fee set forth in the contract.

Staklinski v. Pyramid Elec. Co. (1959) R

Facts: Staklinski was an officer of Pyramid. His contract stated that should he be declared permanently disabled, he would receive compensation for three years, after which his contract would end. The contract also provided that if controversy ensued, the dispute would be submitted to arbitration. Pyramid declared that Staklinski was permanently disabled and Staklinski disagreed. The matter went to arbitration and the arbitrators ordered that Staklinski be reinstated.
Issue: If parties submit a disputed matter to arbitration pursuant to an arbitration agreement contained in their contract, may the arbitrator award specific performance?
Rule: When a valid contract contains a provision requiring arbitration to resolve contract disputes, any arbitration award, even specific performance, that results from such a provision is also valid.

Allgeyer v. Rutherford (1898) R

Facts: Rutherford claimed that he was discharged without cause and sued to recover wages due under his employment contract.
Issue: What is the measure of damages available to an employee for an employer's breach of contract?
Rule: An employee is entitled to the contract price of the remaining period of the contract, less what he earned or could have earned through other employment during that period.

Koplin v. Faulkner (1956) R

Facts: Faulkner agreed to drill 20,000 feet of hole in an oil field for Koplin. Faulkner was to contact Koplin to determine the exact locations for drilling. Faulkner did not contact Koplin for six months and, when he did, Koplin told Faulkner that someone else had drilled the holes for him. Faulkner sued Koplin to recover damages for breach. Koplin argued that their agreement was a contract for personal services and that Faulkner had a duty to mitigate damages by seeking alternate employment.

Issue: Does a party seeking damages for breach of contract have a duty to mitigate damages by seeking alternate contracts?

Rule: A nonbreaching party has no duty to mitigate damages arising from a contract breach by seeking alternate contracts, unless the contract is one for personal services. The proper measure of damages for breach of an entire contract is the nonbreaching party's expectation interest, e.g., the difference between the contract price and the reasonable cost of performance. The court found that the contract in this case was not a contract for personal services.

Chapter 3

CONSIDERATION

Review Requirements of a Contract:

Mnemonic: **Mother Adores Cigars After Dinner**

(1) **M**utual **A**ssent
(2) **C**onsideration
(3) **A**bsence of **D**efenses

I. ELEMENTS OF CONSIDERATION

It would be unfair for courts to hold people to every promise that they make because many promises are made in jest or without sufficient forethought. Thus, to be legally enforceable, a promise must be made in return for *consideration*, which consists of two general elements: *bargained-for exchange* and *legal detriment*.

A. Bargained-for Exchange
A performance or return promise is bargained-for if it is sought by the promisor in exchange for his promise, *and* it is given by the promisee in exchange for that promise. (Rest. 2d. § 71(2).) The bargain requirement serves the purpose of distinguishing between enforceable promises and ordinary gifts.

1. Gifts
   A promise to make a gift is unenforceable, not only because it is not bargained-for but also because the offeree suffers no legal detriment. Example: A says to B, "I promise to buy you a new car." A is not legally bound to buy B a car because A's promise was not made as part of a bargain in exchange for some return benefit from B. There is no consideration for A's promise.

2. Bargain v. Precondition
   Performance of a bargain benefits the promisor and therefore is valid consideration. Performance of a precondition does not benefit the promisor and is not consideration. Example: X promises his sister a place to raise her family if she comes to visit

him. She incurs the expense of moving, but X changes his mind. X is not legally bound to keep his promise, because no consideration was given for it. The moving expenses were incurred as a precondition to fulfilling his request. X did not bargain that he would give his sister a place to stay in exchange for her incurring moving expenses.

3. Benefit

    a. The benefit a promisor receives as part of a bargain does not have to be economic in nature. Example: A promises B $100 if B does not smoke.

    b. However, the benefit must be more than just altruistic pleasure or love. Example: There is no consideration if A promises to pay B's debts as a gesture of gratitude for all the happiness B has given A. Moral obligation does not constitute legal consideration.

4. Adequacy of Consideration

    a. Nominal Consideration
    Often an agreement between two parties will state something like "A promises B … in consideration of $1.00 paid to A." Although courts will not ordinarily examine the adequacy of consideration, courts will do so in cases involving purely token consideration, in order to thwart attempts to make gratuitous promises appear legally enforceable. Nominal or sham consideration is usually evidence that a gift is masquerading as a bargained-for exchange.

    b. Recited Consideration
    A majority of courts allow a promisor who is opposing enforcement of a contract to prove that the consideration recited in the agreement was not actually given. Nonpayment of recited consideration may be used as partial evidence that there was no bargained-for exchange.

c. Past Consideration

As a general rule, "past consideration is no consideration." Logically, a current promise cannot be exchanged for some benefit that the promisor has already received. Example: A promises to pay B, A's employee, $100 a week "in consideration" of B's many years of hard work, or A promises to pay B $1,000,000 after B saves A's life. In both cases, A has received the benefit before he made the promise, and thus nothing was actually given in exchange for the promise. There are some exceptions to the general rule:

i. Pre-existing Debt

A promise to repay a pre-existing debt that was excused because of a technical defense, such as the running of the statute of limitations, is enforceable without consideration. (Rest. 2d. §§ 82, 83.)

ii. New Promise for Benefits Received

A new promise to pay for benefits received will sometimes be enforceable without consideration on grounds of moral obligation to prevent injustice. (Rest. 2d. § 86.)

B. Legal Detriment

The second requirement for valid consideration is that it must constitute a legal detriment to the promisee. Legal detriment is liberally construed to mean either a promise to do something that one is not legally obligated to do (e.g., cross the street) or to refrain from doing something that one has a right to do (e.g., stop smoking). There is no requirement that the promisee suffer any actual hardship. Likewise, the benefit that the promisor receives is not necessarily related to pleasure or advantage. All that is required is that the promisor does something he does not have to do.

1. Minority View

Some courts broaden the test such that valid consideration exists if the promisor received a benefit, even if the promisee did not "suffer" a detriment.

2. Bilateral Contract
   In a bilateral contract, the detriment is in the form of a promise.

3. Unilateral Contract
   In a unilateral contract, the detriment is in the form of an action. No consideration exists prior to performance.

4. Pre-existing Duty Rule
   Generally, there is no legal detriment if a party promises to do something that he is already obligated to do, or forbears from doing something that he is not legally entitled to do. (Rest. 2d. § 73.) Example: A promises not to use illegal drugs. Many courts dislike the pre-existing duty rule and have avoided its application in many ways. A promise to perform an act that one is already legally obligated to do may be consideration under certain circumstances.

   Mnemonic: **DUCk PiNS**

   a. **D**ispute
      If there is an honest dispute as to whether the promisor is already legally obligated to do the promised act, the promise or act may be consideration.

   b. **U**nforeseen **C**ircumstances
      Unforeseen circumstances make it "fair and equitable" to allow a promisor to modify an agreement without giving new consideration. (Rest. 2d. § 89.)

   c. **P**re-existing Duty to a Third Party
      The promise is made to a third party outside the contract. Example: A contracts with B to construct an elevator in the building that B is erecting for C. B quits the job, but A promises C that he will continue the job if C pays him. The promise is enforceable, even though A already had a legal obligation to build.

d. New or Different Consideration Promised
Even a slight change in the terms of a pre-existing duty will satisfy the requirement of consideration.

e. Sale of Goods
Under UCC § 2-209, which applies only to the sale of goods, modifications of existing contracts can be made without new consideration.

5. Partial Payment as Satisfaction of a Debt
A promise to pay part of a debt, instead of the whole, is not consideration for a return promise by the creditor to relinquish the debt, because the debtor is obligated to pay anyway ("pre-existing duty"). This rule has been overruled by the UCC and by some jurisdictions. Also, courts will consider a promise of partial payment to be valid consideration if:

a. The payment terms are slightly changed.

b. The debtor refrains from declaring bankruptcy.

c. There is an honest dispute as to the debt.

d. A check marked "payment in full" is cashed.

i. At common law, a creditor forfeited no rights to the rest of the debt still outstanding.

ii. Under the UCC, the entire debt is discharged unless a creditor expressly reserves his rights by writing "with recourse," or something to that effect, on the check. (UCC § 1-207.)

6. Forbearance to Bring Suit
A promise not to sue, made in exchange for some return benefit, is valid consideration if either;

a. The claim was valid, or

    b. The claim was not valid, and

        i. The parties reasonably believed the claim was valid (majority rule), or

        ii. The validity was uncertain or the promisor subjectively believed that it was valid (Rest. 2d. § 74).

II. MUTUALITY

Mutuality requires that *each* party to a contract must provide consideration to the other in exchange for the other's promise.

A. Illusory Promises
An illusory promise is not sufficient consideration, because it only appears to bind the promisor when, in fact, it commits him to nothing at all. (Rest. 2d. § 77.) Example: A promises to be B's agent. B agrees, but reserves the right to terminate at any time. There is no mutuality, because A received no consideration for his promise.

B. Alternative Promises
A promise that allows the promisor to choose among several alternative performances will satisfy mutuality only if each alternative has valid consideration. (Rest. 2d. § 77.)
Example: A promises to give B either $1,000 or his car in exchange for B's car. The promise is enforceable because both alternatives embody valid consideration.

C. Right to Withdraw from the Agreement
A promise that gives the promisor the right to terminate the agreement can still be valid consideration for a return promise if:

1. Termination is allowed after performance is rendered.
Example: A promises to be B's agent. B accepts (promises to hire A) but reserves the right to fire A upon 30 days notice. B's promise is consideration for A's promise because the agency agreement must last at least 30 days before B can fire A.

2. Termination is dependent on ability to perform.
   Example: A promises to sell his house to B. B promises to buy subject to his ability to obtain financing. B's promise satisfies mutuality because it is not dependent on his willingness to perform but rather on his ability.

3. Termination occurs with notice.
   If the only limitation on termination is the requirement that notice be given, modern courts are likely to recognize such a promise as valid consideration. Some courts will even go so far as to imply a notice requirement, the idea being that if notice is required, performance must occur for the notice period, at least. Example: A promises to clean B's house in exchange for $100 a day, subject to A's right to terminate with seven days notice. The promise is valid consideration because A must perform for at least seven days.

D. Voidable Promises
   A promise that is voidable at a party's election (promises made by minors, incompetents, etc. are voidable if the promisor so chooses) is valid consideration and satisfies the requirement of mutuality. (Rest. 2d. § 78.)

E. Conditional Promises
   A promise that makes performance of an act dependent on the occurrence of a future event is valid consideration if:

   1. Condition is Outside Promisor's Control
      There is valid consideration, even if a promisor eventually does not have to perform, unless the promisor knows that the condition cannot occur. Example: A promises to pay B $100 for her baseball glove if it rains on Tuesday. This is valid consideration even if it does not rain on Tuesday.

2. Condition is Partially Within Promisor's Control
A court will imply such a promise to mean that the promisor will use reasonable efforts to satisfy the condition. Example: B promises to sell his house to A if he can find a new house within a year. If A agrees, B's promise will be construed to mean that B will make best efforts to find a new home. Otherwise, B's promise is illusory.

F. Option Contracts
A promisee who receives an irrevocable offer (an option contract or a firm offer) is not always required to give consideration in exchange for that offer. (Rest. 2d. § 87; UCC § 2-205.) Even in cases where consideration is recited, courts do not require that it be paid.

G. Requirements and Output Contracts

1. Traditional Rule
A promise to buy goods from a specific seller over a period of time was insufficient consideration for the return promise to supply those goods, if the quantity term was to be determined by what the buyer required over that period (as opposed to a preset amount). Mutuality was lacking because, although the seller had to provide the goods, the buyer did not have to buy if he required nothing.

2. Modern/UCC Rule
Such promises are valid consideration and do not lack mutuality of obligation. UCC § 2-306 implies that the buyer has a good faith duty to ...

a. Maintain reasonable requirement levels,

b. Buy exclusively from that seller, and

c. Not take advantage of the seller by increasing demand to benefit from fluctuating market prices.

3. Output Contract
Seller promises all of his output to one buyer. A mutuality problem exists because the seller never promised to have any output, let alone a certain amount. Such contracts are now valid because UCC § 2-306 implies that sellers have a good faith duty to maintain a certain level of output.

4. Unilateral Contract
Part performance of a unilateral contract is sufficient consideration to keep a promise open, even though the promisee is not obligated to complete performance. Once part performance is rendered, however, the promisor cannot withdraw his promise unless the promisee revokes.

III. PROMISSORY ESTOPPEL (Rest. 2d. § 90)

Promissory estoppel is an equitable doctrine that is used to avoid injustice by enforcing otherwise unenforceable promises. It "estops" the promisor from claiming that no consideration was given.

A. Requirements for enforcement of a promise with estoppel:
Mnemonic: **Robin hood Finds Danger Inviting**

1. That there was actual **R**eliance on the contract or promise,

2. That the reliance was **F**oreseeable to the breaching party,

3. That it was clearly **D**etrimental, and

4. That **I**njustice can only be avoided by enforcement.

B. Exemplary Situations:

1. Promise to Make Gift
A promises to pay B, his son, $1,000 a week for life. B quits his job in reliance on the promise. A cannot revoke the offer if it would cause injustice, such as if B is unable to obtain new employment.

2. Charitable Subscriptions
   Promises to make donations are enforceable absent consideration, even if there is no detrimental reliance.

3. Bids by Subcontractors (Rest. 2d. § 87)
   subcontractor who submits a "sub-bid" to a general contractor for use in computing the general contract bid must give the contractor a reasonable amount of time to accept, even if no consideration is given to keep the offer (bid) open.

CASE CLIPS

Hamer v. Sidway (1891) DHH, KGK, FE, MS, CPB

Facts: A young man's uncle promised to pay him $5,000 if he abstained from drinking, smoking, swearing and gambling until the age of 21. The uncle's executor refused to honor the promise, claiming that no consideration was given to the uncle in exchange for his promise.

Issue: Does voluntary forbearance of a legal right constitute consideration?

Rule: Forbearance of a right is a sufficient legal detriment to satisfy the requirement of consideration.

Fischer v. Union Trust Co. (1904) DHH, KGK

Facts: A father deeded some property to his daughter and promised to pay the outstanding mortgages on it. The daughter jokingly gave her father one dollar as consideration. At the father's death, the estate refused to continue the mortgage payments, claiming the promise was not binding for want of consideration.

Issue 1: Can a dollar that is transferred in jest to a promisor be consideration?

Rule 1: The passing of a dollar that is treated as a joke is not consideration.

Issue 2: Is a promisor's love and affection for his daughter and his desire to provide her with support consideration?

Rule 2: A promisor's love, affection and desire to provide support for his daughter is not sufficient consideration to bind a promise.

Batsakis v. Demotsis (1949) DHH, FE, KC

Facts: During World War II, Batsakis loaned Demotsis 500,000 Greek drachmas (worth about $25) to get back to America. Demotsis promised to pay Batsakis $2,000. Demotsis refused to repay the debt, claiming that inadequate consideration was given for her promise.

Issue: Is a contract void if the consideration furnished by one party is substantially disproportionate to that given by the other?

Rule: Inadequacy of consideration does not void a contract, as long as the consideration had some value. A party that receives the "benefit" it seeks will not be relieved from a bad bargain.

Duncan v. Black (1959) DHH

Facts: Part of Black's contract to sell Duncan farm land included a clause specifying that Duncan was to receive a 65-acre cotton allotment. Duncan was allotted a lesser area of cotton, and he threatened to sue. To settle the dispute, Black gave Duncan a $1,500 promissory note. Black stopped making payments when he discovered that under the existing cotton allotment quota, Duncan was not entitled to the amount of cotton for which he had contracted. Duncan sued to enforce the note.

Issue: May forbearance to bring a lawsuit constitute consideration for a promissory note?

Rule: Forbearance to assert an action is not sufficient consideration when the underlying claim is illegal and against public policy, such as a violation of the Agricultural Adjustment Act.

Martin v. Little, Brown and Co. (1981) DHH, R

Facts: Martin offered proof to Little, Brown, a publisher, that a portion of one of its books had been plagiarized. When Little, Brown prosecuted the plagiarists, Martin sought one-third of the recovery amount. Although it had never promised Martin anything, Little, Brown gave him a $200 honorarium.

Issue: Absent any express promises, can a party recover for the value of services that were volunteered?

Rule: One who volunteers information or services is generally not entitled to restitution.

Mills v. Wyman (1825) DHH, KGK, FE, KC, MS, R

Facts: Mills provided board, nursing, and care to Wyman's 25-year-old son who became ill while traveling. After the services had been rendered,

Wyman wrote to Mills, promising to pay for them. Wyman later refused to pay.

Issue: Is moral obligation sufficient consideration to support a promise?

Rule: Moral obligation is not sufficient consideration to enforce a promise to pay for services already rendered. Past consideration is no consideration.

Webb v. McGowin (1935) DHH, KGK, FE, KC, MS, CPB, R

Facts: Webb was crippled in the course of a heroic act to prevent harm to McGowin. Consequently, McGowin promised Webb $15 every two weeks for the rest of Webb's life. McGowin made payments until his death, whereupon his estate refused to honor the promise.

Issue: Is moral obligation sufficient consideration to enforce a promise?

Rule: Moral obligation is sufficient consideration to support a subsequent promise when the promisor received a material benefit.

Note: This is the minority rule; the majority view is that moral obligation is no consideration. (See *Mills v. Wyman.*)

Kirksey v. Kirksey (1845) DHH, KGK, FE, KC, MS, CPB

Facts: The defendant wrote to his sister-in-law, "If you will come down and see me, I will let you have a place to raise your family." Two years after her relocation, he changed his mind and made her leave. The plaintiff claims that the expenses she incurred in moving were valid consideration.

Issue: Is an act necessary to accept a promise simply a precondition to a gratuitous act or consideration given in exchange for the promise?

Rule: Acts that are required before fulfillment of a promise are preconditions to accepting the promise, not valid consideration.

Note: A famous example of this rule involved a man who told another, "If you go to the shop around the corner, you can buy a coat on my credit." The walk around the corner is a precondition to accepting the promise. It was not done "in exchange" for the coat.

Allegheny College v. Nat'l Chautauqua County Bank (1927) DHH, KGK, KC, MS

Facts: Allegheny received a $5,000 pledge that was to become effective 30 days after the donor's death. It was agreed that the money would be used either as part of a general fund or to create a special fund named after the donor. The donor made a partial payment of $1,000 while she was still alive. Allegheny set the money aside until the rest of the pledge would be

received. Before her death, the donor repudiated her pledge. Allegheny sued the donor's executor, National Chautaqua, to recover the rest of the pledge.
Issue: Does acceptance of part of a donation imply a promise to perform the donor's wishes, such promise being valid consideration to bind the promisor?
Rule: The acceptance of a charitable subscription is an implied promise by a college to comply with the wishes of the donor which, in turn, constitutes valid consideration to bind the donor.
Note: Consideration is not required to enforce a promise of a charitable contribution.

East Providence Credit Union v. Geremia
(1968) DHH, CPB

Facts: The Geremias secured a loan from East Providence by using their car as collateral. The loan agreement provided that if the Geremias' insurance lapsed, East Providence could make the payments and add the amount to the balance owed. On one occasion, the Geremias agreed to East Providence paying the premium, which it failed to do. The uninsured car was destroyed in an accident.
Issue: May the doctrine of estoppel be applied to promises to act in the future?
Rule: The doctrine of promissory estoppel, expressed in Restatement § 90, provides that a promise to act in the future, that the promisor should reasonably expect to induce reliance, will be enforced, if the promise induced reliance, and injustice can only be avoided by enforcement of the promise.

Seavey v. Drake (1882) DHH, KGK

Facts: Seavey, wishing to help his son, Drake, orally agreed to give him a strip of land. In return, Drake tore up a $200 debt his father owed him. Drake spent $3,000 to improve the land and paid all taxes on it. After Seavey's death, his executor sought to evict Drake, claiming no consideration was given for Seavey's promise because the oral agreement violated the statute of frauds.
Issue: Can an oral promise to convey land be enforced if the promisee has given the required performance?
Rule: A parol contract to convey land will be enforced in favor of the promisee if the failure or refusal to convey the land would operate as a fraud upon him. The bar of the statute of frauds is removed upon the grounds that

it is a fraud for the promisor to insist upon the lack of a written document after he has allowed partial performance of the contract.

Forrer v. Sears, Roebuck & Co. (1967) DHH

Facts: Sears promised Forrer "permanent employment" if he agreed to give up his farming work. Forrer sold his livestock, rented his barn at a loss, and began working for Sears. He was fired without cause four months later.

Issue: Can an employee who is promised "permanent employment" recover if he is terminated?

Rule: A contract for permanent or life employment actually amounts to indefinite employment, terminable at will by either party, unless the employee furnishes additional consideration other than performance of services.

Stearns v. Emery-Waterhouse Co. (1991) DHH

Facts: Defendant's president promised Stearns, 50 years old, employment to the age of 55 he if would quit his job of 27 years and start working for the defendant. Stearns was terminated before he reached the age of 55.

Issue: May an employee avoid the statute of frauds by claiming detrimental reliance on an oral contract which cannot be completed within one year?

Rule: Promissory estoppel may not be used to avoid the statute of frauds where there is an oral employment contract that requires longer than one year to complete, unless the employer engages in fraudulent conduct. In the absence of a written contract or proof of fraud, a multi-year employment contract is unenforceable.

Goodman v. Dicker (1948) DHH, KGK, FE

Facts: The defendant, a representative of a franchisor, encouraged the plaintiff to apply for a franchise and incorrectly told him that it would be granted. Relying on the defendant's assurance, the plaintiff invested money in setting up a store.

Issue: Can a party be compensated for expenses that were incurred because of reasonable reliance on the words or actions of another party?

Rule: A party that incurs expenses as a result of reasonably foreseeable reliance on the statements of another party can recover the value of those expenses under the theory of promissory estoppel, even in the absence of an actual contract between the parties. However, the plaintiff can only recover for expenses made in reliance, not for the value of lost profits.

Obering v. Swain-Roach Lumber Co. (1927) DHH

Facts: Both Obering and Swain-Roach were interested in purchasing the same parcel of land for different purposes. They agreed that if Swain-Roach succeeded in buying the land, it would sell it immediately to Obering, with some rights reserved. Obering refused to honor the agreement after Swain-Roach purchased the land and tendered it to him. Obering claimed that the condition precedent, Swain-Roach obtaining the land, made their contract too indefinite to be valid.

Issue: Is a contract that cannot become effective without the occurrence of a condition precedent too indefinite to be enforceable?

Rule: A contract that cannot become effective absent a condition precedent does not fail because of indefiniteness.

Wood v. Lucy, Lady Duff-Gordon (1917)
DHH, KGK, FE, KC, MS, CPB, R

Facts: Lady Duff-Gordon, a famous designer, agreed with Wood that he would have exclusive agency to place her endorsements on clothing designs, to place her designs on sale and to license others to market them. In exchange, Wood promised to keep the books and to split the profits evenly with Duff-Gordon. Duff-Gordon breached by endorsing designs herself and keeping the profits. In defense, she claimed that Wood's promise was illusory, as she had granted him exclusive agency, but he was not obligated to find designs or to sell her labels.

Issue: Is a contract void for lack of mutuality because one party did not promise to use reasonable efforts to perform his duties?

Rule: A promise to use reasonable efforts can be implied from a contract and, therefore, a contract does not fail for lack of mutuality because it does not contain explicit clauses requiring good faith efforts (UCC § 2-306(2)).

Petroleum Refractionating Corp. v. Kendrick
Oil Co. (1933) DHH

Facts: Petroleum accepted an order from Kendrick for 1.5 million gallons of grade-C oil. The contract provided that, should Petroleum stop manufacturing such oil for whatever reason, it could terminate the contract upon five days notice. Kendrick terminated the contract, after it had received 62,000 gallons of substandard oil. During the suit, it claimed that it was void for lack of mutuality because Petroleum's promise was illusory.

Issue: Does a contract become void for lack of mutuality if one of the parties retains power to terminate the contract at its discretion?

Rule: A promise to perform a contract is valid consideration even if a party retains the power to terminate at its discretion, so long as that party incurs some legal detriment. A party incurs such a detriment if it is required to give notice before termination, or if termination will mean giving up a legal right (i.e., to produce grade-C oil).

Feld v. Henry S. Levy & Sons, Inc.
(1975) DHH, FE, MS, R

Facts: The defendant agreed to sell to the plaintiff the entire output of bread crumbs at its factory for one year. Each party had the right to cancel upon six months notice. The defendant stopped production because his obsolete equipment was uneconomical, and offered to resume production at a higher price.

Issue: Must a seller who signs an output contract continue to produce goods for the term of the contract?

Rule: A party to an output contract is obligated to act in good faith and may cease production as long as it is acting in good faith. Whether a party acted in good faith is a jury question.

Note: The case was remanded for further proceedings.

Sheets v. Teddy's Frosted Foods, Inc. (1980) DHH

Facts: Sheets claimed he was wrongfully discharged in retaliation for his efforts to ensure that Teddy's products would comply with statutory health requirements.

Issue: Does an employer have a complete and unlimited right to terminate the services of an at-will employee?

Rule: An employer can terminate an at-will employee without showing just cause, unless the employee can show that the termination was against public policy.

Noble v. Williams (1912) KGK

Facts: Teachers voluntarily spent their own money to keep a public school in operation by buying provisions and paying the rent. They sued the school board for failing to provide the funds.

Issue: Can one recover expenses voluntarily incurred on behalf of another?

Rule: One cannot unilaterally make another his debtor.

Davis & Co. v. Morgan (1903) KGK

Facts: Davis' employee, Morgan, was offered a higher salary by another company. When Morgan informed Davis of the offer, Davis promised to pay Morgan more if he stayed until the expiration of his contract. Morgan agreed, but Davis fired him just before the expiration date and refused to pay the extra wage.

Issue: Is a promise to raise wages under an existing employment contract enforceable if the employee's duties did not also change?

Rule: A promise to pay additional compensation under an existing employment contract fails for lack of consideration if there is no reciprocal change in the employee's duties.

Schwartzreich v. Bauman-Basch, Inc. (1921) KGK, CPB, R

Facts: Bauman-Basch hired Schwartzreich for one year at $90 a week. Before beginning the work, Schwartzreich was offered $115 a week by another employer. Bauman-Basch offered to raise Schwartzreich's weekly salary to $100 which he accepted. Another contract was made reflecting the new salary provision, and the old one was simultaneously torn up. Bauman-Basch fired Schwartzreich before the year passed, claiming the second contract was unenforceable for lack of consideration.

Issue: Is a new contract that replaces a prior contract with terms that are similar, but more favorable to one party, enforceable?

Rule: Any change from an existing contract must have new consideration to support it. Where an existing contract is terminated by mutual consent, and a new one is executed in its place, the mutual promises of the parties constitute consideration.

Great Northern Ry. v. Witham (1873) KGK, R

Facts: Great Northern entered into a one-year contract to buy "any quantity that they may need" of train fenders from Witham. Witham later refused to perform, claiming the contract was invalid for lack of mutuality (i.e., Great Northern was not obligated to buy any set amount and could, if it wished, buy nothing, whereas Witham had to sell if Great Northern asked).

Issue: Does a requirements contract fail for lack of consideration if a party was not obligated to place an order?

Rule: Placing an order is sufficient consideration to bind a party to a requirements contract.

Westesen v. Olathe State Bank (1922) KGK

Facts: Westesen, in planning a vacation, obtained credit from Olathe, as needed, up to $5,000. In return, Westesen signed $5,000 worth of promissory notes. Olathe reneged on the deal claiming lack of mutuality because Westesen was not obligated to "need" any money.

Issue: Has the requirement of mutuality been met by a promise to use a product or service "as needed" when the need would not necessarily arise?

Rule: A "promise" is valid consideration fulfilling the requirement of mutuality when one is committed to use a product or service as needed, even if he is not required by the contract to use the product or service.

Swindell & Co. v. First National Bank
(1905) KGK

Facts: Swindell gave the bank promissory notes in exchange for a credit line that could be used according to its needs. The bank advanced some of the money but then canceled the agreement, claiming that it was void for lack of mutuality. The lower court ruled for the bank, and Swindell appealed.

Issue: Can a contract be valid if only one party is obligated to perform?

Rule: A contract dependent on mutual promises must contain reciprocal obligations in order for it to have the requisite consideration.

Note: This is not the modern rule regarding requirements contracts.

Lima Locomotive & Machine Co. v.
National Steel Castings Co. (1907) KGK

Facts: Lima entered into a requirements contract to purchase steel castings from National at a set price. National stopped performance before the agreed time and sued to recover for the value of goods already shipped. Lima counterclaimed that National was in breach.

Issue: Is a promise to buy all that one requires void for lack of mutuality?

Rule: A contract to buy all that one requires in a particular manufacturing business will not fail for lack of mutuality, because consideration is given in the form of forbearance from the right to buy from anyone else (even though the buyer is not obligated to buy without need).

Eastern Airlines v. Gulf Oil Corp. (1975) KGK

Facts: Gulf contracted to fulfill Eastern's jet fuel requirements on a long-term basis. The parties agreed that price would be determined by an index of posted fuel prices. In 1974, when oil prices skyrocketed as a result of an

OPEC embargo of foreign fuel sources, posted prices were kept below the market level by government regulation. Gulf refused to perform, claiming lack of mutuality because Eastern was not obligated to buy a set amount.

Issue: Are requirements contracts void for lack of mutuality?

Rule: Requirements contracts, entered into in good faith, are not void for lack of mutuality. According to UCC § 2-306, such contracts are valid so long as the requirements are not varied in bad faith or grossly disproportionate to a reasonably foreseeable figure.

Utah International Inc. v.
Colorado-Ute Electric Assn., Inc. (1976) KGK

Facts: Utah, a mining company, and Colorado-Ute signed a 35-year requirements contract for coal which contained maximum sales and minimum purchase obligations. To determine the purchase obligations and price terms under the contract, Utah used the size of Colorado-Ute's generators to calculate the average amounts of coal they would consume. Before the contract was signed, Colorado-Ute decided to use larger generators without telling Utah. The price of coal had risen since the capacity determinations had been made, and Colorado-Ute wanted to take advantage of the contract's lower prices. Utah sued, claiming that the capacity change constituted breach. Colorado-Ute answered that as long as its orders did not exceed Utah's maximum sales obligation, there was no breach.

Issue: Does an intentional increase in the amount of a buyer's "requirements" that does not exceed the maximum sales obligation violate a requirements contract?

Rule: A requirements contract that contains minimum and maximum quantity provisions implies an obligation and right to consume the minimum amount and an obligation to consume only what is required by the buyer's operations, as specified in the contract, up to the maximum amount. Requirements may be modified but not in a bad faith effort to take advantage of market changes.

Schlegel Manufacturing Co. v.
Cooper's Glue Factory (1921) KGK

Facts: Schlegel primarily did work involving solicitation of orders for the goods of other companies. It entered into a contract with Cooper's to purchase the amount of glue it needed to fill orders. The quantity was to be determined by the orders Schlegel received. Copper's later refused to honor the agreement, claiming lack of mutuality because Schlegel was not obligated to have orders.

Issue: Will a requirements contract be voided when the buyer does not have requirements?

Rule: The mere possibility of a future need for a product, by one who does not normally require the product, is not sufficient consideration to fulfill the mutuality requirement of a valid contract.

Note: This case illustrates the minimal requirement that a buyer in a "requirements" contract must have good reason to believe he will have some needs.

Hammond v. C.I.T. Financial Corp. (1953) KGK

Facts: C.I.T. granted Hammond the exclusive right to sell the assets of one of its subsidiaries. The agreement gave C.I.T. the power to terminate if it was dissatisfied with Hammond's efforts. C.I.T. sold the subsidiary to another company without any assistance from Hammond. When Hammond sued to recover a commission, C.I.T. claimed that the contract was invalid for lack of consideration because its promise was illusory.

Issue: Is a promise illusory and unenforceable when one party reserves the right to terminate if it is dissatisfied with the other party's efforts?

Rule: An agreement is not illusory when one party reserves the right to cancel the agreement because of dissatisfaction with the other party's performance.

Note: The condition of satisfaction is subject to a requirement of good faith.

Sylvan Crest Sand & Gravel Co. v. United States
(1945) KGK, R

Facts: Sylvan was awarded a contract to supply traprock for an airport. The contract specified that the U.S. could cancel at any time. Other provisions, including penalties for refusal or failure to perform, clearly indicated that the parties supposed they were entering an enforceable contract. The U.S. later refused to take custody of a delivery of rock, claiming its reservation of an unrestricted power of termination made the contract wholly illusory and nonbinding.

Issue: Is a contract that allows cancellation at any time void for lack of consideration?

Rule: A contract provision allowing cancellation at any time is to be interpreted as an implied promise to either perform according to the contract or to give notice of cancellation within a reasonable time. The alternative of giving notice, while not usually difficult, is sufficient consideration to support a contract.

Carlton v. Smith (1936) KGK

Facts: Carlton agreed to sell his business to Smith subject to the condition that Smith would be able to get a lease for the premises from Carlton's landlord. Smith did not get a lease, although he was offered the same terms as Carlton. Carlton sued for breach of contract.

Issue: If a contract depends on the fulfillment of a condition, can a party avoid the contract by making no effort to fulfill the condition?

Rule: A party to a contract is impliedly required to make a reasonable, good faith effort to fulfill a precondition to a contract that has been signed.

Reinert v. Lawson (1938) KGK

Facts: Lawson contracted to buy Reinert's gin plant, subject to the condition precedent that Lawson successfully purchase a farm from a bank. Although the farm negotiations went well, Lawson refused to buy it. Reinert sued to recover liquidated damages provided for in the contract.

Issue: Can one recover damages from a party who did not act in good faith to fulfill a condition precedent to the contract?

Rule: When a contract is subject to a condition precedent, the language of which does not imply a promise to actually fulfill the condition but only to fulfill it before the contract may exist, there can be no liability for breach of contract.

Bernstein v. W.B. Mfg. Co. (1921) KGK

Facts: The plaintiff's contract to sell the defendant swim suits contained a clause that provided, "All orders accepted, to be delivered to the best of our ability. ... [We are not] liable for failure to deliver any portion of orders taken." The plaintiff sued after the defendant refused to accept delivery of an order. The defendant claimed the contract was void for lack of mutuality.

Issue: Is a bilateral contract void for lack of mutuality when one party is not bound to perform?

Rule: When one party is not bound by a bilateral contract, the agreement is void at its inception due to a lack of mutuality.

Gurfein v. Werbelovsky (1922) KGK

Facts: Gurfein accepted Werbelovsky's order of glass, stipulating that Werbelovsky had "the option to cancel the above order before shipment." Gurfein later refused to ship.

Issue: Is an agreement that allows one party to cancel unenforceable for lack of mutuality?

Rule: An agreement will not be void for lack of mutuality when one party had the power at some point to bind the other party.

Roberts-Horsfield v. Gedicks (1922) KGK

Facts: Horsfield's aunt, Gedicks, gave Horsfield land and helped her to build a house on it. Horsfield occupied the house and made improvements. After Gedicks died, her husband's second wife tried to evict Horsfield.

Issue: Is an oral gift of realty enforceable if the donee occupied the realty and paid for improvements?

Rule: A parol gift of land is invalid, but when the gift is accompanied by possession, and the donee has been induced by the promise of the gift to make valuable improvements of a permanent nature, the gift will be enforced on equitable principles.

Devecmon v. Shaw (1888) KGK, FE

Facts: While working for his uncle, Devecmon took a trip unrelated to business to Europe at his uncle's request after his uncle promised that he would be reimbursed. The uncle's estate refused to pay.

Issue: Is a party bound by a promise from which no direct benefit was received?

Rule: A gratuitous promise that induces the promisee to incur an expenditure in reasonable reliance on the promise is enforceable even if no benefit is received by the promisor.

Ricketts v. Scothorn (1898) KGK, KC, MS, R

Facts: Ricketts signed a note promising his granddaughter $2,000 on demand so that she would not have to work. She quit her job in reliance on the promise. The administrator of Ricketts' estate refused to honor the note after Ricketts' death, claiming that no consideration was given for his promise.

Issue: When will a gratuitous promise bind a promisor?

Rule: The doctrine of equitable estoppel provides that a right may accrue to a promisee if the promisee changed her position in accordance with the real or apparent intention of the promisor.

De Cicco v. Schweizer (1917)
KGK, FE, CPB

Facts: Schweizer promised his daughter's fiancé $2,500 per year if they married. Schweizer paid the annuity for ten years after the marriage before stopping. When the husband sued, Schweizer claimed the promise was unenforceable for lack of consideration.

Issue: Is a promise made by a third party to encourage two parties to marry enforceable?

Rule: A promisee who forbears from the right to modify or withdraw from an agreement has incurred legal detriment.

Gillingham v. Brown (1901) KGK

Facts: The defendant gave the plaintiff a promissory note which he never paid, and the statute of limitations expired. The defendant later gave the plaintiff part of the money and promised to pay the rest in installments, which he did not do. The jury found that the defendant had to pay all of the outstanding debt. The defendant claimed he only had to abide by the terms of his new promise and pay for those installments that were actually overdue.

Issue: Is a party who promises to pay a debt that is unenforceable due to a legal technicality required to abide by the conditions of the old debt?

Rule: A new promise to pay an old debt will be enforceable only according to the terms of the new promise.

Lampleigh v. Brathwait (1615) KGK

Facts: After he was convicted on murder charges, Brathwait asked Lampleigh to try to obtain a pardon from the King. Brathwait made no reference to payment. Lampleigh expended great effort on behalf of Brathwait, but was unsuccessful. After Lampleigh's efforts, Brathwait promised to reimburse him, then later changed his mind.

Issue: Is a promise to pay for services voluntarily performed in the past enforceable?

Rule: A promise to pay for services voluntarily performed in the past will usually fail for lack of consideration unless such services were performed pursuant to the request of the promisor.

Eastwood v. Kenyon (1840) KGK

Facts: The executor of an estate to which the defendant's wife was the sole heir borrowed some money on behalf of the estate. The defendant subsequently promised to reimburse the plaintiff for his services.

Issue: Is a promise to pay for services performed prior to the promise enforceable?

Rule: Unless the services were rendered at the request of the promisor, a later promise to compensate for services already performed is unenforceable.

C_ v. W_ (1972) KGK

Facts: C_, the mother of W_'s child, sued W_ for breaching two contracts for child support and other payments. C_ and W_ were never married, and W_ claimed that his promise was unenforceable for lack of consideration (i.e., he received no "benefit" for making the promise). Under common law in this jurisdiction, a father was under no legal duty to support an illegitimate child.

Issue: Is a child support agreement between an unmarried couple unenforceable?

Rule: A child support agreement, executed by a father under no legal obligation to support his illegitimate child, is unenforceable due to the absence of consideration.

Perreault v. Hall (1946) KGK

Facts: Perreault's boss made several oral promises that she "would have a good living for the rest of her life" if she stayed with the business and did not marry. At her retirement, Perreault received a letter granting her a pension of $20 a week "in consideration" of 40 years of good work. The pension was paid until Perreault's employer died. Hall, as executor of the decedent, refused to honor the pension, claiming no consideration was given.

Issue: Can a contract containing only an indefinite recital of consideration be enforced?

Rule: An agreement in which recital of consideration is too vague for enforcement can become binding by partial performance.

Note: Although the executor is correct that past consideration is no consideration, the court chose to enforce the oral promises, which were initially too vague but were made clear by the written promise and the plaintiff's performance after they were made.

In Re Schoenkerman's Estate (1940) KGK

Facts: After his wife died, Schoenkerman asked his relatives to come live with him and raise his children which they did. Schoenkerman gave each a promissory note ten years later "in consideration" of their past services which his estate refused to honor.

Issue: Can a promise made for past services be enforceable?

Rule: A promise made for past consideration can be enforced if there is a moral obligation to pay. Moral obligation operates as consideration for a promise whenever the promisor has received value under circumstances giving rise to a moral obligation to pay for that which he has received.

Elbinger v. Capitol & Teutonia Co. (1932) KGK

Facts: Elbinger, a real-estate broker, performed services for Capitol pursuant to an oral agreement. Capitol paid Elbinger part of the money and gave him a written note for the balance. The statute of frauds required real estate transactions to be written in order to be valid. Capitol refused to pay the rest of the fee, claiming it received no consideration after the written agreement was made.

Issue: Can a promise given for past consideration be enforced on grounds of moral obligation?

Rule: The promise of an owner, made after the services were rendered, is sufficient to constitute a legal obligation to pay the broker for services, even though the original oral contract violated a statute and did not give rise to a legally enforceable obligation. The value received prior to the promise gives rise to a moral obligation, which satisfies the contractual element of consideration (Rest. 2d. § 89).

Medberry v. Olcovich (1936) KGK

Facts: Medberry's son was injured while riding in a car driven by Olcovich's son. Out of sympathy, Olcovich promised to pay all Medberry's medical bills but later refused to do so, claiming his promise was unenforceable due to lack of consideration.

Issue: Can a gratuitous promise be enforced on the basis that a moral obligation acts as consideration?

Rule: Moral obligation acts as consideration for a gratuitous promise if the promise is relied upon.

Note: The promisee in this case incurred expenses in reliance on a secure source of financial backing.

Lawrence v. Oglesby (1899) KGK, MS

Facts: Oglesby's father wanted to build a $1,500 house for her, but was unable to do so during his life. Before he died he asked his son, Lawrence, to promise to pay his sister $1,500. Lawrence promised, but later claimed he received no consideration for his promise.

Issue: Can a gratuitous promise be enforced?

Rule: When a party is under moral obligation and makes a gratuitous promise, the honesty and rectitude of the promise is consideration.

Haigh v. Brooks (1840) KGK, MS

Facts: Brooks gave Haigh and another a promissory note for £10,000 owed to them by a third party. Neither party realized that the note was void because it lacked a proper seal. Brooks promised Haigh £10,000 for the return of the note but refused payment when he found out the document was worthless, claiming that he received no consideration for his promise.

Issue: Is an agreement void for lack of consideration if the "value" given by one party turns out to be worthless in fact?

Rule: Consideration exists when a party is induced to part with something he might have kept, even if the parties later discover that the "value" of the inducement was not as expected.

Cook v. Wright (1861) KGK

Facts: A local statute required homeowners to pay for repairs to streets adjoining their homes. The agent of one of the homeowner's refused to pay but acceded when threatened with legal action. The district commissioner agreed to accept a smaller fee from the agent. The agent defaulted and argued that the compromise was nonbinding for lack of consideration because the commissioner's claim was invalid, and thus the promise to refrain from bringing suit was frivolous.

Issue: Is a promise to resist from instituting a baseless legal action adequate consideration for a contract?

Rule: A promise to refrain from pursuing a legal claim serves as sufficient consideration to an agreement even if the claim is not credible. The promise to resist from bringing a legal action constitutes a detriment to the promising party.

Marks v. Gates (1907) DHH

Facts: Gates gave Marks a 20 percent interest in all property that Gates might acquire in Alaska, for recited consideration of one dollar. Gates later refused to share the property he acquired, which was worth $750,000. Marks introduced evidence that he gave additional consideration, including cancellation of Gates' $11,225 prior indebtedness and a $1,000 payment to Gates. (The court was not convinced of the veracity of this additional consideration.)

Issue: If inadequacy of consideration is so gross as to render the contract unconscionable, can specific performance be denied?

Rule: If consideration is grossly inadequate, equity does not require the granting of specific performance in case of breach, and the parties are left to their remedies at law, if they have any.

Embola v. Tuppela (1923) KGK, R

Facts: In return for the $320 that Embola advanced him, Tuppela promised to give Embola $10,000 if he ever successfully recovered his mining properties in a lawsuit. Embola sued to collect the money promised when Tuppela's trustee reneged.

Issue: Does a large disparity in the value of consideration given and received make a contract unenforceable?

Rule: A contract that compels the payment of a large amount of money upon the occurrence of a specific contingent event is enforceable even if only a small amount of money is advanced as consideration for the agreement. The small sum is adequate consideration because of the risk that the money advanced may be lost if the contingency never occurs.

United States v. Bethlehem Steel Corp.
(1942) KGK

Facts: Bethlehem was able to negotiate extremely favorable contract terms to build ships for the U.S. because it owned the only plant with the necessary facilities to fulfill its needs, and because an overall shipping shortage existed due to World War I. The U.S. sued in equity for an accounting and for a refund of amounts paid in excess of just and reasonable compensation. Bethlehem sued for breach of contract.

Issue: Is a contract enforceable if it allows one of the parties to realize excessive profits?

Rule: Without a showing of fraud or duress, a contract is valid even if one of the parties enjoys excessive profits to the detriment of the other.

Dissent: Taking advantage of desperate circumstances constitutes duress, which leads to unconscionable contract terms. (UCC § 2-302.)

Thomas v. Thomas (1842) KGK, MS, CPB

Facts: Before he died, the husband told his wife in front of witnesses that she could either take their house or £100 from his estate. His estate accepted the validity of the promise, reasoning that his motive to help his wife was consideration. His wife was required to pay £1 rent per year in return for using the house. One of the executors later changed his mind and tried to revoke the promise, claiming that the husband received no consideration.

Issue: Does motive constitute valid consideration?

Rule: Motive is different from, and does not replace, consideration. However, a promise to pay £1 a year in rent is valid consideration.

Murphy, Thompson & Co. v. Reed (1907) KGK

Facts: Reed gave Murphy options to buy his land. The options recited consideration of $1. Reed later refused to sell his land, claiming he received no consideration for the options.

Issue: Is an option given for nominal consideration enforceable?

Rule: Nominal consideration will not make a contract enforceable.

Real Estate Co. of Pittsburgh v. Rudolph (1930) KGK

Facts: For $1, Rudolph granted Real Estate a written option to buy his property. Real Estate was also promised a three percent commission if it succeeded in selling Rudolph's home. Rudolph later attempted to revoke the option.

Issue: Is an option given for one dollar binding?

Rule: Valuable consideration, no matter how small or nominal, if given or stipulated in good faith, is binding in the absence of fraud.

Note: The court reasoned, alternatively, that Rudolph had given Real Estate an offer to enter into a unilateral contract by finding a buyer.

Wheat v. Morse (1961) KGK

Facts: A long-term option to purchase land was given in exchange for $1 consideration.

Issue: Can a long-term option to buy land given in exchange for nominal consideration be terminated?

Rule: An option given for consideration, however small, cannot be terminated without the consent of the other party during the option period.

Warren v. Lynch (1810) KGK

Facts: The defendant gave the plaintiff a handwritten promissory note which recited that it was under the defendant's "hand and seal."

Issue: Can handwritten words qualify as a seal?

Rule: A scrawl with a pen is not a seal, which must be in wax.

Note: This case and others following discuss the rules of the seal. These rules have been abolished virtually everywhere and are of little relevance today. Some jurisdictions that still require seals do not require that they be in wax.

Krell v. Codman (1891) KGK

Facts: A deceased signed a covenant under seal to bind her estate to make cash distributions after her death to certain parties, including the plaintiff. The defendant refused to honor the covenant, claiming no consideration was given.

Issue: Is a covenant to pay money after one's death valid?

Rule: A covenant for the payment of money after one's death will be valid, even if the requirements of a will are not met, if the covenant was written and signed.

Goulet v. Goulet (1963) KGK

Facts: The plaintiff executed a covenant under seal that she would not sue her husband for injuries sustained in a car accident. The plaintiff was given one dollar as consideration. She later decided to bring suit.

Issue: Must consideration be given when a contract is executed under seal?

Rule: Neither the absence nor the failure of consideration will overcome the binding legal effect of a seal.

Aller v. Aller (1878) KGK, DHH

Facts: The defendant executed a promissory note to his daughters under seal. He did not receive consideration.

Issue: Is a note executed under seal enforceable, despite the absence of consideration?

Rule: A note executed under seal is enforceable regardless of whether consideration was exchanged.

Schnell v. Nell (1861) KGK, FE

Facts: Nell was granted $200 in a will made by Schnell's wife. The will was invalid, but Schnell promised to make the payment in exchange for one cent consideration. Schnell revoked his promise.

Issue: May one cent be acceptable consideration?

Rule: Plainly nominal consideration is not effective.

Cochran v. Taylor (1937) KGK

Facts: The defendant gave an option for the purchase of land for $1 consideration. The option was executed under seal.

Issue: Must consideration be more than nominal if an option is given under seal?

Rule: An option executed under seal is enforceable, regardless of whether actual or nominal consideration is given.

Pillans & Rose v. Van Mierop & Hopkins (1765) KGK

Facts: Pillans & Rose extended credit to a third party in reliance on Van Mierop & Hopkins' written promise to guarantee the debt. The latter was given no consideration for its promise. Both parties were financial institutions.

Issue: Is a written contract between merchants valid without the exchange of consideration?

Rule: A commercial contract between merchants does not fail because consideration was not given (UCC § 2-209).

Dougherty v. Salt (1919) FE

Facts: The plaintiff received a promissory note from his aunt for $3,000. The note was on a printed form that contained the words "for value received." No consideration was in fact given.

Issue: Is the printed clause "value received" sufficient evidence of consideration to render a note enforceable?

Rule: An inference of consideration that is drawn from the form of a note can be overcome by other evidence suggesting that no consideration was in fact given.

Hancock Bank & Trust Co. v. Shell Oil Co. (1974) FE

Facts: Shell had a lease that included a clause providing that "Shell may terminate this lease at any time by giving lessor at least ninety days notice." Hancock tried to invalidate the lease on grounds of lack of mutuality.

Issue: Will a lease be void due to a lack of mutuality when one party has the option of canceling upon providing ninety days notice?

Rule: When a contract is supported by some consideration, the contract will not be voided because of a bad or uneven bargain.

Newman & Snell's State Bank v. Hunter (1928) FE

Facts: Hunter's husband owed money to Newman & Snell's, and at his death, his insolvent estate could not repay his debts. Hunter made an agreement to repay her husband's debt to Newman & Snell's, in exchange for the bank surrendering her husband's promissory note and interest due.

Issue: Does a spouse's promise to pay the debts of a deceased, insolvent spouse fail for lack of consideration?

Rule: A spouse's promise to pay the debts of her insolvent, deceased spouse will not be enforced if she did not receive consideration for her promise. The submission of a worthless debt does not constitute consideration.

Springstead v. Nees (1908) FE

Facts: Springstead, Nees and others were siblings. Their father died intestate (without a will) leaving behind two parcels of real estate. One was held in trust exclusively for Nees and another defendant. The other was to be divided equally among all the parties. In reaction to Springstead and others' disapproval, Nees and another defendant promised to give their share of the common property to Springstead and the others if the plaintiffs would not bother them about their inheritance (to which they had no right). The defendants later changed their mind.

Issue: Does forbearance from asserting an invalid claim constitute consideration?

Rule: Forbearance of a claim does not constitute consideration if the party forbearing the claim was aware that the claim was unfounded.

Miller v. Miller (1887) FE

Facts: A husband and wife contracted to "refrain from scolding, fault-finding and anger." The wife agreed to "keep her home and family" in return for the husband's promise to support the family and provide his wife with $200 per year for her "individual use." The wife sued because her husband spent money on other women and did not meet the terms of their financial agreement.

Issue: Is a marriage contract invalid because it is without consideration and against public policy?

Rule: Although a marriage contract does not fail for lack of consideration, it will fail because public policy prohibits a judicial inquiry into matters between husband and wife.

Scott v. Moragues Lumber Co. (1918) FE

Facts: Scott agreed to charter a vessel to Moragues on the condition that Scott was able to buy it. Scott purchased the vessel, but rented it to a third party. Scott claimed its agreement with Moragues was void for lack of mutuality because it was not obligated to buy the vessel, but Moragues was obligated to rent it if it was available.

Issue: Is a contract void for lack of mutuality of consideration when it is conditioned upon an event whose occurrence is at the will of one of the parties?

Rule: A contract that is conditioned upon the occurrence of an event which is at the will of a party to the contract is not void for lack of consideration. Once the condition is met, an obligation to fulfill the contract exists.

Wickham & Burton Coal Co. v. Farmers' Lumber Co.
(1920) FE

Facts: Wickham & Burton agreed to supply Farmer's with the coal it "would want to purchase." Wickham & Burton later renounced the contract, claiming lack of mutuality of obligation. Farmer's counterclaimed for damages.

Issue: Does a contract lack mutuality of obligation if it allows one party to choose the quantity it will purchase?

Rule: A requirements contract is void for want of mutuality if the quantity to be delivered is conditioned entirely on the will, wish or want of the buyer and not dependent on the buyer's needs.

Grouse v. Group Health Plan, Inc.
(1981) FE, CPB

Facts: Grouse resigned from his job because he received an employment offer from Group Health. The offer was later revoked.

Issue: Are damages resulting from revocation of an at-will employment offer recoverable?

Rule: Under the doctrine of promissory estoppel, a promise that the promisor should reasonably expect to induce action or forbearance on the part of the promisee, and which does induce such action, is binding if nonenforcement would result in injustice.

Gray v. Martino (1918) FE

Facts: The defendant offered the plaintiff, a police officer, a reward if he could determine the identity of persons who had stolen her jewels. The defendant refused to pay the plaintiff.

Issue: Can a public servant enforce a private offer of a reward for performing duties encompassed by that person's employment?

Rule: Public policy forbids outside remuneration for official duties performed by a public servant.

Lingenfelder v. Wainwright Brewery Co.
(1891) FE

Facts: Wainwright hired an architect to build its new brewery. The architect walked off the job after Wainwright awarded a different job to his competitor. Pressed for time, Wainwright promised to pay him extra compensation if he resumed work. Wainwright reneged on this promise, claiming it received no consideration for its promise.

Issue: Does the resumption of work one was contractually obligated to perform constitute sufficient consideration for a promise that induced the return to work?

Rule: A new contract that was signed to prevent one party from breaching an earlier agreement will fail for lack of consideration.

Note: This is the "pre-existing duty" rule.

Foakes v. Beer (1884) FE

Facts: Beer agreed to forgive all the interest on Foakes' debt if he paid a quarter of the principal at once and the rest in installments. After Foakes completed the installments Beer sued for the interest.

Issue: Will an agreement to forgo the interest due on a loan in exchange for payment of the principal fail for lack of consideration?

Rule: A creditor's agreement to forgo interest on a debt in exchange for repayment of principal fails for lack of consideration because the debtor only agreed to do that which he was already obligated to perform (pre-existing duty rule).

Angel v. Murray (1974) FE, CPB

Facts: After he signed a five-year garbage collection contract, Maher requested an increase in pay because a construction boon substantially increased the number of homes from which he had to collect garbage. The city council agreed to pay Maher more. Several years later, Angel and other taxpayers brought suit claiming that no consideration was given for the promise to pay more.

Issue: Can a contract be modified because of unanticipated difficulties?

Rule: If a party to a contract encounters unanticipated difficulties, and the other party, not influenced by coercion or duress, voluntarily agrees to pay additional compensation for work already required to be performed under the contract, the contract will be enforced despite the pre-existing duty rule.

Central London Property Trust Ltd. v. High Trees House Ltd. (1946) FE

Facts: High Trees leased premises from Central London at a rate of £2,500 a year. During World War II, Central London agreed to halve the rent because of the poor economic situation. After the war, it sought to restore the rent and to recover the discount it gave High Trees.

Issue: Can an agreement to lower the rent of a written lease be enforced if the lessee relies on the modification?

Rule: A promise to accept a smaller sum in discharge of a larger sum is binding if the promisee relied on the promise despite failure of consideration.

Roth Steel Prod. v. Sharon Steel Corp. (1983) FE, CPB

Facts: Sharon threatened to breach its contract to supply steel if Roth did not agree to price increases. Although Sharon's motive was rising costs, it did not offer this explanation until the case came to trial.

Issue: Is an attempted contract modification to compensate for rising costs ineffective if the party did not act in good faith?

Rule: Contract modification must be obtained in good faith, by conduct that is both consistent with "reasonable commercial standards of fair dealing in the trade" and "honesty in fact," to be enforceable. (UCC § 2-103(1)(b).)

Flambeau Prod. Corp. v. Honeywell Info. Sys. Inc. (1983) FE

Facts: Flambeau, in an attempt to prepay an installment purchase contract, paid Honeywell in full except for an amount agreed upon for services that

Flambeau did not actually use. Honeywell cashed the check but claimed that Flambeau still owed it the service fee.

Issue: Does a vendor's acceptance of a check marked "in full payment" constitute accord and satisfaction, discharging the obligations of the vendee?

Rule: If a check marked "in full payment" is submitted in good faith as an offer to settle a disputed claim, cashing the check constitutes acceptance, or accord and satisfaction, and settles the claim.

Clark v. West (1908) FE, MS

Facts: West Publishing promised to pay Clark $6.00 per page for an acceptable manuscript if he did not drink and $2.00 per page if he did. West discovered that Clark was drinking alcohol during the term of the contract but told him not to worry. After the book was finished West offered to pay only $2 per page. Clark claimed that the alcohol provision was a condition to the contract, which was expressly waived by West. West claimed abstinence was consideration for the contract.

Issue: May a condition to a contract be waived?

Rule: A condition to a contract can be expressly waived. Merely accepting a party's performance does not constitute waiver, but if an express waiver is made, it is valid.

Wisconsin Knife Works v. National Metal Crafters
(1986) FE, CPB, R

Facts: Wisconsin's purchase order included a provision that stated that the contract could not be modified without its written assent. National missed the delivery deadlines, but Wisconsin accepted the late shipments and issued a new set of orders (later rescinded). Wisconsin later terminated the contract after National missed more of the original deadlines. National claimed Wisconsin "waived" the written modification requirement by acceptance of late shipments. In consequence, National continued to produce the goods.

Issue: Absent a writing, when does a contract modification "operate as a waiver" (UCC § 2-209(4)) so as to be effective despite a clause that forbids modification other than in writing?

Rule: Absent a writing, an attempted modification of a contract that contains a clause forbidding modifications other than in writing is effective as a waiver only when it is reasonably relied upon.

Jones v. Jones (1965) FE

Facts: A separation agreement between a wife and husband called for a payment of $100,000 to the wife, and an additional $50,000 one year later. Neither payment was made, but the husband did make payments to support the wife. Suit on the separation agreement was barred by the statute of limitations. The wife claimed that her husband's promise to support her was a new promise to pay the $150,000.

Issue: Will a new promise to pay a debt barred by the statute of limitations bind the promisor?

Rule: A new promise by a debtor to his creditor to pay a debt, which is unenforceable by operation of a statute of limitations, will be enforceable, despite the lack of any new consideration.

Langer v. Superior Steel Corp. (1932) MS

Facts: Upon his retirement Langer was promised a pension "as long as [he] preserve[d] his present attitude of loyalty to the company and its officers and [was] not employed in any competitive occupation." Pension payments were discontinued after four years. Superior claimed that its promise was unenforceable due to lack of consideration.

Issue: Can forbearance of a right constitute consideration?

Rule: Forbearance of a right, such as the right to be employed by a former employer's competitor, is a detriment of a definite and substantial character and is valid consideration.

Stonestreet v. Southern Oil Co. (1946) MS

Facts: Stonestreet leased property to Southern. When the water supply was partly depleted, both agreed to pay half the cost of digging a new well. Southern's agent later promised Stonestreet that if Southern exercised its option to buy Stonestreet's property, it would pay for the whole well. Stonestreet did not respond to the promise. Southern exercised the option but only paid for half the well.

Issue: Is a promise enforceable if it is made without consideration?

Rule: A bare promise, for which no consideration is received, creates no legal rights and imposes no legal obligations.

Bogigian v. Bogigian (1990) MS

Facts: When David and Hazel Bogigian dissolved their marriage, Hazel received a judgment on the family home of $10,300, to be paid when David sold the real estate. David sold the home, but because he had no equity in the property, he gave Hazel a paltry $5, and Hazel released her judgment. Hazel brought suit the following year to reinstate the judgment, claiming that her release was not supported by consideration because she did not understand what she was doing.

Issue: Can parties give or receive valid consideration if they are not aware that they are doing so?

Rule: Because consideration must actually be bargained for, a benefit received or a detriment suffered cannot be consideration unless the parties agree that the benefit or detriment is consideration.

Jones v. Star Credit Corp. (1969) MS

Facts: Jones and other welfare recipients were to pay over $1,400 (including tax, finance charges, and insurance) for a freezer that ordinarily retailed for less than $300. UCC § 2-302 provided that a court may refuse to enforce a contract or excise an objectionable clause if it finds that the contract or clause was unconscionable at the time it was made.

Issue: Can a contract be void for unconscionability because the price term is excessive?

Rule: A court may refuse to enforce an excessive price term on the grounds of unconscionability.

In Re Greene (1930) MS

Facts: Greene, a married man, signed an agreement to pay his mistress $1,000 monthly plus insurance and rent upon the termination of their relationship. Consideration of one dollar was recited in the agreement.

Issue: Does nominal consideration suffice to bind a promise?

Rule: Token consideration will not suffice to make an agreement binding. The past "illicit intercourse" of the parties is not consideration either.

Fiege v. Boehm (1956) MS, CPB

Facts: Fiege agreed to pay medical and other expenses of Boehm provided that Boehm would not institute a paternity suit. After Boehm gave birth, Fiege used blood tests to prove he was not the father. He then refused to honor his promise, claiming absence of valid consideration.

Issue: Does forbearance to bring suit qualify as consideration if the suit would not have been successful?

Rule: Forbearance to assert an invalid claim is sufficient consideration if the forbearing party had an honest intention to prosecute the litigation and reasonably believed it was valid.

Levine v. Blumenthal (1936) MS

Facts: The defendant contracted to lease a store for two years at a rate of $175 per month in the first year and $200 per month in the second. At the end of the first year, the defendant claimed that due to financial difficulties, he would have to go out of business if his rent was increased. The plaintiff accepted $175 per month, then sued for the balance.

Issue: Is an agreement to accept payments below the agreed upon amount binding when a party is in financial difficulties?

Rule: Partial payment of a larger debt is not consideration for an agreement to excuse the full debt, because the debtor is obligated to repay his debt anyway (pre-existing duty). The fact that a financially weak debtor agreed not to breach is not adequate consideration.

Alaska Packer's Assoc. v. Domenico (1902) MS, DHH

Facts: Sailors contracted to work for Alaska Packer's as fishermen in Alaska at a rate of $50 for the season, plus two cents for each fish caught. Upon arrival in Alaska, they refused to work unless they received higher wages. Alaska Packer's agreed because of the unavailability of alternative fishermen, and subsequently refused to pay the higher wages.

Issue: Is an agreement to increase compensation for services that the promisee is already contractually obligated to perform enforceable?

Rule: A new promise to increase the compensation of one already contractually obligated to perform is invalid if new consideration is not given (pre-existing duty rule).

Rehm-Zeiher Co. v. F.G. Walker Co. (1913) MS

Facts: Reim-Zeiher, a seller of whiskey, entered into a four-year contract to purchase whiskey from F.G. Walker, a distiller. A clause in the contract provided that if Reim-Zeiher "finds they cannot use the full amount of the above-named goods," they would only be required to buy what they wanted. Walker broke the agreement claiming lack of mutuality of consideration made it void.

Issue: Is a contract that allows one party to refuse to purchase void for lack of mutuality?

Rule: A contract that allows one party to perform at its own discretion fails for lack of mutuality.

McMichael v. Price (1936) MS

Facts: Price, an experienced sand salesman, formed a new company and contracted to buy all the sand his company would be able to resell from McMichael for 60 percent of the market price. Although Price's company was not established, McMichael was aware of Price's experience.

Issue: Is an agreement to purchase all of one's requirements void for lack of mutuality?

Rule: A contract to buy all of one's "requirements" will not be void for lack of mutuality when both parties assume that a purchase would be made.

Note: In light of Price's experience and likely connections, it is sufficiently probable that his business would have requirements.

Omni Group, Inc. v. Seattle-First Nat'l Bank (1982) MS

Facts: Omni contracted to buy land from the Clarks subject to the requirement that Omni would be satisfied with a feasibility report made by its engineers and architects. The Clarks refused to sell, claiming lack of consideration because Omni's promise was illusory.

Issue: Does a condition precedent involving the satisfaction of a party render the said party's promise to perform illusory?

Rule: A condition precedent that requires a party's subjective satisfaction does not render a contract unenforceable, because it imposes a duty of good faith upon the said party in exercising good judgment.

Bailey v. West (1969) MS

Facts: The defendant bought a lame horse which he tried to return to the seller. During several months of arguments between the defendant and the seller, the plaintiff, aware of the dispute, voluntarily cared for the horse and sent bills to both. The plaintiff sued the defendant for the value of the services rendered.

Issue: Is a person who voluntarily renders a service entitled to recovery in quasi-contract?

Rule: A person who voluntarily renders a service is usually not entitled to restitution.

Spooner v. Reserve Life Insurance Co. (1955) MS

Facts: Reserve offered its employees a bonus for improved sales performance but expressly reserved the right to cancel the arrangement without notice. Reserve refused to pay the bonuses, claiming no contract was formed because its promise was illusory.

Issue: Is a promise illusory if the promisor's performance is entirely discretionary?

Rule: A promise is illusory if it is accompanied by a provision that makes performance optional or entirely discretionary on the part of the promisor.

Duncan v. Akers (1970) MS

Facts: Duncan contracted to have a house built on his property. The builder erroneously built on Akers' land, due to a surveyor's error.

Issue: Is one who erroneously improves another's land entitled to restitution from the owner of the land?

Rule: An innocent builder who mistakenly improves another's real estate may recover on the theory that a constructive contract was made. The builder recovers restitution for the unjust enrichment of the owner.

Manwill v. Oyler (1961) MS

Facts: Defendant orally agreed to pay a debt that had been barred by the statute of limitations. The defendant later claimed that his promise was unenforceable due to lack of consideration.

Issue: Is a promise to repay a debt that is legally unenforceable due to a technicality void for lack of consideration?

Rule: Moral obligation does not suffice as consideration.

Note: Courts are split on this issue.

Harrington v. Taylor (1945) MS, CPB

Facts: The defendant's wife took refuge in the plaintiff's home after the defendant assaulted her. The defendant entered the plaintiff's house. His wife succeeded in knocking him down and was about to hit him with an axe when the plaintiff deflected the blow, mutilating her hand as a result. The defendant promised to pay for the plaintiff's damages but reneged after making a few payments, claiming that no consideration was given for his promise.

Issue: Is a promise to pay for damages made subsequent to an accident unenforceable for lack of consideration?

Rule: A voluntary humanitarian act is not consideration for a promise made at a later date. Past consideration is no consideration.

Miles Homes Div. of Insilco Corp. v. First State Bank of Joplin (1990) MS

Facts: Ames purchased land on which to build a Miles Homes kit house, financing much of the purchase with a mortgage from First State. Miles Homes sent a credit inquiry to First State, requesting that it notify Miles if Ames was delinquent in his mortgage payments and that it provide Miles with an opportunity to make the payments before foreclosure. Based on this pledge from First State, Miles Homes approved Ames' credit for the kit house. Ames defaulted on the mortgage, First State auctioned off the property and Miles Homes lost its security for the loan.

Issue: May a creditor who loans funds on the basis of a third party's promise, which is not supported by consideration, recover losses resulting from the third party's failure to keep that promise?

Rule: Under the doctrine of estoppel, a promise, which the promisor should reasonably expect to induce action on the part of the promisee and which does induce such action, is binding if injustice can be avoided only by enforcement of the promise.

Note: Here, First State knew that Miles Homes would furnish the building materials dependent on its promise to give notice of delinquency, and First State's failure to keep the promise caused Miles Homes to lose its security interest.

Kibler v. Frank L. Garrett & Sons, Inc. (1968) CPB

Facts: In response to a dispute over how much money he owed the plaintiff for harvesting wheat, the defendant sent a check for what he felt he owed. A clause, written in fine print, stated that cashing the check would constitute full satisfaction of the debt. The plaintiff accepted the check without noticing the fine print and sued for the rest of the debt.

Issue: If there is a disputed claim, is it necessary to show that the defendant actually manifested his intention not to pay more than he remitted?

Rule: When partial payment of a debated debt is intended to be full satisfaction, it must be clearly brought to the attention of the payee.

RMP Industries, Ltd. v. Linen Center (1986) CPB

Facts: RMP, a subcontractor, and Brown, a contractor for the Linen Center, disagreed over the amount of money due at the completion of a project. Brown sent a check to RMP which stated that it was "payment in full" upon cashing. RMP cashed the check after writing "under protest" on the face of it and sued for the difference.

Issue: Does the common law accord and satisfaction doctrine bar any suits for further payment for the same work if payment was conditionally accepted?

Rule: The acceptance of a payment offered under the condition that it represents settlement of all disputes constitutes a binding agreement and any language claiming acceptance "under protest" is irrelevant.

Note: The issue of whether the UCC alters the common law was not reached but the court suggested in a footnote that § 1-207 was not meant to alter the common law accord and satisfaction doctrine.

Austin Instrument, Inc. v. Loral Corp. (1971) CPB

Facts: Loral had a contract to produce radar sets for the Navy. The sets had 40 parts of which Austin, a subcontractor, produced 23. When Loral received a second contract from the Navy, Austin bid on all 40 parts, threatening to stop delivery of all parts on the first contract if it did not receive a price increase and the subcontract for all 40 parts of the second contract. After unsuccessfully checking with all the other subcontractors on its approved list, Loral acceded to Austin's demands so as to avoid breaching its contract with the Navy.

Issue: Is a contract modification enforceable if it was agreed to by a party who was deprived of free will under circumstances amounting to economic duress?

Rule: A contract is voidable if the party claiming duress was forced to agree by means of a wrongful threat precluding the exercise of its free will. The existence of economic duress is demonstrated by proof that immediate possession of needed goods is threatened and that the goods could not be obtained from another source.

Texas Gas Utilities Company v. S.A. Barrett
(1970) CPB

Facts: Texas Gas was assigned a contract to supply natural gas to Barrett and others. The lower court held that the contract was unenforceable for lack of mutuality of obligation because an article of the contract relieved Texas Gas of its obligation to furnish gas in specific situations.

Issue: Does an exculpatory clause which excuses a party from performance of the contract automatically violate the requirement of mutuality of obligation between the parties?

Rule: The requirement that a contract be mutually binding is not violated by an exculpatory clause which provides specific circumstances in which a party is not bound to perform.

Mezzanotte v. Freeland (1973) CPB

Facts: Mezzanotte contracted to purchase a tract of land together with improvements and facilities. The contract was contingent on Mezzanotte securing a second mortgage under conditions which would enable it to satisfactorily complete the contract. Freeland contended that the promise to buy was "illusory" since it depended on Mezzanotte's efforts to obtain financing.

Issue: Can there be valid consideration in a contract which is contingent on a conditional promise of one of the parties?

Rule: A conditional promise accompanied by an implied promise of good faith and reasonable effort constitutes valid consideration.

Miami Coca Cola Bottling v. Orange Crush Co.
(1924) CPB

Facts: Under a licensing agreement, Miami Coca Cola had the exclusive right to manufacture and distribute Orange Crush soda. In return, it was required to purchase a specified quantity of concentrate and promote and sell the soda. The license was perpetual but contained a provision allowing Orange Crush to cancel at any time. A year later, Orange Crush canceled the agreement.

Issue: Is a contract void for lack of mutuality when one party is given an option to terminate without providing any consideration to the other party for this term?

Rule: For an unlimited cancellation provision to be valid it must be supported by consideration.

Central Adjustment Bureau, Inc. v. Ingram (1984) CPB

Facts: After being hired at CAB, a collection agency, Ingram and two colleagues were made to sign noncompetition agreements if they wished to continue working there. Several years later, they resigned and formed a competing collection agency with CAB's client lists, claiming that the noncompetition agreement was void for lack of consideration.

Issue: Is a noncompetition agreement invalid for failure of consideration if it was signed after at-will employment had begun?

Rule: Continued employment constitutes valid consideration for a noncompetition agreement signed after at-will employment has begun.
Note: Despite this rule, courts are generally hostile to noncompetition agreements which are not sufficiently limited in scope of location and time.

R.A. Weaver and Assoc., Inc. v. Asphalt Construction, Inc.
(1978) CPB

Facts: Weaver contracted to supply limestone to Asphalt Construction, a subcontractor on a government project. Before any limestone had been ordered, the government canceled the provision for it with the general contractor. Consequently, Asphalt informed Weaver that none would be ordered. Based on the government bid documents, Weaver contended that the contract was for a specified quantity of limestone. However, Asphalt contended that it was a requirements contract in which quantity depended on the need for limestone.
Issue 1: Under what conditions will a contract which indicates specified quantities be considered a requirements contract?
Rule 1: When a contract contains provisions specifying that only work completed or goods which have actually been ordered and delivered will be paid for, it is transformed into a requirements contract.
Issue 2: Is it a breach of a requirements contract for a party to cease or reduce their need to zero?
Rule 2: UCC § 2-306(1) defines "requirement" in terms of good faith and does not preclude good faith reductions that are disproportionate to normal prior requirements or stated estimates.

Sheldon v. Blackman (1925) CPB

Facts: The deceased, Wilkinson, left a written promise to pay Sheldon a large sum of money in compensation for services rendered. Sheldon had cared for the elderly Wilkinson and his wife for many years.
Issue: When the value of a deliberately made agreement is indefinite or indeterminate, should the court substitute its own judgment for what constitutes valid consideration?
Rule: When the value of services is largely a matter of opinion, the court will not substitute its own judgment for that of the contracting parties because it would be a denial of the right of parties to make their own contract.

Feinberg v. Pfeiffer Co. (1959) CPB

Facts: Pfeiffer agreed to pay Feinberg $200 per month for life when she retired. Feinberg worked for a few more years and retired. Her pension was terminated after several years when she refused to have it reduced to $100 per month.

Issue: Can a promisor withdraw a promise that was given without consideration?

Rule: Past employment is considered past and invalid consideration. However, if one acts to her detriment (quitting work) in justifiable reliance on a promise, the promise will be enforced if an injustice would otherwise result.

Salsbury v. Northwestern Bell Telephone Co. (1974) CPB

Facts: Northwestern pledged a sum of money to support the establishment of a new city college. Salsbury, chairman of the college's board of trustees, sued to enforce the pledge.

Issue: Can a charitable subscription be enforced?

Rule: As a matter of public policy, charitable subscriptions are enforceable even without a showing of consideration or detrimental reliance.

Note: The court takes a modern approach to charitable subscriptions by applying the tentative draft of the Restatement (Second) of Contract § 90(2).

Maryland National Bank, et al. v. United Jewish Appeal
(1979) CPB, KC

Facts: Polinger signed a written pledge to pay the United Jewish Appeal a large sum of money. He died before he completed payment and the charity organization sued for the difference.

Issue: Can a charitable subscription which lacks valid consideration be enforced?

Rule: Valid consideration is essential for a contract to be enforceable and charitable subscriptions are not an exception.

Note: Taking the more traditional approach to charitable subscriptions, the Court held § 90 of the Restatements (Second) does not allow any contract to escape the requirement of consideration.

Drennan v. Star Paving Co. (1958) CPB

Facts: Drennan, a contractor, used a bid from Star Paving, a subcontractor, to calculate the costs of a larger bid it submitted to a third party. After Drennan was awarded the job, Star informed it that its "sub-bid" was erroneously low and refused to work at that price. Although Drennan had not formally accepted the offer, it had relied on the price, as is customary in the construction industry. Drennan sued to recover the difference between Star's original price and the amount paid to another subcontractor to do the work.

Issue: May a party be required to perform by the terms of an offer that was never actually accepted?

Rule: If an offeror should reasonably expect that his offer will induce reliance by the offeree to take an action or forbearance of a substantial and definite character (such as basing a contract price on subcontractor bids), the offer is enforceable even if the reliance occurs prior to a formal acceptance of the offer.

Werner v. Xerox Corp. (1984) CPB

Facts: A District Court held that Werner had reasonably relied upon the representation of a Xerox agent that Werner would become a parts manufacturer for Xerox. Having received parts-producing machines from Werner, Xerox terminated their relationship and prepared to make the parts in its own factory. The Court awarded reliance damages having found that the reliance was foreseeable to Xerox, that Werner actually relied and that nonenforcement of the promise would be unjust.

Issue: What standard will a court apply in reviewing the three elements of promissory estoppel?

Rule: Foreseeability of reliance and actual reliance are matters of fact which will not be reversed unless clearly erroneous; whether injustice will result from nonenforcement is a matter of law to be reversed only in a case of abuse of discretion.

Goldstick v. ICM Realty (1986) CPB

Facts: ICM retained Goldstick and his partner to seek a reduction in past-due real estate taxes on a piece of property. Goldstick successfully reduced the taxes by a substantial amount but ICM did not pay the legal bill for $290,000. The property had financial problems and ICM negotiated with a third party to invest fresh capital, who then refused to close the deal unless Goldstick and his partner released their claim for legal fees. Goldstick signed a release which stated that $250,000 would be paid over a number of years out of the profits of the property. However, Goldstick refused to sign until an agent for ICM assured him that something would be worked out. Goldstick assumed this meant that he would receive payment regardless of

profits, but no further agreements were made, and the property was never profitable. Goldstick and his former partner sued for the original $290,000.
Issue: May a party recover under promissory estoppel when the promise is unambiguous on the minimum value but vague on any higher value?
Rule: If a promise is unambiguous as to the minimum value but vague on any higher value, the question of whether a party may recover on the basis of promissory estoppel is one for the trier of fact.

Glenn v. Savage (1887) KC

Facts: Defendant Savage owned a stack of lumber that he stored near the Columbia River. In his absence, the lumber fell into the river and was almost carried off by the water. At his own expense, Glenn saved the lumber and sued Savage for the reasonable value of his services.
Issue: If a person voluntarily performs a service for another without the recipient's knowledge, can the actor sue the recipient for the reasonable value of the service?
Rule: A person who voluntarily performs a service for another without the recipient's knowledge cannot sue the recipient for the value of that service because the law deems such acts to be gratuitous acts of courtesy.

In Re Estate of Crisan (1961) KC

Facts: Crisan, an 87-year-old widow, collapsed in a grocery store. She was rushed to a public hospital and admitted. She stayed there for 14 days and was then transferred to another public hospital, where she remained until she died 11 months later. Crisan never recovered consciousness after her initial collapse. After her death, the City of Detroit sued her estate for the medical expenses she had incurred.
Issue: Will the law imply a promise to pay for emergency services rendered to an unconscious patient?
Rule: The law will imply a promise to pay for emergency services rendered to an unconscious patient if the services are necessary to prevent serious bodily harm or pain, if the recipient is unable to give consent, if the provider intends to charge for the services, and if the provider has no reason to know that the recipient would not have given their consent. This rule encourages emergency medical treatment by assuring providers that they will be paid for their services.

Flooring Systems, Inc. v. Radisson Group, Inc. (1989) KC

Facts: Radisson chose Five Star Services to be the general contractor for renovations to be performed at one of Radisson's resorts. Five Star subcontracted with Flooring to perform some carpeting work. Flooring completed the carpeting work, but Five Star failed to pay the full amount due to Flooring under the subcontract. Because of Five Star's failure to pay Flooring, Radisson withheld $25,000 that was due to Five Star under the general contract. Flooring sued both Radisson and Five Star under an unjust enrichment theory, but Five Star was dismissed as a party when it filed for bankruptcy.

Issue: May a subcontractor sue the owner of subcontracted work under an unjust enrichment theory, even though no contract exists between the owner and the subcontractor?

Rule: A subcontractor may sue the owner of subcontracted work under an unjust enrichment theory if it can be shown that the work was not intended or expected to be performed gratuitously.

Greiner v. Greiner (1930) KC

Facts: Mrs. Greiner promised to give her son some land if he and his family would move from one county to another and live in a house that she owned. Frank and his family moved. His mother then told him that if he would move the house to another 80 acre tract that she owned, she would give him both the house and the tract. Frank moved the house and spent money on improvements. Mrs. Greiner then promised to leave the land to Frank in her will, but later agreed to give him the deed outright. A family squabble occurred and the deed was never given to Frank. Instead, Frank's mother tried to evict Frank and his family from the land. Frank counterclaimed for the deed.

Issue: If a promisee acts in reasonable reliance on a promise, is the promisor obligated to perform?

Rule: A promise binds the promisor if the promisee acts in reasonable reliance on the promise and injustice can only be avoided by enforcement of the promise.

Katz v. Danny Dare, Inc. (1980) KC

Facts: Katz worked for Dare. Katz was injured attempting to foil a robbery attempt at one of Dare's stores, and Dare tried to convince Katz to retire. After negotiating for over a year, Katz agreed to retire upon Dare's promise of a lifetime pension. Dare would have fired Katz had he not agreed to retire. Dare paid Katz the pension for three years and then stopped.

Issue: Does the doctrine of promissory estoppel require a promisee to give up something to which the promisee is legally entitled before a promise can be enforced?

Rule: Promissory estoppel does not require a promisee to give up something to which the promisee is legally entitled before a promise can be enforced. If a promisee reasonably relies on a promise to the promisee's detriment and injustice can only be avoided by enforcement of the promise, the promise is enforceable.

Universal Computer Systems, Inc. v. Medical Services Assn.
(1980) KC

Facts: Medical Services solicited bids for the lease of a computer and specified a deadline for receipt of all proposals. To meet the deadline, Universal arranged to send the bid by airplane and asked Gebert, Medical Service's agent, if he could arrange to have the bid picked up at the airport. While the bid was in flight, Gebert told Universal he had changed his mind and could not pick up the bid. Universal attempted to find an alternate courier, but was unable to meet Medical Services' deadline. Medical Services returned Universal's bid unopened.

Issue: If a company's agent makes a promise and the promisee detrimentally relies on that promise, is the company bound by the agent's promise?

Rule: If a promisee reasonably believes that a company's agent has the authority to make a promise and detrimentally relies on that promise, the company is bound by the agent's promise.

Ray v. William G. Eurice & Bros., Inc. (1952) KC

Facts: Eurice submitted a three-page proposed contract to build Ray's house. Ray did not approve of Eurice's proposal, so he had his own lawyer draft a contract, consisting of five pages of specifications that differed from Eurice's proposal. Both Ray and Eurice signed this contract. Subsequently, Eurice refused to perform, arguing that when John Eurice signed the contract, he thought it was identical to the three-page proposal that Eurice had submitted and did not contain any new specifications.

Issue: Does a unilateral mistake as to the contents of a contract discharge the party from his contractual obligations?

Rule: A unilateral mistake as to the contents of a contract does not discharge the party from his contractual obligations. Absent fraud, duress or mutual mistake, a party who has the capacity to understand a written document is bound by his signature.

St. Landry Loan Co. v. Avie (1962) KC

Facts: Defendant Skinner endorsed a promissory note that Avie owed to St. Landry. Avie defaulted, and St. Landry sued Skinner for the debt. Skinner claimed that he was not liable because he did not understand the provisions of the note.

Issue: Is a party who signs a written contract bound by the contract even if that party is ignorant of the contract's terms?

Rule: A party who signs a written contract is bound by the contract, absent fraud or misrepresentation, because he is presumed to know its terms.

Baehr v. Penn-O-Tex Oil Corp. (1960) KC, R

Facts: Plaintiff leased filling stations to Kemp. Kemp, in debt to Defendant, assigned Defendant his accounts receivable. Plaintiff asked Defendant to pay Kemp's past due rent on the filling stations, and Defendant agreed. When Defendant failed to pay the debt, Plaintiff sued the Defendant to recover the rent.

Issue: Is a promise to pay a debt of another sufficient to constitute a contract?

Rule: A mere promise to pay a debt does not create a contract because there is a lack of mutual consideration.

E.I. Du Pont De Nemours & Co. v. Clairborne-Reno Co. (1933) KC

Facts: Reno contracted to be the exclusive distributor of Du Pont's products. The contract stated that Du Pont would continue to perform so long as Reno's services proved satisfactory. Du Pont terminated the contract. Reno claimed that its services were satisfactory and therefore Du Pont's actions constituted a breach.

Issue: Can a party who promises continued performance terminate the contract at will, when the other party is not similarly bound?

Rule: A party who promises continued performance can terminate the contract at will when the other party is not also bound, because this lack of mutuality is unfair to the party who is bound.

Plowman v. Indian Refining Co. (1937) KC

Facts: Indian promised to pay retirement benefits to Plaintiffs, and stopped paying after one year. Plaintiffs claimed that Indian promised that the payments would continue for life, and that their past performance and their promise to pick up the checks themselves constituted consideration.

Issue 1: Can consideration be based on past performance?

Rule 1: Past performance cannot be consideration for a promise, because consideration is something given in exchange for a promise or in reliance on a promise.

Issue 2: Can consideration be based on moral obligations?

Rule 2: Moral consideration cannot be used to enforce a promise.

Issue 3: Can consideration be based on an act imposed on the promisee as a condition for the promise?

Rule 3: Acts imposed on the promisee, which are merely necessary conditions for obtaining the gratuitous promise, are not consideration. These conditions are benefits to the promisees, not detriments.

Berryman v. Kmoch (1977) KC

Facts: Berryman and Kmoch signed an option contract which stated that Berryman, for $10 and "other valuable consideration," would grant Kmoch a 120 day option to purchase real estate. However, the $10 was never paid. Kmoch attempted to exercise his option after he learned that Berryman sold the land to someone else.

Issue: When is an option contract valid?

Rule: An option contract is valid only when there is sufficient consideration, or when promissory estoppel can be invoked as a substitute for consideration. If the option contract is void, then there is merely an offer to sell, revokable anytime before the offeree accepts.

De Los Santos v. Great Western Sugar Co. (1984) R

Facts: De Los Santos agreed to transport all the beets loaded into its trucks by Great Western to designated factories. Before all the beets had been transported, Great Western terminated its contract with De Los Santos.

Issue: Can a promisor be held liable for terminating a contract that does not specify a quantity of goods?

Rule: Where a promisor agrees to purchase services from a promisee on a per unit basis, but the agreement does not specify a quantity or an intent to have the promisee perform all of the promisor's needs, the promisor may terminate the agreement at anytime.

Mattei v. Hopper (1958) R

Facts: Mattei agreed to buy Hopper's shopping center. The agreement called for a $1,000 down payment and the balance to be paid within 120 days subject to Mattei obtaining satisfactory leases. Hopper refused to complete the sale, claiming Mattei's promise was illusory because he was not actually bound: Hopper was obligated to sell, but Mattei only had to buy if he was satisfied with the leases.

Issue: Does a contract lack consideration if the assent of one party to the agreement is conditioned by a satisfaction clause?

Rule: An agreement that contains a satisfaction clause is not illusory (lacking consideration or mutuality of obligation) if performance of the condition can be judged by a reasonable person standard or if the party subject to the satisfaction clause acts in good faith.

Charter Township of Ypsilanti v. General Motors Corp. (1993) R

Facts: Ypsilanti granted numerous tax abatements to General Motors, based on promises by General Motors that its production line would remain in the area. When General Motors announced that it was going to move its production line elsewhere, Ypsilanti alleged that the company breached a contract created by the tax abatement statute.

Issue: Do promises made in an effort to solicit tax abatements constitute an enforceable contract?

Rule: The fact that a corporation solicits a tax abatement and persuades a municipality to grant them with assurances of jobs cannot be evidence of a promise, and thus may not be used to estop action by the beneficiary of the tax abatement.

Keller v. Holderman (1863) R

Facts: Keller gave Holderman a $300 check for a watch owned by Holderman. The watch had an actual value of $15, and Keller had never expected to actually be held to the deal, as evidenced by the lack of funds in his account. The check was not honored, and Holderman sued.

Issue: Is a contract enforceable when the parties contracted in jest?

Rule: When a trial court finds that a transaction is a "frolic and a banter," such that the plaintiff does not expect to sell a good, and the defendant does not intend to buy it, no contract has been made.

Brown v. Finney (1866) R

Facts: The parties met at a restaurant, and their conversation turned to coal prices. Although there was no mutual intent to contract, the plaintiff made a "bantering proposition" to the defendant, that was orally accepted. Plaintiff brought action for breach of the contract.

Issue: Is a contract formed when two parties meet, and an agreement is proposed in the absence of the intent to create a binding contract?

Rule: If a proposition is made and accepted, and no expectation to create a binding contract exists, a court must look at the specific circumstances of the case to decide if there was mutual assent to the agreement.

Maughs v. Porter (1931) R

Facts: Porter held an auction that included a drawing for a new car. Maughs gave $5 to participate in the drawing, and her name was chosen. Porter ordered the car, but when it was ready for delivery, he refused to pay for it or to give Maughs the value of the car.

Issue: When is a promise to give a gift enforceable?

Rule: Where a promisor derives a benefit from a promise to give a gift, and the promisee incurs a corresponding detriment, the promise is supported by consideration and enforceable.

Clark v. Elza (1979) R

Facts: Plaintiffs brought suit against defendants for injuries sustained in a car accident. The parties verbally agreed upon a settlement figure, which was later rescinded by the plaintiffs. Defendants filed a motion to enforce the settlement.

Issue: When does a settlement agreement become binding on the parties?

Rule: In order to enforce a settlement agreement, a court must decide whether it constituted an agreement for the future discharge of an existing claim (an executory accord), or one that immediately discharged the original claim (a substitute contract). Unless there is clear evidence to the contrary, an agreement to discharge a pre-existing claim is regarded as an executory accord, and thus will not discharge the underlying claim until it is performed.

Mazer v. Jackson Insurance Agency (1976) R

Facts: Homeowners, represented by Mazer, sued for an injunction against developers of an office park. The homeowners claimed that the action proposed by the developers to clear-cut woodlands constituted a breach of a promise to maintain the area as a 100-foot buffer zone between the office park and their property, and contended that the developer was estopped from developing in a manner inconsistent with its previous assurances.

Issue: May a party claim estoppel due to detrimental reliance on another's actions?

Rule: A party is estopped from denying the validity of a promise when the promise is reasonably expected to induce action or forbearance on the part of the promisee and does induce such action or forbearance, if injustice can be avoided only by enforcement of the promise. Rest. 2d § 90.

Chapter 4

OFFER AND ACCEPTANCE

To create a valid contract, three general requirements must be met.

Mnemonic: **M**other **A**dores **C**igars **A**fter **D**inner

(1) **M**utual **A**ssent
(2) **C**onsideration
(3) **A**bsence of **D**efenses

This chapter primarily deals with mutual assent, also called a "meeting of the minds." It embodies the idea that all parties should have a similar understanding of the contract they agree to enter. To achieve mutual assent, the parties often undergo a negotiated process whereby each makes proposals and counterproposals until they arrive at a mutually acceptable arrangement. The process ends when one side *accepts* the other side's *offer* (proposal).

I.   OFFER

An offer is a manifestation of willingness to enter into a bargain which invites another person's assent to the bargain which assent will, in turn, conclude the arrangement (Rest. 2d. § 24). One who makes an offer is the offeror, and the person to whom it is made is the offeree. To be a valid offer (i.e., to constitute an offer), a manifestation of intent to enter a bargain must have "the 3 C's:"

Commitment or promise by the offeror to enter into a contract
Certainty and definitiveness of essential terms
Communication by offeror to offeree

A.   Commitment or Promise
The first requirement for an offer is that it embody a promise or commitment, as opposed to a statement of present intention or preliminary negotiation. Statements such as "I intend to sell you my car" or "come talk to me about buying my car" are not offers. Saying "if you pay me $100, I will sell you my car" is a valid offer.

1. Objective Test
   Whether a statement is an offer depends on whether a reasonable person would so understand it, regardless of the parties' subjective understanding. For example, given the trade customs of an industry, would a reasonable person think that an offer was made? The courts consider several factors:

   Mnemonic: **LIMPS**

   a. **L**anguage
      Have the words "offer" or "promise" been used? Courts also consider the definitiveness of the terms and language of a proposal to help decide whether it is an offer. "First come, first served" may indicate an offer because it provides buyers with a clear means of accepting by buying first.

   b. **I**ndustry Customs
      Courts determine whether the type of language and manner of the proposal is usually considered to be an offer in a specific industry.

   c. **M**ethod of Communication
      Communications made by mass media (i.e., TV, newspaper, billboard) are often held to be invitations for offers, not actual offers. For example, a TV ad announces that a dealer has 100 cars for sale for $1000 each. The dealer did not make an offer to the entire TV audience (which could be millions) to buy his cars for $1000. Rather, he "invited" members of the audience to offer to buy his cars.

   d. **P**rior Practices Between the Parties
      If the parties had prior transactions, the courts will consider the significance of the questioned statements in light of statements made in previous dealings.

   e. **S**urrounding Circumstances
      Courts also consider the manner and context in which a statement was made (e.g., in jest, with anger, etc.), and whether

it was reasonable to construe the statement as an offer under those circumstances.

2. Commitments/promises are distinguished from opinions.
A hired B to pick A's crops, partly because B told A that the task would take approximately two or three weeks. B has not made an offer to pick the crop in two to three weeks, unless he actually guaranteed that he could do it in that time.

3. Price Quotations
A price quotation is not an offer to sell unless:

  a. The quoter specifies the quantity he is willing to sell, not merely the per-unit cost, and

  b. The quote is made to a specific person, not the general public.

4. Auctions
An auctioneer solicits bids; he does not make offers.

B. Certainty of Terms
The subject matter of a proposal must be definite and certain; otherwise, a court would be unable to determine the terms if the offer evolves into an enforceable contract. The consequences of missing or vague terms are as follows:

1. Time of Payment and Performance
The absence of these terms is not fatal because the court can imply that performance is due within a reasonable time. (UCC § 2-309.)

2. Identity of the Parties and Subject Matter
These must be certain.

3. Quantity Must be Specified
Quantity is a required term except for output and requirement contracts (see below). An employment contract that has no specific duration is considered to be terminable at will.

4. Price
   Price and other missing terms can be implied. (UCC § 2-305.)
   However, if the parties clearly show the absence of agreement on
   price, price will not be implied, and there will be no contract.

5. Part Performance or Acceptance
   Vagueness and uncertainty of terms can also be overcome if there
   is part performance or acceptance.

   a. Part Performance
      If the parties have already begun performing the contract, the
      manner in which they acted upon vague terms can be determi-
      native of their meaning.

   b. Acceptance
      If the contract terms are uncertain, acceptance of one possible
      interpretation will establish the terms.

   c. Terms to be Agreed Upon
      Offers that include some of the terms and state that other terms
      will be agreed upon in the future are too vague if the omitted
      terms are material to the agreement (e.g., quantity), and a
      contract will not be formed even if this "offer" is "accepted."

6. Output and Requirements Contracts
   Output and requirements contracts are valid despite an absence of
   definite terms, so long as both parties act in good faith.

   a. Requirements Contract
      Airline contracts with Refinery to supply it with "all the jet fuel
      it needs." There is no definite quantity, but if Airline makes a
      good faith effort to buy a certain amount of fuel and Refinery
      makes a good faith effort to provide it, the contract is valid.

   b. Output Contract
      A cereal company contracts with Farmer to buy "all wheat
      grown in year X." Neither knows how much wheat will be
      sold, but the absence of a specific quantity is not fatal in such
      a situation.

C. Communication to the Offeree
The offeree must have knowledge of the offer.

II. TERMINATION OF AN OFFER

Once an offer is made, the power of acceptance is created in the offeree; if he accepts the offer, the offeror must perform. Termination of the offer extinguishes this power. An offer can only be terminated before the offeree accepts it. Termination can occur by an act of either party or by operation of law.

A. Revocation by the Offeror
An offeror can revoke his offer so long as it has not been accepted by the offeree. An offer can be terminated in various ways:

1. Communication to the Offeree
Communication of termination of an offer can be direct or indirect. Indirect communication may involve a third party who notifies the offeree of the offeror's revocation. The indirect communication must be correct, given by a reliable source and understandable to a "reasonable person." Example: A makes an offer to B then sells the item to C before B accepts. The act of selling to another is a reasonable indication of revocation if B is aware of the sale. However, if B is not *notified* of A's revocation – either directly or indirectly – before he accepts, then the acceptance is valid and A must sell to B.

2. By Publication
Offers that are made by publication can be revoked by publication. Unlike direct and indirect communications, the revocation is effective when published, not when it is received by the offeree.

B. Irrevocable Offers
An offeror can generally terminate his offer, even if he promised not to do so. However, offers cannot be revoked under certain circumstances.

Mnemonic: **DROP FU**

1. **Detrimental Reliance**
   Offers are irrevocable for a reasonable time period if the offeree relied to his detriment on the offer being held open, and it is reasonably foreseeable to the offeror that the offeree would so rely. Example: A general contractor relies on a sub-contractor's offer in determining the costs of the overall job.

2. **Options**
   If the offeree gave consideration for the promise that the offer would be kept open, it must be. It is, in essence, a contract to contract. Example: A gives B $20 not to revoke his promise for two weeks. Section 87 of the Restatement (Second) holds an option contract valid even if there is no actual consideration, so long as consideration is recited in a written and signed document.

3. **Partial Performance of a Unilateral Contract**
   Traditionally, a unilateral contract was revocable at any time prior to completion of the requested performance. For example, A promises to pay B $100 if B crosses a bridge. B "accepts" only by crossing the bridge. A can revoke at any time before B reaches the other side. Today, the majority and Restatement (Second) view is that a contract is formed when performance begins (i.e., when B starts crossing), provided that it is completed within a reasonable time. The offeror cannot revoke, but the offeree can discontinue his performance at any time. However, preparation to begin performance is not considered to be partial performance (e.g., when B puts on his bridge-crossing shoes and says his pre-crossing mantra).

4. **Firm Offers (UCC § 2-205)**
   A signed writing by a merchant to buy or sell goods that has firm terms and assures that the offer will be held open is enforceable, even without consideration. Duration:

   a. Period stated
      If the period is actually stated, the offer will remain open for the stated period or three months, whichever is less.

b. Period not stated
If the period is not stated, the offer remains open for a "reasonable time," not to exceed three months.

C. Termination by the Offeree
An offeree can terminate an offer in three ways:

1. Express Rejection

2. Counteroffer
A counteroffer occurs when an offeree tries to add or change terms in the original offer. This is considered a rejection of the original offer, as well as a new offer. Example: A offers to sell his car to B. B makes a counteroffer to buy the car if A repaints it. A's original offer to sell has been rejected, and B's offer to buy with additional conditions is the new offer. A is actually the offeree now.

a. Mere Inquiry
A "mere inquiry" is not a counteroffer. As long as offeree suggests that he is still considering the original offer, a counteroffer has not been made. Example: B tells A, "I'm still thinking about buying your car, but I would like to know how you feel about lowering the price."

b. Irrevocable Offer
A counteroffer does not revoke an irrevocable offer.

c. Date Effective
A rejection is effective when it is received by the offeror, who then can extend a new offer to another party.

d. "Battle of the Forms" Exception
See Acceptance, below.

3. Passage of Time
If an offer specifies a time within which it must be accepted, failure to accept within that time period will constitute a rejection. If no time period is specified, a reasonable time period is given for

response. In either case, the time period starts when the offeree actually gets the offer.

D.   Termination by Law

1. Death or Incapacity
    The death or incapacity (e.g., insanity) of either party before the offer is accepted will terminate the offer. The death or incapacity does not have to be communicated to the other party. Irrevocable offers are not terminated by death or incapacity. (Rest. 2d. § 48.)

2. If the subject of the offer, such as the goods offered for sale, is destroyed prior to acceptance, the offer is terminated. (Rest. 2d. § 35.)

3. If the contract becomes contrary to law prior to acceptance, the offer will be terminated. (Rest. 2d. § 35.) Example: A offers to sell liquor to B. While the offer is open, Congress outlaws alcohol consumption. A's offer is terminated. Had B already accepted, the contract would become void.

III.   ACCEPTANCE

An acceptance is a manifestation of assent to the terms of an offer in the manner required by the offer. A contract is created once an acceptance is communicated. To be valid an acceptance must meet the following requirements:

A.   Acceptor
Only the specific person to whom the offer was made can accept. The power of acceptance cannot be assigned. Exception: an option can be assigned.

B.   Communication
Acceptance of an offer for a bilateral contract is not effective until it is communicated to the offeror.

1. Objective Manifestation of Assent Required
   The offeree's subjective state of mind is irrelevant. However, the offeree must realize that an offer was made. Absent such knowledge, his acceptance is invalid.

2. Acceptance Received by the Offeror
   The obvious situation is where the offeree conveys acceptance to the offeror, either by telephone communication or in person. But problems can develop if there is a delay between the time the offeree accepts and the time the offeror receives the communication, such as when the offeree accepts by mail.

   a. Mailbox Rule (majority)
      An acceptance is effective (and a contract is thus formed) upon the dispatch, not the actual receipt, of the acceptance. Exceptions:

      i. The offer explicitly states that acceptance is not effective until actually received.

      ii. Options
          Exercise (i.e., acceptance) of an option contract is only effective upon receipt by the offeror.

   b. An offeror can specify the means of acceptance of his offer (e.g., only upon actual receipt or in a specified place).

   c. If offeror does not specify the method of conveying acceptance then any reasonable means is valid. Even if a specific method is given, an acceptance that is conveyed in a different way is valid if it is actually received by the offeror before he revokes the offer.

   d. Acceptance Lost in Transmission
      An acceptance that is lost in transmission is valid if it was properly sent, but may be excused if it will cause hardship to the offeror, such as if the offeror already sold the property.

e. Restatement (Second) § 40 Exception
In general, a rejection becomes effective upon receipt, and an offer is effective upon dispatch. However, where an offeree dispatches a rejection and then dispatches an acceptance, the acceptance is only effective if received before the rejection. Examples:

   i. Rejection Before Acceptance
   An offeree mails a rejection on Monday and an acceptance on Tuesday. Both letters are delivered on Wednesday. The acceptance is effective only if the offeror gets it before he receives the rejection.

   ii. Acceptance Before Rejection
   Offeree mails acceptance on Monday and it is delivered on Thursday. Offeree also mails a rejection on Tuesday and it arrives on Wednesday.

      (1) Majority Rule
      Under the mailbox rule, acceptance is effective as of Monday unless the offeror limited the manner of conveying the acceptance. However, the offeror may be able to prevent the contract under the theory of estoppel by showing that he relied on the rejection to his detriment.

      (2) Minority Rule
      Some courts rule that if an offeror actually receives the rejection first, no contract can be created.

f. "Crossing" Communications
If two parties send identical offers to each other, neither one knowing of the other's offer, a contract is not formed when the offers "cross in the mail." There must be knowledge of an offer before a contract can be formed.

g. Mistake in Transmission
If an offer is mistakenly changed *during* the process of transmission to the offeree (e.g., teletype or clerical error) and

the offeree does not know and could not reasonably have been expected to know of the error, then the offer can be accepted on its mistaken terms (majority view).

3. Exceptions to the Requirement of Communication of Acceptance

   Mnemonic: **Search And Will Destroy**

   a. **Silence**
      If an offeree does not respond to an offer but accepts the benefits of the offer, and prior dealings or custom would lead a reasonable person to believe that this is the way in which an acceptance is made, then silence can constitute acceptance.

   b. **Act**
      If an offeror specifies that performance of a certain act will constitute acceptance, performing the requisite act will form a contract. Note: This is not a unilateral contract – an act in return for a promise; rather, the act here is used to symbolize the promise.

   c. **Waiver Expressly Contained in the Offer**
      The offeror may expressly waive communication of acceptance.

   d. **Dominion**
      In general, if an "offeree" accepts unsolicited goods and exercises dominion over them, he has accepted an offer (to purchase the goods) and formed a contract. However, some states have statutes that classify unsolicited goods as gifts to the recipient.

4. Unilateral Contracts
   In the context of unilateral contracts, performance of an act (as opposed to making a promise for bilateral contracts) constitutes acceptance of the offer. The offeree's act must be consummated:

    a. With the knowledge of the offeror and motivation from the offer.

    b. Completely
    The offeree must completely perform the requisite act. Partial performance merely creates an option for the offeree to complete the performance and form a contract.

    c. With notification to the offeror (majority rule).
    The offeree must notify the offeror, even after completing performance, if the offeree's performance would not otherwise come to the offeror's attention.

C. **Variations from Offer's Terms**
Variations from the terms of the offer do not necessarily invalidate an acceptance.

    1. Common Law View
    Any variation in the acceptance constitutes a rejection of the offer and an extension of a counteroffer. This was sometimes called the "last shot rule" because contracting parties often varied their acceptances in an effort to get the "last shot"; that is, by sending a counteroffer instead of an acceptance, each side would try to manipulate the terms of the final agreement to its favor.

    2. UCC § 2-207
    A written acceptance of an offer for the "sale of goods" is valid, notwithstanding terms that vary from the offer, unless acceptance is expressly conditioned on assent to the additional or different terms. This has been referred to as the "first shot rule:" there is some incentive to send out the first form, against which the consistency of future terms is to be judged.

    3. Battle of the Forms and Related Problems
    In routine business transactions, most parties use standardized printed forms. However, one company's standard forms rarely match the other's. A "battle of the forms" results when courts have to decide whose forms govern.

a. Conditional Acceptance
   If a party sends an acceptance that is conditional upon the offeror's assent to new or conflicting terms that are included in the acceptance, there is no contract until and unless the original offeror manifests his acceptance.

b. Acceptance Contains Additional Terms

   i. Neither party is a merchant –
      The contract terms are those of the original offer.

   ii. One party is not a merchant –
       The additional terms become part of the contract if the offeror explicitly assents.

   iii. All parties are merchants –
        The additional term becomes part of the contract unless the offeror objects or the term is a material alteration.

c. Offer and Acceptance Differ on a Particular Issue (varying but not additional terms)

   i. Knockout Rule (majority)
      The disputed terms are "knocked out" of both the offer and acceptance, and UCC standard "gap fillers" (e.g., implied time of performance) control.

   ii. Minority Rule
       Offeror's clause overrides ("first shot").

d. Written Confirmation of Oral Agreement

   i. Under UCC § 2-207, additional terms contained in a written confirmation are treated the same as additional terms contained in an acceptance (see above).

   ii. When the confirmation contains terms that differ from the oral agreement, the terms of the oral agreement usually control.

e. If an acceptance materially deviates from the offer, it will not be effective.

   i. Material deviations usually involve price, quality, quantity, or delivery terms.

   ii. Although the writings of the parties do not establish a contract, conduct by both parties recognizing the existence of a contract is sufficient to establish a contract. The terms consist of those terms on which the writings agree, together with gap fillers from the UCC. (UCC § 2-207(3).)

f. If the parties use custom-written offer and acceptance forms, as opposed to standardized contract forms, then the traditional offer and acceptance rules apply without variation.

CASE CLIPS

Embry v. Hargadine-McKittrick Dry Goods Co.
(1907) DHH, FE, MS

Facts: Embry, a fired employee, claimed that McKittrick had promised to renew his contract. McKittrick denied that he ever made such a promise. The judge told the jury that unless both parties subjectively intended to form an employment contract, no contract exists, even if McKittrick did promise to renew the contract.

Issue: When determining if a contract exists, is a party's assent to be determined by his actual state of mind or by the reasonable outward manifestation of assent?

Rule: One's state of mind is immaterial if that party outwardly manifests assent to the contract.

Kabil Dev. Corp. v. Mignot (1977) DHH

Facts: Kabil conducted oral negotiations with the Mignots regarding the provision of helicopter services. Kabil sued for breach of contract when such service was not provided. Kabil's vice-president was allowed to testify that he "felt" an agreement had been reached.

Issue: Can a party's personal perceptions be introduced as evidence of whether a contract was formed?
Rule: Whether a contract was formed is to be determined by objective manifestations of the parties. Subjective opinions not misleading to the jury may be admissible when illustrative of the behavior and perceptions of the parties and whether such behavior gave reasonable notice of intent to the other party.

McDonald v. Mobil Coal Producing, Inc. (1991) DHH

Facts: McDonald left his employ at Mobil when rumors linking him to the sexual harassment of a co-worker surfaced. It was disputed whether he resigned or was fired. At the beginning of his employment at Mobil, McDonald signed a contract which described his job status as terminable at will. He was later given an employee manual which contained a disclaimer against its use as an employment contract. The manual included information on employee procedure and policies. McDonald challenged his dismissal on the ground that the manual to modified his initial at-will contract to one of termination only for cause.
Issue 1: What is necessary to create a legally effective disclaimer?
Rule 1: For a disclaimer to be effective it must be conspicuous (e.g., set off from other text, placed under a specific sub-heading, written in a different font, and capitalized.)
Issue 2: Can an employee manual modify an at-will employment contract?
Rule 2: In the absence of a conspicuous disclaimer, the objective theory of contract formation allows for the modification of an at-will employment contract if the employer's actions create a reasonable reliance by the employee. Subjective intent to contract is irrelevant. In this case, the court found that the manual modified the contract, since there was no conspicuous disclaimer.

Moulton v. Kershaw (1884) DHH, KGK

Facts: The defendant, a salt dealer, sent a letter to another dealer, offering to sell him salt in shipments of 80 to 95 barrels at the price of $.85 per barrel. The plaintiff ordered 2,000 barrels, but the defendant refused to fill the order.
Issue: Is a letter that solicits the sale of goods considered to be an offer?
Rule: A general letter or circular is not construed to be a firm offer to sell. The absence of a specific quantity in the letter prevents it from being an offer.

Note: The defendant had stated the size and cost of a shipment, but had not offered to provide a certain number of shipments. Thus, it is unfair to construe the letter as an offer.

Joseph Martin Jr. Delicatessen v. Schumacher
(1981) DHH, FE, MS, CPB

Facts: A clause in the lease agreement stated that "the tenant may renew this lease for an additional period of five years at annual rentals to be agreed upon." When the tenant sought to exercise the option, the landlord doubled the rent. The tenant sued for specific performance at a reasonable rent, and the landlord brought an action for eviction.

Issue: Is a clause in a realty lease that specifies "rent will be agreed upon" too vague to be enforced?

Rule: A lease renewal clause that does not specify the rent to be paid, or some specific manner of calculating the rent, is merely an "agreement to agree" and is not enforceable.

Empro Manufacturing Co., Inc.
v.
Ball-Co Manufacturing, Inc. (1989) MS, R

Facts: Empro was negotiating for the purchase of Ball-co's assets. Empro sent Ball-co a three page letter of intent that contained detailed terms, including the price and payment schedule. The letter also contained "general terms and conditions" and stated that a definitive agreement was "subject to" a variety of conditions, including shareholder approval. Upon learning that Ball-co was negotiating with another party, Empro contended that the parties intended to be bound by the letter of intent.

Issue: May parties be bound to a document that memorializes essential terms of an agreement, but anticipates future negotiation?

Rule: Because intent in contract law is objective, parties who make their pact "subject to" a later definitive agreement manifest an intent not to be bound, which under the parol evidence rule becomes the definitive intent, even if one party later says otherwise.

Wheeler v. White (1965) DHH, KC

Facts: White contracted to finance construction on Wheeler's property. White later encouraged Wheeler to demolish the buildings existing on the property which he did. White then backed out, claiming that the contract terms were too indefinite.

Issue: Can a promise be enforced even if a valid contract was not formed?
Rule: Where a promisee acts to his detriment in reasonable reliance upon an otherwise unenforceable promise, he may be entitled to recover damages incurred by the reliance if necessary to avoid injustice.

Raffles v. Wichelhaus (1864) DHH, KGK, FE, MS, R

Facts: The defendant contracted to buy Indian cotton from the plaintiff which was to arrive on a ship called the *Peerless*. Unknown to both parties there were two ships named *Peerless* that delivered cotton from India. The ship the defendant was expecting arrived in October. The ship the plaintiff sent the cotton aboard arrived in December. The defendant refused the later shipment.
Issue: If parties to a contract are unaware of an ambiguity, is the contract void because there was no "meeting of the minds"?
Rule: When parties to a contract are unaware that they have different understandings of a material ambiguity, the agreement is unenforceable because there was no "meeting of the minds."

Cobaugh v. Klick-Lewis, Inc. (1989) DHH

Facts: Cobaugh arrived at the ninth tee of a golf course to find a 1988 Chevrolet Beretta on display, as well as signs purporting to award the car to anyone who could make a hole-in-one. Cobaugh subsequently shot a hole-in-one and attempted to claim his prize. The signs had originally been put up for a charity event that had been played two days previously, and had been mistakenly left standing.
Issue: Can a court enforce a unilateral promise which was not intended to be offered to the eventual claimant?
Rule: The apparent intent of the offeror, not his subjective intent, determines the power of acceptance. The promoter of a contest is bound to perform his promise if a person acts on it before the offer is withdrawn. In this case, the act of shooting for the hole-in-one constituted acceptance of the offer.

Allied Steel and Conveyors, Inc. v. Ford Motor Co. (1960) DHH, MS

Facts: Ford ordered machinery from Allied with its own order form which stated that the order was not binding until accepted and "acceptance should be executed on acknowledgment copy which should be returned to the buyer." A clause in the purchase order provided that Allied was to be liable for all injuries resulting from negligence in the installation of the machinery. It began installing the machinery without sending the acknowledgment copy as formal acceptance. An Allied employee was injured as a result of the negligence of Ford's employees in connection with Allied's work. Allied claimed it was not liable, because it did not formally accept the offer.

Issue: Can the beginning of performance act as an acceptance to an offer that provides a specific means of communicating acceptance?

Rule: Beginning performance with the knowledge, consent, and agreement of the offeror is a valid means of accepting an offer. "Acceptance should be executed on acknowledgment copy" is merely a suggestion.

Note: Although this case seems to contradict *White v. Corlies and Tift*, both courts were actually looking to whether the offeror knew of the acceptance.

Davis v. Jacoby (1934) DHH, KGK, FE

Facts: Whitehead wrote to his niece, Davis, that if she and her husband came to care for his sick wife and help with the business, they would "inherit everything." Davis immediately accepted the proposition, but Whitehead committed suicide before Davis and her husband arrived. Davis cared for Mrs. Whitehead until her death a week later. When Whitehead's will was opened it revealed that he had left everything to his nephews. Davis argued that she was entitled to the property based on the contract made prior to Whitehead's death.

Issue: Is an offer presumed to be bilateral or unilateral in the absence of any indication by the offeror?

Rule: When there is doubt as to whether an offer is for a unilateral or bilateral contract, the law will presume the offer was for a bilateral contract. An offer requesting a response by mail is more likely an offer for a bilateral contract than a unilateral contract.

Note: If the contract had been unilateral and thus accepted by performance, Davis would not have recovered, since the death of Whitehead would have acted as revocation before acceptance.

Petterson v. Pattberg (1928) DHH, FE, MS, KGK, CPB

Facts: Pattberg offered Petterson the chance to pay the balance of his mortgage at a discount by a certain date. When Petterson attempted to pay the balance before the deadline (and thus to accept Pattberg's offer), Petterson told him that he had already sold the mortgage to a third party who was unwilling to reduce the payment.

Issue: Can an offer for a unilateral contract be withdrawn?
Rule: An offer for a unilateral contract can be withdrawn until the moment the requested act is performed.

Brackenbury v. Hodgkin (1917) DHH, CPB
Facts: Hodgkin promised her daughter and son-in-law, the Brackenburys, that she would bequeath her farm to them if they would move in and take care of her. The Brackenburys moved in and cared for Hodgkin until disputes arose, and Hodgkin ordered them to leave.
Issue: Can an offer of a unilateral contract be withdrawn after the offeree has performed part of the requested act?
Rule: A unilateral contract is accepted by performance. The offer is no longer revocable once the offeree has begun performance of the requested act. Completion of the act obligates the offeror to perform its promise.

Thomason v. Bescher (1918) DHH
Facts: Bescher executed a writing, under seal, that created an option for Thomason to purchase a tract of Bescher's land. The writing stated that payment of $1 was given as consideration, although in actuality the payment was never made. To complete the sale, Thomason was required to demand the deed and tender the contract price before a specified date. Before tender was made, Bescher notified Thomason that the offer was withdrawn. Thomason sued for specific performance.
Issue: May an offer creating an option contract be revoked before tender is made?
Rule: An option contract is a binding agreement, and irrevocable within the time designated, as long as the terms of the contract are fair and equitable.
Note: The use of the seal has been abolished in most states, (as well as under UCC § 2-203), but under traditional usage no consideration was required to support a contract under seal. The Restatement (Second) requires that an option contract be a signed writing, but does not require consideration to be actually delivered.

James Baird Co. v. Gimbel Bros., Inc. (1933)
DHH, KGK, KC, MS
Facts: The defendant sent a "sub-bid" for the cost of installing linoleum to the plaintiff, a general contractor, who used the sub-bid in calculating its costs for the overall project. The sub-bid expressly stated that acceptance

should be conveyed only after (and if) the contractor was awarded the project. The defendant later realized that its bid was incorrect and notified the plaintiff that it was withdrawing it. The plaintiff had already sent in its bid. When the plaintiff won the project, it accepted the offer of the defendant who refused to perform.

Issue: Can an offer, for which no consideration was received, be revoked prior to acceptance even if the offeree relied on it?

Rule: If no consideration is received for an offer which was clearly not intended to be a binding promise, it is revocable even if the offeree relied on it to his detriment.

Drennan v. Star Paving Co. (1958) DHH, KGK, KC, FE, MS, R

Facts: Drennan, a contractor, used a bid from Star Paving, a subcontractor, to calculate the costs of a larger bid it was submitting to a third party. After Drennan was awarded the job, Star Paving claimed that its "sub-bid" was erroneously low and refused to work at that price. Although it had not formally accepted the offer, Drennan had relied on the price, as is customary in the construction industry. It sued to recover the difference between the Star bid and the amount paid to another subcontractor.

Issue: May a party be required to perform by the terms of an offer that was never actually accepted?

Rule: If an offeror should reasonably expect that his offer will induce justifiable reliance by the offeree of a substantial and definite nature, the offer is enforceable even if the reliance occurs prior to a formal acceptance of the offer.

Hoffman v. Red Owl Stores (1965) DHH, FE, KC, MS, R

Facts: Relying on Red Owl's repeated advice and promises that he would be able to obtain a Red Owl supermarket franchise, Hoffman sold his existing business, moved to a new town, bought and sold a small grocery, and took out a loan. Red Owl later informed Hoffman that there would be no deal. Hoffman sued to recover lost income and expenses he incurred in reliance on Red Owl's promise. Red Owl claimed it was not liable because there was no contract, as it had never made Hoffman an offer.

Issue: Can a party be liable under the theory of promissory estoppel for breaking a promise, even though the terms of the promise were too vague and indefinite to constitute an offer?

Rule: A party will be liable for a promise made during preliminary negotiations if the promisor should reasonably expect to induce an action or forbearance of a definite and substantial nature by the promisee, the promise does induce such action or forbearance, and injustice would result if relief were not granted.

Livingstone v. Evans (1925) DHH

Facts: Evans offered to sell his land to Livingstone for $1,800. Livingstone sent a counteroffer to buy at a lower price. Evans rejected Livingstone's offer, saying, "cannot reduce price." When Livingstone agreed to pay $1,800, Evans refused to sell.

Issue: Does an offeree who has made a counteroffer still have the power to accept the original offer?

Rule: A counteroffer is a rejection of the offer and it cannot be accepted at a later date. The original offer can only be accepted if it is renewed.

Note: The court held that Evans' statement that he "cannot reduce price" was itself a reaffirmation of his earlier offer, which Livingstone validly accepted.

Idaho Power Co. v. Westinghouse Elec. Corp. (1979) DHH, R

Facts: Westinghouse sent Idaho Power its standardized list of product which also contained certain conditions, including a disclaimer of liability for damages resulting from defective products. Idaho ordered a voltage regulator with its standardized order form (acceptance), which stated that it "superseded all previous agreements" but was silent as to liability. The regulator was defective.

Issue: What is the legal effect of an agreement when the terms of the offer and acceptance vary?

Rule: Under UCC § 2-207, a contract between merchants is valid even if the terms of the offer and acceptance are not identical, unless acceptance is conditioned upon assent to the different terms.

Note: Thus, Idaho's acceptance was not a counteroffer and, because it was silent as to liability, Westinghouse's disclaimer applies.

Morrison v. Thoelke (1963) DHH, CPB

Facts: The plaintiff mailed an acceptance to the defendant. Before the acceptance was received, the plaintiff called to revoke acceptance.

Issue: When does an acceptance become effective?

Rule: According to the mailbox rule, acceptance becomes effective at the time it is posted. Therefore subsequent revocations are not effective even if received before the acceptance.

Note: Some courts hold that acceptance becomes effective upon receipt.

H.B. Toms Tree Surgery, Inc. v. Brant (1982) DHH

Facts: Plaintiff performed substantial landscaping work on the defendant's property. The parties' dealings were informal, and the defendant continuously directed the plaintiff to do work above and beyond any written estimates. Defendant paid the plaintiff the full amount due, in excess of written estimates for work done in the fall and winter, but refused to pay the necessary amount for work done in the summer.

Issue: May a party recover for the value of expenses incurred absent an express contract?

Rule: The conduct of parties to an agreement may establish an implied contract which is legally binding on both parties, as long as there is no inconsistent express contract.

Note: This is an extension of the objective view of contract formation.

Hobbs v. Massasoit Whip Co. (1898) CPB

Facts: Massasoit had bought eel skins from Hobbs on four or five prior occasions. On this occasion, Hobbs sent skins which Massasoit did not want. Massasoit neither notified Hobbs nor returned the skins, and eventually destroyed them.

Issue: May a party's conduct serve as an acceptance regardless of that party's state of mind?

Rule: When the silence or inaction of an offeree warrants the offeror's belief that the goods were accepted, that conduct serves as an acceptance regardless of intent.

Morone v. Morone (1980) DHH, R

Facts: The parties were an unmarried couple who lived together for 20 years, holding themselves out to the community as husband and wife. Together they had two children. After they separated, the plaintiff sued under implied contract to get her share of the couple's earnings and assets. She also claimed that the defendant had expressly promised that he would support her in return for her domestic services.

Issue 1: May a contract regarding earnings and assets be implied from a relationship of an unmarried couple?

Rule 1: An implied contract between an unmarried couple living together is too indefinite to be enforced as well as contrary to statutes that have abolished common law marriage.

Issue 2: Is an express contract between such a couple enforceable?

Rule 2: An express contract is enforceable so long as illicit sexual relations were not part of the consideration of the contract.

Hurley v. Eddingfield (1901) KGK

Facts: A physician refused to help the plaintiff who then died.

Issue: Are physicians bound to render their services to all persons who are in need of help?

Rule: A physician is not required to render services to everyone who requests them.

Poughkeepsie Buying Service, Inc. v. Poughkeepsie Newspapers, Inc. (1954) KGK

Facts: The plaintiff sued because the defendant refused to allow the plaintiff to advertise in his newspaper. The defendant published the only general daily paper in Poughkeepsie.

Issue: May a newspaper be compelled to run an advertisement?

Rule: The newspaper business is a private enterprise, and absent statutory regulation to the contrary, newspaper publishers generally have the right to publish or reject a general advertisement submitted to them.

Continental Forest Products, Inc. v. Chandler Supply Co. (1974) KGK

Facts: Chandler placed an order for two carloads of plywood with North America Millwork. Unbeknownst to Chandler, the North America employee who took the order left his position and gave the order to his new employer, Continental. When Continental's shipment arrived, Chandler sought to deduct from the purchase price a trade debt owed to it by North America.

Issue: May courts fashion equitable remedies without regard to the express or implied terms of an agreement?

Rule: Justice and equity may sometimes require courts to impose an obligation without reference to the intent or agreement of the parties.

Note: In the instant case, justice requires that Chandler only pay the amount that it would have paid had the transaction gone the way the company had intended.

Watteau v. Fenwick (1892) KGK

Facts: Humble sold his pub to the defendant, but stayed on as manager. Humble's name remained on the door and license. The plaintiff sold goods to the pub which Humble accepted even though the defendant had not authorized him to do so. The defendant refused to pay for the goods.

Issue: Is a principal liable for an unauthorized purchase by his agent if the seller was unaware of the principal-agent relationship?

Rule: A principal is liable for all acts of an agent that are within the authority usually confided to an agent, even if the principal placed a limitation on the agent's authority.

Balfour v. Balfour (1919) KGK, CPB

Facts: The plaintiff lived in a different country from her husband for health-related reasons. He had agreed to pay her a living allowance to support her. Their relationship deteriorated, and they eventually separated. The plaintiff sought to enforce their agreement.

Issue: Is any agreement between a husband and wife enforceable in a court of law?

Rule: Agreements between family members are usually unenforceable because, at the time they are made, the parties to the agreements usually do not have the "intent" to enter into an enforceable contract. However, if the requisite intent was present, then the agreement would be enforceable.

Davis v. General Foods Corp. (1937) KGK

Facts: Davis offered to reveal to General Foods a new idea for creating fruit flavors for ice cream. When General Foods agreed to review the idea it did so on the condition that any compensation to Davis would be at it's discretion. It used the product and neved paid Davis.

Issue: Is a promise reserving discretion over compensation too indefinite to be enforced?

Rule: If a promisor retains an unlimited right to control the nature and extent of his performance, the promise is too indefinite to be legally enforceable. This is an "illusory promise," i.e., the promisor seems to have promised something but really has reserved the right to give nothing.

The Mabley & Carew Co. v. Borden (1935) KGK

Facts: As part of her employment benefits, Work was promised that if she was still employed by Mabley & Carew at the time of her death, her designated beneficiary would receive a lump-sum payment. Mabley &

Carew expressly reserved the right to withdraw or discontinue the promise "at any time." Work died while still employed by Mabley & Carew which refused to pay Work's beneficiary, Borden.

Issue: Is an employer's revocable promise of death benefits to its employees unenforceable for lack of consideration?

Rule: The continued employment of an employee in reliance on a promise is valid consideration. If the offer has not been withdrawn during the employee's lifetime, it cannot be withdrawn later.

Note: This is the minority view on "illusory promises." The majority view is that reliance on an illusory promise will not create a contract.

Armstrong v. M'Ghee KGK

Facts: Armstrong, dissatisfied with his valuable horse after a hard ride, sold it to M'Ghee for a nominal amount. He later claimed he was in jest when he made the sale.

Issue: Will an inadequate price of which both parties are aware be grounds for annulling a completed contract?

Rule: If parties' objective signs show intent to make a binding contract, the contract will not be set aside despite any subjective belief to the contrary.

Anderson v. Backlund (1924) KGK

Facts: Backlund, a tenant farmer on Anderson's property, bought cattle to expand his farming activity in reliance on Anderson's "promise" that "there will be plenty of water because it never failed [to rain] in Minnesota." When Anderson sued Backlund on a separate debt, Backlund counterclaimed for the lost value of his cattle caused by a shortage of water.

Issue: Is a vague promise that has no specific terms an enforceable contract?

Rule: Contracts must be certain in terms and not so indefinite and illusory as to make it impossible to say just what was promised. In this case "mutual assent" is lacking because the indefiniteness of the agreement makes it uncertain as to what each party agreed.

Sullivan v. O'Connor (1973) KGK, CPB

Facts: Sullivan sued her surgeon for breach of contract after the plastic surgery performed on her nose failed to "enhance her beauty and improve her appearance" as expressly promised.

Issue: Does a doctor breach a contract if a medical procedure does not produce the desired results?

Rule: If a doctor expressly promises that a procedure will produce certain results, a patient may recover damages if that promise is not fulfilled.
Note: Because of the fear that patients will elevate a doctor's opinion to a promise, some courts require written proof of the promise. Other courts completely deny recovery in such cases.

Shaheen v. Knight (1957) KGK

Facts: Shaheen underwent an operation to be sterilized after which his wife had a baby. The doctor, Knight, had specifically promised that the procedure would be effective.
Issue: Can a contract for specified results exist between doctor and patient?
Rule: While courts are reluctant to require a doctor to guarantee success, a contract which specifies a particular result will be enforced.
Note: The court refused to grant Shaheen damages for the birth of the child on the grounds that it contravenes public policy to assess "damages" for the "fun, joy and affection" of raising a child.

Young and Ashburnham's Case (1587) KGK

Facts: Ashburnham slept and ate at Young's lodge without paying or making any agreement to do so.
Issue: Can one recover in contract absent an express agreement?
Rule: A contract action will not lie when an agreement was never made between two parties as to price or any other term.

Hertzog v. Hertzog (1857) KGK

Facts: A son sued his father's estate for the value of 17 years of uncompensated labor on his father's farm and for an outstanding debt. He claimed that his father had orally promised to pay him. There was no written contract between them.
Issue: Should an employment contract be implied between relatives who work for each other?
Rule: If a special relationship, such as father and son, exists between two parties, courts should be reluctant to imply an employment contract because the actions of the parties may be induced by familial affection.

Barnet's Estate (1936) KGK

Facts: A woman sued her husband's estate for the salary that he had promised to pay her for managing his business. There was no written memorandum of the alleged agreement.

Issue: When will a party recover the value of work performed for a close relative?

Rule: A party seeking to recover from the estate of a decedent with whom she had a close relationship must show that an express agreement with clear and unequivocal terms existed.

Note: Generally, family members, and spouses in particular, are considered to be working for the mutual benefit of the family or for reasons of affection, and courts are reluctant to imply contractual obligations.

Shaw v. Shaw (1954) KGK

Facts: After her "husband" died, the plaintiff discovered that their marriage was void because the decedent was married to another woman at the time of their marriage. As a result, the plaintiff was denied recovery from her husband's estate.

Issue: Can a promise to wed be enforceable in contract?

Rule: By proposing marriage, a man warrants that he is in a position to marry and is not a married man. He is liable if he breaches his promise.

Note: The court allowed the plaintiff to recover from the estate as if she was the decedent's legal wife.

Hewitt v. Hewitt (1974) KGK

Facts: The parties agreed to live together and share assets and earnings as a husband and wife would. The "wife" worked hard to support her husband's education, business and social interests. Common law marriage was not recognized in this jurisdiction. The wife sued to recover half the assets at separation.

Issue: Can two unmarried persons be required to share equally in income and assets if they agreed to such a plan, even though both were aware they were not legally married?

Rule: Courts can determine that the conduct of unmarried persons living together demonstrates an implied contract or an agreement of partnership or joint venture. A nonmarital partner can recover in *quantum meruit* for the reasonable value of services rendered, less the reasonable value of support received, if they can show that services were rendered with the expectation of monetary reward.

Cotnam v. Wisdom (1907) KGK

Facts: Cotnam's decedent was fatally injured after being thrown from a streetcar. Wisdom and another physician were summoned but were unable to save the patient. The physicians sued to recover the value of the services rendered. The trial judge instructed the jury that the size of the decedent's estate was relevant to the issue of the amount of recovery.

Issue 1: Can a physician recover for the value of services rendered when no express contract was made with the patient?

Rule 1: A physician may recover under the theory of quasi-contract for the reasonable value of services provided during an emergency.

Issue 2: What amount can a physician recover for emergency services provided under quasi-contract?

Rule 2: The physician should be granted reasonable compensation for services rendered. The financial standing of the victim is not relevant.

Sommers v. Putnam Bd. of Educ. (1925) KGK

Facts: Sommers lived four and a half miles from the nearest high school and had to transport his children to school daily because Putnam County refused to provide transportation or dormitory space. A state statute imposed an obligation on the county to either provide school facilities within four miles of every home or to provide transportation.

Issue: Can a party recover compensation for performing a duty that belongs to another?

Rule: When one performs a duty that another is required to perform, the value of the performance is recoverable under the theory of quasi-contract provided the legal duty is important to the public, the obligated party knowingly failed to perform the duty and a proper person intervened.

Upton-on-Severn Rural District Council v. Powell (1942) KGK

Facts: When Powell called the Upton Police Department to report that his barn was on fire, the Upton fire brigade was immediately sent out to extinguish the fire. Unknown to both parties, Powell's property was located outside the Upton Fire District, which meant that Powell was not entitled to free services.

Issue: Is one liable in contract for services requested in the belief that the services were gratuitous even though the services could have been received without charge from another party?

Rule: A contractual duty to pay arises when one requests services from a party in the erroneous belief that the services were free, despite the fact that the party was entitled to such services without charge from another party.

Vickery v. Ritchie (1909) KGK

Facts: The plaintiff contracted to build a bathhouse for the defendant. The architect who drew up the contracts defrauded them by writing different price figures on each party's copy: the plaintiff's contract "paid" him $33,721, while the defendant's contract "charged" him only $23,200. The mistake was not discovered until after the plaintiff had built most of the building. The defendant refused to pay more than the price in his contract.

Issue: Can a party to a contract voided due to mutual mistake recover the value of services provided in good faith?

Rule: When a mutual mistake by parties acting in good faith voids their express contract, the party who provided goods or services is entitled to their reasonable value under a theory of quasi-contract.

Michigan Central R.R. v. State (1927) KGK

Facts: Indiana (State) contracted to buy coal from Michigan Central at $3.40 per ton. Michigan delivered a carload of coal that was valued at $6.85 per ton. Michigan reimbursed the owner of the misdelivered coal and sued Indiana for indemnification. The lower court ruled that Indiana only had to pay Michigan at the rate of $3.40 per ton.

Issue: How is recovery in an action in quasi-contract determined?

Rule: In actions to enforce quasi-contractual obligations, the measure of recovery is the value to the defendant of the benefit received, which may be less than the market value of the goods.

Lefkowitz v. Great Minneapolis Surplus Store, Inc.
(1957) KGK, FE, MS, R

Facts: Great Minneapolis advertised in a newspaper that it would sell one lapin stole for $1 on a "first come, first served" basis. It refused to sell to Lefkowitz, who arrived first, claiming that the sale was for women only.

Issue: When is a newspaper advertisement considered an offer?

Rule: A newspaper advertisement that is clear, definite, explicit, and leaves nothing open for negotiation is considered to be an offer. While the offer may be modified, new and arbitrary conditions not in print may not be imposed after acceptance.

Note: UCC § 2-204 recognizes offers even when some issues are left for future negotiations.

Jenkins Towel Serv. Inc. v. Fidelity-Philadelphia Trust Co.
(1960) KGK

Facts: Fidelity requested parties to submit sealed bids for the purchase of land stating that an "agreement of sale" would be tendered to the highest acceptable bidder above $92,000. Although it reserved the right to reject any offer, Fidelity expressly stated that it had a duty to recommend "the most advantageous offer." Jenkins' unconditional bid of $95,600 was rejected in favor of a rival bid, which was as high but conditioned upon changes in the zoning law and further approval. Jenkins claimed that its bid was the highest and most advantageous and that the rival's conditional bid was not an acceptance but rather a counteroffer.

Issue: How is an ambiguous offer interpreted?

Rule: An ambiguous statement that could reasonably be interpreted as an offer is construed against the party who wrote it.

Fairmount Glass Works v. Crunden-Martin Woodenware Co.
(1899) KGK, CPB

Facts: Crunden-Martin asked Fairmount to quote the "lowest price" at which it would sell certain goods. Fairmount provided a price quote sheet with terms and conditions "for immediate acceptance." Crunden-Martin sent in an order, but Fairmount refused to fill it.

Issue: Is a price quote an offer?

Rule: Use of the phrase "for immediate acceptance" in a price quote has the legal effect of making the quote an offer.

Note: Price quotations are generally not considered offers, especially if they are unsolicited.

Channel Master Corp. v. Aluminum Ltd. Sales
(1958) KGK

Facts: The defendant misrepresented that it could supply the plaintiff with 400,000 pounds of aluminum per month. The plaintiff sued to recover damages in tort caused by its reliance on the oral promise. The defendant claimed that since his promise was not written, it was unenforceable because it violated the statute of frauds.

Issue: Is a fraudulent misrepresentation excused if the promise would have been unenforceable because it violated the statute of frauds?

Rule: A party may recover damages arising from a fraudulent misrepresentation in a tort action, even if the fraudulent misrepresentation would have been unenforceable as a contract because it violated the statute of frauds. The tort was committed by the utterance of a falsehood and there is no need to prove the existence of a contract.

Hill v. Waxberg (1956) KGK

Facts: Waxberg helped Hill to prepare for the construction of a building. It was agreed that Waxberg would be awarded the project if Hill succeeded in securing financing. Waxberg did much of the preparatory work (e.g., talked with an architect, rented equipment, calculated costs) which enabled Hill to secure financing, but Hill hired another contractor when the two could not agree on contract terms. Waxberg sued to recover the value of the services provided.

Issue 1: Can one recover for services performed even though a formal contract was never made?

Rule 1: A party can recover for services that were provided in the absence of a formal contract under the theories of "implied-in-fact" (implied) and "implied-in-law" (quasi-) contracts.

Issue 2: What is the measure of recovery for services performed in the absence of a formal contract?

Rule 2: If recovery is based on an implied-in-fact contract, a party will be compensated according to the market value of the services that were provided. Recovery based on an implied-in-law contract is limited to the value of the benefit that was conferred, i.e., both the reasonable value of the services and the granting of financing.

Collins Radio Co. (1941) KGK

Facts: The U.S. government conditionally accepted a bid from Collins Radio to build radios, subject to the "execution of a formal contract." Collins incurred expenses in preparation for manufacturing the radios. Because its needs changed, the government sought to find out what its liability would be if it refused to execute the formal contract.

Issue: Is a party that conditionally accepts a bid, but does not formally execute a contract, liable for expenses incurred by the party that submitted the bid?

Rule: If one party expressly makes it clear that it does not intend to form a contract until it signs a written document, no valid contract exists, and a bidder will not be reimbursed for work performed.

The Sun Printing and Publishing Ass'n. v. Remington
Paper and Power Co., Inc. (1923) KGK

Facts: Sun agreed to buy from Remington 1,000 tons of newsprint per month for sixteen months. The price for the first four months was specified, but the price for the remainder of the contract was to be "reasonably agreed upon" with a limitation that it could not rise above the price the Canadian Export Paper Company (an unrelated party) charged its large customers. When prices rose sharply, Remington refused to sell after the fourth month claiming that the contract was indefinite.

Issue: Is a contract void for indefiniteness when the price term is left open to be determined by the parties at a later date?

Rule: A contract is void for indefiniteness if a material term such as price has been omitted.

Note: The modern view, as expressed in UCC § 2-305, allows enforcement of contracts with open price terms.

Borg-Warner Corp. v. Anchor Coupling Co.
(1959) KGK, MS

Facts: Borg-Warner entered into negotiations for the purchase of Anchor. Anchor's directors assured Borg-Warner that if it made an offer within 50 days (during which time Borg-Warner could survey Anchor) it would accept. Anchor also required that Borg-Warner give suitable assurances that personnel would not be fired and that a "mutually acceptable" arrangement would be made for the continued employment of one of the owners. These conditions were left open to be "agreed upon" in good faith after a contract was executed. Borg-Warner made an offer that was accepted. Anchor later refused to perform.

Issue: Can a contract be formed even though some terms were left open to be decided by the parties at some future time?

Rule: When two parties manifest an intent to contract and reach substantial agreement, a contract is formed, even though minor issues are left to be resolved.

Itek Corp. v. Chicago Aerial Indus. Inc. (1968) KGK

Facts: Itek and CAI signed a "letter of intent" providing that they "shall make every reasonable effort to agree upon" a contract. CAI later broke off negotiations when it received an offer from another company.

Issue: Is a party liable for failure to honor its promise to attempt to reach a contract?

Rule: A party that breaks off negotiations after signing a letter of intent to make every reasonable effort to reach an agreement is liable if it fails to act in good faith.

Prescott v. Jones (1898) KGK

Facts: The defendants, insurance agents, informed the plaintiff that his insurance policy would be automatically renewed unless he specifically objected. The plaintiff did not respond. The defendant neither renewed the policy nor informed the plaintiff. The plaintiff sued to recover for damages for breach of contract after the defendants refused to reimburse him for property lost in a fire.

Issue: Can silence constitute acceptance of an offer?

Rule: Acceptance of an offer must be made by direct communication, even if the offer is so worded as to suggest that acceptance is possible without communication.

Note: This common law rule has been superseded.

National Union Fire Ins. v. Joseph Ehrlich (1924) KGK

Facts: Ehrlich had been insured by National for several years when he received a standard automatic renewal notice and bill. Ehrlich held on to the notice and only rejected his policy two months later when National requested payment.

Issue: Can receipt and failure to return an automatic renewal insurance policy constitute acceptance?

Rule: The receipt and retention of an insurance renewal policy, where the insured individual knows that payment is required in cases of retention, is an acceptance that will create a binding contract even if the insured subjectively wants to reject it.

Austin v. Burge (1911) KGK

Facts: Burge was given a two-year subscription to Austin's newspaper by his father-in-law. Delivery of the paper continued for several years after the subscription expired, even though Burge made several requests that it be cancelled. During this period, however, Burge took the newspapers home and read them. Austin sued to collect the value of the newspapers that were delivered.

Issue: Does the receipt and use of an item shipped through the mail constitute an acceptance by conduct?

Rule: Receipt of an item not requested and use of the item will constitute a valid acceptance of an offer (i.e., to use the item).

Note: This rule has been altered by statute in many states whereby an item received in the mail without request (such as from book clubs) is treated as a gift.

Cole-McIntyre-Norfleet Co. v. Holloway
(1919) KGK, FE

Facts: The defendant's salesman took an order for barrels of meal from Holloway and gave him four months within which to exercise the order (i.e., ask that the meal be shipped). The order contract provided that it was not binding until approved at the home office and that the company could not be bound by its salesperson. When Holloway asked for delivery of the meal, he was told that his order was rejected by the home office. Holloway suffered monetary loss because the price of meal had sharply risen in the meantime.

Issue: Does an unreasonable delay in rejecting an offer constitute an acceptance?

Rule: When the subject of a contract, either by its nature or by virtue of market conditions, will become unmarketable by delay, a delay in notifying the other party of its decision will amount to an acceptance by the offeree.

Langellier v. Schaefer (1887) KGK

Facts: Langellier accepted Schaefer's offer to sell a lot of property but changed the terms. Schaefer rejected Langellier's acceptance.

Issue: Is an acceptance effective if additional terms are added?

Rule: If the parties conduct negotiations by letters there is no mutual assent unless the response to the offer is a similar acceptance that does not introduce any new terms.

Note: This is the common-law "mirror image" rule that requires an acceptance to be identical in its terms to the offer. This approach is modified in UCC § 2-207.

Butler v. Foley (1920) KGK

Facts: Butler ordered Foley to purchase stock in its behalf. Foley's response was erroneously transmitted by the telegraph company, leading Butler to think that Foley had bought the stock. Butler incurred extra costs when it had to purchase the stock on the open market.

Issue: Which party bears the risk of an error by a third party that transmits an acceptance?

Rule: An offeror bears the risk as to the effectiveness of communication if the acceptance is made in the manner either expressly or impliedly indicated by him.

Note: The court found that Foley was the offeror because its response to Butler's offer modified the terms of the offer ("mirror image" rule).

United States v. Braunstein (1947) KGK, R

Facts: The U.S. solicited bids for 9,599 25-pound boxes of raisins. Braunstein offered ten cents a pound. The U.S. accepted Braunstein's offer, but a clerk erred in cabling the response, which stated that U.S. "accepts" ten cents per 25-pound box. Braunstein did not reply to the acceptance. U.S. discovered the error and notified Braunstein who again made no response. The U.S. sold the raisins elsewhere and sued for the loss on the sale.

Issue: If the language accepting an offer leads the other party to believe that the offeree does not intend what he says, is the acceptance effective?

Rule: If either party to a contract knows that the other has made an error and therefore does not intend to be bound by its words, the words or acts do not operate as an offer or acceptance.

Roto-Lith, Ltd. v. F.P. Bartlett & Co. (1962) KGK, MS

Facts: Roto-Lith ordered emulsifier from Bartlett. Bartlett accepted Roto-Lith's offer by sending an "acknowledgment" form and an invoice, both of which disclaimed all warranties in conspicuous type on the front. Roto-Lith accepted the emulsifier, which later turned out to be defective. Roto-Lith claimed that the disclaimer of warranties on Bartlett's acceptance form was a material addition to the terms of the offer and was therefore a rejectable proposal under UCC § 2-207(2).

Issue: Does an additional term on an acceptance that is solely to the offeree's advantage become a part of a binding contract?

Rule: An acceptance that includes an additional term made solely for the offeree's advantage is an acceptance that is expressly conditioned upon the offeror's assent to the additional terms.

Note: Roto-Lith assented to the additional terms by its actions in accepting delivery of the goods with knowledge of the conditions specified in the acknowledgment.

Woodburn v. Northwestern Bell Tel. Co. (1979) KGK

Facts: Woodburn, a physician, sued Northwestern for failing to list him in the yellow pages. Northwestern asserted that it had filed an express limitation of damages with the state commerce commission and a similar limitation was printed on the back of the form Woodburn used to place his order.

Issue: When does a clause that limits liability for damages become part of a contract?

Rule: A contractual limitation of liability is enforceable if there was mutual assent to it. A party is allowed to introduce evidence on whether the other party reasonably was or should have been aware of the contract term.

Air Products & Chem., Inc. v. Fairbanks Morse, Inc. (1973) KGK

Facts: Air Products ordered several electric motors from Fairbanks. Fairbanks returned Air Product's order form with a copy of its acknowledgment form, which contained an additional term that limited Fairbank's liability in case of defect.

Issue: Can a limitation of liability that is contained in a seller's acknowledgment form become part of the contract of sale when the buyer's purchase order contained no such term and the buyer never expressly agreed to such terms?

Rule: A disclaimer for consequential loss is sufficiently material to require express conversation between parties over its exclusion or inclusion in a contract under UCC § 2-207(2)(b).

Siegel v. Spear & Co. (1923) KGK

Facts: Spear's agent gratuitously promised to obtain insurance for the furniture that Siegel had stored with Spear. Spear never insured the plaintiff's goods, which were subsequently destroyed in a fire.

Issue: Is a party liable for a gratuitous promise?

Rule: A party is not obligated to perform a gratuitous promise unless performance has begun. Once started, the performing party is held to full execution of all that has been promised.

Note: In the instant case, the court held that by storing the Siegel's furniture Spear had begun performing the promise and was thus required to complete it by taking out insurance.

Lusk-Harbison-Jones, Inc. v. Universal Credit Co.
(1933) KGK
Facts: Universal contracted to have LHJ, a car dealer, repair and recondition five repossessed cars and store them until they were sold. LHJ did not insure the cars because Universal later told him that it would carry insurance on the cars. The cars were destroyed by fire. Universal claimed that its statement relating to insurance was made after the contract and was not a part of it.
Issue: Is a promise that foreseeably induces reliance by the promisee enforceable?
Rule: A promise that the promisor should reasonably expect to induce action or forbearance by the promisee that induces such action is binding if injustice can only be avoided by the enforcement of the promise.

Fisher v. Jackson (1955) KGK
Facts: The plaintiff quit his job to work for the defendant. The plaintiff sued for breach of contract when the defendant fired him, claiming that the defendant had orally promised to hire him for life.
Issue: Absent consideration other than the rendering of employment services, is a promise of permanent employment enforceable?
Rule: Leaving one job for another job is not sufficient consideration for a promise of life employment; an agreement for life employment is terminable at the will of either party.

Underwood Typewriter Co. v. Century Realty Co. (1909) KGK
Facts: Century modified its lease with Underwood to allow the latter to sublease the premises to an acceptable tenant. With Century's knowlege, Underwood expended time and effort in search of a sub-tenant. When Underwood presented a tenant, Century claimed that the sublease agreement was invalid due to lack of mutual obligation: although Century was obligated to consent to a proper tenant, Underwood was not likewise obligated to look for a tenant.
Issue: May a contract be enforced absent mutuality of obligation?
Rule: A unilateral contract is enforceable even absent mutuality of obligation.

Capital Sav. & Loan Assn. v. Przybylowicz (1978) KGK
Facts: Capital S & L granted and drew up the terms of a $34,500 residential mortgage loan to the Przybylowiczs, which stated that the

Przybylowiczs were required to repay the loan in 300 monthly payments of $251.76. Unknown to both, Capital had miscalculated the terms. The payments should have been $289.53 per month. In reliance upon the loan, the Przybylowicz sold their home and contracted to build a new one. Capital sought to reform the contract.

Issue: Can a written contract be reformed because of an error by one of the parties?

Rule: When a party relies on an erroneous statement made by the other party to a contract, and the first party could not have been expected to discover the error, the contract will be enforced if the other party is a professional who regularly engages in the activity involved.

Chapman v. Bomann (1978) KGK

Facts: The Chapmans signed an agreement to buy the Bomann's property. Mrs. Bomann orally promised that they would also sign, but later Mr. Bomann changed his mind. In reliance upon the promise the Chapmans refinanced their home. The Bomanns claimed that the promise was unenforceable as a violation of the Statute of Frauds.

Issue: Is a separate ancillary promise to sign a contract to buy property enforceable?

Rule: On principles of equity, a party is estopped from asserting the Statute of Frauds to deny the enforceability of a separate, ancillary oral promise, otherwise binding, to sign a written document that would not satisfy the Statute of Frauds if it were left unsigned.

Note: The Chapmans also prevailed on a theory of promissory estoppel.

Feinberg v. Pfeiffer Co. (1959) KGK, FE, MS

Facts: Pfeiffer agreed to pay Feinberg $200 per month for life when she retired. Feinberg worked for a few more years and retired. Her pension was terminated after several years when she refused to have it reduced to $100 per month.

Issue: Can a promisor withdraw a promise that was given without consideration?

Rule: Past employment is considered past consideration, which does not constitute adequate legal consideration. However, if one acts to her detriment by quitting lucrative employment in justifiable reliance on a promise, the promise will be enforced if an injustice would result otherwise.

Dickinson v. Dodds (1876) KGK, FE, MS

Facts: On June 10, Dodds offered to sell Dickinson a parcel of land and promised to keep the offer open until June 12. On June 11, Dickinson learned that Dodds intended to sell the land to another person. That afternoon Dickinson left a note accepting the offer.

Issue: What is the effect of an offer upon notice to the offeree that the offeror has made an offer to another party?

Rule: Information that leads an offeree to reasonably conclude that an offer has been withdrawn voids the offer.

Jordan v. Dobbins (1877) KGK

Facts: Dobbins guaranteed the credit of a third party to Jordan. Before discovering that Dobbins had died, Jordan made some sales to the third party which were never repaid. Jordan sued to recover from Dobbins' estate.

Issue: Is a guaranty terminated at the death of the guarantor?

Rule: The death of a guarantor operates as the revocation of the guaranty; the person holding it cannot recover against the guarantor's estate for goods sold after the guarantor's death.

Loranger Constr. Corp. v. E.F. Hauserman Co. (1978) KGK

Facts: The plaintiff, relying on an "estimate" given by the defendant, submitted a bid that was later accepted. The defendant refused to perform.

Issue: Is a party bound by an "estimate" that was given without consideration?

Rule: An estimator is bound to perform according to its "estimate" (bid) if reliance upon it is foreseeable and if injustice can only be avoided by enforcement of the "estimate" (bid) (Rest. 2d. § 89(b)(2)).

Southern California Acoustics Co. v. C.V. Holder, Inc. (1969) KGK

Facts: Southern, a subcontractor, submitted a bid to Holder, a contractor, who submitted its overall bid along with a list of subcontractors that included Southern. After Holder was awarded the project, a local trade newspaper published the names of all the subcontractors. When it saw its name in the trade paper, Southern assumed it was part of the project and did not seek other jobs. Holder received approval to replace Southern with another subcontractor.

Issue: Can a contractor substitute subcontractors after the contractor's bid has been accepted?

Rule: A contractor cannot substitute a listed subcontractor, absent a proper reason such as the subcontractor's insolvency, failure or refusal to perform, or failure or refusal to meet bonding requirements.

Note: This rule is based on the Subletting and Subcontracting Fair Practices Act. Today a subcontractor that is listed due to a clerical error can be substituted.

Cushing v. Thomson (1978) KGK

Facts: Cushing's mailed acceptance was postmarked April 5 but dated April 3. Thomson withdrew the offer on April 4. Cushing represented that it was customary office procedure for letters to be sent out the same day that they were placed in the outbox, April 3, in this case. The court found for Cushing.

Issue: Can a party introduce evidence beyond the postmark, as to the date an acceptance was mailed?

Rule: A party is allowed to introduce evidence as to when an acceptance was mailed if the postmark is insufficient.

Rhode Island Tool Co. v. United States (1955) KGK

Facts: After the U.S. mailed an acceptance of Rhode Island's bid, but before Rhode Island received it, Rhode Island notified the defendant of an error in the bid.

Issue: May an erroneous bid be withdrawn after acceptance is posted?

Rule: When one has the right to withdraw a bid because it is erroneous, a binding contract will not result from posting of an acceptance.

Note: This court is in the minority that rejects the "mailbox" rule.

Palo Alto Town & Country Village, Inc. v. BBTC Co.
(1974) KGK

Facts: The defendant's lease contained an option to renew, to be exercised five months before the end of the term of lease. The defendant sent a properly stamped, addressed notice of exercise of the option six months before the lease expired, but the plaintiff never received the notice.

Issue: Is notice by an optionee of his exercise of an option effective upon its deposit in the mail or upon its receipt by the optionor?

Rule: Absent any provisions in the option contract to the contrary, the exercise of an option becomes effective at the time written notice of acceptance is deposited in the mail.

Postal Telegraph-Cable Co. v. Willis (1908) KGK

Facts: Willis, a cotton dealer, telegraphed an offer to sell cotton which was accepted. The acceptance was telegraphed but delivery was delayed by Postal. The acceptance was later revoked by the offeree because it was the custom of the cotton industry that acceptances were only effective upon actual receipt. Willis sued Postal to recover for the loss he incurred in selling elsewhere. Postal appealed.

Issue: Does a contrary "custom and usage" of an industry overrule the "mailbox" rule?

Rule: A legal rule will not be overruled by "custom and usage" of a trade.

Caldwell v. Cline (1930) KGK

Facts: Cline mailed an offer for the purchase of Caldwell's land on January 29 that provided that Caldwell had eight days to accept or reject the offer. Caldwell received the offer on February 2 and wired an acceptance on February 8. Cline refused to perform claiming that Caldwell had accepted ten days after the offer was mailed.

Issue: If an offer contains a time limit, does the clock start when the offer is sent or when it is received?

Rule: Since an offer becomes effective when received, the acceptance period also begins when the offer is received, not when it is sent.

Carlill v. Carbolic Smoke Ball Co.
(1893) KGK, FE, MS, CPB

Facts: Carbolic offered a cash reward to anyone who contracted influenza after using its medical product. Carlill followed the product's usage instructions, but contracted the flu anyhow.

Issue: When a company advertises a reward if its product performs unsatisfactorily, must the consumer notify the company that he is accepting the offer before he uses the product?

Rule: If the advertisement is sufficiently specific as to the requirements for getting the reward (i.e., what the plaintiff can or cannot do) then its "offer" can be "accepted" by any person who fulfills the conditions of the advertisement, and there is no requirement to notify the company before using its product.

Taft v. Hyatt (1919) KGK

Facts: Taft posted a reward for information leading to the capture of a suspected murderer. Hyatt, a lawyer, was approached by the fugitive but not retained by him. Hyatt then went to the police. In the meantime the fugitive was turned in by other defendants who were unaware of the reward.

Issue: Can one recover a reward if he acted without knowledge of the reward?

Rule: An offer to pay a reward constitutes a unilateral contract, which can only be accepted by performing the requisite act with knowledge of and intent to claim the reward.

Strong v. Sheffield (1895) KGK

Facts: Sheffield guaranteed her husband's debt to Strong on the condition that he would forbear from demanding payment for an unspecified period of time. Strong forbore for two years before presenting the note for collection. Sheffield claimed her guarantee was unenforceable for lack of consideration, because Strong's promise was illusory. Payment could have been demanded at any time without violating the letter of his promise to ask for the money when he wanted it.

Issue: Does a promise to forbear from collection of a debt for an unspecified period of time constitute valid consideration?

Rule: Forbearance to collect on a note is illusory and insufficient consideration if the forbearer had the option of demanding payment at any time.

Hay v. Fortier (1917) KGK

Facts: Fortier was a surety for a bond owed to Hay by a third party. When the third party defaulted, Fortier, legally bound to pay, made a promise to pay in installments if Hay promised not to bring suit. Hay agreed, but Fortier made only one payment. Hay sued to enforce Fortier's promise. Fortier claimed that because she was already obligated to pay, there was no new consideration for Hay's promise not to sue. Since Hay could have sued at any time to enforce her original promise to pay, there was no mutuality of obligation.

Issue: Does the fact that there is a lack of mutuality of obligation necessarily mean that a promise to pay a debt is unenforceable?

Rule: If a contract not originally binding due to a lack of mutuality is performed by the party not originally bound thereby conferring a benefit on the other party, the other party will be estopped from refusing performance.

Crook v. Cowan (1870) KGK

Facts: Cowan sent a carpet dealer, Crook, a detailed, unconditional order for carpets. Crook accepted the order and shipped the carpets without notice to Cowan. Cowan had made other arrangements, thinking that Crook had not accepted.

Issue: Must one offering property for sale convey a formal acceptance?

Rule: A party who holds its property out for sale is not required to send a formal acceptance if it receives a detailed and unconditional order (offer).

Note: The dissent viewed this as a unilateral contract and required formal notice.

Bishop v. Eaton (1894) KGK, FE

Facts: Eaton promised that he would guarantee any loans that Bishop made to the Eaton's brother. Bishop repaid a debt of Eaton's brother and sent properly addressed and stamped notification to Eaton, who resided in a distant land. Eaton claimed that he never received the letter.

Issue: What constitutes acceptance of an offer for a unilateral contract where it is unlikely the offeror will find out whether the offeree performed?

Rule: Where one performs in response to an offer for a unilateral contract, and the offeror is unlikely to know whether the offeree has performed, the offeror will be bound if the offeree makes a reasonable and seasonable effort to notify the offeror of his performance. The offeror need not actually receive the notification.

White v. Corlies (1871) KGK, FE

Facts: White submitted an estimate to perform work for Corlies and Tift. Corlies and Tift then sent White an offer to do the work. White began work without formally communicating acceptance of the offer. Corlies and Tift changed its mind and revoked the offer.

Issue: Can an offer be accepted by beginning performance without giving any other indication of assent?

Rule: Acceptance of an offer must be actually communicated to the offeror.

Note: The resolution of this case turned on whether Corlies and Tift required return performance or a return promise in response. The court ruled that this was not a unilateral contract and therefore a return "promise" was required.

Los Angeles Traction Co. v. Wilshire (1902) KGK

Facts: Wilshire executed a note to L.A. Traction, payable upon completion of a road. L.A. Traction immediately paid $1,505 to get a franchise from the city to do the work. Wilshire revoked the offer before L.A. Traction completed performance.

Issue: May an offer for a unilateral contract be withdrawn at any time?

Rule: An offer of a unilateral contract cannot be withdrawn after the offeree has expended time and money in reliance upon the contract. The offeree must be compensated for his costs.

Baumgartner v. Meek (1954) KGK

Facts: After agreeing to list their property exclusively with Baumgartner, a broker, the Meeks attempted to withdraw their property from the listing.

Issue: Can a property owner revoke an agreement to exclusively list property with a broker?

Rule: An agreement to exclusively list one's property with a broker is irrevocable for the term of the agreement.

Lucy v. Zehmer (1954) FE, MS, CPB

Facts: Zehmer signed a memorandum agreeing to sell his family farm to Lucy. Zehmer claimed that it was part of a joke he was playing on Lucy.

Issue: Can a contract be avoided if one party claims that the "whole matter was a joke"?

Rule: The intention of a party to a contract is judged by his words and acts (objective standard), not by his unexpressed state of mind (subjective standard).

Frigaliment Importing Co. v. B.N.S. Int'l Sales Corp. (1960) FE

Facts: B.N.S. agreed to supply Frigaliment with 100,000 lbs. of chicken. While Frigaliment interpreted "chicken" to mean only young chickens suitable for broiling and frying, B.N.S understood it to mean any bird of that genus that met the contractual specifications of weight and quality.

Issue: How does a court resolve conflicting interpretations of a key word in the contract?

Rule: If a party seeks to introduce a narrower definition of a word in the contract, it bears the burden of proving that its definition was accepted by the other party or that it is the acceptable trade use of the term.

Spaulding v. Morse (1947) FE

Facts: As part of his divorce settlement, Morse was required to pay $1,200 per year to a trust fund for the education and maintenance of his son. The amount was to rise to $2,200 for the four years the son spent in college. The son was drafted when he graduated from school. Morse refused to pay the $1,200 during the son's tenure in the army, claiming he was not required to do so by the agreement.

Issue: In interpreting the meaning of a contract, can a court look at the circumstances surrounding its formulation in addition to its express terms?

Rule: A written contract is to be interpreted with a view to the circumstances of the parties at the time of its making. If the purpose was to provide support for the son, who is now being maintained and educated by the army, the promisor's duties are relieved.

Lonergan v. Scolnick (1954) FE, KC, MS, CPB

Facts: The defendant advertised his property for sale and responded to the plaintiff's inquiries by describing the location of the property and stating his lowest price. The defendant's reply carried the caption "this is a form letter." The plaintiff made a second inquiry, but received the defendant's response only after the property was sold.

Issue: Is a form letter an offer?

Rule: A contract is not formed when the minds of the parties have not met and mutually agreed upon some specific thing. A contract does not exist if it is clear that the parties do not intend to bind themselves without further negotiations.

Akers v. J.B. Sedberry, Inc. (1955) FE

Facts: Sedberry did not respond when Akers and another employee offered to resign during a meeting. Several days later, Sedberry accepted the offer to resign.

Issue: Does an offer made during a conversation end with the conversation?

Rule: Ordinarily, an offer made by one to another in a face-to-face conversation is deemed to continue only to the close of the conversation and cannot be accepted thereafter. If there is no express provision, an offer must be accepted within a reasonable time, which depends on the circumstances surrounding the offer, business usage, or nature of the contract.

Ardente v. Horan (1976) FE

Facts: The Horans accepted Ardente's bid for their home. In signing the contract, Ardente added a condition that some of the furniture be left in the home.

Issue: Is a conditional acceptance of an offer valid to create a contract?

Rule: A contract is not formed by a conditional acceptance unless the original offeror assents to the additional conditions (Rest. 2d. § 39).

Ryder v. Wescoat (1976) FE

Facts: Wescoat had sold an option to buy property to Ryder. Ryder informed Wescoat that he would not be exercising the option. As a result, Wescoat made some preparations to purchase the property himself without making any legal commitments. Ryder changed his mind before the option expired and sought to exercise it himself.

Issue: Does an option expire when its holder indicates that he does not intend to accept it?

Rule: An option obtained in exchange for consideration will not expire when it is rejected unless the party giving the option relied on the rejection to its detriment.

Payne v. Cave (1789) FE

Facts: The highest bidder at an auction withdrew his bid before the auctioneer pounded his gavel.

Issue: Can a bid be withdrawn at an auction?

Rule: A bid at an auction is not binding and can be revoked before the auctioneer drops his gavel.

Shuey v. United States (1875) FE

Facts: The United States used newspapers to publicize a reward for the arrest of an accomplice in the murder of President Lincoln. The offer was later revoked in the same manner. Shuey, unaware of the revocation, gave information that led to the arrest of the accomplice. She was given a smaller reward.

Issue: How may a general offer that is made to unknown persons via the mass media be revoked?

Rule: An offer of a reward made by means of a published proclamation can be revoked in the manner in which it was made or through similar publicity. There is no legal duty to satisfy an acceptor who does not know of the revocation.

Marchiondo v. Scheck (1967) FE, MS, CPB

Facts: The defendant offered to pay the plaintiff, a broker, a certain commission if the plaintiff succeeded in selling the defendant's property to a specified buyer within six days. The defendant revoked the offer on the sixth day. The plaintiff obtained the buyer's agreement on that same day.

Issue: Can an offer to enter a unilateral contract be revoked at any time?

Rule: When an offer specifies acceptance by performance, the offer is for a unilateral contract and cannot be revoked once the offeree begins performance (e.g., by beginning to solicit the buyer).

Adams v. Lindsell (1818) FE, MS, R

Facts: The defendant's offer was delayed in the mail because he addressed it incorrectly. The plaintiff sent out an acceptance immediately. The defendant sold the goods to a third party after the acceptance was mailed but before he received it.

Issue: When does an acceptance sent by mail become effective?

Rule: An acceptance sent by mail becomes effective as of the moment it leaves the offeree's control, i.e., when it is mailed.

Lewis v. Browning (1881) FE

Facts: The plaintiff, lessor, offered the defendant terms for a leasing agreement and told the defendant, "If I do not hear from you by the 18th or 20th I shall conclude your answer is no." The defendant's acceptance never reached the plaintiff.

Issue: Can an offeror require actual communication of acceptance?

Rule: An offeror can require that the formation of a contract be dependent on actual communication of acceptance. (This is one way to circumvent the "mailbox" rule.)

Falconer v. Mazess (1961) FE

Facts: Falconer made an offer to Mazess, a broker, to buy all of the stock owned by a third party. Falconer left a deposit with Mazess and gave him five days to accept in writing. The acceptance was posted on time but received after the deadline. Falconer sued to recover his deposit, claiming no contract was formed.

Issue: Must an acceptance be received to be effective?

Rule: When the use of the mails is authorized as a method of acceptance, the acceptance is valid upon posting unless the offer explicitly provided that an acceptance would only take effect upon receipt. (For the current rule, see UCC § 2-206, and Rest. 2d. § 64(b).)

Klockner v. Green (1969) FE

Facts: Klockner's stepmother orally promised Klockner and his daughter that they would receive her estate if they cared for her during her lifetime. Klockner provided care as his stepmother had asked but claimed he would have cared for her even if no promise was made. The stepmother twice drew up a will but never signed it because of superstition. After her death, Klockner sued to recover on the oral promise.

Issue: What is the intent required to accept an offer?

Rule: A valid enforceable contract can be made, obligating one to bequeath her property, even if the services given in exchange for the bequest would have been provided absent the promise.

Holman Erection Co. v. Orville E. Madsen & Sons, Inc. (1983) FE

Facts: Madsen incorporated Holman's bid for a subcontract in its bid for a general contract. Madsen received the general contract but subcontracted the work to someone else.

Issue: Does a general contractor accept a subcontractor's offer if that subcontractor's offer is used in preparing an offer for a general contract that is later obtained?

Rule: The use of a subcontractor's bid in preparing the general bid does not constitute acceptance of the subcontractor's offer.

Phillips v. Moor (1880) FE

Facts: The defendant contracted to buy the plaintiff's hay. Before delivery or payment, the hay was destroyed.

Issue: With whom lies the risk of loss of goods that are sold but not yet delivered?

Rule: After the terms of sale are agreed upon and the bargain is struck, the property and risk of accident to the goods vest in the buyer.

Note: Under UCC § 2-509, "the risk of loss passes to the buyer on his receipt of the goods if the seller is a merchant; otherwise the risk passes to the buyer on tender of delivery."

McGlone v. Lacey (1968) FE

Facts: McGlone sent Lacey, an attorney, an offer to handle her personal injury case on a contingent fee basis. Lacey's partner replied that Lacey was away and would contact McGlone as soon as he got back in March. Lacey did not respond until May, when McGlone inquired again. By then the statute of limitations had expired. McGlone sued for malpractice.

Issue: Does silence constitute acceptance of an offer?

Rule: Acceptance must be unequivocal in order to create a contract; silence will not constitute an acceptance absent a duty to speak.

In Re Crisan Estate (1961) FE

Facts: Crisan collapsed in a store and was taken to a hospital where she remained unconscious until her death 11 months later.

Issue: Will the law imply a promise to pay for emergency services rendered to an unconscious patient by a public hospital?

Rule: A party can recover the value of emergency services given to an unconscious person in quasi-contract if the party acted with the intention of being compensated, provided essential services, and there was no reason to think that the unconscious, injured party would have refused the services.

Day v. Caton (1876) FE, CPB

Facts: The plaintiff claimed that the defendant expressly agreed to pay for half the value of a wall between their properties. The defendant, who had silently watched the work in progress, denied any such agreement.

Issue: Does a party's silence when witnessing beneficial services rendered on his property obligate him to pay for those services?

Rule: A promise to pay for valuable beneficial services will be inferred if a party voluntarily accepted them, knowing that they were rendered with an expectation of compensation.

Bastian v. Gafford (1977) FE

Facts: Gafford inquired whether Bastion would be interested in building on Gafford's property. Bastion orally agreed and prepared the plans but was denied the job because his payment schedule was unsatisfactory to the bank financing the construction. Bastion sued to recover the cost of drafting his unused plans, claiming that the parties had an implied-in-fact contract.

Issue: When can a party recover for services rendered in preparation for a contract?

Rule: To recover for services rendered in preparation for a contract, a party must show that the circumstances suggest an implied agreement to pay, or an implied-in-fact agreement.
Note: The case was remanded to determine the existence of an implied-in-fact contract, or agreement to pay for the services; the court below applied the standard of unjust enrichment which is relevant only in the context of quasi-contract, not implied-in-fact contract.

Pine River State Bank v. Mettille (1983) FE

Facts: Pine River fired Mettille, an at-will employee. Pine River had given Mettille an employee handbook that contained disciplinary procedures.
Issue: Do disciplinary procedures in an employee handbook, distributed after employment begins, become part of an employee's contract of employment?
Rule: Where an employment contract is for an indefinite duration, continued employment acts as acceptance of new terms of a unilateral contract as embodied in a personnel manual.

Arnold Palmer Golf Co. v. Fuqua Indus., Inc. (1976) FE

Facts: Palmer and Fuqua signed a memorandum stating the intent of the two to combine their businesses. The "Memorandum of Intent" provided that the obligations of the parties were subject to the preparation of a definitive agreement for the proposed combination of businesses satisfactory to both parties and to the approval thereof by Fuqua's board of directors.
Issue: Under what circumstances will a memorandum of intent indicate a binding agreement?
Rule: Both parties must have a clear understanding of the terms of an agreement and an intention to be bound by its terms before an enforceable contract is created. This is a factual issue to be determined by an evaluation of the circumstances surrounding the parties' negotiations.

Channel Home Centers v. Grossman (1986) FE

Facts: Channel Home Centers and Grossman signed a letter of intent providing that they would negotiate in good faith for Channel to lease premises in a mall which was being purchased by Grossman, and that Grossman would withdraw the premises from the market. Grossman used the letter to obtain credit and then rented the premises to Channel Home's competitor.

Issue: Is a letter of intent in which the parties promise to bargain in good faith enforceable?
Rule: An agreement to negotiate in good faith is enforceable if the parties intended to be bound, and there are definite terms and consideration.
Note: In the instant case, the letter was enforceable because it was evidence of an intent to be bound, the terms were detailed in the letter, and the credit obtained by use of the letter was consideration.

Poel v. Brunswick-Balke-Collender Co. of New York
(1915) FE, KC

Facts: After extensive negotiations, Poel offered rubber at $2.40 a pound. Brunswick's acceptance contained a printed clause that stated the acceptance would not be effective without confirmation by Poel. Brunswick backed out of the contract.
Issue: How does adding a clause affect an acceptance?
Rule: An attempt to accept an offer is ineffective if the acceptance varies from the terms of the offer.
Note: See UCC § 2-207 for the modern view.

Dorton v. Collins & Aikman Corp. (1972) FE, CPB

Facts: The Carpet Mart made an oral offer to Collins & Aikman to buy carpeting. Collins & Aikman sent its standard acceptance form, which included an arbitration clause to settle disputes. When a dispute arose, it sought to settle by arbitration. The lower court ruled that since the acceptance included new terms, a contract was formed by the conduct of the parties, and inconsistent terms should be "knocked out" as per UCC § 2-207.
Issue: Are parties bound by an arbitration clause included on the back of an acceptance form?
Rule: Under the "battle of the forms" rule of UCC § 2-207, a document can be an acceptance even if it is not a "mirror image" of the offer, provided that the conflicting term is not a material alteration.
Note: Some courts hold arbitration clauses to be material alterations.

C. Itoh (America) Inc. v. Jordan Int'l. Co. (1977) FE

Facts: Itoh submitted a purchase order which was accepted by Jordan, subject to conditions printed on the reverse of the acceptance. The reverse contained an arbitration clause, which Jordan sought to enforce when a dispute subsequently arose. Itoh was unaware of the provision.

Issue: Does performance of a defective agreement give rise to a contract?
Rule: When two parties acted under the belief that they had formed a contract, and the parties were unaware that the contract was defective, they have formed a contract based only on the terms to which they had actually agreed.

Daitom, Inc. v. Pennwalt Corp. (1984) FE

Facts: Pennwalt issued a preprinted purchase order for machinery with standard conditions. Daitom issued a standard preprinted sales form with a different warranty.
Issue: Where a vendor and a vendee issue different preprinted forms stating different terms for service and warranty, what provisions are given effect?
Rule: In a battle of the forms, differing terms knock each other out, and the UCC supplies standard provisions.

Cohen v. Cowles Media Co. (1990) MS

Facts: Cohen offered politically inflammatory documents to reporters on the condition that his identity be kept anonymous. The reporters intended to fulfill the promise, but their editors insisted on printing his name. Cohen received negative media coverage for his disclosure and lost his job.
Issue 1: May one recover on the grounds of fraudulent misrepresentation if a party fails to keep a promise?
Rule 1: For fraud, there must be a misrepresentation of a past or present fact. Thus, a representation as to a future act only supports an action for fraud if the promisor had no intention of performing at the time the promise was made, not merely because the represented act did not occur.
Issue 2: Is an enforceable contract formed where information is given to a reporter in exchange for confidentiality?
Rule 2: An enforceable contract is not formed where information is given to a reporter in exchange for confidentiality, because in the special milieu of news gathering, a source and a reporter do not ordinarily believe that they are making a legally binding contract.
Issue 3: May a political news source recover in estoppel if a promise of anonymity is broken?
Rule 3: A political news source may not recover in estoppel if a promise of anonymity is broken, because the potentiality for civil damages in this context would violate the First Amendment by interfering with editorial judgment and chilling public debate.

Fisher v. Bell (1960) MS

Facts: The defendant placed a knife with a price tag in his store window. A statute prohibited offering such knives for sale.

Issue: Is an article that is placed in a shop window being "offered" for sale?

Rule: Display of an article for sale is not considered an offer, even if the article has a price tag. It is only an invitation to negotiate.

Southworth v. Oliver (1978) MS

Facts: Southworth entered into preliminary talks with Oliver for the sale of Oliver's land. Southworth claimed the parties agreed to give the matter further consideration. Soon afterward Oliver sent Southworth and three other ranchers a written document stating a price and terms for the sale of the land. Southworth accepted, but problems arose when another rancher also wanted part of the parcel. Oliver claimed that no offer was made to Southworth, so the acceptance was invalid.

Issue: By what standard does a court determine whether statements constitute an offer?

Rule: Whether an offer exists depends on what a reasonable person in the position of the offeree would have believed. While a price quotation is usually not an offer, it can be under certain circumstances. A court will also look at the language used, the definiteness of the terms, and whether the offeree is named.

La Salle Nat. Bank v. Vega (1988) MS

Facts: La Salle sued Vega for specific performance and damages resulting from breach of a real estate contract. As a defense, Vega denied the existence of the contract. The document in question provided that the "attached rider is part of this contract." The attached rider provided that "upon execution of this contract by seller, this contract shall be presented to the trust for full execution." The seller signed the document, but a trustee did not.

Issue: May an offeror require written acceptance of an offer by a third party?

Rule: An offeror has complete control over an offer and may condition acceptance to the terms of the offer.

Ever-Tite Roofing Corp. v. Green (1955) MS

Facts: Green's request to have Ever-Tite re-roof his house stated that acceptance could be given in writing or by commencing work. As Green requested that the entire job be done on credit, Ever-Tite had to verify his credit worthiness which took eight days. Ever-Tite's workmen arrived to start work the next day and found that Green had revoked the offer and hired another company two days earlier. Green claimed that Ever-Tite waited too long to accept.

Issue: In the absence of an express provision, what is the time limit within which an offer must be accepted?

Rule: The power to create a contract by acceptance of an offer terminates at the time specified in the offer or, if no time is specified, at the end of a reasonable time. Where the offeror should be aware of the source of delay in the offeree's acceptance (e.g., to get credit approval), it is reasonable to allot more time for acceptance.

Corinthian Pharmaceutical Sys., Inc. v. Lederle Laboratories (1989) MS

Facts: Lederle periodically issued price lists to customers stating that all orders were subject to acceptance at the home office, prices were subject to change without notice, and unfilled current orders would be invoiced at the price in effect at the time of shipment. Aware that Lederle was going to drastically increase the price of DTP vaccine in the near future, Corinthian ordered 1,000 vials. Lederle acknowledged receipt of the order, shipped 50 vials at the lower price, and sent a letter stating that the remaining 950 vials would be invoiced at the increased price if Corinthian still wanted them.

Issue 1: Does acknowledgment of a receipt of a sales order constitute acceptance?

Rule 1: An offer to make a contract invites acceptance in any manner and by any medium that is reasonable in the circumstances, but the offeree must do some act that manifests the intention to accept the offer and make a contract. An automated and ministerial acknowledgement that an order has been received is not a communication or act that is sufficient to constitute an acceptance.

Note: The court here found that under the circumstances, acceptance occurred when the goods were shipped.

Issue 2: If a buyer makes an offer and the seller ships nonconforming goods without otherwise manifesting acceptance, what are the consequences?

Rule 2: An order to buy goods is accepted by a prompt shipment of goods, even if they are non-conforming goods. However, when a shipment of nonconforming goods is accompanied by seasonable notice that the shipment is not an acceptance but an accommodation to the buyer, the shipment is a counteroffer.

Note: The court in this case found that a shipment of 50 vials did not conform with an order for 1,000 vials, and that the letter was seasonable notification that the shipment was not an acceptance of the original order. Thus, the defendant did not have to sell the remaining 950 vials at the lower price.

Hendricks v. Behee (1990) MS

Facts: On March 3, Behee's agent mailed an offer to the Smiths to purchase real estate. On March 4, the Smiths signed the proposed agreement. Before Behee was notified of the acceptance (ca. March 6), he notified the real estate agent that the offer was withdrawn.

Issue: Does an offeree accept an offer for a bilateral contract by communicating acceptance to his agent?

Rule: An offer for a bilateral contract that is not supported by consideration may be withdrawn if acceptance has not been communicated to the offeror, even if the offeree has already communicated an intent to accept to its own agent.

Glover v. Jewish War Veterans of United States (1949) MS

Facts: Jewish War Veterans offered a reward for information leading to the arrest of a murderer. Glover, unaware of the reward, provided the information during a police interrogation.

Issue: Is a person who accepts an offer without knowledge of the existence of the offer legally entitled to the benefits of the offer?

Rule: There can be no contract unless an acceptance is made with knowledge of an offer and an intention to accept it.

"Industrial America," Inc. v. Fulton
Indus. Inc. (1971) MS, CPB

Facts: Industrial, a broker specializing in mergers and acquisitions, responded to Fulton's advertisement to acquire other companies by introducing one of its clients to Fulton. The client and Fulton agreed to a merger without the use of Industrial's services or payment of a commission. Fulton's advertisement had proclaimed that "brokers [were] fully protected."

Issue: If an offer states that acceptance can be made by performance, must the offeree also show an intention to accept?

Rule: When acceptance can be accomplished by performance of an act (e.g., finding a company that wants to merge), such performance alone will constitute an acceptance unless there is a manifestation to the contrary.

Russell v. Texas Co. (1956) MS

Facts: Russell was the surface owner of a parcel of land to which Texas Co. had underground rights. Texas also made use of the surface area which prompted Russell to offer a revocable permit that would be "accepted" if Texas continued to use the roadway, water, or materials on the land. Texas did not stop using the land, but claimed that no contract was formed because it had not intended to accept Russell's offer.

Issue: Does the use of the benefits of an offer constitute an acceptance?

Rule: If an offeree exercises dominion over things that were offered to him, such exercise of dominion, in the absence of other circumstances showing a contrary intention, is an acceptance. The test is not the offeree's subjective intent, but rather what the offeror could reasonably conclude from the offeree's actions.

Ammons v. Wilson & Co. (1936) MS

Facts: Ammons placed an order (offer) with Wilson's salesman subject to approval by Wilson's home office. In past dealings, Ammons received a response from the defendant within a week. Wilson rejected the offer after 12 days of silence.

Issue: Can acceptance be implied from silence?

Rule: Where previous dealings or other circumstances give an offeror reason to believe that silence or inaction is intended by the offeree as a manifestation of assent, silence and inaction operate as an acceptance.

Smith-Scharff Paper Co. v. P.N. Hirsch & Co. (1988) MS

Facts: Smith-Scharff orally agreed to sell Hirsch bags specially designed for it and stamped with its name. The parties enjoyed a thirty-six-year business relationship, during which Smith-Scharff, with Hirsch's knowledge, often stockpiled bags with Hirsch's logo. Smith-Scharff, concerned that Hirsch was terminating its business, demanded assurance that Hirsch would purchase the remaining inventory of bags marked with its logo. Although Hirsch did buy a portion of the stockpiled bags, Smith-Scharff sued to recover for the balance.

Issue 1: Do prior dealings between customers give rise to an implied contract in the absence of a written agreement?

Rule 1: The course of dealings between parties can create an implied contract.

Issue 2: Does an unreasonable response to a request for assurance justify suspension of performance?

Rule 2: A customer's unreasonable response to a request for assurance of contract fulfillment justifies a supplier suspending performance.

Harris v. Time, Inc. (1987) MS, R

Facts: Harris' son opened an envelope that indicated that Time would give him a free watch simply for opening the envelope. The contents revealed that he would also have to subscribe to a magazine to obtain the watch. Harris, a prominent public-interest lawyer, sued Time for $15,000,000 on theories of breach of contract, promissory estoppel as well as several tort claims.

Issue: Do junk-mail envelopes create unilateral contract offers?

Rule: Although a misleading promise on an envelope may technically support a breach of contract action, where the only detriment suffered is the act of opening the envelope, the action will be dismissed as *de minimis.*

Minneapolis & St. Louis Ry. Co. v. Columbus Rolling-Mill Co. (1886) MS

Facts: In response to a query, Columbus provided the Minneapolis & St. Louis Railroad with a price quote for the purchase of 2,000 to 5,000 tons of iron rails. The railroad was given 12 days to accept. It ordered only 1,200 tons at the quoted price, and Columbus refused to fill the order. Before the 12 days were up, the railroad made a second order for 2,000 tons, and Columbus again refused.

Issue: Is an "acceptance" that changes the terms of the offer, such as quantity, a rejection of the offer and a counteroffer?

Rule: Responding to an offer with an "acceptance" that changes a material term has the legal effect of being a rejection of the offer and a counteroffer. The original offeror now has the power to reject or accept.

Leonard Pevar Co. v. Evans Prods. Co. (1981) MS

Facts: Pevar called Evans for a price quotation. Pevar claims it ordered plywood and entered into an oral contract for sale. Evans admits there was a phone call but denies that it accepted an order. Two days later, Pevar sent a written purchase order to Evans specifying price, quantity and shipping instructions but making no reference to warranties. Evans sent an acknowledgment to Pevar, which stated in boilerplate fashion that the sales contract would be expressly contingent upon Pevar accepting all terms in the document including a disclaimer of all warranties.

Issue: How should courts resolve the "battle of the forms"?

Rule: If a court determines that an oral agreement has been reached and the parties send each other additional terms which do not materially alter the oral agreement, then the terms will be incorporated into the agreement. If the terms materially alter the agreement, they will not be incorporated, and standardized "gap filler" provisions of the UCC will provide the terms of the contract.

If a court determines that in the absence of an oral contract the parties have exchanged writings that do not contain identical terms and there is a clause conditioning acceptance on assent to the additional or different terms, there is no contract and either party may walk away from the deal.

If the writings of the parties do not establish a contract but the conduct of both parties indicates they recognize the existence of a contract, a court will imply a contract. The terms will include those on which the parties' writings agree, and the remainder will be provided by UCC "gap fillers."

Note: The court remanded the case to determine which of the above rules was applicable to the facts.

Board of Control of Eastern Michigan Univ.
v. Burgess (1973) MS

Facts: Burgess signed an option that gave the University 60 days to buy her land. The document stated that Burgess received consideration, but no consideration had been given in fact. Burgess rejected the University's attempt to exercise the option.

Issue: Can a written option be revoked?

Rule: An option that is given without consideration is revocable at the will of the offeror.

Note: UCC § 2-205 enforces such options in certain cases.

Humble Oil & Refining Co. v. Westside Investment Corp.
(1968) MS

Facts: Westside granted Humble an exclusive and irrevocable option to purchase land in exchange for consideration of $35,000. Humble suggested amending the terms of the sales contract but later tried to exercise the option on its original terms.

Issue: Does the rule that a qualified acceptance acts as a rejection also void an option secured in exchange for consideration?

Rule: An option secured in exchange for valuable consideration will remain in effect, even after its holder makes a counteroffer.

Electrical Construction & Maintenance Company, Inc. v. Maeda Pacific Corporation (1985) MS

Facts: Maeda was preparing a bid for a prime contract. When asked to submit a sub-bid, ECM replied that it would only submit a bid if Maeda agreed to award it the subcontract, and if ECM gave the lowest bid and Maeda was the successful bidder on the prime contract. Maeda was awarded the prime contract, but it did not hire ECM for the subcontract.

Issue: Is submission of a bid sufficient consideration to create a condition that the bid be accepted if it is the lowest?

Rule: Because a potential subcontractor is under no legal obligation to submit a bid, undertaking the time and expense to prepare and submit a bid is sufficient consideration to create a condition that the bid be accepted if it is the low bid and if the general contractor is awarded the prime contract.

Varney v. Ditmars (1916) MS

Facts: In February 1911, the plaintiff, an architect, was told that he would receive a raise immediately and a bonus if he stayed through the year and completed certain projects. Upon falling sick in November, the plaintiff was discharged. He sued for wages to the end of the year and for his bonus.

Issue: Is an executory contract enforceable if it is silent as to the price term enforceable?

Rule: An executory contract which is silent as to the price term is too indefinite to be binding.

Note: The court only considers the issue of the bonus. Cardozo, in dissent, argues that the court ignored that the employment contract was to run to the end of the year and that the plaintiff should have been compensated accordingly.

Community Design Corp. v. Antonell (1984) MS

Facts: Antonell was employed by CDC as an architect. The president of CDC promised a bonus to any employee still working at Christmas time. The amount of the bonus was to be determined by the vice-president of

CDC, who had also promised Antonell a one-week paid vacation if drawings were completed on time. Antonell received neither. CDC argued that the agreement was too indefinite to be enforced because the amount of the bonus and the degree of completion were indefinite.

Issue: Is an oral employment agreement too vague to be enforceable if the exact job requirements and compensation rate are missing?

Rule: Where one party has received the benefit of the other's performance and the existence of a contract is clear, the benefitted party must act in good faith to fulfill its promises. Reasonable compensation is to be determined by the jury.

Metro-Goldwyn-Mayer, Inc. v. Scheider
(1976) MS

Facts: MGM made an initial oral contract to hire Schneider to act in a television series. In the weeks that followed, most of the essential terms were settled. Schneider acted in and was compensated for the pilot film, but refused to act in the series to follow. Schneider claimed that the contract was never set as the starting date for filming the TV series was not specified.

Issue: Is an employment contract unenforceable if it is missing an essential term?

Rule: If the parties have agreed to what they regard as the essential elements of an agreement, and performance has begun on the good faith understanding that agreement on the unsettled matters will follow, courts will find and enforce a contract even though the parties have expressly left certain elements for future negotiation, provided the elements can be objectively determined.

Oglebay Norton Co. v. Armco, Inc. (1990) MS

Facts: For many years, Oglebay shipped iron ore for Armco. Armco relied upon Oglebay to ship its goods, and Oglebay made expensive capital improvements to accommodate Armco's shipping needs. The contract had a pricing mechanism whereunder Armco would pay the shipping rates recognized by leading ore shippers for that season. If there was no recognized rate, the parties were to agree upon a rate, based upon the rate being charged for similar transportation by leading independent shippers. The parties could not agree upon a rate.

Issue: May a court fill in a price term when a contractual pricing mechanism fails to establish a price?

Rule: Where parties clearly intended to be bound by a contract, but the price term was to be fixed by some agreed market mechanism which fails to do so, a court may set a reasonable price based on market conditions at the time of performance.

Earhart v. William Low Co. (1979) MS

Facts: William Low contracted with Earhart to build a mobile-home park on two adjoining tracts of land, one of which it owned and the other it planned to buy. The agreement was conditioned upon Earhart succeeding in obtaining financing and Low securing a construction bond. At Earhart's urging, Low started work on the tract that was not Earhart's, so as to preserve the license to use it. Earhart later told Low that he had obtained financing and to work on both tracts, but never actually promised to pay. After a week, Earhart claimed he did not have the financing and that he had hired another contractor. Low sued in *quantum meruit* and recovered the value of his services except for the work done on the second tract.

Issue: Can a party recover in *quantum meruit* for work that indirectly benefitted the other party?

Rule: One who induced the performance of another is liable under the theory of *quantum meruit*, even if a third party benefitted from the performance. (Rest. 2d. § 90.)

Konic Int'l Corp. v. Spokane Computer Servs., Inc. (1985) MS

Facts: Spokane was searching for a surge protector. It had found several units priced between $50 and $200, but none served its needs. Konic had an appropriate unit, which it offered for sale for the price of "fifty-six, twenty." The defendant accepted. The unit was delivered, installed, and used for a short period, until the parties realized that Konic had meant $5,620, and Spokane had understood $56.20.

Issue: What is the status of a contract when the parties have different, reasonable understandings of a price term?

Rule: When parties have different understandings of a material contract term (such as a hundred fold discrepancy in price), and the term is expressed in an ambiguous form to which both meanings could apply, there is no meeting of the minds and therefore no contract.

Boise Junior College District
v. Mattefs Construction Co. (1969) MS

Facts: Mattefs made a clerical error when computing a bid and therefore underestimated its costs by $10,000, or 14 percent. Although Mattefs' bid was much lower than the $150,000 Boise had expected to pay, Boise still paid only $149,000 to the next lowest bidder. Boise sought to keep enough of the bid bond to cover the difference between Mattefs' bid and the bid that Boise had to accept.

Issue: Is a contractor entitled to withdraw without penalty a bid that has a material clerical error?

Rule: One who errs in preparing a bid for public works is entitled to rescission of the bid if the mistake was material and did not result from violation of a legal duty or culpable negligence, enforcing the bid would be unconscionable, the party to whom the bid was submitted will not be prejudiced except by loss of bargain, and prompt notice of the error was given.

Beachcomber Coins, Inc. v. Boskett (1979) MS

Facts: Beachcomber, a coin dealer, sought rescission of a coin purchase by him from Boskett. At the time of purchase neither party knew that the coin was actually counterfeit. Beachcomber had inspected the coin prior to buying.

Issue: Is a contract voidable for a mutual mistake of fact?

Rule: A contract is voidable by either party when both parties are under a misapprehension regarding a fact assumed by both as the basis of their transaction. Moreover, negligent failure of a party to know or discover the erroneous fact does not preclude rescission.

Lenawee County Bd. of Health v. Messerly (1982) MS, FE, R

Facts: Unknown to the Messerlys, a previous owner of their land had installed an illegal underground septic tank. The Messerlys then sold the property, which included a three-unit apartment building, to Pickles. The contract had an "as is" clause, which shifted the risk of unknown defects to Pickles. Six days after the sale, sewage from the tank oozed up to the surface of the property, and the county condemned the property until the sewage system could conform to the sanitation code. The Pickles sought rescission of the sales contract.

Issue: Is a hidden defect sufficient grounds for rescission of a contract on the basis of mutual mistake?

Rule: A rescission on the grounds of mutual mistake may be granted when the mistake relates to a basic assumption of the parties upon which the contract is made and which materially affects the agreed performances of the parties. However, where both parties are equally innocent and have allocated the risk of loss, rescission will not be granted.

Note: Courts are divided on the effectiveness of "as is" clauses. (Rest. 2d. § 124.)

Ayer v. Western Union Tel. Co. (1887) MS

Facts: Western Union made an error while transmitting Ayer's offer. Ayer complied with the erroneous offer and sued to recover its loss from Western Union.

Issue: Is an offeror obligated to comply with an offer whose terms are incorrectly transmitted?

Rule: The party that selects the means of communication of its offer bears the risk of loss caused by errors in transmission (i.e., must comply with the mistaken terms). However, it can recover its loss from the negligent transmitter of the message.

Greene v. Howard University (1969) CPB

Facts: Five non-tenured faculty members believed that they were to be reappointed based on course assignments, oral indications and the passing of the deadline for notification. Although there was no contractual provision, the Faculty Handbook provided that all persons would be given reasonable notice and a hearing before dismissal for misconduct. Following their involvement in campus disturbances, the five plaintiffs were dismissed without a hearing.

Issue: Can customs and usages incidental to a contract create additional contractual rights and obligations?

Rule: Customs and practices can create additional contractual obligations where reasonable reliance has been induced by written assurances.

K. D. v. Educational Testing Service (1976) CPB, R

Facts:. While registering to take the LSAT, K.D. signed a stipulation stating that the Educational Testing Service (ETS) "reserve[d] the right to cancel any test score if ... there is adequate reason to question its validity." Finding a suspiciously high correlation between K.D. and a nearby student, ETS offered a free retest as an alternative to canceling K.D.'s score. In seeking to enjoin the ETS from canceling his score (he refused the retest),

K.D. claimed that he was not bound because it was a contract of adhesion, as he was unable to negotiate its terms or contract elsewhere.
Issue: When may a contract be voided on the grounds that it was an adhesion contract?
Rule: An offending clause of a contract of adhesion may be voided if it is found to be unfair and unreasonable.
Note: Here, the court found that ETS had taken a reasonable measure to protect its reputation for accurate aptitude forecasting.

Craft v. Elder & Johnston Co. (1941) CPB

Facts: The Elder & Johnston Company advertised a sewing machine for $26 as a "Thursday Only Special." It refused to sell the machine to Craft.
Issue: Is an advertisement an offer that a member of the public can accept?
Rule: An advertisement is not an offer. It is an invitation to negotiate and receive offers.

Hoffman v. Horton (1972) CPB

Facts: The auctioneer at a land sale closed on Hoffman's initial bid of $177,000. Prior to or simultaneously with the auctioneer's act of closing the bidding, a higher bid was placed by another party. The auctioneer reopened the bidding; Hoffman finally bought the land at a higher price and sued to recover the difference.
Issue: May an auctioneer reopen bidding for land when a higher bid is made just prior to or simultaneously with the falling of the hammer?
Rule: UCC § 2-328 provides auctioneers with discretion to reopen the bidding when it is apparent to them that a higher bid has been made "prior to or simultaneously with" the falling of the hammer.
Note: Although the UCC is technically applicable only to the sale of goods, it is considered guiding in the sale of land.

United States v. Briggs Manufacturing Co. (1972) CPB

Facts: Briggs quoted shipping prices to Toombs to induce Toombs to purchase housing.
Issue: May an estimated price be regarded as a term of an offer?
Rule: When both parties anticipate that an estimated price is reasonably accurate and will be relied upon, the doctrine of equitable estoppel may preclude one party from passing on damages not foreseen from the offer. Briggs was estopped from claiming damages not listed as potential costs.

Winston v. Mediafare Entertainment Corp. (1985) CPB

Facts: Winston, an intermediary promised a finder's fee by Mediafare, sought to enforce a settlement agreement still in the draft stages. Both parties placed significant weight in their correspondence during the negotiation process on an "Execution Date" that was never reached.

Issue: Can a binding agreement between two parties be reached prior to execution of a final document satisfactory in every respect to both sides?

Rule: The parties' intended time of binding each other may be revealed by express or implied elements of negotiation, such as an express reservation that a final, mutually acceptable contract be executed, a partial performance of the agreement, an absence of any remaining points of negotiation or the size and complexity of the agreement as an indication of the need for written execution. If either party indicates an intent not to be bound before a final agreement is executed, then no oral agreement will constitute a binding agreement.

Texaco, Inc. v. Pennzoil, Co. (1987) CPB

Facts: Pennzoil sought to recover damages from Texaco for tortious interference with a contract between Pennzoil and the "Getty entities" (Getty Oil Co., the Sarah C. Getty Trust and the J. Paul Getty Museum). The jury found that the Getty entities intended to bind themselves to an agreement providing for the purchase and division of their assets by Pennzoil. On appeal, Texaco claimed that as a matter of law the agreement's language reflected an intent to be bound only at a later point upon execution of a formal, final agreement.

Issue: Is the determination of whether an informal agreement is binding a matter of fact for the jury or one of law for the court to decide?

Rule: When a question of the parties' intent to be bound is not clear from their writings, the matter is left to the jury.

Note: Four factors are used to determine whether a party intended to be bound only by a formal, signed agreement: express stipulation of binding conditions, partial performance, remaining negotiable terms and the complexity and magnitude of the agreement as requiring a final, formal writing.

Bettancourt v. Gilroy Theatre Co. (1953) CPB

Facts: Bettancourt sold the Gilroy Theatre Co. a plot of land adjacent to his land on the condition that the defendant erect a "first-class theatre." Gilroy resold the land for profit having never built a theatre. Bettancourt sued to recover the enhancement in value that would have accrued to the nearby land he owned if the theatre had been built.

Issue: How definite must a contractual provision be in order to be enforceable?

Rule: The terms of an agreement need only be definite enough to determine that damages should be awarded to the plaintiff.

Note: Specific performance might have required a more definite agreement, but this remedy was not available as Gilroy was no longer in possession of the land.

Haines v. City of New York (1977) CPB

Facts: In 1924, the City of New York agreed with the Town of Hunter and Village of Theater that the City would provide and maintain sewage treatment plants in order to prevent the release of untreated sewage into the City's reservoir, while the Town and Village would maintain the appropriate easements. In addition, the agreement provided that the City would extend sewage lines as growth required. Haines, a developer, brought this action to compel the City to extend its lines to new properties, and if necessary, to expand or rebuild the facilities to meet the new capacity requirements.

Issue: In the absence of a clause designating duration, how long are parties bound by a contract?

Rule: Where the parties have not expressly provided for the duration of an agreement, the court shall imply that the parties intended performance to continue for a reasonable time.

Note: This rule does not apply to employment, exclusive agency, distributorship or requirements contracts.

McGinnis Piano and Organ Co. v. Yamaha Internat'l Corp. (1973) CPB

Facts: Yamaha established an implied distributorship agreement with the McGinnis Piano and Organ Co., a retailer. For several years, McGinnis participated in dealer meetings, restricted sales to the territory assigned and made expenditures until eventually, it sold only Yamaha instruments.

Issue: May a distributorship agreement of unspecified duration be terminated at will?

Rule: A distributorship agreement that does not specify duration is terminable at will by either party upon reasonable notice, with reasonableness defined as the time necessary to close out the dealership or to recoup investments. There is no implied agreement to continue as long as the distributor performs satisfactorily.

Note: This rule is consistent with UCC § 2-309.

Wagenseller v. Scottsdale Memorial Hospital (1985) CPB

Facts: Catherine Wagenseller enjoyed a good relationship with her manager, Kay Smith, and her employer, Scottsdale Hospital. Wagenseller and Smith took a trip together during which Wagenseller refused to join in the lewd behavior, such as public excretion and "mooning," of Smith and their other companions. Following the trip, the relationship between Wagenseller and Smith deteriorated until Wagenseller was terminated by Smith. Wagenseller brought this action for reinstatement and other remedies.

Issue: Are there any limitations on the employment-at-will doctrine, which provides that an employer may fire an employee for any reason, including one unrelated to job performance?

Rule: An employee whose contract does not specify duration is terminable for good cause or no cause, but not for "bad" cause. Termination for refusal to violate public policy, such as statutes banning indecent exposure, are bad causes.

Southwest Engineering Co. v. Martin Tractor Co.
(1970) CPB

Facts: Martin agreed to supply Southwest with a generator and other equipment. A memorandum of the agreement made on Martin stationery specified most of the terms besides the manner of payment. Martin later refused to perform, claiming that the contract was too indefinite, and that it violated the Statute of Frauds.

Issue 1: Is an agreement that is recorded in a memorandum valid?

Rule 1: A written memorandum that is signed, contains terms for a contract for the sale of goods, and specifies the quantity involved will satisfy the writing requirement of the Statute of Frauds.

Issue 2: Does a valid agreement that lacks some terms fail as being too vague?

Rule 2: A court can enforce a contract that has some missing terms if the essential terms are present and the parties intended to enter into a contract. Missing terms can be implied by the court [UCC § 2-310, 2-204(3)].

Note: "Signed" includes any symbol or printing that is intended to authenticate the writing.

Eckles v. Sharman (1977) CPB

Facts: The owner of the Utah Stars, a professional basketball team brought this action for breach of contract against the team's former coach, Sharman. The contract stated generally that Sharman would receive a pension plan and an option to buy 5 percent of the Stars and that failure to resolve one portion of the contract would not void the rest. The specifics of the option and pension were negotiated but never resolved during the year that Sharman coached the Stars. Sharman then left to coach another team, claiming the contract was invalid.

Issue: When does failure to agree on terms of a contract render the contract invalid?

Rule: Failure to agree on terms will invalidate a contract if the terms are essential. Essence depends on the intent of the parties.

Broadnax v. Ledbetter (1907) CPB

Facts: Having recaptured a criminal without knowledge of any reward for doing so, the plaintiff brought this action to compel delivery of the reward.

Issue: Must a party have knowledge of an offer before acting in order to satisfy the meeting of the minds requirement and bind the offeror?

Rule: An offeror is only bound by a promise if such promise induced action in another party. If a party acted without knowledge, there is no meeting of the minds and that action cannot serve as acceptance of the offer.

Wilhoite v. Beck (1967) CPB

Facts: Ruth Beck, a cousin of Lawrence, brought this action against Lawrence's estate for room, board, care and companionship rendered during the twenty years Lawrence lived in Beck's home.

Issue: May an implied contract to pay for valuable services be inferred between relatives?

Rule: An implied contract to pay for services will be found where there is evidence that the parties intended to arrange for payment.

Note: Blood relationships do not in and of themselves raise a presumption of gratuity. However, a blood relationship between parties living together as a family may raise a rebuttable presumption of gratuity. In this case, the evidence suggested that Lawrence intended to compensate Beck for services, that she did not do so in her will, and that the relationship between them did not raise a presumption of gratuity.

Fujimoto v. Rio Grande Pickle Co. (1969) CPB

Facts: Jose Bravo and George Fujimoto were hired by Rio Grande Pickle Co. to perform jobs with significant managerial authority. In order to encourage Bravo and Fujimoto to work hard and to stay with the company, the president of Rio Grande offered each a written contract containing a promise of a bonus of 10 percent of company profits. After receiving the offers, the two continued to work for fourteen months. Rio Grande refused to deliver the bonuses, claiming that Bravo and Fujimoto never accepted the offers.

Issue: How may an offer be accepted if no provision for acceptance has been specified?

Rule: The mode of expressing assent is inconsequential so long as it effectively makes known to the offeror that the offer has been accepted.

Note: In this case, the employees' assent by continuing to work should have been unmistakable to Rio Grande.

Swift & Co. v. Smigel (1971) CPB

Facts: Smigel promised Swift & Co. that he would make good any bills for provisions incurred by Pine Haven, the corporation of which he possessed a one-half stock interest. During the period Swift was delivering merchandise to Pine Haven, Smigel was found by a court to be incompetent.

Issue: Does an offer terminate upon adjudication of an offeror's incompetence?

Rule: An offer accepted in good faith without knowledge of the offeror's incompetence is valid until notice is given.

Diamond Fruit Growers, Inc. v. Krack Corp. (1986) CPB

Facts: When sued by the Diamond Fruit Growers, Inc. for the value of fruit lost when a Krack cooling system failed, the Krack Corp. sued Metal-Matic, its tubing supplier. Metal-Matic had expressly conditioned its tubing sales on a clause limiting liability to refunds, replacements or costs of repairs to defective tubing. Although a discussion of the liability clause ended in Metal-Matic's refusal to change its terms, the two continued to do business together.

Issue: When disagreements over terms remain after the bargaining process has ended, which terms govern?

Rule: All agreed upon terms constitute the contract, and the gaps are to be filled by the UCC, unless the disputed terms are so material as to void the contract.

Note: In this case, the evidence was sufficient to support the imposition of third-party damage liability on Metal-Matic. This case is a sound rejection of the common law last-shot rule in favor of the neutrality of UCC § 2-207(3).

Plantation Key Developers, Inc. v.
Colonial Mortgage Co. of Indiana, Inc. (1979) CPB

Facts: Colonial Mortgage agreed to make permanent mortgages available for one year for purchasers of Plantation Key Developers condominiums for a $60,000 fee. The contract provided Plantation with an option to extend the arrangement at rates to be adjusted by Colonial only as market conditions demanded. The terms of the extension were to be secured with an additional $30,000 upon renewal. Plantation sued for breach of the option contract when Colonial nearly tripled the loan service fee for the six-month extension without market impetus.

Issue: In an option contract, what responsibility does the offeror have to maintain the terms promised to the offeree?

Rule: If the offeree has secured the contract with consideration (here, $60,000), the offeror is required to keep the option open on the terms originally specified.

Henthorn v. Fraser (1892) KC

Facts: Defendant offered to sell property to Plaintiff. Plaintiff mailed an acceptance of the offer to Defendant and Defendant mailed a revocation of the offer to Plaintiff on the same day. Plaintiff's acceptance was postmarked before he received Defendant's revocation. Plaintiff sued for specific performance of the sales contract.

Issue: When is an acceptance sent by mail deemed complete?

Rule: An acceptance sent by mail is complete as soon as it is postmarked if the mail is a reasonable means of corresponding under the circumstances, and it is within the contemplation of the parties that the mail will be used.

Normile v. Miller (1985) KC

Facts: Normile made an offer to purchase real estate from Miller. The offer contained a time limit for acceptance. Miller rejected the offer and made a counteroffer with no time provision. Before Normile answered the counteroffer, Miller contracted to sell the land to a third party. After Normile found out that Miller had revoked her counteroffer by selling to the third party, Normile signed the counteroffer and returned it to Miller within the time limit stated in the original offer.

Issue: Does a time limit provision from an original offer apply to a counteroffer that does not expressly adopt it?

Rule: A time limit provision in an original offer is not incorporated into a counteroffer if it is not expressly adopted, because the counteroffer serves as a rejection of the original offer.

Bishop v. Eaton (1894) KC

Facts: Eaton offered to guaranty any loans that Bishop assisted in obtaining for Eaton's brother, Harry. Bishop signed a promissory note as Harry's surety and sent a letter to Eaton informing him of the transaction. Eaton never received the letter and refused to guarantee Harry's loan. Bishop repaid Harry's note and then sued Eaton for the guarantee payment.

Issue: Is the mail a sufficient means to inform an offeror that the offer has been accepted?

Rule: Notice of the act which constitutes acceptance of an offer must be given in a reasonable manner. When communication by mail is reasonable, mailing the notice of acceptance is sufficient. The party who mails the notification is not responsible for the letter actually getting to the other party.

Mid-South Packers, Inc. v. Shoney's, Inc. (1985) KC, R

Facts: Mid-South negotiated to sell pork products to Shoney's and wrote a "proposal." The proposal stated the pork price and required that 45 days notice be given prior to any price adjustment. Without accepting or rejecting the proposal, Shoney's purchased pork from Mid-South. Subsequently, Mid-South raised the price of pork and Shoney's paid the increased price, but withheld money on their final order. Shoney's claimed that according to the terms of the original contract, it did not have to pay the higher price until 45 days after notice of the increase. Mid-South claimed these transactions were not covered by the original proposal.

Issue: Does a proposal become a binding contract when the parties begin transacting before the proposal is accepted or rejected?

Rule: A proposal is considered at most a firm offer, which will only be binding for three months according to UCC § 2-205. After three months, the parties can alter the contract.

Brown Machine, Inc. v. Hercules, Inc. (1989) KC

Facts: Brown sent Hercules a proposal containing a price quote for the sale of a press. This proposal contained a clause stating that Hercules would indemnify Brown if Brown was held liable for any claims arising from the operation or misuse of the press. Hercules responded with a purchase order with no indemnification clause rejecting all additional terms proposed by Brown. Brown sent back an order acknowledgment which contained the same indemnity clause as the original proposal. Brown delivered the press. A Hercules employee was injured while using the press, and recovered against Brown. Brown sued Hercules for indemnification, claiming that its original proposal containing the indemnity clause was an offer which Hercules accepted. Hercules claimed that it never accepted Brown's proposal. Rather Hercules' purchase order without the indemnity clause was the offer which Brown accepted.

Issue 1:   Is a proposal containing a price quotation an offer, or an invitation to make an offer?

Rule 1:   A price quotation is not an offer, but rather an invitation to enter into negotiations, unless it is sufficiently detailed to be construed as an offer creating the power of acceptance.

Issue 2:   Do additional terms in an acceptance constitute a counteroffer?

Rule 2:   An acceptance with additional terms will be considered a counteroffer only if the acceptance is expressly made conditional on assent to the additional terms. The additional terms will be incorporated into the contract only if they do not materially alter it.

Dale R. Horning Co. v. Falconer Glass Industries, Inc. (1990) KC

Facts: Plaintiff AGM, a glass installer, telephoned Falconer, a glass supplier, and ordered glass for a job. The next day, Falconer sent AGM a confirmation containing fine print stating that Falconer was not liable for any consequential damages. Falconer sent AGM a substandard shipment of glass resulting in extra costs to AGM. Falconer refused to pay the extra costs because its confirmation contained the clause limiting damages.

Issue: Do additional terms limiting consequential damages materially alter the contract?

Rule: Pursuant to UCC § 2-207, additional terms limiting consequential damages materially alter the contract. The test is whether the additional terms result in surprise or hardship.

Note: Some jurisdictions hold that additional terms limiting consequential damages do not materially alter the contract. The test is very fact specific.

Walker v. Keith (1964) KC

Facts: Plaintiff leased a lot from Defendant. The lease contained a renewal option which stated the rent for the additional term would be agreed upon if the option was exercised. The option failed to provide a method as to how future rent should be fixed. The parties were unable to agree upon the new rent.

Issue: Is a provision stating that the parties will agree upon future rent, which lacks a method as to how the rent should be fixed, so indefinite that it is not binding?

Rule: A renewal option that fails to specify either an agreed rent, or an agreed method by which to fix the rent, is unenforceable because it is too indefinite.

Pennsylvania Co. v. Wilmington Trust Co. (1960) KC

Facts: Wilmington signed a letter agreeing to sell stock to Pennsylvania. Subsequently, Wilmington sold the stock to a third party. Pennsylvania claimed the letter was a binding contract.

Issue: When determining if the parties to an agreement meant to be bound, should the court examine evidence not in the text of the document?

Rule: If intent is not clearly expressed, then other evidence is admissible to aid in ascertaining intent.

Teachers Insurance & Annuity Association of America v. Butler (1986) KC

Facts: Butler signed a binding commitment letter to borrow money from Teachers. Butler refused to close the loan because a provision not included in the commitment letter was included in the closing document. Teachers claimed that Butler breached the contract by failing to negotiate the provision in good faith and close the contract.

Issue: Can a party escape its duty to perform a binding agreement because of a dispute concerning a final term?

Rule: Where the parties are under a definite duty to perform, the parties have a duty to negotiate in good faith so that a party may not escape from an obligation he has contracted to perform.

Favrot v. Barnes (1976) R

Facts: Favrot and Barnes signed a prenuptial agreement stipulating they would limit sexual intercourse to once a week. Favrot filed for divorce because his wife demanded intercourse more than three times a day.

Issue: Is a contract term which attempts to modify marital obligations enforceable?
Rule: The law does not authorize contractual modifications of marriage obligations. Marriage obliges each spouse to fulfill certain obligations, including sex, which cannot be altered by a pre-marital agreement.

Morone v. Morone (1980) DHH

Facts: The parties were an unmarried couple who lived together for 20 years, holding themselves out to the community as husband and wife. Together they had two children. After they separated, the plaintiff sued under implied contract to get her share of the couple's earnings and assets. She also claimed that the defendant had expressly promised that he would support her in return for her domestic services.
Issue 1: May a contract regarding earnings and assets be implied from a relationship of an unmarried couple?
Rule 1: An implied contract between an unmarried couple living together is too indefinite to be enforced as well as contrary to statutes that have abolished common law marriage.
Issue 2: Is an express contract between such a couple enforceable?
Rule 2: An express contract is enforceable so long as illicit sexual relations were not part of the consideration of the contract.

Nebraska Seed Co. v. Harsh (1915) R

Facts: Nebraska Seed alleged that a seed-purchase contract was formed when it accepted an offer it received in a letter from Harsh. Harsh denied that the letter was an offer.
Issue: Does a letter to a dealer discussing price and quantity constitute a binding offer by the seller?
Rule: A letter is not an offer if the language used is general and not intended to be an offer. The court ruled that the letter was not an offer.

Arcadian Phosphates, Inc. v. Arcadian Corp. (1989) R

Facts: Plaintiff claimed that a memorandum describing the sale of Defendant's fertilizer business was a binding contract. The memorandum documented a number of terms, but some terms remained to be negotiated. Plaintiff sued based on breach of contract and promissory estoppel.
Issue: Is a preliminary agreement binding when the parties have not yet committed to all of the terms?

Rule: A preliminary agreement is binding if the language of the agreement manifests an intent to be bound. Other indications of intent are: the context of negotiations, the existence of open terms, partial performance, and the necessity of putting the agreement in final form. Promissory estoppel may also be used to enforce a commitment to a preliminary agreement by showing a clear and unambiguous promise, a reasonable and foreseeable reliance by the promisee, and an injury sustained by the promisee.

Elvin Associates. v. Franklin (1990) R

Facts: Aretha Franklin orally agreed to star in a Broadway show being produced by Elvin. Elvin hired designers and cast members, and incurred many expenses during the drafting stages of the contract. Franklin never signed the final contract and never showed up for rehearsals. Production was suspended, and when a second attempt at mounting the show failed, Elvin claimed breach of the original agreement and promissory estoppel.

Issue: Can a plaintiff recover under the theory of promissory estoppel when there is no cause of action for breach of contract?

Rule: When a party justifiably acts in reliance on another's oral promises, it would be unconscionable not to compensate the relying party for any losses sustained as a result of the broken promise.

Giant Food, Inc. v. Ice King, Inc. (1988) R

Facts: Giant negotiated to have Ice King supply it with ice. Ice King argued that it was led to believe that they were negotiating to supply Giant with ice regularly, but Giant only considered Ice King to be a safety valve, to be used only if its own plant was not operational.

Issue: Is there a cause of action for the tort of negligent misrepresentation when a party issues statements which induce reliance?

Rule: There is a duty to furnish correct information when a relationship gives one party the right to rely upon the other. When information is negligently misrepresented, and reliance is justified, a party has a right to relief.

Marsh v. Lott (1908) R

Facts: Marsh sought specific performance for the sale of real estate. Marsh claimed that he gave consideration of 25 cents in exchange for the option to purchase land for $100,000.

Issue: What constitutes sufficient consideration for an option to purchase real estate?

Rule: Any money consideration, however small, paid in exchange for an option to purchase property at its adequate value, is binding upon the seller for the time specified.

Beard Implement Co., Inc v. Krusa (1991) R

Facts: Beard alleged a breach of contract by Krusa for the purchase of a combine, claiming that Krusa had signed a purchase order and issued a check as a down payment. The purchase order, however, was not signed by Beard's representative.

Issue: Is there an acceptance if a purchase order is signed by the buyer but not by the seller?

Rule: If a purchase order clearly requires the signature of the seller's authorized representative, no contract exists.

American Parts Co., Inc. v. American Arbitration Assoc. (1967) R

Facts: Deering Milliken orally agreed to sell fabric to American Parts. Deering sent American Parts two "confirmation of order" forms that contained a price term and an arbitration provision. American Parts claimed that the price term was incorrect but accepted shipment from Deering and paid the incorrect price. American Parts eventually stopped purchasing from Deering, and Deering tried to invoke the arbitration provision in the "confirmation of order." However, American Parts claimed that each shipment was a separate transaction and denied that the "confirmation of order" was a contract. American Parts sued for a stay of arbitration proceedings.

Issue: Does a written "confirmation of order" which contains an additional term operate as a modification to a prior oral contract?

Rule: If the seller and purchaser are both merchants, and a firm oral agreement is reached, the seller's written confirmation of order acts as a modification of the contract if the confirmation's changes are immaterial to the contract, and the seller performs the contract as written.

Farley v. Champs Fine Foods, Inc. (1987) R

Facts: Farley, who managed four of Champs' restaurants, negotiated for the purchase of some of the restaurants. Champs told Farley over the telephone that it would not enter into any agreement with him. After this conversation, Farley sent a letter of acceptance to a prior offer.

Issue: Is there a contract if an offer has been orally withdrawn before acceptance?

Rule: An offeror may revoke a proposal at any time before its acceptance is communicated to him, but not after. Thus, if a party mails a letter of acceptance after he learns that a proposal has been withdrawn, revocation is valid.

Buschman v. Diamond Shamrock Corp. (1970) R

Facts: Buschman sought to recover for services rendered as a business broker. Buschman claimed reliance on a suggested agreement and an attached cover letter sent to him by Diamond. The cover letter was signed by Diamond's vice-president but the agreement was not.

Issue: Is a suggested agreement binding prior to formal execution by both parties?

Rule: The parties' intentions determine whether a suggested agreement is binding. If the parties do not intend to be bound until an agreement is reduced to writing and signed by both parties, they are not bound until the event takes place.

Chapter 5

INTERPRETING CONTRACTS
(Parol Evidence, Contract Language,
Omitted Terms)

I. PAROL EVIDENCE RULE

The parol evidence rule is substantive law that renders preliminary negotiations, written documents, conversations, and verbal agreements inadmissible at trial because they are merged into and superseded by the subsequent written contract. Even if a court allows such evidence, its veracity still has to be proved to the jury. The rule controls only what type of evidence is allowed, not whether such evidence is credible.

A. Integration
A writing is integrated if it is adopted by the parties as "a final expression of one or more of the terms of an agreement." (Rest. 2d. § 209(1).)

1. A writing is partially integrated if the parties did not intend for it to include all the terms of the agreement.

2. A writing is completely integrated if the parties intended it to include all the terms of the agreement.
(Rest. 2d. § 210(1).)

B. When Parol Evidence is Admissible

1. Evidence of prior agreements or negotiations may supplement a partially integrated agreement, provided this evidence does not contradict a term of the writing.

2. When an agreement is completely integrated, not even evidence of a consistent additional term is admissible to explain or supplement it. (Rest. 2d. § 216.)

3. Some courts treat contemporaneous oral agreements as prior oral agreements. Others assert that the existence of a contemporaneous

oral agreement automatically proves that the writing is only partially integrated.

4. Parol testimony is admissible to prove a condition precedent to the legal effectiveness of a written contract if the condition does not contradict the express terms of such written agreement.

5. Even if the writing is a complete integration, parol evidence is admissible to show fraud, mistake, or duress in the inducement of the contract. Most courts hold that a merger clause should not be held a bar to actions for fraud.

6. Evidence of subsequent oral agreements will not be barred by the parol evidence rule. The rule only applies to agreements made prior to the final contract.

   a. To avoid the admission of this type of evidence, some parties insert no-oral-modification clauses which find statutory support from UCC § 2-209(2).

   b. An attempted oral modification of a contract that contains a no-oral-modification clause is effective as a waiver only if it is reasonably relied upon.

C. The UCC Version

1. A writing intended to be a final expression of an agreement may not be contradicted by evidence of a prior written or oral agreement or of a contemporaneous oral agreement. (UCC § 2-202.)

2. The writing may be explained or supplemented by course of dealing or usage of trade even if it is a complete integration, unless the course of dealing or trade usage is carefully canceled by the contract's terms. (UCC § 2-202(1).)

3. The writing may be explained or supplemented by evidence of consistent additional terms unless the court finds the writing to be complete and exclusive. (UCC § 2-202(2).)

D. Judge Makes All Parol Evidence Decisions (Rest. 2d § 209(2))
There is concern that juries would be more sympathetic to oral
testimony and not realize that written evidence is more accurate.

    1. Partial v. Complete Integration

        a. The strict view asserts that this question should be answered
through an examination of the writing only (four-corners
approach).

           i. According to this view, a clause that states that the writing
represents the complete agreement between the parties
(merger clause) will usually lead to a determination that the
writing is a complete integration, unless it is obviously clear
that it is not.

           ii. If a writing is seemingly complete on its face, evidence of
a prior oral agreement is admissible only if it is one that the
parties would not ordinarily be expected to embody in the
writing (see *Mitchell v. Lath*).

        b. A more permissive approach looks to extrinsic circumstances
along with the face of the writing (see *Lee v. Joseph E.
Seagram & Sons, Inc.* and *Masterson v. Sine*).

           i. The important consideration is the intent of the parties.

           ii. A general merger clause is merely evidence of intent.

        c. UCC § 2-202, comment 3
Parol evidence of additional terms is not admissible as above
unless "the additional terms are such that, if agreed upon, they
would certainly have been included in the document."

    2. Judges decide whether or not the writing is an integration (i.e., a
final expression of accord). Some courts look to the writing; others
look to the parties' intent.

3. Judges also determine if the oral additional terms are contradictory or consistent with the writing. The judge must evaluate the oral testimony.

II. INTERPRETING CONTRACT LANGUAGE

In addition to disputes as to whether a term is actually part of a contract, parties may also disagree as to the meaning of those terms that are part of the contract. Difficulties may arise because the parties do not speak the same language or because certain words may have a special "trade meaning" of which one of the parties is not aware.

A. Role of Judge and Jury

1. Although the meaning of language is a question of fact, it has frequently been removed from the jury by calling it a question of law because of a distrust of uneducated and unsophisticated jurors and a desire for uniformity in interpretation.

2. The test of admissibility of extrinsic evidence to explain the meaning of a written instrument is not whether the instrument appears to be plain and unambiguous on its face, but whether the offered evidence is relevant to prove a meaning to which the language of the instrument is reasonably susceptible (see *Pacific Gas & Electric Co. v. G.W. Thomas Drayage & Rigging Co.*).

B. The party that seeks to have a contract term interpreted in a narrower sense that is more favorable to him bears a substantial burden of proof. (See *Frigaliment Importing Co. v. B.N.S. Int'l Sales Corp.*)

C. Objective and Subjective Theories of Interpretation

1. Objectivists and subjectivists agree that where the parties have in fact attached different significance to their language, the objective standard should be used in determining the meaning of the language.

2. Objectivists also argue that even where parties have attached the same meaning to their language, an objective standard should

determine the meaning, even if it is different from that which the parties intended.

3. In reality, courts allow parol evidence to help them determine the intended meaning of ambiguous words in a written contract.

D.   Restatement (Second) § 201

1. Where all parties have attached the same meaning to an agreement or a term, it is interpreted in accordance with that meaning.

2. Where the parties have attached different meanings to an agreement, it is interpreted in accordance with the meaning attached by one of them if at the time the agreement was made that party did not know or have reason to know of any different meaning attached by the other, and the other knew or had reason to know the meaning attached by the first party.

3. There is no binding contract if the parties unknowingly assign different subjective meanings to an important contract term because there was no meeting of the minds. (See *Raffles v. Wichelhaus*; Rest. 2d. § 20.)

E.   Rules in Aid of Interpretation

1. Words and conduct are interpreted in light of all the surrounding circumstances. The principal purpose of the contract is given great weight if it is ascertainable in light of all the circumstances. (Rest. 2d § 202(1).)

2. Maxims, such as "the term is to be strictly construed against the draftsman," can be used.

3. Contracts will be construed to serve the public interest.

a. An interpretation that gives a reasonable, lawful, and effective meaning to all the terms is preferred to an interpretation that leaves a part of the contract unreasonable, unlawful, or of no effect. (Rest. 2d § 203(a).)

b. Contracts that restrain trade or land use are narrowly construed.

4. Specific terms and separately negotiated terms are given greater weight than general language and standardized terms, respectively. (Rest. 2d. § 203(c-d).)

5. Interpret terms with the aid of any relevant course of performance, course of dealing and usage of trade. (Rest. 2d. § 202(5); UCC §§ 1-205, 2-208.)

F. Hierarchy of Extrinsic Aids (Rest. 2d. § 203(b); UCC § 2-208(2))

1. Express Terms
Look at the contract terms themselves.

2. Course of Performance
If the contract has been partially performed, the court will consider how the ambiguous terms were treated.

3. Course of Dealing
If the parties have made other contracts in the past, the court will consider whether similarly ambiguous terms were used and how they were interpreted by the parties.

4. Trade Usage
Whether the ambiguous or disputed terms have a common interpretation in the specific industry or trade in which the parties are engaged will be considered.

5. These standards are inapplicable if the contract specifically bars their use.

III. OMITTED TERMS

How the courts deal with problems that are not addressed by the parties.

A. When the parties to a bargain sufficiently defined to be a contract have not agreed with respect to a term that is essential to a determination of their rights and duties, a term that is reasonable in the circumstances is supplied by the court. (Rest. 2d. § 204.)

1. The reasonable omitted term may be supplied even if the writing is completely integrated (see parol evidence rule).

2. Although extrinsic evidence may be inadmissible to supply the omitted term (e.g., the writing is completely integrated), it may be used to determine what is "reasonable."

B. There are many instances where a court will supply omitted terms (see Chapters 7 and 8 for court-implied conditions and extraordinary events that make performance impracticable):

1. Obligation of Good Faith

   a. Every contract or duty imposes an obligation of good faith in its performance and enforcement. (UCC § 1-203; Rest. 2d. § 205.)

   b. Requirements and Output Contracts
      There is an obligation of good faith when demanding or tendering requirements or outputs pursuant to the agreement. (UCC § 2-306(1).)

      i. This obligation is satisfied if the buyer's demands are in accordance with established course of performance and dealing between the parties and the established usage of trade. (See *Eastern Air Lines, Inc. v. Gulf Oil Corp.*)

      ii. A requirements or output contract usually does not include an implied obligation to continue the business.

2. Best Efforts

   a. A lawful agreement for exclusive dealing, unless otherwise agreed, imposes a return obligation to use best efforts to promote the product. (See *Wood v. Lucy, Lady Duff-Gordon;* UCC § 2-306(2).)

b. A clause requiring "best efforts to maintain a high volume of sales" is violated by the philosophy that profit motivation should override sales volume in the absence of consideration.

c. A promise to publish implies a good faith effort to promote the book, including a first printing and advertising budget adequate to give the book a reasonable chance of achieving success. However, while publishers must perform honestly, there is no requirement to perform skillfully.

3. Percentage Lease
   Rent is fixed as a stated percentage of the lessee's receipts or profits.

   a. If based on gross receipts, a conflict is created. The lessor wants the lessee to maximize gross receipts, while the lessee wants to maximize net profits.

   b. When no minimum rent is reserved, a percentage lease must be construed as including an implied covenant to continue the business.

   c. Such an obligation is not implied if the lessor is protected by a substantial minimum rental provision.

4. Agreements Without End

   a. Employment Contracts
      The majority of states have not implied a duty to terminate employment contracts in good faith.

   b. Franchise Agreements
      There is a three-way division among courts:

      i. Franchisors cannot terminate without cause.

    ii. Franchisors must give reasonable notice of termination.

    iii. Franchisors must allow the franchisee a reasonable opportunity to avail himself of the primary efforts and expenditures incurred in setting up the franchise.

5. Course of Performance, Course of Dealing and Trade Usage
Extrinsic evidence relating to the usage of trade and the parties' course of dealing is admissible to supplement an unambiguous and complete written contract as long as it does not contradict the written agreement's express terms. (UCC § 2-202.)

6. UCC Gap-Fillers
If it has not been agreed upon, courts determine:

    a. Reasonable price terms. (UCC § 2-305(a).)

    b. Place for delivery. (UCC § 2-308.)

    c. Date payment is due. (UCC § 2-310.)

CASE CLIPS

Mitchill v. Lath (1928) DHH, KGK, FE, MS, CPB
Facts: The Laths orally promised to remove an icehouse in exchange for Mitchill's written agreement to buy land. The written agreement excluded the Laths' earlier promise. Mitchill sought to introduce evidence of the promise for its enforcement.
Issue: Will a written contract be modified by evidence of a prior oral agreement that addresses and modifies the same issues and obligations?
Rule: An oral agreement is allowed to be in variance of the written contract if the agreement is collateral, it does not contradict express or implied provisions of the written contract, and the parties would *not* ordinarily be expected to embody it in the writing.

Hatley v. Stafford (1978) DHH

Facts: Stafford leased farmland to Hatley with the option that Stafford could buy out Hatley at a figure not to exceed $70 per acre. Six months into the lease, Stafford tried to buy out Hatley but Hatley refused to sell, claiming that the parties had made a contemporaneous oral agreement stipulating that the buy-out option would be effective from 30 to 60 days only. The lease was negotiated without the use of lawyers.

Issue: Will parol evidence be admitted to prove the existence of an oral agreement if it is not inconsistent with the express terms of a written contract that was formed by unsophisticated parties?

Rule: Parol evidence to prove the existence of an oral agreement will be admitted by the court if the oral agreement is not inconsistent with the express terms of the written agreement, and if it is such an agreement that would naturally be made as a separate agreement by the parties situated in their specific circumstances.

Long Island Trust Co. v. International Inst. for Packaging Educ., Ltd. (1976) DHH

Facts: When International failed to repay the recently renewed loan, the Long Island Trust sued four of the five guarantors and International. The guarantors tried to introduce parol evidence of a contemporaneous oral agreement that the endorsement of all the guarantors was required for renewal of the loan. Only four endorsed.

Issue: May a party use parol evidence to attempt to prove the existence of an oral condition that would bar the enforcement of the written agreement if not performed?

Rule: An oral condition precedent may be proved by parol evidence if it in no way contradicts the express terms of the written agreement.

Lipsit v. Leonard (1974) DHH

Facts: Leonard's contemporaneous oral promises to give Lipsit a share of the business induced Lipsit into entering a series of one-year employment contracts. Lipsit sued for fraud and breach of contract after he was fired.

Issue: Can an action in tort based on a fraudulent oral promise be maintained if the promise itself cannot be enforced because proof of its existence is barred by the parol evidence rule?

Rule: Even if a party cannot establish the existence of an oral promise because it falls under the parol evidence rule, an action in fraud based on the oral promise may be sustained. The measure of damages for fraud is limited to out-of-pocket expenses.

LaFazia v. Howe (1990) DHH

Facts: The Howes entered into negotiations to purchase a delicatessen from the LaFazias. After receiving and reviewing the LaFazias' tax returns, the Howes decided against the purchase. The Howes were eventually persuaded to purchase by the LaFazias' representations that the tax returns did not reflect the true value of the business. The Howes purchased the business under a signed contract containing a disclaimer which stated "The Buyers rely on their own judgment as to … profits … and does [sic] not rely on any representations of the seller." The Howes were subsequently forced to sell the delicatessen after a lack of business made it impossible to complete payment of the contract price. The LaFazias instituted suit for recovery of the remaining contract price, and the Howes counterclaimed, asserting misrepresentation.

Issue: Can a written disclaimer be used to uphold a contract that may otherwise be voidable for fraud?

Rule: A specific disclaimer provision that is read and understood by the party asserting fraud estops all allegations made by the complainant which are contrary to the disclaimer, unless the provision itself was procured by fraud.

Note: This rule allows contracting parties to agree that one is not relying on the representations of the other, a form of freedom of contract.

Hoffman v. Chapman (1943) DHH

Facts: A draftsman, who was acting as an agent for both parties, made a mistake in writing the deed which resulted in the conveyance of more land to the Hoffmans than agreed upon. When the mistake was detected, the Hoffmans refused to reconvey the unsold land.

Issue: Will a court reform a written agreement to reflect the real intention of the parties?

Rule: A written instrument will be reformed to conform to the real intention of the parties if there is clear and convincing evidence of a mutual mistake.

Pacific Gas & Elec. Co. v. G.W. Drayage & Rigging Co.
(1968) DHH, MS, FE, CPB, R

Facts: The contract to repair Pacific's steam turbine contained an indemnity clause requiring Drayage to pay for all property damage arising out of performance of the contract. When Drayage damaged the exposed rotor of a turbine, Pacific sued. Drayage sought to introduce extrinsic evidence to show that the indemnity clause only held it liable for damages to the property of third parties, not to that of Pacific.

Issue: Is evidence of the parties' intention admissible to help explain the meaning of a written instrument?

Rule: Extrinsic evidence of the parties' intention is admissible when relevant to prove a meaning to which the language of a written instrument is reasonably susceptible. Even when the meaning of the instrument appears plain and unambiguous on its face, extrinsic evidence having the above effect is admissible.

Thompson v. Libby (1885) KGK, KC

Facts: Thompson brought an action for the purchase price of logs sold. Libby offered oral testimony to prove the existence of a warranty of the quality of the logs.

Issue: May a party use parol evidence to prove the existence of a warranty allegedly made at the time of sale?

Rule: A warranty is an item and term of the contract of sale, not a separate and independent collateral contract, and therefore cannot be added to a complete written agreement by oral testimony.

Crawford v. France (1933) KGK

Facts: The plaintiff contracted to design plans for the defendant's proposed hotel. The defendant later abandoned the project and refused to pay the plaintiff's fees because the proposed design was too expensive to build. The defendant sought to introduce evidence of a contemporaneous oral agreement by which the parties agreed that the project would be abandoned if too costly. The written contract lacked several important terms.

Issue: Is parol evidence permitted to supplement a contract that is incomplete on its face?

Rule: Parol evidence is admissible to establish other conditions of a contract where the writing is incomplete on its face and to reduce ambiguities where uncertainty exists on the face of a contract.

Danann Realty Corp. v. Harris (1959) KGK

Facts: The plaintiff sought damages because he was induced to enter into a lease as a result of the defendant's fraudulent oral misrepresentations. However, the contract included a disclaimer of all oral misrepresentations.

Issue: If a contract clause disclaims all oral misrepresentations, may a party bring an action for fraudulent misrepresentation?

Rule: When a contract contains a clause that specifically disclaims all oral misrepresentations, a party may not institute a suit for damages because he entered the contract as a result of fraudulent misrepresentations.

Dissent: A disclaimer clause should not be held a bar to actions for fraud.

Zell v. American Seating Co. (2d. Cir. 1943) KGK, R

Facts: Zell orally agreed to procure government contracts for American Seating during the war, in exchange for a flat fee and commissions. A written contract followed omitting the commissions because of government disfavor toward such arrangements. The parties orally agreed, however, that the first oral agreement was the actual contract. American Seating later refused to pay commissions.

Issue: Will the parol evidence rule bar a party from submitting proof of an oral agreement that renders a writing, complete on its face, not binding?

Rule: A purported written agreement, which the parties design as a mere sham, lacks legal efficacy, and extrinsic parol or other written evidence will always be received on the issue.

American Seating Co. v. Zell (S. Ct. 1944) KGK

Facts: See preceding case.

Issue: See preceding case.

Rule: (Per Curiam): If a written agreement is complete and unambiguous on its face, the parol evidence rule will bar all evidence that is inconsistent with its terms.

Lee v. Joseph E. Seagram & Sons, Inc. (1977) FE, CPB, R

Facts: The Lees claimed that there was a contemporaneous oral agreement that if they sold their liquor distributorship to Seagram under a written contract, Seagram would relocate Lee's sons in another distributorship. Lee, who had enjoyed a good friendship with Seagram, brought suit when Seagram refused to execute its oral promise. An integration clause was not included in the written contract.

Issue: Does the parol evidence rule bar proof of an oral agreement that does not contradict the written contract if the writing contained no integration clause?

Rule: Proof of an oral collateral agreement that is not contradictory to any terms of a written contract will not be barred by the parol evidence rule if the parties would not be expected to incorporate the oral agreement into the written contract.

Hunt Foods & Indus., Inc. v. Doliner (1966) FE, MS

Facts: When Hunt sought to enforce a written option contract to purchase stock at a certain price, Doliner attempted to introduce evidence of a contemporaneous oral agreement that the option would only be exercised if Doliner tried to solicit a higher offer elsewhere.

Issue: Is proof of prior or contemporaneous oral agreements admissible if it is consistent with the written contract and would not be expected to be included within its terms?

Rule: Proof of an oral agreement that is consistent with the terms of the written contract is not barred by the parol evidence rule if it would not be expected to be included in the written agreement.

Lusk Corp. v. Burgess (1958) FE

Facts: Before the Burgesses purchased land under a written contract that contained a merger clause, Lusk orally represented to the plaintiffs that the use of the adjoining plot (also owned by Lusk) would be restricted. Six days later, Lusk sold the adjoining land to a third party with no restrictions.

Issue: Is parol evidence admissible to prove actionable fraud in the inducement of a fully integrated written contract?

Rule: Although inadmissible to vary a fully integrated written contract, parol evidence is admissible to show fraud in the inducement of a contract.

Hicks v. Bush (1962) FE

Facts: Hicks and Bush contracted to combine their business interests to effect a more efficient operation. Hicks performed his obligations, but Bush did not. Bush sought to introduce evidence that the parties had made a contemporaneous oral agreement stipulating that the contract would only be binding if they obtained financing, which was not forthcoming. The writing was silent on this issue.

Issue: Is parol testimony admissible to prove the existence of a condition precedent to a written agreement?

Rule: Parol testimony is admissible to prove a condition precedent to the legal effectiveness of a written agreement if the condition does not contradict the express terms of such written agreement "in a real sense."

Steuart v. McChesney (1982) FE

Facts: The Steuarts granted the McChesneys a right of first refusal, or right to make a bid if the Steuarts found a purchaser for a parcel of farmland. The property was appraised at $50,000, and the defendants received offers of over $30,000. However, the McChesneys sought to exercise their right for $7,820, twice the value listed on the tax rolls maintained in the county. The contract provided that county records were to be the source of the McChesneys' offer.

Issue: When an agreement's meaning is clear and unambiguous and yet produces an inequitable result, can extrinsic evidence be introduced to supply another meaning?

Rule: The plain meaning of an unambiguous contract will be enforced despite inequitable results. Plain meaning cannot be distorted to produce ambiguity simply because fairness might warrant a different outcome.

Hayden v. Hoadley (1920) FE

Facts: The parties contracted in writing to exchange their properties, and Hoadley agreed to make repairs on his land at no charge to the Haydens. When the Haydens brought suit to enforce this provision, Hoadley attempted to introduce evidence of contemporaneous oral agreements that limited the time and costs of repairs.

Issue: Can oral testimony be admitted to vary or contradict a written contract that contains no latent ambiguity?

Rule: A written contract that contains no latent ambiguity cannot be qualified, controlled, contradicted, enlarged or diminished by evidence of any contemporaneous or antecedent understanding or agreement.

Masterson v. Sine (1968) FE, MS

Facts: Masterson sold a ranch to Sine (his sister) with an option reserved to repurchase the property. Masterson's trustee in bankruptcy sought to utilize the option, but Sine attempted to prove that there was a prior oral agreement barring assignment of the option to anyone outside of the family.

Issue: When is parol evidence of an oral collateral agreement admissible?

Rule: Evidence of oral collateral agreements are excluded only when the fact finder is likely to be misled. If it appears that the oral collateral agreement might naturally be made as a separate agreement, proof of the collateral agreement is permitted, but if the additional agreed upon terms logically would have been included in the document, the evidence must be excluded. (UCC § 2-202.)

Berwick & Smith Co. v. Salem Press, Inc. (1954) FE

Facts: The plaintiff submitted a bid to bind the defendant's two-volume book. The defendant, a newcomer to the printing industry, was unaware that according to industry custom and usage, each book of a multivolume work was considered a copy. The defendant thought "copy" referred to the entire work.

Issue: Is a party obligated to perform its part of an agreement as defined by the "custom and usage" of a trade when it was unaware of the trade definition of the term?

Rule: When parties to a contract are engaged in the same trade, terms of the agreement are interpreted according to the "custom and usage of the trade." (UCC § 1-205.)

Nanakuli Paving & Rock Co. v. Shell Oil Co., Inc.
(1981) FE, KC

Facts: Nanakuli entered into a long-term contract to buy asphalt from Shell. Although not explicitly required to do so, Shell gave Nanakuli price protection for five years in accordance with industry-wide custom in Hawaii. Due to rising costs, Shell raised its prices.

Issue: Will trade usage that is reinforced by the course of dealings between the parties be incorporated into an agreement?

Rule: A course of dealings that complies with a prevalent trade usage of which the parties are or should be aware will be incorporated into an agreement provided it is consistent with the express terms of the contract.

Alaska Northern Development., Inc. v. Alyeska
Pipeline Serv. Co. (1983) MS

Facts: Alaska Northern Development (AND) sent Alyeska a proposal to purchase Alyeska's entire inventory of Caterpillar parts. No price was mentioned. Alyeska responded with its own letter of intent, also without a price term, which included the words "subject to the final approval of the owner committee." AND claimed the language referred only to the price term but Alyeska contended it referred to the whole deal. The lower court found that the contract was partially integrated.

Issue: What definition of inconsistency is to be applied to determine whether parol evidence should be admitted to interpret a partially integrated contract?

Rule: Inconsistency, for purposes of admitting parol evidence, means the absence of reasonable harmony in terms of the language and respective obligations of the party.

Note: Other jurisdictions hold that to be inconsistent, a term must actually contradict or negate a term of the writing.

Luther Williams, Jr., Inc. v. Johnson (1967) MS

Facts: The defendants testified that they signed the contract for improvements to their home believing it was merely an estimate and not an obligation until they procured the financing. The contract had a merger clause.

Issue: Is parol evidence admissible to prove the existence of an oral agreement that acts as a condition precedent to a written contract?

Rule: Parol evidence is admissible to prove the existence of an oral agreement that acts as a condition precedent to a written contract if the parol condition does not contradict the terms of the writing. The merger clause is an indication, not conclusive, of the intent of the parties with regard to the completeness of their agreement.

In Re Soper's Estate (1935) MS

Facts: Soper deserted his wife (the plaintiff), married a widow who later died, and then married a third time to a woman who survived him at his death. Prior to his death, he had entered a stock insurance plan with the proceeds to be paid to his "surviving wife" upon his death.

Issue: Is parol evidence of a party's intent admissible to help interpret the meaning of an ambiguous term in a written contract?

Rule: Parol evidence is admissible to help determine the intent behind ambiguous words in a written contract.

A. Kemp Fisheries, Inc. v. Castle & Cooke, Inc. (1988) MS

Facts: Kemp contracted with a subsidiary of Castle & Cooke to charter a commercial fishing vessel for the season. The contract provided that (1) the subsidiary would deliver the vessel in good, inspected condition, (2) acceptance is conclusive evidence that the Kemp deemed the vessel seaworthy and suitable for its intended use, and (3) delivery would constitute full performance by the subsidiary. The freezing system broke

down during the season, forcing Kemp to sell his fish at reduced rates. The trial judge admitted parol evidence to find that the subsidiary had orally warranted that the freezing system would meet the Kemp's requirements.
Issue: When should extrinsic evidence be admitted to interpret the language of a contract?
Rule: The parol evidence rule requires that courts consider extrinsic evidence to determine whether a contract is ambiguous, but if the evidence leads to an interpretation that is contrary to a reasonable interpretation of the contract language, the evidence is not admissible.

Frigaliment Imp. Co. v. B.N.S. Int'l Sales Corp. (1960) KC, MS

Facts: Frigaliment rejected International's delivery of "stewing chickens" because it said that the contract called for "young chickens." International defended that the contract allowed for it to deliver "any bird of that genus," and that its prices were too low to suggest that it was selling "broilers."
Issue: How does the court determine the meaning of an ambiguous contract term?
Rule: The party who seeks to have a contract term interpreted in a narrower sense that is more favorable to it bears the substantial burden of persuading the court. In order to determine the meaning of an ambiguous term, the court looks to the contract language, prevalence and actual knowledge of the trade usage and the dealings between the parties.

Gray v. Zurich Insurance Co. (1966) MS

Facts: Zurich Insurance refused to defend Gray on the ground that the complaint alleged an intentional tort, which fell outside the coverage of the policy as stated in an unclear exclusionary clause.
Issue: Is an unclear exclusionary provision buried in the fine print of an insurance policy invalid so that the reasonable expectations of the insured are not disappointed?
Rule: In interpreting an insurance policy, doubts as to meaning must be resolved against the insurer, and any exception to the performance of the basic underlying obligation must be stated clearly to apprise the insured of its effect.

Paymaster Oil Mill Co. v. Mitchell (1975) CPB

Facts: Paymaster contracted with Mitchell to buy 4,000 bushels of soybeans at a set price. This oral agreement was later corroborated in writing. A severe drought damaged Mitchell's crop preventing full delivery.

Issue: Is parol evidence concerning a written contract admissible if it does not conflict with the written contract?

Rule: Parol evidence may be used to further explain or supplement the terms of a written contract so long as it is not contradictory to the terms of a written agreement intended as the final expression of a contract.

Note: Parol evidence may not be used if there has been an adjudication that the writing was intended as the exclusive statement of the agreement.

Trident Center v. Connecticut General Life Insurance Co. (1988) CPB

Facts: Trident Center obtained a $56.5 million commercial loan from Connecticut General at an interest rate of 12.25 percent. The agreement provided that Trident not prepay the loan during the first 12 years. A few years later, interest rates greatly decreased and Trident sought to refinance, but Connecticut General refused to allow it to prepay. Trident claimed that extrinsic evidence could be introduced to show that the agreement struck was actually different from the written language of the contract.

Issue: Under California law, may parol evidence be introduced even when the written contract is clear and unambiguous?

Rule: Even when the terms of a contract are clear, a party must always have the opportunity to introduce parol evidence because language has no objective meaning.

Note: Under traditional contract principles, extrinsic evidence is usually inadmissible to interpret, vary or add to the terms of an unambiguous, integrated written instrument. California law is an exception to the normal rule.

Raffles v. Wichelhaus (1864) CPB, R

Facts: The contract stated that the plaintiff was to deliver the goods on the ship *Peerless*. Unknown to both parties there were two different ships bearing the same name but sailing at different times. The defendant refused the plaintiff's goods because he expected the delivery to be made on the *Peerless* which sailed earlier.

Issue: Is there a contract if each party gives a different meaning to a material ambiguity in the contract?

Rule: There is no binding contract if the parties unknowingly assign different meanings to an important contract term. Parol evidence may be given to prove that the parties attributed different meanings to a term.

Columbia Nitrogen Corp. v. Royster Co. (1971) CPB

Facts: Columbia contracted to purchase a minimum of 31,000 tons of phosphate each year for three years from Royster. The contract set the price per ton, subject to an escalation clause based on production costs. Because phosphate prices tumbled, Columbia could not resell it at a competitive price and consequently ordered less than a tenth of the contract amount in the first year. Columbia sought to introduce evidence that, despite the express terms of the contract, contracts of this type were meant to be mere projections of price and quantity.

Issue: May parol evidence pertaining to the usage of the trade and the parties' course of dealing be admitted when the terms of the written agreement are unambiguous?

Rule: Even when an agreement is unambiguous, extrinsic evidence about the usage of trade and the parties' course of dealing is admissible.

Note: Such parol evidence should be excluded when it cannot be reasonably construed as consistent with the terms of the contract, but it may be introduced even when the writing was intended to be a complete statement of the terms of the agreement.

Southern Concrete Services, Inc. v. Mableton Contractors, Inc. (1975) CPB

Facts: Southern contracted to sell Mableton 70,000 cubic yards of concrete. During the time period involved, Mableton ordered only 12,542 cubic yards. Southern sought to recover profits lost and costs incurred in purchasing and delivering raw materials to the job site.

Issue 1: Under the "usage of trade" language of UCC § 2-202(a), can the written price and quantity terms of a contract be challenged?

Rule 1: The specifications of the contract are intended to be observed by the parties; any major departure from these specifications must be expressly agreed to in the contract.

Issue 2: Does UCC § 2-202(b) permit the introduction of evidence of additional terms which are inconsistent with the original agreement?

Rule 2: Section 2-202 requires that written contracts not be contradicted by evidence of agreements outside of the written contract.

Note: Written contracts may be explained or supplemented by evidence of "consistent additional terms" if the court finds the contract was not meant to be the complete statement of the agreement.

Monge v. Beebe Rubber Co. (1974) KC

Facts: Monge had an oral terminable at will employment contract with Beebe. Monge's foreman asked Monge out on a date and she refused. During the next eight months, the foreman, with the "connivance" of the personnel manager, transferred Monge to lower paying positions, took away her overtime, and eventually fired her. Monge sued for breach of contract.

Issue: When is the termination of an at will employment contract a breach of contract?

Rule: The termination of a contract for employment at will is a breach of contract when the termination is motivated by bad faith, malice, or retaliation, because such a termination is not in the best interest of the economic system or the public good.

Howard v. Dorr Woolen Company (1980) KC

Facts: Defendant, Dorr Woolen Company, fired Baldwin for reasons of "economic necessity." At the time Baldwin was fired, he was 50 years old and suffered from angina. Baldwin claimed that he was terminated because of his age and illness.

Issue: Is a discharge for reasons of age or illness considered a discharge motivated by bad faith, malice, or retaliation?

Rule: A discharge for reasons of age or illness is not motivated by bad faith, malice, or retaliation because it is not in response to the employee's performance of an act which public policy would encourage, or refusal to perform an act which public policy would condemn.

Note: This case narrows the rule in Monge v. Beebe Rubber Co. to cases in which the employee is discharged for acting or refusing to act in a manner that can be justified on public policy grounds.

Cloutier v. The Great Atlantic & Pacific Tea Co. (1981) KC

Facts: Plaintiff managed one of Defendant's stores. Company policy required store employees to make bank deposits twice each day. However, Plaintiff's supervisor told the plaintiff that deposits could be skipped and the money placed in the store safe at night or during weekends if store employees were afraid to go to the bank unescorted. One day, after the deposit had not been made and the money had been placed in the store vault, the store was burglarized. The defendant fired the plaintiff for failing to require his employees to make the required daily deposits.

Issue: If an employee claims to have been wrongfully discharged for acting in a manner justified by public policy, does the public policy need to be based on statutory authority?

Rule: If an employee claims to have been wrongfully discharged for acting in a manner justified by public policy, the public policy need not be based on statutory authority. The validity of the articulated public policy may be determined by the jury.

Note: This case further clarifies the "public policy" prong of the Monge-Howard wrongful discharge test.

Leibel v. Raynor Manufacturing Co. (1978) KC

Facts: Raynor and Leibel made an oral distributorship agreement. Raynor agreed to sell its goods to Leibel at the factory distributor price if Leibel agreed to sell, install and service Raynor products exclusively. After two years of decreasing sales, Raynor informed Leibel that their relationship was terminated, effective immediately. Leibel agreed that the relationship was terminable at will, but claimed that reasonable notice of termination was required.

Issue: Under the UCC, may an oral distributorship agreement be terminated without reasonable notice?

Rule: UCC § 2-309 requires reasonable notice before an oral distributorship agreement may be terminated. Reasonable notice is required to assure the dealer an adequate opportunity to sell its existing inventory.

K.M.C. Co. v. Irving Trust Co. (1985) KC

Facts: K.M.C. had a financing agreement with Irving that extended K.M.C. a line of credit in exchange for, among other things, a security interest in all of K.M.C.'s accounts receivable and inventory. K.M.C. requested funds against the line of credit. Even though the loan would not have increased K.M.C.'s balance beyond its credit limit, Irving refused to grant the request. K.M.C. was caught short without any funds and its business collapsed. K.M.C. claimed that Irving's refusal of credit without notice breached a duty of good faith performance. Irving claimed the refusal was well within its discretionary rights, as expressed in their agreement.

Issue: Is there a duty of good faith requiring a party to provide reasonable notice before exercising its contractually granted discretionary right to withhold performance?

Rule: If a contract grants a party a discretionary right to withhold performance, the party has a good faith obligation to provide reasonable notice before exercising that right. Reasonable notice affords the refused party an opportunity to make substitute arrangements and minimizes damages.

Thompson v. St. Regis Paper Co. (1984) KC

Facts: St. Regis hired Thompson as a terminable at will employee. Thompson worked in a variety of positions with the company, earning merit raises and promotions. After 17 years of service, St. Regis fired Thompson and refused to give any reason for his discharge, except to say that Thompson had "stepped on somebody's toes." Thompson sued for wrongful discharge, arguing that the company policy handbook and his past performance created an implied "discharge for cause only" term in his employment contract. He also alleged that he was fired for instituting accurate accounting procedures that were mandated by federal law.

Issue: Is an employer's right to fire a terminable at will employee restricted?

Rule: An employer does not have a duty to discharge a terminable at will employee only for cause. However, an employer may not discharge a terminable at will employee if the discharge contravenes public policy. In addition, if the employer's promises of specific treatment in specific situations (e.g., specific guidelines outlined in an employee handbook) imply that an employee will only be terminated for cause, and an employee relies on that implication, the employer may be found to have modified the original employment contract accordingly.

Note: Jurisdictions vary with respect to whether they will recognize the good faith, public policy, and "implied term through specific guidelines" theories of discharge limitation.

McDonald v. Mianecki (1979) KC

Facts: Mianecki was a construction engineer who placed a newspaper ad offering to build a home on a particular parcel of land. The McDonalds accepted Mianecki's offer. While the house was being built, the McDonalds noticed that the water supply was discolored. Tests revealed that the water was not potable. Repeated attempts to cure the problem, before and after the McDonalds took possession of the house, failed to correct the problem.

Issue: Is there an implied warranty of habitability and reasonable workmanship in the sale of a house by a builder-vendor?

Rule: Builder-vendors impliedly warrant that a home that they construct will be of reasonable workmanship and habitability. Home buyers have inferior bargaining power and must rely on the builder-vendor's representations that he is qualified to build a home. In addition, the builder-vendor is responsible for placing the home into the stream of commerce and has both the expertise and the opportunity to prevent, detect, and correct the occurrence of major problems.

Note: Traditionally, the common law doctrine of caveat emptor applied to home buyers.

Doe v. Travenol Laboratories, Inc. (1988) KC

Facts: Doe, a hemophiliac, underwent an operation requiring a prophylactic infusion of a blood-clotting protein that had been manufactured by the defendant. The blood-clotting protein was contaminated by HIV, and Doe subsequently developed AIDS-Related Complex. Doe sued under breach of warranty, strict liability and negligence theories.

Issue: Does a contaminated blood product constitute a breach of warranty by its manufacturer?

Rule: The manufacturer of a contaminated blood product is shielded from liability under breach of warranty or strict liability theories for reasons of public policy. Such liability could drive blood products manufacturers out of business, significantly reducing the availability of vital blood products.

Joyner v. Adams (1987) KC

Facts: Adams entered into a lease with Joynder that required Adams to completely subdivide and "develop" the leased property by a certain date. The lease required Adams to pay a flat rate rent. However, if Adams failed to subdivide and "develop" all of the leased property by the specified date, Adams was required to pay back rent in the amount that would have been due under a higher rent formula. On the specified date, Adams had completely developed and subdivided all the land, with the exception of a single lot, which had been subdivided and prepared, but upon which no buildings had yet been erected. The parties disagreed as to whether the word "develop" required Adams to complete construction of all buildings or to develop the property to the point that building construction could begin.

Issue: If the parties to a contract attribute different meanings to an ambiguous term, which interpretation should apply?

Rule: If A knows or has reason to know the meaning that B attaches to a term, and B does not know or does not have reason to know the meaning that A attaches to that term, the court will interpret the term in accordance with B's interpretation.

Hershon v. Gibraltar Building & Loan Association, Inc. (1989) KC

Facts: Hershon had financed a condominium purchase by executing a promissory note payable to Gibraltar Building & Loan. Hershon and Gibraltar became parties to five lawsuits that were unrelated to the condominium sale and involved a number of other parties. In an effort to settle the pending lawsuits, Hershon, Gibraltar, and the other parties drew up a "Mutual Release and Discharge Agreement." The Release included expansive language that released all parties from "any and all Claims" the parties might have against one another. Hershon claimed that the explicit and expansive language of the release barred Gibraltar from bringing an action for payment on the condominium promissory notes. Gibraltar, relying on evidence from the settlement negotiations, claimed that the Release only barred claims related to the five settled lawsuits.

Issue: Does the parol evidence rule permit the use of extrinsic evidence to contradict the clear and ordinary meaning of the language of a contract?

Rule: The parol evidence rule does not permit the use of extrinsic evidence to contradict the clear and ordinary meaning of the language of a contract, but does permit the use of extrinsic evidence to reveal an ambiguity in the language of a contract.

Berg v. Hudesman (1990) R

Facts: The landlord of a 99-year ground lease claimed that the tenant had not paid him the proper amount due under the lease for several years. The terms of the contract were ambiguous as to how the rent should be calculated.

Issue: What is the proper way to interpret an ambiguous contract term?

Rule: Extrinsic evidence is admissible as to the entire circumstances under which a contract was made, as an aid to ascertain the parties' intent as to the meaning of particular contract terms. Subsequent conduct of the contracting parties, as well as the reasonableness of the parties' respective interpretations, may also be a factor in the determination of an ambiguous term.

Frigaliment Imp. Co. v. B.N.S. Int'l Sales Corp. (1960) R

Facts: Frigaliment rejected International's delivery of "stewing chickens" because it said that the contract called for "young chickens." International defended that the contract allowed for it to deliver "any bird of that genus," and that it's prices were too low to suggest that it was selling "broilers."

Issue: How does the court determine the meaning of an ambiguous contract term?

Rule: The party who seeks to have a contract term interpreted in a narrower sense that is more favorable to him bears the substantial burden of persuading the court. In order to determine the meaning of an ambiguous term, the court looks to the contract language, prevalence and actual knowledge of the trade usage, and the dealings between the parties.

Eskimo Pie Corp. v. Whitelawn Dairies, Co. (1968) R

Facts: Eskimo Pie was involved in a contract with Whitelawn and Supermarket Advisory Sales ("SAS"), under which Whitelawn had the right to manufacture ice cream products bearing the "Eskimo" name, and SAS had the right to purchase the products. SAS was given "non-exclusive" purchasing rights, and Eskimo subsequently entered into agreements with other parties. SAS brought suit for breach, and proposed to bring in parol evidence to prove the "non-exclusive" clause neither allowed Eskimo to grant licenses to independent companies, nor to compete with SAS in the sale of Eskimo ice cream products.

Issue: Should parol evidence be admitted to ascertain the intended meaning of a contract term?

Rule: The admission of parol evidence is determined by the ambiguity of the contractual language. The admission of parol evidence concerning unambiguous contract language hinges on whether the language might objectively be recognized by a reasonably intelligent person acquainted with the general usage, customs and surrounding circumstances as having special meaning. Where language is ambiguous, a party may use surrounding circumstances, common usage and custom as to the meaning attributed to the language, and the subsequent conduct of the parties, but evidence of subjective understanding will not be admissible.

Shaw v. Leff (1967) R

Facts: A memorandum from an attorney to his client read in its entirety, "Mr. Ted Leff – <u>Divorce</u> Retainer 750.00 Court Time 150.00 per day plus costs – William W. Shaw."

Issue: May extrinsic evidence be introduced to help explain an attorney's retainer letter?

Rule: When an attorney's retainer letter is ambiguous and incomplete, extrinsic evidence may be introduced to explain it.

Chapter 6

POLICING THE BARGAIN

I. CAPACITY TO CONTRACT

Certain classes of individuals lack full capacity to contract. Contracts they form are often voidable at their option.

A. Minors

Minors can disaffirm any contract, except for necessities, during minority and within a reasonable time after reaching majority. (Rest. 2d. § 14.)

1. Exceptions are statutory or involve contracts that deal with duties imposed by law (e.g., marriage contract, agreement to support an illegitimate child).

2. Upon a minor's disaffirmance, the non-infant party is limited to restitution, and only if the minor still possesses the goods.

3. A minor can ratify after a contract coming of age, expressly or by conduct that causes reliance by the other party.

B. Mental Incompetents

Mentally incompetent parties can disaffirm a contract if, by reason of mental illness or defect:

1. They are unable to understand in a reasonable manner the nature and consequences of the transaction, or

2. They are unable to act in a reasonable manner in relation to the transaction, and

3. The other party has reason to know of the condition. (Rest. 2d. § 15.)

C. An intoxicated party can also avoid contractual duties if he does not understand the transaction (majority rule).

II. REVISIONS OF CONTRACTUAL DUTY

A.   Pre-existing Duty Rule
If one party promises another that he will do what he is already legally obligated to do, the promise is not a detriment sufficient to satisfy the requirement of consideration. (Rest. 2d. § 73.)

1.   Courts have held that modifications of rents and wages are invalid because of a pre-existing duty.

2.   Foakes v. Beer Rule
An agreement to accept payment of a lesser sum on or after the due date of a money debt is not binding for lack of consideration.

   a.   This rule is severely criticized because it discourages settlements. It has been overruled in some jurisdictions.

   b.   Most jurisdictions follow it, but hold that sufficient detriment exists if payment of a lesser sum is accompanied by some additional act of the debtor.

3.   Pre-existing Duty Rule Not Applicable:

   a.   Original contract is rescinded and a new contract is executed, with the mutual promises serving again as consideration.

   b.   Contract modification is a partial rescission and therefore supported by consideration (Watkins & Sons v. Carrig).

   c.   Some new detriment can be found for consideration.

   d.   Rest. 2d. § 89(a) allows a modification to be binding if compelled by unforeseen circumstances.

   e.   Under promissory estoppel, a modification is binding to the extent that justice requires enforcement because of reliance on the modification.

  f. Some state statutes allow modifications without consideration as long as written and signed.

  g. UCC § 2-209(1) repudiated the rule by providing that a modification requires no consideration to be binding.

  h. Dropping an invalid claim serves in most courts as consideration for modification if the party has a genuine and reasonable subjective belief that the surrendered claim is valid.

 4. Third-party Situations
  If C, an outsider to the contract, promises compensation to a party to fulfill a contract with another,

  a. Majority holds that the agreement with C is invalid since the party is merely promising to perform his legal obligation.

  b. Minority, which includes the Restatement, holds that a valid contract with C is formed.

B. Economic Duress

 1. Rule
  A contract is voidable if a party was forced to agree to it by use of a wrongful threat precluding his exercise of free will.

 2. Proof
  A party must show that immediate possession of needful goods is threatened and that the goods could not be obtained from another source.

 3. The remedy is usually restitution.

 4. Exercise of a legal right, such as the right to dispute the value of services, is not economic duress.

C.   Check Tendered as Payment in Full

    1. Common law Rule
    If there is a good faith dispute over the amount of a debt and the debtor tenders a check for a lesser amount than creditor's claim, cashing the check, even "under protest," discharges the debt.

        a. A debtor's intention that the check be full satisfaction of the debt must be clearly indicated to the creditor.

        b. Partial payment by a fiduciary (an agent who holds the assets of another) will not result in an accord and satisfaction.

    2. UCC § 1-207

        a. A creditor can cash a check tendered as "payment in full" and still reserve the right to sue for the balance of the debt by writing words of protest on the check.

        b. This rule protects creditors.

        c. Some jurisdictions ignore this rule because it makes settlement of claims difficult.

III.   OVERREACHING IN THE BARGAINING PROCESS

A.   Concealment

    1. In the absence of a fiduciary relationship, there is no liability for bare nondisclosure of known latent defects.

    2. However, half-truths are actionable as whole lies and constitute grounds for contract rescission.

B.   Misrepresentation

    1. Innocent misrepresentations (i.e., negligent, unintentional) are actionable.

2. The misrepresentation must be of a material factor in the contract.

3. The complainant must show justifiable reliance.

4. The misrepresentation must be of facts, not opinions or law.

    a. Opinion is actionable if a fiduciary relationship exists.

    b. Restrictions on relief from misrepresentations of law and opinion are increasingly being relaxed. There is a disposition to treat the nature of the statement (fact or opinion) as only one part of the broader issue of whether reliance was justified.

C.   Confidential Relation
A confidential relation is grounds for avoiding a contract if it is used to contravene the bargaining process.

1. Exemplary relationships include guardian and ward, principal and agent, doctor and patient, etc.

2. A confidential relation is deemed to exist whenever the relative positions of the parties gives one the power and means to take advantage or exert undue influence over the other.

3. Factors that determine such a relation are disparities in age, education, or business experience.

4. If the claimant in an action is the party in whom confidence was placed, he must prove that the bargain was fair and at arm's length (without a confidential relation, however, fraud is not presumed).

D. Relief from Mistake (Rest. 2d. § 152)

1. Mutual Mistake

    a. The mistake under which both parties are acting must have a material effect on the agreed exchange.

        i. Proof that one would not have entered the contract but for the mistake is not sufficient.

        ii. It must be unfair to require performance.

        iii. Availability of other remedies may lead a court to decide that the mistake's effect is not "material."

    b. The mistake must involve a basic assumption.

        i. Determinative factors are the magnitude of the mistake, the degree of certainty in the minds of the parties and the attitude toward the type of transaction involved.

        ii. Belief that the thing bargained for in the contract actually exists is considered to be a basic assumption.

        iii. Courts are divided as to whether the quality of the agreement's subject matter is a basic assumption (see *Sherwood v. Walker, Wood v. Boynton*).

    c. The adversely affected party must not "bear the risk of the mistake." (Rest. 2d §§ 152, 154.)

apportionment

        i. Risk can be allocated by the contract terms.

        ii. Risk is allocated to a party if he enters a contract despite having doubts about the facts to which the mistake relates.

iii.   Risk can be allocated by the court if it is reasonable to do so.

iv.   Negligent failure of a party to know or discover facts as to which both parties are under a mistake does not preclude rescission (see *Beachcomber Coins, Inc. v. Boskett*).

d.   Remedy: Usually, rescission of the contract.

2.   Unilateral Mistake (Rest. 2d. § 153)

a.   Courts are less willing to grant rescission in cases where only one party is mistaken because the remedy deprives the non-mistaken party of the benefit of the bargain.

b.   Elements:

i.   Unilateral mistake requires the same three elements that are needed for mutual mistake: basic assumption, material effect on the exchange, and the risk must not have been allocated to the adversely affected party, *and*

ii.   Either the enforcement of the agreement would be unconscionable, or the other party had reason to know of the mistake or actually caused it.

c.   Courts are more likely to grant rescission for a clerical error than a mistake in judgment (see *Elsinore Union Elementary Sch. Dist. v. Kastorff*).

3.   Warranty

a.   Parties that try to avoid a contract by pleading concealment or mistake sometimes have the option of claiming breach of warranty (implied or express).

    b. Warranty analysis is used mostly in sale-of-goods cases.

        i. Look to UCC § 2-312.

        ii. The risk of mistake is placed on the seller unless the warranty is excluded in the contract pursuant to the code's provisions.

    c. Implied warranties were recently extended to personal injury claims and to transactions involving the sale of houses.

IV. INEQUALITY OF EXCHANGE

A. An unequal exchange will not usually void a contract in an action *at law*, especially if the parties deal at arm's length.

B. Courts will deny equitable relief (i.e., specific performance) to protect a party that refuses to perform its part of a highly disproportionate exchange. (See *Campbell Soup v. Wentz.*)

C. The adequacy of consideration is judged as of the time of the transaction. Example: In an arm's-length agreement, A promises to sell ten law guides to B in exchange for $100. The goods are to be delivered and paid for in 30 days. To the surprise of both parties, the fair market value of law guides increases to $1,000 each by the date of the actual exchange. Although the consideration is vastly disproportionate at the time of the actual exchange, it was adequate at the time the contract was made.

V. UNCONSCIONABILITY AND ADHESION CONTRACTS

A. Unconscionability
The doctrine of unconscionability is used to avoid oppression and unfair surprise, but not to disturb the allocation of risk in contract formation. (UCC § 2-302, comment 1.)

1. UCC § 2-302:

   a. Judges decide the issue of unconscionability as a matter of law.

   b. Unconscionability is determined by circumstances at the time the contract was made.

   c. Parties are entitled to a reasonable opportunity to present evidence of the circumstances ("commercial setting, purpose and effect") to aid the court in making its decision.

   d. The doctrine is used mostly in consumer cases, but there are occasional business applications (see *Gianni Sport Ltd. v. Gantos, Inc.*).

   e. Rest. 2d. § 208, using similar language as UCC § 2-302, allows a court to refuse to enforce all or part of an unconscionable agreement.

2. Types of Unconscionability

   a. Procedural
      Unfairness in the bargaining process. Courts usually require some kind of procedural unconscionability before refusing to enforce a contract.

   b. Substantive
      Unfairness in the bargaining outcome. Substantive unconscionability is criticized for interfering with the private right to contract at arm's length.

      i. Unconscionability has been recognized to include an absence of meaningful choice on the part of one of the parties, together with contract terms that are unreasonably favorable to the other party. (See *Williams v. Walker-Thomas Furniture Co.*)

ii. Courts have used price unconscionability, a type of substantive unconscionability, to invalidate agreements. (See *Jones v. Star Credit Corp.*)

c. Waivers of defenses and cross-collateral clauses have been found unconscionable.

3. Remedies
   If the agreement, or part of it, is unconscionable, the court may:

   a. Refuse to enforce the whole contract,

   b. Refuse to enforce the unconscionable part of the contract, or

   c. Limit the application of an unconscionable clause to avoid an unconscionable result.

   d. When Remedies are Limited:

      i. UCC § 2-719(2)
         When a limited remedy "fails of its essential purpose" because of the circumstances, "remedy may be had as provided in this Act." The Comment states that this section is to be applied when the limitation of the remedy works in an "unconscionable manner." (See *Wilson Trading, Corp. v. David Ferguson, Ltd.*)

      ii. UCC § 2-719(3)
         Consequential damages may be limited or excluded, unless the limitation or exclusion is unconscionable. Limitation of consequential damages for personal injury in a consumer-goods case is *prima facie* unconscionable.

B.   Standard Form Contracts (Contracts of Adhesion)

1. Primary Advantages:

   a. Save time and reduce uncertainty.

   b. Allow parties to control risks.

2. Courts will void provisions in form contracts which were not actually understood and agreed to by the party not writing (see *Henningsen v. Bloomfield Motors*).

3. Unconscionability will invalidate a form-contract provision if a stronger party uses superior bargaining power to introduce contract provisions that cause the lesser party great hardship.

4. Nondrafters usually do not realize that printed slips and tickets are contracts to limit the liability of the issuer.

   a. Rest. 2d. § 212 deals with this difficulty, providing that a paper binds a party only if he "signs or otherwise manifests assent."

   b. If the issuer has reason to believe that the party manifesting assent would not do so if he knew that the writing contained a particular term, the term is not part of the agreement. (Rest. 2d. § 211(3).)

5. Measures for Reducing the Problems of Adhesion

   a. Legislation, which is usually aimed at correcting imbalances of bargaining power:

      i. Statutes require contracts to be written in "plain language" and regulations to control the terms of the exchange and remedies.

  ii.   The main problem with such statutes is inflexibility.

 b. Judicial Control
 Judicial control is more flexible, but incapable of revising underlying patterns of market relationships.

 c. Administrative Control
 Administrative control creates quasi-judicial responsibility and power within a limited jurisdiction (i.e., to investigate charges against common carriers and to exercise control over contract terms in insurance contracts). Administrative control is fairly flexible because administrative decisions carry less precedential value than judicial decisions.

 C. Home-solicitation Sales

  1. State statutes provide a cooling-off period, during which a buyer can cancel his purchase.

  2. Uniform Consumer Credit Code allows the buyer to cancel "until midnight of the third business day" after a home-solicitation sale.

VI.   ILLEGALITY

A.   Courts will also void agreements that are valid from the perspective of contract law, but are otherwise in violation of public policy (illegal contracts).

B.   Criminal sanctions are a more effective way to handle illegal agreements.

C. Claims for restitution are usually precluded, but sometimes allowed if:

1. The claimant is not *in pari delicto* (equally blameworthy) with the defendant, or

2. The claimant is *in locus poenitentiae* (withdrew before consummation of the illegal bargain).

D. Remitter's Liability
A mere agent or depository of the proceeds of an illegal transaction is not permitted to assert the defense of illegality in an action to recover the proceeds by a party to the illegal transaction.

E. Types of Illegal Contracts and Effects of Illegality:

1. Covenants Not to Compete
Unless made in bad faith, courts enforce such covenants up to the point that is reasonably necessary to protect the employer's interest without imposing undue hardship on the employee.

2. Inducing Official Action

a. Contingent fee arrangements for services in securing the passage of legislation are strictly scrutinized.

b. Contingent fees for lawyers are permissible because they ensure the most humble citizen equal justice under the law.

3. Bribery

a. A contract in which an employee is bribed to take official action is illegal and unenforceable. Most courts will not enforce such a contract even if one party was unjustly enriched.

b. If a party bribes a third party in order to help him perform his obligations under a contract, the contract will not be enforced if public policy is strongly frustrated.

4. Licensing
   If the purpose of a licensing requirement is protection of the public, the want of a license will render the contract for the unlicensed services unenforceable (e.g., uncertified doctor, lawyer, etc.).

5. Usury
   Loan agreements that charge interest rates in excess of the legal limit are unenforceable.

6. Wagering
   Although courts are unwilling to enforce private gambling contracts, they will grant restitution if

   a. The claimant is not *in pari delicto* with the defendant, or

   b. The claimant was *in locus poenitentiae*.

CASE CLIPS

Mundy v. Lumberman's Mut. Cas. Co. (1986) DHH
Facts: Mundy, an assistant district attorney, was robbed of silverware from his home. The insurance policy in effect at the time of the robbery limited recovery for the loss of silverware to $1,000, although an earlier edition of the policy had contained no such limit. A copy of the new insurance policy, which had been sent to Mundy, contained multiple references to changes made from the old policy, including a one-page summary of the changes, each identified in a separate paragraph and set off from the others by added space and black dots. Mundy argued that the insurance company's notice was inadequate, and thus entitled him to full recovery.
Issue: How should a court decide whether changes made to an insurance policy are binding upon the insured?
Rule: Where a casual reading of the material would give a party notice of changes in an insurance policy (e.g., written in large print or bold type), the insured is bound by limits of the new policy upon receipt, regardless of whether actual notice is effected.

Henningsen v. Bloomfield Motors, Inc.
(1960) DHH, KGK, FE, MS

Facts: Henningsen purchased a new car from Bloomfield Motors. His wife was injured when the steering failed ten days after the car was delivered. All implied warranties of merchantability were disclaimed by a clause buried in the fine print on the back of the contract.

Issue: In an adhesion contract, can a manufacturer or dealer disclaim all warranties of merchantability?

Rule: When there is vastly unequal bargaining power between the parties to a contract, contract clauses that disclaim the implied warranty of merchantability are void as against public policy.

Ellsworth Dobbs, Inc. v. Johnson (1967) DHH

Facts: Ellsworth Dobbs, a real-estate broker, drew up a sales contract between two parties, the defendants, which was conditioned on the acquisition of adequate financing by one of the parties. Ellsworth Dobbs' commission was to be paid by the seller. After the deal collapsed because of the inability of the buyer to arrange financing, Ellsworth Dobbs sued for its commission.

Issue: Is a sales contract term, drawn up by a broker, valid if it charges a commission without regard to whether the sale is actually consummated?

Rule: A contract clause resulting from the superior bargaining power of a broker is invalid if it requires a seller to pay a commission whether or not title passes to a buyer.

Broemmer v. Abortion Services of Phoenix (1992) DHH

Facts: Broemmer desired to receive an abortion from the defendant clinic. Upon her arrival at the clinic, Broemmer was directed to complete three forms, one of which contained an agreement to arbitrate any dispute arising between the parties as a result of the procedure. The clinic made no attempt to explain the agreement, nor did it provide copies of the form, and Broemmer could not recall signing the agreement. Broemmer was injured by the procedure, and attempted to bring suit in state court.

Issue 1: What is an adhesion contract?

Rule 1: An adhesion contract is a standardized form offered on a 'take it or leave it' basis, where the offeror does not afford the consumer a realistic opportunity to bargain, and refuses service to the consumer unless the contract is agreed to.

Issue 2: When is a provision contained in an adhesion contract enforceable?

Rule 2: An adhesion contract is fully enforceable according to its terms, unless the contract falls outside the reasonable expectations of the adhering party, or the contract is unconscionable. Since the provision in this case was neither negotiated for nor explained, it would be unreasonable to enforce.

Halbman v. Lemke (1980) DHH

Facts: Lemke sold a car to Halbman, a minor. Halbman took the car to a garage for repairs but refused to pay the bill. Halbman later disaffirmed the purchase contract, and the garage sold parts of the car to recover its money. The car was also vandalized. Halbman sued to recover the purchase price.

Issue: Is a minor who disaffirms a contract for an item that is not a necessity and tenders the property to the seller liable for damage to the property prior to the disaffirmance?

Rule: Absent misrepresentation or tortious damage to the property, a minor who disaffirms a contract for the purchase of an item that is not a necessity may recover his purchase price without liability for use, depreciation, damage, or other diminution in value.

Faber v. Sweet Style Mfg. Corp. (1963) DHH

Facts: Faber, who suffered from manic-depressive psychosis, underwent an almost total character change, freely spending his money on cars and investments, including the purchase of vacant land from Sweet Style. There was conflicting testimony by psychiatrists on the effect of the psychosis on Faber's judgment.

Issue: May a contract be voided due to incompetence if a party enters it under compulsion of a mental disease?

Rule: Incompetence to contract arises not only when capacity to understand is hindered, but also when a contract is entered into under the compulsion of a mental disease or disorder but for which the contract would not have been made.

Odorizzi v. Bloomfield School Dist. (1966) DHH, KC

Facts: Odorizzi, a teacher, was arrested for alleged homosexual activity. Immediately after he was released on bail, Bloomfield school district officials came to his home and made him sign a resignation, promising that if he did so, his "crime" would be kept quiet. Odorizzi was later acquitted of the charges and sued to rescind the resignation on grounds of undue influence by the school district.

Issue: Can a weak and vulnerable party rescind a contract that it assented to because of excessive pressure used by a dominant party?

Rule: A contract can be rescinded for undue influence if circumstances show that the agreement was reached through use of excessive persuasion by a dominant party against a weak and vulnerable one. Factors used to determine if excessive force was used are discussion or consummation of the transaction at an unusual place or time, insistent demands to get the business done at once, use of multiple persuaders against a single servient party and absence of and dissuasion of the need for third-party advisers to the servient party.

Austin Instrument, Inc. v. Loral Corp. (1971)
DHH, KGK, MS, CPB

Facts: Loral had a contract to produce radar sets for the Navy. The sets had 40 component parts, of which Austin, a subcontractor, produced 23. When Loral received a second contract from the Navy, Austin bid on all 40 parts, threatening to stop delivery of all parts on the first contract if it did not receive a price increase and the subcontract for all 40 parts of the second contract. After unsuccessfully checking with all the other subcontractors on its approved list, Loral agreed to Austin's demands so as to avoid breaching its contract with the Navy.

Issue: Is a contract modification enforceable if it was agreed to by a party who was deprived of free will under circumstances amounting to economic duress?

Rule: A contract is voidable if the party claiming duress was forced to agree by means of a wrongful threat precluding the exercise of his free will. The existence of economic duress is demonstrated by proof that immediate possession of needed goods is threatened and that the goods could not be obtained from another source.

Alaska Packer's Assoc. v. Domenico (1902) DHH, KC

Facts: Sailors contracted to work for Alaska Packer's as fishermen in Alaska, at a rate of $60 for the season plus two cents for each fish caught. Upon arrival in Alaska, the sailors refused to work unless they received higher wages. Alaska Packer's agreed, due to the unavailability of alternative fishermen. Alaska Packer's subsequently refused to pay the higher wages.

Issue: Is an agreement to increase compensation for services that the promisee is already contractually obligated to perform enforceable?

Rule: A new promise to increase the compensation of one already contractually obligated to perform is invalid (pre-existing duty rule).

Brian Constr. & Dev. Co. Inc. v. Brighenti (1978) DHH

Facts: The plaintiff, a contractor, hired the defendant, a subcontractor, to excavate, grade and landscape a foundation for a building. Unanticipated difficulties arose when the defendant unexpectedly discovered rubble from another building on the site which made the work much more costly. The plaintiff orally promised to pay more after the defendant refused to continue. The defendant returned to work but quit after a week. He claimed he did not breach the contract because he did not give new consideration for the plaintiff's oral promise.

Issue: If unanticipated events make the required performance excessively burdensome, and the parties agree to adjust the compensation, does a valid new contract exist?

Rule: Where a subsequent agreement imposes upon the one seeking greater compensation an additional obligation or burden not previously assumed, the agreement is supported by consideration and is valid and binding upon the parties.

Note: This case illustrates the "unforeseen circumstances" exception to the pre-existing duty rule.

Universal Builders, Inc. v. Moon Motor Lodge, Inc.
(1968) DHH, FE, MS

Facts: Universal's construction contract with Moon provided in part that all requests for building modifications had to be written and signed by Moon or its architect. Moon's agent orally requested modifications and promised to pay. Although the agent watched the work being done, Moon refused to pay.

Issue: Is an unwritten contract modification that was agreed upon by both parties valid if a contract requires that modifications must be in writing?

Rule: The effectiveness of a non-written modification, in spite of a contract condition that modifications must be in writing, depends upon whether enforcement of the condition is or is not barred by equitable considerations. When one party materially changes its position in reliance on the other party's waiver of a contract condition that modifications must be in writing, the condition will not be enforced.

Hackley v. Headley (1881) DHH, KGK

Facts: Hackley hired Headley to cut logs. Hackley disputed Headley's bill at the end of the job and tendered a smaller sum, which Headley was forced to accept due to financial difficulties. Headley signed a release accepting Hackley's payment as full satisfaction of the debt. Headley sought to rescind the release claiming it was obtained through economic duress.

Issue: Is it economic duress to merely refuse to pay a debt?

Rule: The exercise of a legal right, such as the right to honestly dispute the value of services, does not constitute economic duress.

Headley v. Hackley (1883) DHH

Facts: To settle a disputed debt he owed Headley, Hackley tendered a smaller sum which was accepted. Headley claimed the settlement was void because Hackley manufactured a dispute in bad faith to extort a compromise.

Issue: Is a compromise agreement binding if a party negotiates in bad faith to obtain favorable terms?

Rule: A compromise agreement is unenforceable if one party obtained favorable terms by acting unfairly or oppressively and asserting claims that it knew to be void of right.

Marton Remodeling v. Jensen (1985) DHH

Facts: Jensen hired Marton to do remodeling work on his home. The parties disagreed over the amount of the bill. Jensen sent a check for a smaller sum with the condition that endorsement of the check on the back by Marton would constitute full satisfaction. Marton cashed the check after writing "not full payment" on it and sued for the balance owed.

Issue: Has an accord and satisfaction occurred if a check marked "payment in full" is cashed with express protest?

Rule: An accord and satisfaction occurs even if a "payment in full" check is cashed under protest.

Note: UCC § 1-207 does not displace the common law rule of accord and satisfaction.

Denney v. Reppert (1968) DHH, R

Facts: In response to a reward offered by a bank, Denney and many other bank employees gave information that led to the conviction of bank robbers. The reward was given to Reppert, a policeman from another jurisdiction, who assisted in the conviction. Denney sued to receive part of the reward.

Issue: Can a reward offered to the general public be claimed by employees or public officials who acted within the scope of their employment or official duties?

Rule: If a party is already under a legal obligation to perform an act being rewarded, he has not provided consideration for the reward. A policeman is not legally obligated to assist in law enforcement outside of his jurisdiction, and such actions can therefore constitute consideration for a reward.

Jackson v. Seymour (1952) DHH

Facts: Jackson, in need of money, sold a tract of land to her brother, Seymour, for $275. Unknown to both, the land contained valuable timber, on which Seymour made a profit of $2,300. Jackson wished to rescind her sale.

Issue: Can a contract be annulled because the consideration furnished by a party substantially exceeded the value of the consideration it received?

Rule: Generally, inadequate consideration is not grounds for rescinding an agreement. However, if the inadequacy is such as to shock the sensitivities, an agreement can be annulled on grounds of constructive (not actual) fraud. Factors to be considered are the relationship of the parties, the inadequacy of the price, the parties' financial positions and the relative knowledge of the parties.

Note: The court granted Jackson rescission of the sale on the basis of these factors.

Sherwood v. Walker (1887) DHH, KGK, FE

Facts: Both parties believed that the cow Sherwood was buying from Walker was barren. Just before Walker delivered the cow he realized it was impregnated and, therefore, worth about ten times as much. Walker tried to rescind the contract.

Issue: Can a contract be rescinded if both parties are mistaken as to a material fact about the substance of the transaction?

Rule: No contract exists if the parties act under a mutual mistake of fact which is central to the "very nature" of the contract. Mistakes relating to "mere quality" are not grounds for rescission.

Laidlaw v. Organ (S.Ct.1817) KGK

Facts: Organ was negotiating to buy tobacco from Laidlaw. Organ heard news of the Treaty of Ghent which ended the War of 1812 and the British blockage of New Orleans, and would cause an increase in the price of tobacco. When Laidlaw asked Organ if he had heard any news which would raise the price of the tobacco, Organ said that he did not. Subsequently, Organ bought the tobacco, but Laidlaw retrieved it after he heard of the Treaty and the resulting increase in the price of tobacco. Organ sued to recover the tobacco, and Laidlaw argued that Organ committed fraud by not disclosing news of the peace treaty.

Issue: Does a vendee have a duty to disclose information exclusively in his possession that is relevant to the price of a commodity?

Rule: (Marshall, C.J.) A vendee has no duty to disclose information exclusively in his possession that is relevant to the price of a commodity. It would be difficult to fashion a rule that compels disclosure when the methods of obtaining information are equally accessible to both parties.

Edwards v. Trinity & Brazes Valley Ry. Co. (1909) DHH

Facts: The defendant contracted to remove at least 5,000 cubic yards of gravel and sand from the plaintiffs' property each month. The defendant stopped its operations when it realized that the cost would be far more expensive than contemplated. The plaintiffs sued to recover royalties they would have been paid if the minimum amount of gravel and sand had been removed.

Issue: Can a party rescind a contract it entered into under a unilateral mistake?

Rule: A contract can be rescinded due to unilateral mistake that goes to the very essence of the contract (i.e., the existence of its subject matter).

Elsinore Union Elementary School District v. Kastorff
(1960) DHH, KGK, FE

Facts: Kastorff, a contractor, submitted an erroneous bid for work that was being contracted out by the school district. Kastorff had told the school district that the figures were correct because he did not know of the error. He notified the school district upon learning of the error, which was caused by a clerical mistake. The school district "accepted" the bid despite knowing of the error. Kastorff refused to do the work.

Issue: Is a party relieved of its obligation to perform because its offering price was erroneously calculated?

Rule: A party may be relieved of the obligation to perform according to its offer if the party to whom the offer was made knew, or had reason to know, of a material error in calculation of the price.

Note: Although courts grant relief for clerical errors, this is not the case with errors of judgment, i.e., if a contractor underestimates his costs.

Hinson v. Jefferson (1975) DHH

Facts: The defendants sold land to the plaintiff that was restricted by its deed to residential use only. The plaintiff had to build a septic tank to handle sewage. Before beginning work on the septic tank, the plaintiff was informed that she would have to spend several hundred thousand dollars to prepare the land for the tank because of a nearby marsh. The defendants did not know of the problem when they sold the land.

Issue: Is rescission appropriate if there is a mutual mistake at the time of contract as to the suitability of land for its intended use?

Rule: Although the doctrine of mutual mistake is not applicable in this jurisdiction (North Carolina), a contract may be rescinded where a deed contains restrictive covenants, and subsequent discoveries, which were unknown and not reasonably discoverable by the seller at the time of contract, show that the property cannot be put to the limited use permitted.

Johnson v. Healy (1978) DHH

Facts: Johnson bought a house built by Healy, relying on Healy's assertions that the house was made of the best material and was without defects. After purchase, the house began to settle in such a way as to cause major displacements in foundation walls, and damage to sewer lines. Healy had no knowledge of the faulty construction when he sold the house.

Issue 1: What is the scope of liability for innocent misrepresentation (e.g., misleading statements made without knowledge or intent to deceive)?

Rule 1: Under Connecticut law, strict liability is imposed for innocent misrepresentation, as long as the statements can be reasonably understood as an assertion that the vendor has sufficient factual knowledge of the product, and could reasonably induce reliance by the purchaser.

Issue 2: What is the proper measure of damages for breach of warranty by a vendor?

Rule 2: Damage awards for breach of warranty should serve to place a party in the same position as they would have enjoyed had the good been as warranted.

Cushman v. Kirby (1987) DHH, R

Facts: Plaintiffs purchased a home from Mr. and Mrs. Kirby. During an inspection of the premises, the plaintiffs asked about the quality of the water on the lot, to which Mrs. Kirby answered, "It's good. It's fine. It's a little hard, but the system downstairs will take care of it." Mr. Kirby, who was present, remained silent. Upon moving into the home, the plaintiffs discovered the water was actually sulfur water, which, due to its foul smell and taste, required treatment to become "tolerable." Instead of using the water on the lot, the plaintiffs chose to hook up to the city water supply and sue for misrepresentation.

Issue 1: What is the legal standard to be applied to determine the ocurrence of an intentional misrepresentation?

Rule 1: When a vendor asserts that she has full information, and discloses only part of the information with the intent to deceive, she is guilty of fraud if the statements are relied upon by the purchaser.

Issue 2: When does a vendor's silence rise to the level of misrepresentation?

Rule 2: Silence alone is insufficient to constitute fraud, unless there is a duty to speak. A duty to speak is created where material facts are accessible to the vendor only, and he knows they are not available to the purchaser.

American Home Improvement Co. v. MacIver (1964) KGK

Facts: American Home, a contractor, hired to make improvements to MacIver's home, persuaded MacIver to apply for financing for the work. MacIver was obligated to pay nearly $2,600, with the additional financing charges, for work whose actual value was $960. MacIver canceled the contract, and American Home sued for breach. MacIver moved to dismiss because American Home failed to disclose all the finance charges in violation of a state statute.

Issue: Is a contract that does not reveal the presence of significant financing charges to the paying party invalid?

Rule: A contract is void as unconscionable if it fails to reveal charges that contribute significantly to the contract price. This is sufficient ground for contract invalidation, independent of any statutory violations that may exist.

Williams v. Walker-Thomas Furniture Co.
(1965) KGK, FE, KC, MS, R

Facts: Walker-Thomas sold a number of household items to Williams, on an installment plan. The sales contract had an "add on" clause, which stated that all of Williams' purchases were consolidated into a single debt, and that any payment would be credited equally, among all the items. The effect of the clause was that Williams would only own an item after she has paid for *all* of them. In case of default, the furniture was to be repossessed. Walker-Thomas sued to replevy the items, and Williams contested the contract.

Issue: Can a court refuse to enforce an unconscionable contract?

Rule: Where the element of unconscionability is present at the time the contract is made, the contract should not be enforced. Unconscionability has generally been recognized to include an absence of meaningful choice on the part of one of the parties in conjunction with contract terms unreasonably favorable to the other party. (UCC § 2-302.)

Patterson v. Walker-Thomas Furniture Co. (1971) KGK

Facts: Patterson defaulted on installment payments for goods she bought from Walker-Thomas, a furniture store. Patterson claimed the price of the goods was unconscionably high. She introduced no other factual support for her claim.

Issue: Is an unsupported, conclusory allegation of excessively high prices sufficient to establish unconscionability?

Rule: Sufficient facts surrounding the commercial setting, purpose and effect of a contract at the time it was made must be alleged to establish a valid claim of unconscionability and discovery of evidence to support that claim should be allowed. Unconscionability consists of both an excessively high price and absence of meaningful choice.

Jones v. Star Credit Corp. (1969) KGK

Facts: The Joneses, welfare recipients, were to pay $1,234.80 (including tax, finance charges, and insurance) for a freezer that ordinarily retailed for less than $300. UCC § 2-302 provided that a court may refuse to enforce a contract or excise an objectionable clause if it finds that the contract or clause was unconscionable at the time it was made.

Issue: Can a contract be void for unconscionability because the price term is excessive?

Rule: A court may refuse to enforce an excessive price term on the grounds of unconscionability.

Kugler v. Romain (1971) KGK

Facts: Romain sold educational books at two and one-half times the retail maximum price using a form contract. Romain's sales solicitations, consciously directed toward consumers of limited education and economic means, represented the exorbitant price as a competitive market rate. Pursuant to a state statute, Attorney General Kugler sued claiming fraud and misrepresentation.

Issue: Is a contract unenforceable if its price is unconscionable in relation to the cost to the seller and the value to the buyer?

Rule: A sales contract is invalid if a price, unilaterally fixed and not open to negotiation, is unconscionable in relation to the cost to the seller and the value to the consumers.

Stilk v. Myrick (1809) KGK

Facts: After two sailors jumped ship, the defendant captain offered to divide their pay among the rest of the crew if they would finish the voyage shorthanded. Upon the captain's refusal to pay the extra wages a member of the crew sued.

Issue: Is an agreement for higher wages brought about as a result of an emergency situation enforceable?

Rule: Adjustments of an employment contract which are prompted by emergency situations are void for want of consideration under the pre-existing duty rule.

Lingenfelder v. Wainwright Brewery Co. (1891) KGK

Facts: Wainwright hired an architect to design and supervise the construction of its brewery. The architect walked off the job after Wainwright awarded a different job to his competitor. Pressed for time, Wainwright promised to pay the architect extra compensation if he resumed work. Wainwright claimed it received no consideration for its promise. The architect's executor sought to enforce the modification.

Issue: Does the resumption of work one was contractually obligated to perform constitute sufficient consideration for a promise that induced the return to work?

Rule: A new contract that was signed to prevent one party from breaching an earlier agreement will fail for lack of consideration.

Note: This is the "pre-existing duty" rule.

Goebel v. Linn (1882) KGK

Facts: The plaintiff, an ice supplier, informed the defendants, brewers, that it could not supply the contractually required amount because of a shortage in the ice crop. The beer brewers needed the ice and agreed to pay more. The ice company sued after the brewers defaulted on the payments.

Issue: Is an agreement for a party to receive additional compensation for contractual duties enforceable?

Rule: Absent a showing of duress, an agreement for a party to receive additional payment for pre-existing contractual duties is enforceable.

Schwartzreich v. Bauman-Basch, Inc. (1921) KGK, KC, R

Facts: Schwartzreich contracted to work for Bauman-Bausch for one year at $90 a week. Before beginning work, Schwartzreich was offered $115 a week by another employer. Bauman-Basch offered to raise his weekly salary to $100, and Schwartzreich accepted. Another contract was made, reflecting the new salary provision, and the old one was simultaneously torn up. Bauman-Basch fired him before the year passed, claiming the second contract was unenforceable for lack of consideration.

Issue: Is a new contract that replaces a prior contract with terms that are similar but more favorable to one party enforceable?

Rule: When an existing contract is terminated by mutual consent and a new one is executed in its place, the mutual promises of the parties constitute consideration. Any changes to an existing contract must have new consideration to support it.

Skinner v. Tober Foreign Motors, Inc. (1963) KGK

Facts: Tober sold Skinner and other plaintiffs an airplane on an installment plan. When Skinner had to replace a faulty engine and was unable to bear the financial burden, Tober orally agreed to reduce the installment payments for the first year. Tober reneged on its promise claiming it was unenforceable for lack of consideration.

Issue: Is an oral modification invalid because it is not supported by consideration?

Rule: According to UCC § 2-209(1), an agreement that modifies an existing contract between merchants needs no consideration to be binding.

Foakes v. Beer (1884) KGK

Facts: Beer, Foakes's creditor, agreed to forgive all the interest on Foakes's loan if he paid a quarter of the principal at once and the rest in installments. After Foakes completed the installments, Beer sued for the interest.

Issue: Will an agreement to forego the interest due on a loan in exchange for payment of the principal fail for lack of consideration?

Rule: A creditor's agreement to forego interest on a debt in exchange for repayment of principal fails for lack of consideration because the debtor only agreed to do that which he was already obligated to perform (pre-existing duty rule).

Fitts v. Panhandle & S.F. Ry. (1920) KGK

Facts: Fitts signed a release of claims in exchange for a recited consideration of $1 and one day's employment after he was injured by Panhandle's negligence. Fitts sued for his injuries claiming the $1 was not paid.

Issue: Is a contract rendered invalid when small recited consideration is not actually paid?

Rule: Although small consideration may be adequate to support a contract, the failure to actually pay the recited consideration will invalidate the agreement.

Note: Hiring a party is not consideration for a separate contract, because the party's labor is given for the wages.

Ricketts v. Pennsylvania R.R. (1946) KGK

Facts: When Ricketts sued under the Federal Employer's Liability Act, the railroad denied liability because Ricketts signed two releases of his claims for damages. Ricketts claimed that both releases were falsely represented to him by his agent as receipts for back wages and tips.

Issue: Is a party bound by a release that was secured by the false representations of his own agent?

Rule: A party is not bound by a release that was secured through the misrepresentations of his own agent who was acting beyond the scope of his authority.

Consolidated Edison Co. of New York, Inc. v. Arroll
(1971) KGK, R

Facts: After disputing the amount of his electric bills, the defendant arbitrarily selected the amount he thought the bills should have been and sent checks that bore the legend "this check is in full payment and satisfaction." Con Edison cashed the checks and sued to recover what it felt was still owed.

Issue: Does writing the phrase "full payment and satisfaction" on a check that is tendered for less than the disputed amount of a debt result in a full accord and satisfaction?

Rule: When an amount due is in bona fide dispute, and the debtor sends a check for less than the amount claimed and clearly expresses his intention that the check has been sent as payment in full, cashing or retention of the check by the creditor is deemed an acceptance by the creditor of the conditions stated and operates as an accord and satisfaction of the claim.

Note: Under UCC § 1-107, a creditor can reserve his rights to the outstanding debt.

Hudson v. Yonkers Fruit Co., Inc. (1932) KGK

Facts: The plaintiff asked the defendant to procure a purchaser for the plaintiff's apples, which it did. The plaintiff claimed that the service was offered free of charge while the defendant claimed an express commission agreement was made. The defendant deducted a 10 percent commission and sent the balance by check to the plaintiff, who cashed it and sued to recover the commission.

Issue: Does acceptance of a check for less than the full amount owed by a fiduciary agent result in a settlement?

Rule: A fiduciary's payment of less than the full amount owed to the principal does not result in an accord and satisfaction.

Note: Among the court's considerations was the fact that the principal was actually receiving his own money.

Petterson v. Pattberg (1928) KGK

Facts: Pattberg held a mortgage on Petterson's property and offered to reduce it if Petterson paid off the mortgage by a certain time. Petterson tendered payment according to the terms of the offer, but Pattberg had already sold the mortgage to another party. The plaintiff was the executrix of Petterson's estate.

Issue: Is an offer to enter into a unilateral contract revocable before the other party performs the act requested?

Rule: An offer to enter into a unilateral contract is revocable at any time before the other party performs the requested act.

Goldbard v. Empire State Mutual Life Ins. Co.
(1958) KGK, CPB

Facts: Goldbard, a barber, filed for insurance benefits after he was infected by a fungus. The insurer disputed the claim, and Goldbard filed a complaint with the State Insurance Department. The insurer offered to settle the claim for a lesser amount. Goldbard telephoned the department representative and, without any discussion of precise terms, accepted the insurer's offer to settle the claim. But when the insurer sent a release form to execute the settlement, Goldbard ignored it and sued for the entire claim.

Issue: When does a subsequent agreement substitute for an existing contract?

Rule: For a subsequent agreement to supersede an existing contract, the parties must objectively manifest such an intent and all the requirements for an enforceable contract must be satisfied (such as a writing where compelled by statute).

Boshart v. Gardner (1935) KGK

Facts: Boshart, the assignee of the Gardners' promissory note and mortgage, agreed to reduce the Gardners' debt by half if they took out a loan to pay the amount immediately. After the Gardners had expended a substantial sum in complying with the settlement offer, Boshart instituted an action in foreclosure when the Gardners' application for the loan was delayed.

Issue: Is a contract of novation supported by sufficient consideration if a party expends a substantial sum of money in an attempt to comply with the terms of the agreement?

Rule: A contract of novation is supported by valid consideration when a party detrimentally relies on the terms of the substitute agreement. The offeror has to wait for a reasonable time (60 days) before revoking his offer.

Raffles v. Wichelhaus (1864) KGK, R

Facts: The contract stated that the plaintiff was to deliver the goods on the ship *Peerless*. Unknown to both parties there were two different ships bearing the same name but sailing at different times. The defendant refused the plaintiff's goods because he expected the delivery to be made on the *Peerless* which sailed earlier.

Issue: Is there a contract if each party gives a different meaning to a material ambiguity in the contract?

Rule: There is no binding contract if the parties unknowingly assign different meanings to an important contract term. Parol evidence may be given to prove that the parties attributed different meanings to a term.

Miller v. Stanich (1930) KGK

Facts: The defendant leased one of the plaintiff's properties for a term of five years, retaining an option for an additional five-year term. At the end of the period, the defendant notified the plaintiff's lawyer that he wished to exercise his option, and suggested the inclusion of a similar option in the new lease. The lawyer told the defendant that he did not believe his client would wish to include the option in the lease again. The defendant mailed two copies of the lease to the plaintiff, identical in all respects except for the inclusion of the option in one. The plaintiff mistakenly signed and returned the copy of the lease that included the option.

Issue: May a party seek rescission of a contract based on a unilateral mistake?

Rule: Absent fraud by the nonmistaken party, a contract may not be rescinded on the ground of unilateral mistake.

Wood v. Boynton (1885) KGK, CPB

Facts: Wood sued for rescission when she learned that a stone she sold to Boynton for $1 was worth $700.

Issue: Can a seller rescind a sale if both parties were mistaken as to the value of the product sold?

Rule: If there is no evidence of fraud, a mutual mistake as to the value of the product sold is not grounds for rescission of the sale.

McRae v. Commonwealth Disposals Commission (1951) KGK

Facts: The McRaes' offer to purchase a grounded oil tanker was accepted. It was found later that the specified tanker never existed and that before the sale the seller, the Commission, had no more definite information as to the existence of the tanker than a previous single offer and "mere gossip." The Commission claimed mutual mistake when the McRaes sued for salvage preparation expenses they incurred.

Issue: May a party exempt itself from liability by relying on its own mistake regarding the terms of a contract?

Rule: A party may not avoid a contract due to mistake when the mistake was induced by the serious fault of its own servants.

Swinton v. Whitinsville Sav. Bank (1942) KGK

Facts: The Whitinsville Bank knew the house that Swinton was purchasing from it was infested with termites but it did not disclose this information to Swinton.

Issue: Is a party to a contract obligated to reveal known latent defects to the other party?

Rule: There is no liability for bare nondisclosure when parties deal at arm's length, provided a false representation or attempt to conceal the condition was not made.

Sardo v. Fidelity & Deposit Co. (1926) FE

Facts: Sardo wished to obtain theft insurance for jewelry in his store. The defendant issued an insurance policy that covered securities instead of jewelry, even though there were no securities in Sardo's store. Sardo did not read the policy and mistakenly assumed that it covered jewelry. Sardo's store was robbed, and the defendant refused coverage. Sardo brought suit and had the policy reformed to include jewelry.

Issue: In the absence of fraud, when may a contract be reformed?

Rule: A contract may be reformed, in the absence of fraud, when after the parties have come to a "meeting of the minds," a mutual mistake is made in drafting the contract such that the writing does not reflect the actual intent of the parties. An assumption by one party made without reading a contract does not amount to mutual mistake.

Johnson v. United Investors Life Ins. Co. (1978) FE

Facts: The insurance company's agent assured Johnson's husband that his insurance policy would provide double indemnity coverage for death resulting from piloting a private aircraft. After he died while engaged in this activity, the insurance company showed that the policy did not provide such coverage. Johnson sued for reformation of the policy on the ground of mutual mistake.

Issue: Will an insurance policy be reformed if the mutual intent of the parties is not expressed in the agreement's provisions?

Rule: An insurance policy will be reformed if it is proved by a preponderance of clear and convincing evidence that, through mistake, the policy failed to express the mutual intent of the parties.

Gerhardt v. Continental Ins. Co. (1960) FE

Facts: Statements printed in large type in Gerhardt's insurance policy led her to believe that the coverage she desired was contained in the agreement. The insurance company demonstrated that the coverage Gerhardt desired was excluded by provisions buried in confusing fine print.

Issue: Is an obscure and inconspicuous provision of an insurance policy, which excludes coverage the policy seems to offer in large type, binding?

Rule: If an insurance policy contains obscure and inconspicuous provisions that exclude coverage that a party rationally expects, the party will not be bound by the terms of the policy because of the unequal bargaining positions and expertise of the insurance company.

Weaver v. American Oil Co. (1971) FE, MS, CPB

Facts: Unknown to Weaver, a clause in his standardized lease compelled him to indemnify American Oil, the lessor, for any damages or loss incurred as a result of American Oil's own negligence. The clause, which was never explained to Weaver, was written in small print and contained no title heading. Weaver claimed the clause was unconscionable after one of American's employees negligently injured Weaver and an assistant on the leased premises.

Issue: Is a contract clause obtained by the abuse of a party's superior bargaining position unconscionable?

Rule: The doctrine of unconscionability will invalidate a contract provision if, unknown to the lesser party, a stronger party uses his superior bargaining power to his advantage in instituting a contract provision that causes the lesser party great hardship (e.g., by unknowingly waiving valuable rights).

Toker v. Westerman (1970) FE, CPB

Facts: Westerman argued that he paid an "unconscionable" price for a refrigerator. Westerman was charged $1,229.76 for an appliance with a fair market value of between $350 and $400. Toker, the assignee of the seller, sued when Westerman refused to make full payment.

Issue: Can a contract be voided because its terms are "unconscionable?"

Rule: A contract can be voided because the price was unconscionable. (UCC § 2-302.)

Griffith v. Brymer (1903) FE

Facts: Griffith contracted to rent a room from Brymer for the purpose of viewing a coronation procession. Neither party was aware that the coronation had been canceled prior to the formation of the contract.

Issue: Is a contract void if there is a mutual mistake as to facts central to the purpose of the agreement?

Rule: A contract is void where both parties are under a misconception with regard to the existing state of facts about which they were contracting.

Lenawee County Bd. of Health v. Messerly (1982) FE, KC, CPB, R

Facts: Unknown to the Messerlys, a previous owner of the land had installed an illegal underground septic tank. The Messerlys then sold the property, which included a three-unit apartment building, to Pickles. The contract had an "as is" clause, which shifted the risk of unknown defects to Pickles. Six days after the sale, sewage from the tank oozed up to the surface of the property, and the county condemned the property until the sewage system could conform to the sanitation code.

Issue: Is a hidden defect sufficient grounds for rescission of a contract on the basis of mutual mistake?

Rule: A rescission on the grounds of mutual mistake may be granted when the mistake relates to a basic assumption of the parties upon which the contract is made, and which materially affects the agreed performances of the parties. However, where both parties are equally innocent and have agreed to allocate the risk of loss, rescission will not be granted.

Note: Courts are divided on the effectiveness of "as is" clauses. (Rest. 2d. § 124.)

Obde v. Schlemeyer (1960) FE

Facts: Schlemeyer knowingly sold a building without notifying the buyers, the Obdes, that it was infested with termites.

Issue: Is a seller of property under a duty to disclose known latent defects to prospective purchasers?

Rule: A seller of property must disclose the existence of known hidden defects to prospective purchasers, regardless of the latter's failure to ask any questions relative to the possibility of defects.

Travelers Ins. Co. v. Bailey (1964) FE

Facts: Travelers Insurance printed Bailey's correct descriptive information on the wrong life insurance policy form, giving Bailey more extensive coverage than he paid for. Bailey refused to accept Travelers' attempt to amend the policy so as to correct its mistake.

Issue: Is a party entitled to reformation of a contract where it is penalized by its own erroneous rendition of the agreement?

Rule: Where it is established beyond a reasonable doubt that a contractual agreement between parties was erroneously executed, the party penalized by the error is entitled to reformation, provided there has been no prejudicial change of position by the party benefitting from the mistake.

Bowling v. Sperry (1962) MS

Facts: Bowling sought to disaffirm a contract for the purchase of an automobile on the grounds that he was a minor. Sperry alleged the defenses that Bowling was accompanied by adults when he made the purchase, that Bowling damaged the car and that the car was a necessity.

Issue: Is a contract of a minor voidable if he was accompanied by an adult at the time of purchase?

Rule: Contracts of minors, except for necessities, are voidable even if the minor is accompanied by an adult at the time of purchase and/or the seller is not returned to the status quo.

Bobby Floars Toyota, Inc. v. Smith (1980) MS

Facts: The defendant, a minor at the time he bought an automobile, tried to disaffirm his contractual obligations with Bobby Floars by voluntarily relinquishing the car, ten payments and ten months after he attained majority.

Issue: Can a party disaffirm a contract, made while a minor, after he has reached majority?

Rule: A minor's privilege of disaffirmance may be lost where the infant affirms or ratifies the contract after reaching majority or if it attempts to disaffirm the contract after an unreasonable time.

Heights Realty, Ltd. v. Phillips (1988) MS

Facts: Gholson (the original defendant), an aged woman, signed a contract with Heights Realty, under which it listed Gholson's property for sale and found a buyer. Heights Realty was to receive a commission on the sale. The buyer offered an amount greater than the asking price, but Phillips, the conservator of her estate, refused to sell. Heights Realty sought its commission, and the defendant claimed mental incapacity as a defense.

Significant, but inconclusive evidence was presented to establish Gholson's incompetency and the trial court found for her.

Issue: May a party succeed with a defense of mental incompetence if there is conflicting evidence that indicates she understood the general purpose of the contract and possibly understood the specific terms?

Rule: There is a presumption of mental competency that can only be overcome by clear and convincing evidence. However, where a trial court has weighed all evidence and concluded that a party was mentally incompetent to contract, the presence of conflicting evidence is insufficient to overturn the decision on appeal.

Morta v. Korea Insurance Corp. (1988) MS

Facts: Morta was injured and his car was totaled by a driver who was insured by the defendant. Korea Insurance offered Morta $900, stating that it could offer no more. Morta accepted after consulting with a lawyer and released Korea Insurance from liability for all accident-related injuries, present and future. About a week after the settlement, Morta collapsed and awoke in a hospital, where he was treated for a blood clot and billed $11,000. Morta sued to recover damages, disavowing the release on the ground that Korea Insurance's agent misrepresented its contents.

Issue 1: Is a representation that an offer is the best offer a party can make a fraudulent representation if it is not true?

Rule 1: A representation that an offer is the best offer a party can make is the type of statement frequently made during negotiations and simply does not amount to fraud. This is especially true in the instant case because Morta was apprised otherwise by his lawyer.

Issue 2: Does mistake about the contents of a release justify rescission of the release?

Rule 2: When mistake about the contents of a release is caused by the neglect of the party making the mistake, such as a failure to read the release when given ample opportunity to do so, rescission is not justified.

Vokes v. Arthur Murray, Inc. (1968) MS, CPB

Facts: Vokes was unwittingly influenced by a constant and continuous barrage of flattery, false praise, and excessive compliments from Arthur Murray's employees to purchase thousands of hours of dancing lessons at the dance studio.

Issue: Are misrepresentations of opinion by a party possessing superior knowledge actionable?

Rule: A statement of a party having superior knowledge is regarded as a statement of fact, which is actionable if false, even though it would be deemed as opinion if the parties were dealing on equal terms.

Norton v. Poplos (1982) MS

Facts: Norton agreed to buy Poplos' property when Poplos innocently failed to inform him of zoning restrictions that would affect Norton's business. The contract contained disclaimers of liability for restrictions that were on record.

Issue: May a party rescind a contract because he relied on innocent material misrepresentations by the other party?

Rule: A party entering into a contract, justifiably relying upon an innocent but material misrepresentation of the other party, is entitled to rescission regardless of merger clauses or boiler-plate provisions to the contrary.

Hill v. Jones (1986) KC, MS

Facts: The Hills sued to rescind an agreement to purchase a house from the Jones, alleging that the Joneses had made misrepresentations concerning termite damage to the house, and had failed to disclose the existence of the damage and the history of termite infestation.

Issue: Does a seller of residential property have a duty to disclose defects?

Rule: Where the seller of a home knows of facts materially affecting the value of the property, which are not readily observable and are not known to the buyer, the seller is under a duty to disclose them to the buyer. The instant case was remanded for a jury determination of whether the termite damage was material and whether it was readily observable.

McRae v. Bolstad (1984) MS

Facts: The McRaes agreed to buy a house from the Bolstads. The Bolstads, their broker and the McRaes' broker all knew that the neighbor's sewage often spilled onto the property. The McRaes did not know this. However, they did find standing water on the front lawn and were required to have the property inspected in order to qualify for financing. When there was a sewage eruption in the house, the McRaes sued under the Consumer Protection Act.

Issue: When may a private individual institute an action under the Consumer Protection Act?

Rule: A private individual may institute an action under the Consumer Protection Act when the conduct complained of is unfair or deceptive, within the sphere of trade or commerce and impacts the public interest. The presence of public interest is demonstrated when the defendant induces the plaintiff to act or refrain from acting, the plaintiff suffers damages from such action or inaction and the defendant's deceptive acts or practices have the potential for repetition.

Note: The McRaes' action was sustained because the failure of a salesperson to disclose material facts is an inducement, damages were established, and the salesperson had publicly listed the house on several occasions and was likely to do so again.

Machinery Hauling, Inc. v. Steel of W. Virginia (1989) MS

Facts: Machinery Hauling was hired to deliver seventeen loads of steel for Steel. When all but three were delivered, Steel informed Machinery Hauling that the buyer had rejected the product. Steel directed Machinery Hauling to return the last three loads. Steel then instructed the plaintiff to pay it the price of the last three loads ($31,000) "or else it would cease to do business with plaintiff." The potential loss of business was over $1,000,000 per year. Machinery Hauling sought monetary damages for Steel's "extortionate demands."

Issue: Does the threat to discontinue business relations constitute economic duress?

Rule: Economic duress occurs where a party is forced into a transaction as a result of unlawful threats by another party that leaves it with no reasonable alternative but to acquiesce. Economic duress was not found in this case because the plaintiff did not accede to the defendant's demand and pay over the money, and the expectancy of future business prospects (as opposed to present contractual obligations) is not a right on which a claim of economic duress may be anchored.

Cutler Corp. v. Latshaw (1953) MS

Facts: Cutler contracted to remodel Latshaw's home but was told to stop because of defective work. The contract contained confession of judgment clauses buried in a mass of fine-print verbiage on the reverse side of each contract sheet.

Issue: Are important contract provisions, buried inconspicuously within a written agreement, enforceable?

Rule: A significant contract provision is unenforceable if it is concealed within a sea of fine print and inconspicuously located within the written agreement, because its importance must be brought to the attention of the other party.

Zapatha v. Dairy Mart, Inc. (1980) KC, MS

Facts: The Zapathas contracted to operate a franchise for Dairy Mart, whereby Dairy Mart provided the store and equipment and paid the utility bills in exchange for a percentage of gross profits. The contract was terminable without cause on 90 days notice provided Dairy Mart bought back 80 percent of the inventory. Dairy Mart terminated.

Issue: Is a contract clause that permits termination without cause unconscionable?

Rule: A contract provision that provides for termination without cause is not unconscionable if at the time of the execution of the agreement the provision could not result in unfair surprise, was not oppressive, and was not instituted in bad faith toward the allegedly disadvantaged party.

A & M Produce Co. v. FMC Corp. (1980) MS, R

Facts: A & M was a small farming company that was growing tomatoes for the first time. A & M contacted FMC to acquire the necessary packaging equipment. FMC informed A & M that their weight-sizers worked so fast that an additional hydrocooler would not be necessary. This proved to be false, and much of A & M's crop was damaged. The lengthy contract provided by FMC contained an inconspicuous disclaimer of warranties and a limitation on recovery of consequential damages.

Issue: Under what circumstances may terms in a commercial contract be held unconscionable and unenforceable?

Rule: Although there is a presumption that businesspersons have a greater degree of commercial understanding and economic muscle than ordinary consumers, a commercial contract may still be unconscionable if nonnegotiable terms on preprinted form agreements combine with disparate bargaining power to result in a socially or economically unreasonable allocation of commercial risks (i.e., a seller attempting to use waivers to prevent an inexperienced buyer from relying on product performance representations).

Sinnar v. Le Roy (1954) MS

Facts: The plaintiff gave a bribe in return for the defendant's promise to help the plaintiff obtain a liquor license. The defendant reneged, and the plaintiff sued to recover the bribe.

Issue: Is an illegal bargain enforceable?
Rule: Courts will not enforce an illegal bargain but will leave the parties where it finds them. Because these bargains violate public policy to a great degree, relief is denied on the basis of illegality if the issue appears in the evidence. A defendant cannot waive the defense if he wishes to do so.

Pearsall v. Alexander (1990) MS

Facts: Pearsall and Alexander regularly purchased D.C. lottery tickets together, reinvesting their small returns in more tickets. One lucky day, a ticket purchased and scratched by Alexander was a $20,000 winner. Alexander did not want to share the bounty. The Statute of Anne provided that "a thing in action ... or conveyance made and executed be a person in which any part of the consideration is for money ... won by playing any game whatsoever ... or for the reimbursement or payment of any money knowingly lent or advanced [to place a bet] is void. ...."
Issue: Is a claim to a share of lottery winnings enforceable?
Rule: A claim to a share of legal gambling winnings is enforceable where each man gives consideration for a share in the proceeds. The Statute of Anne does not bar such claims, because such consideration does not derive from one man besting the other in a game of chance or from any sort of a loan.

Homami v. Iranzadi (1989) MS

Facts: Iranzadi repaid Homami $40,000 on a $125,000 note that stated, "This note shall bear no interest." Homami claimed that the parties had orally agreed that there would be interest and had included the no-interest provision for the purpose of evading income taxes. The trial court concluded that the payment did indeed constitute interest, not principal and ruled that Homami was entitled to the full amount of the note.
Issue: Can a collateral agreement to pay interest on a note that explicitly states that it does not bear interest be enforced?
Rule: Where a note has no stated interest for the purpose of facilitating tax evasion, a collateral interest agreement will not be enforced because illegal contracts are never enforceable.

Town Planning & Eng'g Assoc., Inc. v. Amesbury Specialty Co., Inc. (1976) MS

Facts: Town was hired to prepare engineering plans for Amesbury. Although Amato, the president and major employee of Town, was not professionally licensed as required by statute, he used professional consultants throughout the work. Town sued for the balance of payments when Amesbury refused to pay.

Issue: Is a contract entered into by a firm unenforceable if its director is not professionally registered as required by statute?

Rule: A contract entered into by a firm is not automatically unenforceable if the person in charge is not professionally registered as required by statute. Although the criminal statute is aimed at protecting the public, other factors must be considered in order to determine the enforceability of the contract, including the extent of the illegal behavior, whether that behavior is a material or only an incidental part of the performance and how serious or deserved the forfeiture suffered by the plaintiff would be.

Colgan v. Agway Inc. (1988) MS

Facts: Colgan contracted with Agway for the construction of a manure storage facility. Under the agreement, Colgan was to prepare a construction site and provide a dirt ledge around the completed structure. Agway was to supply the plans and construct the facility. The contract provided a one-year warranty "for workmanship and materials ... expressly in lieu of any other warranty, expressed or implied." Three years after the facility was completed, one of the walls collapsed.

Issue: May a party contractually limit its liability for negligence?

Rule: A party may contractually limit its liability for negligence, provided that its terms were intended by both parties to apply to the particular conduct that has caused harm. Since the warranty in this case referred to work and materials, it did not limit the defendant's liability for negligent design.

Data Management, Inc. v. Greene (1988) MS

Facts: The defendants, former employees of Data, had signed a covenant not to compete with Data in Alaska for five years after termination. Shortly after the defendants' termination, Data sought an injunction to enjoin the defendants from rendering computing services to various named individuals.

Issue: Should courts enforce overly broad covenants not to compete?

Rule: Whenever possible, overly broad covenants not to compete should be reasonably altered by courts to render them enforceable, unless they were not drafted in good faith. The factors comprising reasonableness are the absence or presence of limitations as to time and space, whether the employee represents the sole contract with the customer, whether the employee is possessed with confidential information or trade secrets, whether the covenant seeks to eliminate unfair competition or ordinary competition, whether the covenant seeks to stifle the inherent skill and experience of the employee, whether the benefit to the employer is disproportionate to the detriment to the employee, whether the covenant operates to bar the employee's sole means of support, whether the talents the employer seeks to suppress were developed during the period of employment and whether the forbidden employment is merely incidental to the main employment.

Watts v. Watts (1987) KC, MS

Facts: The plaintiff and defendant lived together out of wedlock for twelve years in a relationship that produced two children. They shared bank accounts, made joint income tax returns, and were listed as husband and wife on other legal documents.

Issue: Does public policy preclude an unmarried cohabitant from asserting contract and property claims against the other party to the cohabitation?

Rule: Public policy does not necessarily preclude an unmarried cohabitant from asserting a contract claim against the other party to the cohabitation so long as the claim exists independently of the sexual relationship (i.e., is founded in breach of implied or express contract, *quantum meruit*, etc.) and is supported by separate consideration.

Angel v. Murray (1974) MS

Facts: After he signed a five-year garbage collection contract, Maher requested increased remuneration because an unanticipated construction boon substantially increased the number of homes from which he had to collect garbage. The city council agreed to pay more. Several years later, taxpayers, including the plaintiff Angel, brought suit against Murray, the Director of Finance for the city, claiming that no consideration was given for the promise to pay more.

Issue: Can a contract be modified because of unanticipated difficulties?

Rule: The pre-existing duty rule, voiding modification of a contract already in effect if no new consideration is given, will not apply, if a party to a contract encounters unanticipated difficulties and the other party, not influenced by coercion or duress, voluntarily agrees to pay additional compensation for work already required to be performed under the contract.

Roth Steel Prod. v. Sharon Steel Corp. (1983) MS

Facts: Sharon threatened to breach its contract to supply steel if Roth did not agree to price increases. Although Sharon's motive was due to rising costs, it did not offer this explanation until the case came to trial.

Issue: Is an attempted contract modification to compensate for rising costs ineffective if the party did not act in good faith?

Rule: Contract modification must be obtained in good faith by conduct that is both consistent with "reasonable commercial standards of fair dealing in the trade" and "honesty in fact," to be enforceable. (UCC § 2-103(1)(b).)

AFC Interiors v. DiCello (1989) MS

Facts: DiCello gave AFC a check for less than the full amount AFC expected. The check carried the notation that it constituted payment in full. AFC crossed this out and inserted "payment on account."

Issue: May a creditor accept a check but reject a "payment in full" condition?

Rule: If a creditor reserves his rights to disputed amounts, acceptance of the check is not recognized as an accord and satisfaction.

Seubert v. McKesson Corp. (1990) MS

Facts: Seubert signed an agreement that explicitly stated that he would be an at-will employee of the defendant. During the course of Seubert's employment, the defendant instituted a policy that a salesperson could be fired if not at quota for two consecutive quarters. Seubert was below quota for two consecutive quarters and was fired. There was evidence that he would have met the quotas but for the fact that the defendant's merchandise was defective and many customers returned their orders.

Issue: May an employee only be fired in good faith if there was an express written agreement that the employment is at-will?

Rule: While there is a presumption that employment is at-will, that presumption may be superseded by an express or implied contract that limits the employer's right to discharge the employee. The quota policy instituted by the defendant was an implied contract that required cause for termination.

Pettit v. Liston (1920) CPB

Facts: A minor purchased a motorcycle from Liston for $325 of which he paid $125 down, the balance to be paid in $25 monthly installments. After a month, the minor returned the machine and demanded his money back. Liston claimed he had damaged the machine in excess of $150.

Issue: May a minor, who has purchased and taken possession of an article, return it to the vendor and recover his money without paying for any damage?

Rule: When there has been no fraud or undue influence and the contract is fair and reasonable, a minor who has actually paid money on the purchase price and taken and used the article cannot recover the amount of money paid without allowing the vendor reasonable compensation for the use and depreciation of the article while in his hands.

Note: "The privilege of infancy is to be used as a shield and not as a sword."

Ortelere v. Teachers' Retirement Bd.
(1969) CPB, R

Facts: Ortelere's wife, a teacher, built up a reserve of $70,925 in the public retirement system. Ortelere quit his job to care for his wife when she suffered a nervous breakdown. Two months before she died, while suffering from mental illness, Ortelere's wife exercised an irrevocable option to take maximum retirement benefits, depriving him of any right to the remaining portion of her retirement fund at her death.

Issue: Is a contract voidable if a contracting party cannot act reasonably due to mental incapacity?

Rule: A person incurs only voidable contractual duties by entering into a transaction if, by reason of mental illness or defect, she is unable to act in a reasonable manner in relation to the transaction and the other party has reason to know of her condition.

Gallon v. Lloyd-Thomas Co. (1959) CPB

Facts: Gallon claimed that he was coerced into signing an unfavorable employment contract with his employers. In any event, he abided by the terms of the contract for the remaining time he was employed and did not bring legal action for nearly a year.

Issue 1: When is a contract voidable on the grounds of duress?

Rule 1: The contract is voidable when the threats of the person claiming the benefit of the contract eliminated the quality of mind in the victim essential to the making of the contract.

Issue 2: Is a contract entered into as a result of duress ratified after the duress is removed if no claim is made within a reasonable amount of time?

Rule 2: Ratification of a duress-induced contract results if the party who executed the contract under duress accepts the benefits flowing from it or remains silent for any considerable length of time after the opportunity is afforded to render it void.

Francois v. Francois (1979) CPB

Facts: Victor Francois signed a financially disastrous "Property Settlement and Separation Agreement" with his wife because she and her attorney persuaded him that it was the only way to save their marriage. Victor sought rescission of the agreement and reconveyance of all properties transferred to his wife.

Issue: When does the doctrine of undue influence permit the rescission of a contract?

Rule: A contract may be rescinded when a party's assent to an agreement is obtained through the subversion of that party's free will contrary to his own best interests.

Methodist Mission Home of Texas v. N_ A_ B_ (1970) CPB

Facts: Methodist Mission operated as a maternity home and licensed adoption agency to provide care to pregnant unwed females. In addition to board, lodging, and medical care, Methodist Mission provided counselling by trained social workers who strongly encouraged putting the children up for adoption. The lower court held that Methodist Mission used "undue influence" to get N_A_B_ to consent to the adoption of her soon-to-be born son.

Issue: When does the "undue influence" doctrine apply?

Rule: Not all influence is "undue" merely because it is persuasive and effective. The finding of "undue influence" is justified only where the actor's free agency and will have been destroyed or subverted to the extent that her act does not express her own will but instead reflects that of the person exerting the influence.

Cousineau v. Walker (1980) CPB

Facts: Cousineau purchased a 9.1 acre lot from Walker after seeing a listing that it contained a large quantity of gravel and 580 feet in highway frontage. However, there was no mention of the amount of gravel or highway frontage in the purchasing agreement. After signing the agreement, Cousineau discovered there was only 415 feet of highway frontage and a small quantity of gravel. He stopped making payments and sought rescission of the contract.

Issue: Is innocent misrepresentation a basis for the rescission of a contract?

Rule: A party is entitled to rescission of a land purchase contract on the basis of misrepresentation if it in fact relied on the statement, the statement concerned a material fact which a reasonable person might be expected to consider important in making a decision, and the reliance was justifiable.
Note: The court also held that caveat emptor did not apply to a purchaser of land and that the purchaser would only be barred from recovery if his actions in failing to discover the defects were irrational or in bad faith.

White v. Berenda Mesa Water Dist. (1970) CPB

Facts: White submitted a bid to build a reservoir for the District. He underestimated the amount of hard rock to be excavated and consequently his bid was too low. White rescinded his bid but the District had voted to accept it and sought to keep White's bid bond.
Issue: When will rescission be allowed for a unilateral mistake containing elements of fact and judgment?
Rule: While traditionally it is only mistakes of fact which permit a grant of relief, it is the facts surrounding the mistake, not a label of "fact" or "judgment" which should control. The law does require, however, that the mistake has not resulted from a party's neglect of a legal duty.

Bollinger v. Cent. Pennsylvania Quarry Stripping & Constr. Co. (1967) CPB

Facts: A written agreement allowed Pennsylvania Quarry to deposit waste on the Bollingers' property. The Bollingers averred that there was a mutual understanding mistakenly not included in the document that Pennsylvania Quarry would cover the waste with topsoil. Pennsylvania Quarry covered the waste at first, but later stopped.
Issue: Will a contract be reformed if part of the agreement was omitted by mutual mistake?
Rule: A court in equity has the power to reform the written evidence of a contract and make it correspond to the understanding of the parties if the omission was caused by mutual mistake. The fact that one of the parties denies that a mistake was made does not prevent a finding of mutual mistake.

K. D. v. Educational Testing Service (1976) CPB, R

Facts:. While registering to take the LSAT, K.D. signed a stipulation stating that the Educational Testing Service (ETS) "reserve[d] the right to cancel any test score if … there is adequate reason to question its validity."

Finding a suspiciously high correlation between K.D. and a nearby student, ETS offered a free retest as an alternative to canceling K.D.'s score. In seeking to enjoin the ETS from canceling his score (he refused the retest), K.D. claimed that he was not bound because it was a contract of adhesion, as he was unable to negotiate its terms or contract elsewhere.

Issue: When may a contract be voided on the grounds that it was an adhesion contract?

Rule: An offending clause of a contract of adhesion may be voided if it is found to be unfair and unreasonable. Here, the court found that ETS had taken a reasonable measure to protect its reputation for accurate aptitude forecasting.

Hewitt v. Hewitt (1974) CPB

Facts: The plaintiff and defendant agreed to live together and share assets and earnings as a husband and wife would. The plaintiff worked hard to support the defendant's education, business and social interests. Although the parties held themselves out as husband and wife, they were not formally married. Common law marriage was not recognized in their jurisdiction. The plaintiff sued to recover half the assets at separation.

Issue: Can two unmarried persons be required to share equally in income and assets if they agreed to such a plan, even though both were aware they were not legally married?

Rule: Courts can determine that the conduct of unmarried persons living together demonstrates an implied contract or an agreement of partnership or joint venture. A nonmarital partner can recover in *quantum meruit* for the reasonable value of services rendered, less the reasonable value of support received, if s/he can show that services were rendered with the expectation of monetary reward.

Troutman v. Southern Railway Co. (1971) CPB

Facts: The Interstate Commerce Commission issued an order which Southern Railway feared would have a detrimental effect on it and the entire southern economy. The railway turned to Troutman, a personal friend and ally of President John Kennedy, to persuade the President and Department of Justice to enter the case on the side of Southern. Troutman was successful, and the Justice Department helped Southern win in court against the I.C.C. Troutman demanded compensation for his services.

Issue: Is a contract to exert political and personal influence to gain access to an elected official enforceable?

Rule: Although a contract to use political and personal influence on a public official in the exercise of his duties is illegal and unenforceable, a contract is enforceable when it merely calls for a party to use personal and political influence to gain access and appeal to the judgment of a political official on the merits of the case.

Note: The burden of proving the illegality of the contract is on the party asserting the defense.

Northern Indiana Pub. Serv. Co. v. Carbon County Coal Co. (1986) CPB

Facts: NIPSCO, a public utility, entered into a long-term fixed-price contract to buy coal from Carbon County. Over time, this became a very expensive contract for NIPSCO. It sought to escape it on the grounds, among others, that Carbon County's coal sales are in violation of the Federal Mineral Land Leasing Act of 1920 due to an attenuated affiliation it enjoys with a railroad.

Issue: Will the court enforce a contract which contains elements of illegality?

Rule: The court will weigh the relative benefits of under-deterrence and over-deterrence of illegal behavior. If the illegal act is relatively minor, and it has injured neither the party with which it is contracting nor others, the contract will be enforced.

Bateman Eichler, Hill Richards, Inc. v. Berner (1985) CPB

Facts: A registered securities broker employed by Bateman Eichler induced the plaintiffs to invest in over-the-counter stock by divulging false and materially incomplete information about a company on the pretext it was accurate inside information. The investors purchased the stock, which initially increased dramatically but ultimately declined below the purchase price.

Issue: May a party assert the in pari delicto defense barring recovery when both parties are equal wrongdoers in private actions for damages based on federal securities law?

Rule: The in pari delicto defense is not permitted except where, as a direct result of his own actions, the plaintiff bears at least substantially equal responsibility for the violations he seeks to redress, and preclusions of suit would not significantly interfere with the effective enforcement of the securities laws and protection of the investing public.

Singleton v. Foreman (1970) CPB

Facts: Singleton employed Foreman to represent her in a divorce action. The parties signed a contract which contained provisions for retainer and contingency fees. Foreman was so verbally abusive and threatening in his behavior towards Singleton that she sought rescission and restitution of her retainer. Contracts for a contingency fee in divorce cases were void and unenforceable under Florida law.

Issue: May the court aid a party to an illegal contract?

Rule: If a party cannot be considered in pari delicto, the court may aid a party to the extent of returning the consideration which was tendered in performance of its part of the invalid contract.

Cochran v. Dellfava (1987) CPB

Facts: Cochran sought to recover from Dellfava for the money she lost in the so-called "airplane game." This enterprise was a chain distribution game which was prohibited by statute. Knowing it was illegal, Cochran agreed to play. After she had invested money in the scheme, she attempted to withdraw.

Issue: Are there exceptions to the general rule that the court will leave the parties to an illegal contract where their own acts have left them?

Rule: The court will aid a party when the conduct was prohibited by statute rather than by the nature of the conduct, the parties were not in pari delicto, and the plaintiff acted under duress, undue influence or out of good will.

Note: Cochran's claim failed because she intentionally promoted the game by entering it.

Copeland Process Corp. v. Nalews, Inc. (1973) CPB

Facts: Due to a delay in progress on two town projects and an upcoming meeting to account for such delay, Copeland, the contractor, terminated its subcontract with Nalews for labor, materials, and services. The letter of termination was a writing of an oral agreement between Nalews and Copeland stating that Nalews would be compensated for cost under the contract thus far and that otherwise the contract was mutually canceled "without prejudice." The language suggested that Nalews was not responsible for future costs incurred by Copeland in the project's completion.

Issue: What effect does mutual rescission of a contract have on the past and future obligations of the parties?

Rule: The obligations of parties following mutual rescission of a contract are to be determined by the intent of the parties as reflected in circumstances surrounding the contract and rescission.

Dodson v. Shrader (1992) KC

Facts: Dodson bought a truck from the Shraders when he was 16 years old. Nine months later, the truck began to develop engine trouble. Although Dodson was warned by a mechanic that repairs were probably necessary, Dodson ignored the advice and continued to drive the truck. One month later, the truck "blew up" and became inoperable. The truck was damaged further just before the trial, when it was struck by a hit-and-run driver while parked in Dodson's front yard. Dodson told the Shraders he wanted to return the truck, rescind the contract, and obtain a full refund.

Issue: If a party to a sales contract was a minor at the time the contract was made, can the party freely rescind the contract, return the goods, and obtain a full refund?

Rule: If a sales contract to which a minor is a party is freely and fairly formed in good faith, the minor may rescind the contract and obtain a refund, but must allow the vendor reasonable compensation for the depreciation of the goods while they were in the minor's possession.

Estate of McGovern v. State Employees' Retirement Board (1986) KC

Facts: McGovern worked for the Delaware Joint Toll Bridge Commission for 30 years. As McGovern neared retirement age, his wife fell terminally ill with cancer. McGovern was distraught over his wife's condition and refused to admit that she was ill. When McGovern retired from the Commission, he selected a company retirement plan and named his wife as beneficiary. Two weeks after McGovern's retirement, his wife died. McGovern died just five days later. Under the plan selected by McGovern, his estate was entitled to $27,600. If McGovern had named one of his children as beneficiary, $151,311 would have been available to the beneficiary under the plan. McGovern's son sought to have the plan changed, on the grounds that McGovern was mentally incompetent at the time he made his selection.

Issue: When is a person considered incompetent and therefore incapable of forming a contract?

Rule: A person who is unable to understand the terms of an agreement is considered incompetent, and is therefore incapable of forming a contract.

Irrational behavior or unwise judgment alone does not establish incompetence.

Note: The dissent adopts the competing Restatement (Second) § 15 test for incompetency: A person is incompetent when they are unable to act in a reasonable manner in the transaction and the other party has reason to know of the condition.

Totem Marine Tug & Barge, Inc. v. Alyeska Pipeline Service Co. (1978) KC

Facts: Totem agreed to transport materials from Texas to Alaska for Alyeska Pipeline. Totem encountered many unforeseen difficulties that delayed delivery and increased the transportation costs. After Alyeska promised to pay the increased costs, Totem took out short-term loans to finance its performance. However, Alyeska ordered Totem to dock at Long Beach, California, off-loaded the materials, and terminated the contracted without explanation. Totem pressed Alyeska to pay for the transport from Texas to California, but Alyeska resisted. In desperate need of cash to pay off its short-term loans, Totem agreed to release Alyeska from all claims by Totem in exchange for 1/3 of the amount due. After receiving the settlement payment and paying its immediate debts, Totem sued to have the settlement agreement rescinded on grounds of economic duress.

Issue: When may a party to a contract rescind on grounds of economic duress?

Rule: A party may rescind a contract on grounds of economic duress if the party seeking recision involuntarily agreed to the transaction due to the wrongful acts and threats of the other party and circumstances were such that the party had no reasonable alternative but to agree to the terms or face serious financial hardship.

Note: This rule embraces several competing policies: the court's desire to correct inequitable or unequal exchanges between parties of unequal bargaining power, the court's reluctance to interfere with the freedom to contract, and the court's desire to encourage private settlement of disputes.

Syester v. Banta (1965) KC

Facts: The defendants owned a dance studio. Over the course of a year, the defendants sold Syester, a widow in her late sixties, over 3000 hours of dance lessons at a cost of over $29,000. The defendants employed a wide variety of representations to persuade Syester to purchase the lessons, including promises that the lessons would make her a "professional dancer."

The defendant's also exploited Syester's affection for one a young dance instructors to effect the sales. Syester sued the defendants, but the defendants employed similar tactics to persuade Syester to dismiss the suit and sign two settlement agreements. Shortly afterwards, Syester sued again, alleging fraud and misrepresentation in the defendant's sales and settlement negotiations. **Issue:** When may a contract be voided for fraud and misrepresentation? **Rule:** A contract may be voided for fraud or misrepresentation when a party is damaged because she relied on false representations of a material matter intentionally and knowingly made by the other party. The court found that the plaintiff in this case had fallen victim to a calculated course of intentional misrepresentations on the part of the defendants.

Miller v. Sears (1981) KC

Facts: Miller, an attorney, helped the Sears draft incorporation papers for their business, Norlite, Inc. Four years later, Miller offered to sell the Sears his home. During negotiations, the Sears told Miller to name Norlite as the purchasor and obligor in the conveyance because they planned to convert the residence to commercial uses. Miller changed the conveyance and also added an "Indemnity Agreement," in which the Sears personally guaranteed Norlite's performance. The Sears signed the contract. As a result, everything owned by the Sears personally and everything owned by Norlite, Inc. became security for the promissory note executed to Miller for the purchase of the house. After consulting another attorney, the Sears soon discovered the extent of their liability and asked Miller to "just void the contract." Miller refused. The Sears claimed Miller had breached his fiduciary duty as their attorney by failing to explain the legal significance of the "Indemnity Agreement" that they had signed.

Issue: Is a contract between an attorney and his client voidable if the attorney fails to disclose the significance and legal effect of each of the terms of the contract?

Rule: A contract between an attorney and his client is voidable if the attorney fails to disclose the significance and legal effect of each of the terms of the contract. Failure to disclose is a breach of the attorney's fiduciary duty to the client, which requires the attorney not to take advantage of his client's trust, or to deal with his client in such a way as to benefit himself at the client's expense.

Ahern v. Knecht (1990) KC

Facts: During a heat wave, the Aherns' air conditioner stopped cooling. Mrs. Ahern called Knecht to fix the unit. Knecht arrived at the Aherns' home, inspected the air conditioner, and demanded $762 in advance. Mrs. Ahern, who was in hurry to leave for an appointment elsewhere, paid Knecht and left. When she returned, she found that the air conditioner did not function at all. The next day, another repair company fixed the unit for $72. The Aherns demanded their money back, and Knecht refused.

Issue: When is a contract so unconscionable that it may be rescinded or set aside?

Rule: A contract may be rescinded or set aside as unconscionable if their is a gross disparity in the values exchanged by the contract or if there is gross inequality in the bargaining positions of the parties, such that the disadvantaged party has little meaningful choice when faced with unreasonably unfavorable terms.

Note: Some jurisdictions consider application of the unconscionability doctrine based purely on excessive price to be a form of price-fixing beyond the authority of the court.

Derico v. Duncan (1982) KC

Facts: Duncan agreed to repair Derico's home and satisfy Derico's outstanding mortgage in exchange for a cash price, plus interest, and a new mortgage securing Derico's total indebtedness to Duncan. State law required all creditors to obtain a license before making consumer loans. Duncan had no license. Derico sued to invalidate the loan provision.

Issue: Does failure to comply with a regulatory statute render a contract void and unenforceable?

Rule: A contract formed in violation of a regulatory statute is void and unenforceable if the statute was enacted for the protection of the public, and not for the raising of revenue only.

Note: Some jurisdictions will not apply this rule when the statute provides a separate remedy for violation or when application of the rule would lead to inequitable results.

Karlin v. Weinberg (1978) KC

Facts: Dr. Karlin hired Dr. Weinberg, who was fresh out of medical school. Weinberg's employment contract provided that upon termination, Weinberg could not practice within 10 miles of Karlin's office for a period of 5 years without Karlin's written consent. After 2½ years, Weinberg left

Karlin's office, and set up his own practice a few doors away. Karlin sued for an injunction enforcing the restrictive covenant.

Issue: Is a post-employment restrictive covenant between physicians enforceable?

Rule: A post-employment restrictive covenant between physicians is enforceable to the extent that it protects a legitimate interest of the employer, imposes no undue hardship on the employee, and is not injurious to the public.

Note: Restrictive covenants between attorneys are injurious to the public as a matter of law and are thereby unreasonable per se and unenforceable.

Wil-Fred's, Inc. v. Metropolitan Sanitary District (1978) KC

Facts: Wil-Fred's submitted a closed bid and security deposit for a District project. Wil-Fred's was the lowest bidder and was awarded the contract. Because of a mistake by a subcontractor, Wil-Fred's could not perform the contract at its bid price and requested recision of the bid and return of its deposit.

Issue: Can a contract be rescinded because of a unilateral mistake?

Rule: Rescission of a contract for a unilateral mistake is granted if clear and positive evidence shows: that the mistake occurred notwithstanding the exercise of reasonable care; that it is of such grave consequence that enforcement of the contract would be unconscionable; and that the other party can be restored to its original position.

United States ex rel. Crane Co. v. Progressive Enterprises, Inc. (1976) KC

Facts: Crane contracted to sell a machine to Progressive. Later, Crane sought to raise the machine's price and Progressive acquiesced to the higher price without objection. After delivery of the machine, Progressive refused to pay the new price claiming that the modification was not freely entered into.

Issue: When are modifications to sales agreements unenforceable because they were entered into involuntarily?

Rule: Modification of sales agreements are permitted so long as they are executed in good faith. If the buyer is opposed to a modification he must display some protest against it in order to put the seller on notice. This allows the parties to rely on objective, unequivocal manifestations of assent to modifications.

Bovard v. American Horse Enterprises, Inc. (1988) R

Facts: Bovard sued to recover on promissory notes executed in connection with another party's purchase of American Horse Enterprises, which manufactured illegal drug paraphernalia.

Issue: Under what circumstances is a contract illegal and void as contrary to public policy?

Rule: A contract that is contrary to the policy of the express law is illegal and void. Factors which should be considered in determining whether a contract violates public policy include: the nature of the conduct, the extent of public harm which may be involved, and the moral quality of the conduct of the parties in light of the prevailing standards of the community.

Williams v. Patton (1991) R

Facts: Williams failed to pay child support for eight years. Patton filed a motion for contempt for failure to pay, as well as a motion to modify child support. While the suit was pending, Williams and Patton entered a settlement agreement. However, the trial court would not release Williams from his obligation to pay the support in arrears.

Issue: Is a settlement between parents concerning child support payments made before the amount due has been reduced to a final judgment void as against public policy?

Rule: Child support settlements may not be entered into before the unpaid support amount has been reduced to a final judgment. The purpose of this rule is to protect the best interests of the child by encouraging payment of child support, and to protect custodial parents by putting them in a more equal position with non-custodial parents.

Ellis v. Mullen (1977) R

Facts: Ellis, who was illiterate, sought to recover damages for personal injuries he suffered when his car was hit by Mullen. Mullen alleged contributory negligence and pled that his insurance company had issued four settlement drafts, totaling $900, two of which were signed by Ellis, stating that the Ellis' endorsements would constitute "full and complete settlement to all claims."

Issue: Is the endorsement of a written release by an illiterate plaintiff enforceable?

Rule: Illiterate persons who are ignorant of the contents of contracts signed by them may be relieved of their obligations under the contract if it is proven that the other party took unfair advantage of their disability.

S.P. Dunham and Co. v. Kudra (1957) R

Facts: Dunham, a department store owner, leased its fur department to Hurwitz, a third party. Kudra cleaned and stored furs for Hurwitz, a service for which Kudra was owed a large sum of money. Hurwitz went bankrupt, and Dunham, wishing to fill Hurwitz's back orders, asked Kudra for Hurwitz's stored furs. Kudra refused delivery unless Dunham would cover Hurwitz's debt. Dunham complied for fear of losing valuable customers. Dunham brought an action in restitution, alleging its payments had been made under "business compulsion."

Issue: What constitutes "business compulsion" for which a plaintiff is entitled to restitution?

Rule: A plaintiff is entitled to judgment for "business compulsion," a type of duress, when a defendant's actions induce compliance with improper demands, and the plaintiff lacked a complete and adequate remedy in the courts to resist the demands.

Selmer Company v. Blakeslee-Midwest Company (1983) R

Facts: Selmer was a subcontractor on a construction project for Blakeslee. Blakeslee failed to fulfill its contractual obligations entitling Selmer to terminate the contract. Instead, Selmer orally agreed to complete the work, provided that it would be paid for the extra costs of completion. Selmer demanded its payment, but Blakeslee offered to settle for little more than one-half that amount due. Selmer accepted the settlement because it was strapped for cash.

Issue: When is economic duress a legitimate defense to invalidate the settlement of a contract dispute?

Rule: Economic duress occurs when a party is forced to accept a contract modification, or else incur costs for which no adequate legal remedy would be available. Since the threatening party's conduct is the primary concern, financial difficulty on the part of the party claiming duress is not enough by itself to justify setting aside a settlement.

Perdue v. Crocker National Bank (1985) R

Facts: Each of the Crocker's depositors signed a signature card stating that all deposits were subject to the bank's rules, regulations, and charges. No charges or rules were expressly identified on the cards themselves. Perdue filed a class action that challenged the validity of charges imposed by the bank for the processing of checks drawn on accounts with insufficient funds.

Issue 1: Does a signature card create a contract between a bank and its depositors authorizing charges for handling checks written by those who had insufficient funds?

Rule 1: A signature card is a contract between a depositor and a bank that authorizes a bank to impose charges, such as that for the processing of checks drawn from insufficient funds, subject to a bank's duty of good faith and fair dealing in setting or varying such charges.

Issue 2: How does a court determine whether a price term is unconscionable?

Rule 2: A price term may be found unconscionable by looking at the market price, the cost of the good or service to the seller, the inconvenience imposed on the seller, and the true value of the product or service. Further, the absence of meaningful choice, the lack of sophistication of the buyer and the presence of deceptive practices by the seller may also indicate that a term is unconscionable

Stambovsky v. Ackley (1991)

Facts: The Stambovskys, after contracting to purchase a house, discovered that it was widely reputed to be possessed by poltergeists.

Issue: Does the doctrine of caveat emptor apply in situations where it would be unlikely for the buyer to discover any undisclosed details concerning the home he has contracted to purchase?

Rule: Where a condition which has been created by the seller materially impairs the value of the contract and is undiscoverable by or unlikely to be within the scope of knowledge of a purchaser exercising due care, nondisclosure constitutes a basis for rescission as a matter of equity.

National and Int'l Brotherhood of Street Racers, Inc. v. Superior Ct. (1989) R

Facts: A race car driver, who suffered crippling injuries during a race, sued the race organizer (Brotherhood of Street Racers) and the track owner. The defendants claimed that the driver had signed a release form discharging them from all claims and liability.

Issue: What is required for a party to ensure that a release will effectively discharge it from liability?

Rule: A release will be effective if it is clear, unambiguous and explicit, and if it expresses an agreement not to hold the released party liable for negligence.

LaFluer v. C.C. Pierce Co., Inc. (1986) R

Facts: LaFluer entered into a settlment agreement with an insurance company in the amount of $4000, after injuring his foot in a work-related accident. LaFluer sought to have the agreement rescinded after learning that the accident had caused him to contract a disease that required him to have his legs amputated. The agreement was originally made under the mistaken assumption that the wound was not serious.

Issue: May a settlement agreement be set aside on the ground of mutual mistake when the parties were unaware at the time of the agreement that the injured party suffered from a serious and unknown injury?

Rule: The "unknown injury rule" states that a release of claims for personal injuries may be avoided on the ground of mutual mistake if the parties were mistaken as to the existence of an injury when the agreement was signed.

Stare v. Tate (1971) R

Facts: Defendant, former wife of the plaintiff, proposed a settlement agreement that computed the value of the husband's property, but contained a serious accounting error which undervalued the property. A counteroffer was submitted by the husband that merely rounded off the errant settlement term, and did not call attention to the error. The settlement was agreed to, and the wife later brought action to reform the contract.

Issue: May a written contract be revised when one party makes a mistake of which the other party is aware?

Rule: When one party knows that a writing is erroneous and fails to inform the mistaken party, an agreement may be reformed.

Watkins & Son, Inc. v. Carrig (1941)

Facts: Watkins & Son contracted to excavate a cellar for Carrig. After work began, Watkins & Son encountered solid rock and Carrig orally agreed to pay nine times the original excavation price. Carrig later reneged, claiming his promise was unenforceable due to lack of consideration (i.e., there was a pre-existing duty to do the work anyway).

Issue: Is a modification of an agreement unenforceable because of a lack of consideration?

Rule: Modification involves a partial rescission of the prior contract and therefore the promise to do the original work is new consideration.

Note: After classifying modification as a "partial rescission" of the original contract, the court used same analysis as seen above in *Schwartzreich v. Bauman-Basch, Inc.*

Webster v. Blue Ship Tea Room, Inc. (1964) R

Facts: Webster was injured while eating fish chowder served at the Blue Ship Tea Room. A fish bone that was "lurking" in the fish chowder got caught in her esophagus, resulting in two surgeries. Webster sued for damages under a breach of implied warranty theory.

Issue: Does the presence of a foreign substance in restaurant food constitute a breach of an implied warranty?

Rule: Whether a foreign substance in restaurant food constitutes a breach of an implied warranty depends upon the nature of the foreign substance. Foreign substances which make the food unwholesome are likely to constitute a breach. However, foreign substances which are occasionally found within a particular cuisine (such as fish bones in a rich and hearty New England fish chowder) do not constitute a breach, as the consumer should anticipate the potential presence of such substances.

California State Bar Journal (1978) R

Facts: None provided.

Issue: Is it ethical for a lawyer to condition employment upon the potential client agreeing to arbitrate any future malpractice claims by the client against the attorney?

Rule: It is unethical for an attorney to impose upon potential clients an arbitration condition for malpractice claims until the lawyer has advised the client fully as to the possible consequences of an arbitration agreement and has advised the client that the client may consult with independent counsel.

Walton v. Broglio (1975) R

Facts: Broglio was a client of Walton's law firm, although Walton had never met Broglio. Broglio was arrested on criminal charges and Walton was recommended to Broglio by a third party because of Walton's expertise in criminal matters. When they first, met Walton told Broglio the fee would be $15,000. Broglio was not happy with the fee, but allowed Walton to represent him because Broglio was frightened by the severity of the charges and feared that neither Walton nor Walton's firm would represent Broglio if he disputed the fee. Broglio only paid $4000 in cash and executed a $7500 promissory note. After the trial, Walton sued to recover the balance due and Broglio objected to the fee amount.

Issue: Is there a presumption of undue influence (and thus invalidity) of a contract relating to a fee agreement, where there is a preexisting attorney-client relationship?

Rule: A preexisting attorney-client relationship does not give rise to a presumption of undue influence concerning agreements relating to hiring and compensation.

Ingersoll-Rand Company v. Ciavatta (1987) R

Facts: As a condition of accepting employment with Ingersoll, Ciavatta agreed to assign to the company the rights to all inventions based on his work with Ingersoll that he might create within one year of termination. Nine months after being fired, Ciavatta filed a patent application for an invention that was not based on any of Ingersoll's trade secrets or proprietary information, but that was based on the general knowledge Ciavatta had acquired while working for Ingersoll. The company sued to enforce the assignment agreement and obtain the rights to Ciavatta's invention.

Issue: Is a post-employment restrictive agreement enforceable if it requires the employee to assign to his former employer the rights to the employee's post-employment inventions?

Rule: A post-employment restrictive agreement that requires an employee to assign to his former employer the rights to the employee's post-employment inventions is enforceable if it simply protects the legitimate interests of the employer, imposes no undue hardship on the employee, and is not injurious to the public. In this case, the court found that the restrictive agreement extended beyond the legitimate interests of the employer and imposed an undue hardship on the employee, effectively preventing him from finding employment for one year following termination.

Dwyer v. Jung (1975) R

Facts: Jung, Dwyer and Lisbona, all attorneys, formed a partnership. The partnership agreement included a restrictive covenant, effective upon dissolution of the partnership, that divided the client market amongst the attorneys and prohibited each attorney from representing any client that had been allotted to another attorney. The agreement allotted the bulk of the clients to Jung. The partnership dissolved and subsequently Jung brought an action for an accounting against Dwyer and Lisbona, claiming that they were attempting to pirate his clients.

Issue: Are post-employment restrictive agreements that divide the client market between lawyers and prohibit attorneys from representing certain clients valid?

Rule: Post-employment restrictive agreements that divide the client market between lawyers and prohibit attorneys from representing certain clients restrict a client's ability to select the attorney of his choice and are therefore void and unenforceable as against public policy.

Chapter 7

IMPOSSIBILITY, IMPRACTICABILITY AND
FRUSTRATION OF PURPOSE

After a valid contract has been made by the parties, unforeseen developments may make performance of the contract impossible or of no value to one of the parties. In such situations, courts may excuse nonperformance of a party's contractual duties on the grounds of impossibility, impracticability or frustration. These doctrines can be used as defenses by a party who seemingly breaches or refuses to perform.

I. IMPOSSIBILITY GENERALLY

A. Effect
Contractual duties are discharged if their performance becomes impossible.

   1. Temporary impossibility does not completely discharge performance but suspends it until the impossibility ends.

   2. If performance is partially impossible, contractual duties are only discharged to the extent that the impossibility applies.

B. Allocation of Risk
If the parties have expressly allocated the risk of the occurrence of the impossibility, or surrounding circumstances or the conduct of the parties suggest that one party should bear the risk (implied allocation), then the excuse of impossibility is unavailable. In other words, if the contingency is sufficiently foreseeable, it will be included among the parties' contractual risks.

C. Timing
The impossibility must arise after the contract has been formed. Impossibility that results from circumstances existing at the time of the contract (i.e., one of the parties knows that performance of the other's duties will be impossible, but makes the contract anyhow) is treated as fraud or mistake.

D. Objective Test
Courts usually require that performance must be objectively impossible. It must be impossible for anyone to perform, not just the defendant. Exceptions:

1. Where a party cannot perform due to insolvency, it does not matter that a solvent party could have performed.

2. In contracts for personal services, the death of the party required to render the services will dissolve the contract.

E. If performance of a collateral provision is impossible, courts are less likely to excuse nonperformance than if an essential element was involved.

1. Courts require that a party must utilize an alternative mode of performance to satisfy the collateral provision.

2. UCC § 2-614 provides for use of reasonable alternative methods of delivery or payment if those provided for in the contract become impossible to perform.

II. WHEN IMPOSSIBILITY DISCHARGES PERFORMANCE

A. Traditional View
Prior to the nineteenth century, courts did not recognize impossibility as an excuse for nonperformance. The rationale was that a contingency could always have been provided for in the contract.

B. Modern View
If subject matter essential to the performance of the contract is destroyed through no fault of the parties, the contract will be discharged.

1. Construction
If a party contracts to construct a building, he is not ordinarily excused from performance if the building is destroyed through no fault of his own. The builder is said to have assumed the risk of any construction problems.

2. Repair

A party that contracts to repair an existing structure is discharged if the structure is destroyed. The structure to have been repaired is considered to be the "essential subject matter of the agreement," and its existence was a "basic assumption" on which the contract was made.

3. Sale of Goods Contracts (UCC)

If the contract involves specifically identified goods that are destroyed or damaged through no fault of either party, and the buyer has not assumed the risk of such damage, the contract is discharged if the loss is total. In cases of partial damage, the buyer can choose to either void the entire contract or accept the goods with due reduction from the contract price for the damaged goods. (UCC § 2-613.)

a. It is essential that the goods be specifically described in the contract and be unique in some way; otherwise, impossibility will not apply because substitutes are available.

b. If an agreed source of supply is destroyed, nonperformance is excused.

c. Goods not identified

If the contract requires the seller to provide goods from his inventory without specifying the goods and the goods are destroyed, the seller is excused if their existence was a basic assumption of the contract. (UCC § 2-615.)

d. If the shipping terms are "free on board seller's plant," the risk of destruction of the goods is shifted from the seller to the buyer once the goods are placed with the carrier. If seller makes a destination contract ("free on board buyer's business"), risk is shifted only after the buyer receives the goods.

C. Supervening Illegality

A contract that was valid when entered into may be rendered illegal by a subsequent change in the law. This "supervening illegality" is frequently treated as a form of impossibility that discharges performance.

D. Defective Specifications

1. If a buyer/owner prepares defective contract specifications, the manufacturer/contractor is usually excused from performance.

2. If the manufacturer/contractor prepares defective specifications, he is not excused from performance.

E. Third Party's Failure to Perform

1. If a third party's performance or a particular source of supply is either contractually required or assumed to be part of the agreement, performance is discharged if the third party or source of supply cannot perform.

2. The nonperforming party must employ all due measures to try to assure himself that the third party or source of supply will not fail. (UCC § 2-615, Comment 4.)

3. If a third party's performance or a particular source of supply is not contractually required and not assumed to be part of the agreement, performance is not discharged.

III. IMPRACTICABILITY

Modern courts will discharge duties that are commercially impracticable to perform, even though they may be possible.

A. Test to Determine Impracticability

1. An extreme and unreasonable obstacle hinders performance, and

2. The obstacle was unforeseen at the time the contract was made.

B.   Performance Is Discharged If:

1. It is rendered impracticable, without fault of one of the parties, by the occurrence of an event,

2. The nonoccurrence of the event was a "basic assumption" on which the contract was made, and

3. The party did not expressly or impliedly assume the risk of the occurrence. (Rest. 2d. § 261.)

C.   Sale of Goods Context
Nondelivery or delay in delivery by a seller is not a breach if:

1. Performance as agreed has been made impracticable by the occurrence of a contingency,

2. The nonoccurrence of that contingency was a basic assumption on which the contract was made, and

3. The seller did not assume a "greater obligation" (i.e., did not assume the risk of unforeseen developments).

D.   Increased Costs

1. Increased costs are not usually grounds for impracticability unless the cost increase is extreme, and the nonperforming party did not assume the risk of its occurrence.

2. Comment 4 to UCC § 2-615
    Increased cost alone does not excuse performance unless the rise in cost is due to some unforeseen contingency which alters the essential nature of the performance.

    a. Severe shortage of supplies due to war, embargo, local crop failure or unforeseen shutdown of sources of supply usually warrants nonperformance.

b. Neither a rise nor collapse in market prices is in itself a justification.

c. Entire-enterprise Test
In determining whether the negative impact of a price increase is sufficient to render performance impracticable, some courts look to the overall profitability of the organization, including earnings from contracts with other parties.

IV. FRUSTRATION OF PURPOSE

If the essential purpose of a contract is frustrated, each party's duty of performance is discharged, even if performance is not impossible.

A. Elements (Rest. 2d. § 265)

1. A party's principal reason for making the contract is substantially frustrated by a supervening event.

2. Non-occurrence of the event was a basic assumption upon which the contract was made.

3. The party did not expressly or impliedly assume the risk of the occurrence.

B. Sale of Goods

Frustration of purpose is included under the UCC § 2-615 provisions (see commercial impracticability, above).

V. REMEDIES (Apply to all three doctrines.)

A. Restitution and reliance recovery are allowed for part performance prior to discharge of contractual duties. (Rest. 2d. § 377.) The party receives the contract rate or the reasonable value of the part performance.

B. Generally, there is no recovery for reliance that has not conferred a benefit on the other party. However, Restatement (Second) § 272(2) opposes the general rule and allows relief "as justice requires," including protection of the parties' reliance interests.

C.   Reformation
Instead of dissolving a contract whose principal purpose has become frustrated, impossible, or impracticable, some courts will reform the problematic provisions and make the contract performable.

CASE CLIPS

Taylor v. Caldwell (1863) DHH, KGK, FE, MS, CPB
Facts: The plaintiff contracted to rent the defendant's concert hall. The defendant was unable to convey the hall because it had burned down through no fault of his own. The plaintiff claimed that the defendant breached the contract and brought suit to recover advertising expenses.
Issue: Are both parties excused from performance if that which was essential to their performance ceased to exist?
Rule: In contracts in which performance depends on the continued existence of a given person or thing, there is an implied condition that impossibility of performance arising from the destruction of the person or thing excuses performance.

Tompkins v. Dudley (1862) DHH
Facts: The defendants guaranteed the performance of a contractor to construct a schoolhouse. The schoolhouse burned down before it had been completed. The plaintiff sued for the money advanced by them under the contract.
Issue: If a party expressly and unconditionally agrees to erect a building, will his nonperformance be excused if a fire destroys the building before completion?
Rule: Where a party expressly creates a duty upon himself to perform an act, an accident will not excuse nonperformance because the party could have provided against such a contingency in the contract.

Carroll v. Bowersock (1917) DHH

Facts: The plaintiff agreed to construct a reinforced concrete floor in the defendant's warehouse. When fire destroyed the warehouse, the plaintiff sued to recover for work done prior to the fire.

Issue: May a party under contract to do repair work be compensated for work done before the structure was destroyed?

Rule: When a party's obligation to do repair work is excused on the basis of impracticability, the party can receive compensation for work completed under the contract which the owner would have received the benefit of in the absence of the casualty. Preparatory work (work which does not inure directly to the owner) is not recoverable.

Bunge Corp. v. Recker (1975) DHH

Facts: Recker agreed to supply the Bunge Corp. with soybeans. Recker claimed that he was excused from performance because severe winter weather destroyed a large part of his crop. The contract, however, did not indicate that the soybeans had to be produced on the Recker's lands.

Issue: Will an act of God that destroys goods to be delivered under a sales contract relieve the seller of his performance if the goods were only specified in the contract by kind and amount?

Rule: An act of God that destroys goods to be delivered under a sales contract will not excuse nonperformance if the seller could have obtained substitute goods from another source.

American Trading & Prod. Corp. v. Shell Int'l Marine, Ltd. (1972) DHH, KGK, CPB

Facts: American Trading, under contract to transport lube oil for Shell, incurred almost 30 percent higher costs because the Suez Canal was closed due to a political crisis. Although the canal route was mentioned in the contract, it was not considered to be the exclusive route. Also, American Trading's ship had sailed to Suez knowing that potential problems could arise.

Issue: Does an increase in cost render performance impracticable?

Rule: Although extreme or unreasonable difficulty, expense, injury, or loss renders performance impracticable, mere increase in cost alone is not a sufficient excuse for nonperformance. The court found that an increase of less than one-third over the contract price was not sufficient to constitute commercial impracticability. (See *Transatlantic Financing Corp. v. United States.*)

Krell v. Henry (1903) DHH, KGK, FE, MS, CPB

Facts: Henry placed a deposit on a room to be rented to watch the king's coronation. When the coronation was canceled, he refused to pay the balance owed for the rental of the room.

Issue: Are duties under a contract discharged if the essential purpose of the contract is frustrated?

Rule: If the essential purpose for contracting is frustrated, each party's duty of performance is discharged, even if performance is not impossible (i.e., the defendant can still rent the room).

Lloyd v. Murphy (1944) DHH, KGK, MS

Facts: Shortly before World War II, the defendant leased land from the plaintiff with the restriction that it be used only for selling gasoline and new cars. During the war, new-car sales were restricted and the defendant broke the lease claiming frustration of purpose, although the plaintiff waived the land-use restrictions. Prior to the outbreak of war, there had been much public anticipation that future car sales would be limited.

Issue: If a lessee leases land subject to restrictions on its use and subsequent regulations that limited its profitability were foreseeable, is the lessee excused from performance?

Rule: The doctrine of frustration of purpose will only excuse a party from performance if the risk of the frustrating event was not foreseeable and the value of counterperformance is totally or nearly totally destroyed.

Chase Precast Corp. v. John J. Paonessa Co. (1991) DHH

Facts: Paonessa entered into a contract with the Commonwealth of Massachusetts for a highway reconstruction project. Paonessa hired Chase under a subcontract to provide concrete barriers to be used in replacing the grass median strip on the highway. A group of citizens filed suit to stop the installation of the barriers and negotiated a settlement terminating the installation. Paonessa had earlier notified Chase of the impending difficulties and advised it to stop producing the barriers. Paonessa canceled the remaining portion of the contract, although it had paid Chase for the amount of barriers it already had produced. Chase sued to recover the anticipated profits lost from cancellation of the contract.

Issue: May a party be held liable for damages that result from the cancellation of a contract for reasons beyond the party's control?

Rule: The doctrine of frustration of purpose may be used as a defense when an event unforeseeable by either party, the risk of which was not allocated by contract, destroys the object or purpose of the contract. When this occurs, the parties are excused from any further performance under the contract.

Note: Frustration of purpose is nearly identical to UCC § 2-615, commonly referred to as commercial impracticability.

Woollums v. Horsley (1892) DHH

Facts: Horsley, an experienced businessman, contracted to buy the mineral, gas, and oil rights to Woollum's land for 40 cents an acre. Woollums, an uneducated and ill man, refused to convey a deed when he learned that his land was worth much more (about $15 an acre). Horsley sued for specific performance.

Issue: Can a party who was misled or acted under a gross misapprehension avoid specific performance of a contract?

Rule: Courts of equity will not grant specific performance where the contract is founded in fraud, imposition, mistake, undue advantage or gross misapprehension.

Waters v. Min Ltd. (1992) DHH

Facts: Waters entered into a contract to assign her annuity policy, which had a cash value of $189,000, to the defendants in exchange for $50,000. One of the defendants, Beauchamin, who had been romantically involved with Waters, represented her in the negotiations. Beauchamin acted in his own self-interest during the negotiations, causing himself to be named as the beneficiary of the annuity and having some of his debts forgiven by other defendants. Waters brought suit to rescind the contract, and the defendants counterclaimed for specific performance.

Issue: May a court refuse to enforce a contract that would result in oppression or gross disparity of consideration?

Rule: The defense of unconscionability may be used to avoid a contract, where a gross disparity of consideration, oppression, or unfair surprise indicates that the agreement was improperly obtained.

State v. Avco Fin. Service of New York, Inc. (1980) DHH

Facts: Avco's loan agreement forms included a clause that stated that the loan was secured by all the property the borrower owned at the time of the agreement. The New York Attorney General, acting on a consumer complaint, sued to declare the clause unconscionable and void without providing any factual support for the claim.

Issue: Can a court find a contract clause unconscionable without support from factual evidence?

Rule: A determination of unconscionability requires factual evidence presented by the parties to show that the clause involved is so one-sided as to be unconscionable under the circumstances existing at the time of the making of the contract.

Smith v. Price's Creameries (1982) DHH

Facts: The Smiths contracted to be the wholesale distributor of Price's products. After the Smiths invested $100,000, Price's Creameries exercised its right to terminate "for any reason" with 30 days notice pursuant to a clause giving both parties such power.

Issue: Is a clause allowing termination "for any reason" unconscionable?

Rule: Absent an affirmative showing of mistake, fraud, or illegality, a termination-at-will clause is not unconscionable if it was negotiated at arm's length. If a court determines that such a clause is not unconscionable as a matter of law, the motivation for canceling the agreement is immaterial.

Gianni Sport Ltd. v. Gantos, Inc. (1986) DHH

Facts: Gantos' contract to buy women's clothing from Gianni gave Gantos the right to cancel any part of undelivered purchase orders for "any reason whatsoever." Gantos was a much larger company than Gianni and it canceled an order to pressure Gianni to renegotiate the contract and halve the price. Gianni sued for the original contract price after it delivered goods to Gantos.

Issue: Is a contract clause that gives a buyer in a superior bargaining position the right to cancel a purchase order for any reason unenforceable?

Rule: A contract clause allowing a buyer to unilaterally terminate a purchase order is void as unconscionable (UCC § 2-302) if it is unreasonable, and the buyer is in a far superior bargaining position.

Paradine v. Jane (1647) KGK, MS, CPB

Facts: The lessee (the defendant) claimed that he did not have to pay rent because the land was occupied by an invading army, which prevented him from obtaining any profits.

Issue: If the purpose for contracting is frustrated, will a party be bound to the contractual duties he agreed to?

Rule: A party must fulfill a duty he contractually imposes upon himself, notwithstanding any inevitable intervention, because he could have provided against contingencies in his contract.

Savile v. Savile (1721) KGK

Facts: The plaintiff sued the defendant for the balance of the purchase price of a house the defendant agreed to buy, after the defendant had decided to withdraw and forfeit his deposit because the price he had offered later seemed unreasonable.

Issue: When a deposit is thought to be a sufficient pledge, will forfeiture of the deposit be punishment enough for the buyer if he withdraws from the contract?

Rule: When a deposit is thought to be a sufficient pledge, forfeiture of the deposit is punishment enough for the buyer if he withdraws before completing the contract.

Hall v. Wright (1859) KGK

Facts: Wright claimed he was incapable of performing his contract to marry the plaintiff because he had acquired a dangerous bodily disease.

Issue: Does the impossibility of specifically performing a contract relieve a party from paying damages for the breach?

Rule: The impossibility of performing a contract does not relieve the contractor from paying damages for the breach.

School Trustees of Trenton v. Bennett (1859) KGK

Facts: When the schoolhouse Evernham and Hill agreed to build collapsed due to the latent softness of the soil, they refused to complete their obligations under the contract. The School Trustees sued Bennett who was the guarantor for Evernham and Hill.

Issue: Must an agreement be performed if performance is not absolutely impossible, and the contingency was not expressly provided against in the contract's terms?

Rule: An agreement must be performed, no matter what the cost, so long as performance is not absolutely impossible and the contingency complained of was not expressly provided against in the contract's terms.

Butterfield v. Byron (1891) KGK

Facts: A contract required Byron to build a hotel on Butterfield's land, while Butterfield was to complete the grading, excavating, stonework,

brickwork, painting and plumbing for the project. When lightning destroyed the nearly finished structure, Byron refused to complete his obligations.
Issue: When work is to be done on a building for which the contractor is not solely responsible, will the destruction of the building excuse performance under the contract?
Rule: When work is to be done under a contract on a chattel or a building that is not wholly the property of the contractor, or for which he is not solely accountable, the destruction of it without the fault of either of the parties will excuse performance of the contract. The plaintiff is entitled to sue for the payments he has made to the contractor, and the contractor can sue for the work done before the contingency occurred.

Canadian Indus. Alcohol v. Dunbar Molasses Co.
(1932) KGK, MS, R

Facts: Dunbar, a middleman, contracted to supply Canadian Industries with 1,500,000 gallons of molasses. Dunbar could only deliver 344,000 gallons because the refinery both parties relied on had to cut back production. Dunbar did not have a contract with the refinery to guarantee him a minimum supply.
Issue: Is a middleman excused from delivering contracted for goods if it failed to make a contract with the supplier to assure itself of a sufficient supply?
Rule: A party's nonperformance will not be excused if he impliedly bears the risk of the performance becoming difficult.

Kel Kim Corp. v. Central Mkts., Inc. (1987) FE, CPB

Facts: Kel Kim leased a vacant supermarket from Central Markets to be used as a roller rink, under the condition that the Kel Kim obtain a public liability insurance policy. For several months no insurer would extend the requisite coverage to the Kel Kim, who asked to be relieved of the condition, either because performance was impossible or because the inability to procure insurance was within the lease's *force majeure* clause.
Issue: May a condition requiring a lessee to carry insurance be waived on the grounds of impossibility if no insurer is willing to provide coverage?
Rule: Because an insurance requirement is a bargained-for economic protection, and inability to obtain coverage is foreseeable, such a condition may not be excused on the basis of impossibility.

Transatlantic Fin. Corp. v. United States (1956) FE
Facts: Transatlantic was forced to sail 3,000 additional miles to deliver U.S. wheat because the Suez Canal was closed due to war. After receiving only the contract price, Transatlantic sued in *quantum meruit* (i.e., for what it deserved) for the extra expense.
Issue: Will added expense excuse performance of a contract under the doctrine of impossibility?
Rule: Increased cost will not render performance of a contract legally impossible. The impossibility requires that an unexpected contingency occurred, the risk of the occurrence was not allocated, either by agreement or custom, and the occurrence of the contingency rendered performance commercially impracticable, or possible only by excessive and unreasonable cost.
Note: In the instant case, the plaintiff claimed that the closure of the canal made the agreement impossible to perform, and that use of the new route required a new contract. However, the court ruled that there was no contractual requirement to use the Suez Canal.

Stees v. Leonard (1874) FE
Facts: Leonard, following all of the plans and specifications in the contract, tried unsuccessfully twice to construct a building. Leonard sought to be excused from performance because the land was composed of quicksand.
Issue: If confronted with an unforeseen impediment, is a contractor excused from performing his obligations?
Rule: If a party binds himself, by a positive, express contract, to do an act in itself possible, performance is required unless is it rendered impossible by an act of God, the law or the other party to the contract.

Albre Marble & Tile Co. v. John Bowen Co. (1959) FE, KC
Facts: John Bowen Company's general contract with the state was declared invalid because of its improper bidding procedures. The subcontractor, Albre Marble, sued to recover expenditures incurred in preparation of its duties under the subcontract.
Issue: May a party recover reliance damages if the other party's nonperformance has been excused on the basis of impossibility?
Rule: A party may recover the fair value of acts done in conformity with a specific request of the contract if the other party has been relieved of performance on the ground of impossibility. A contributing factor in

allowing the plaintiff to recover in this case was that the event that rendered the defendant's performance impossible was partly caused by the defendant.

Missouri Pub. Serv. v. Peabody Coal Co. (1979) FE

Facts: Missouri Public Service contracted to buy coal from Peabody at a fixed price. Peabody, faced with escalating costs due to global economic events and increased government regulation, later sought to renegotiate the price and said it would discontinue shipments if a better agreement was not reached.

Issue: Does an unforeseen increase in costs caused by extrinsic events excuse a party from performance due to impracticability?

Rule: A bad bargain not caused by the failure of a basic assumption or the essential nature of the performance does not constitute commercial impracticability.

Bolin Farms v. American Cotton Shippers Assoc. (1974) MS

Facts: Bolin Farms, a group of experienced cotton farmers, contracted to sell future crops to American Cotton at prices ranging from 29 cents to 41 cents per pound. The price of cotton unexpectedly skyrocketed to 80 cents per pound. Bolin Farms tried to rescind its contracts.

Issue: Can a sales contract be rescinded if subsequent price changes make the agreement unprofitable?

Rule: A party may not rescind a sales contract if subsequent price changes render it unprofitable.

Mineral Park Land Co. v. Howard (1916) MS, R

Facts: Howard agreed to take all of its gravel requirements for a bridge-building contract from Mineral's land. Howard removed all of the gravel that was above water level but refused to remove any gravel from below water level because to do so would have been very expensive.

Issue: May nonperformance be excused if the cost of performance is extremely high?

Rule: Performance of a contract premised on the assumption that goods are available may be excused for impracticability where the cost is so great that the effect is to make the goods unavailable.

United States v. Wegematic Corp. (1966) MS

Facts: After contracting to provide the United States with a "revolutionary" computer, Wegematic requested discharge of its duties because it could not manufacture the machine.

Issue: Is a manufacturer excused from performance if it does not possess the technology to manufacture a contracted for product after representing that production was possible?

Rule: In the absence of exculpatory language, a manufacturer is not excused from performance on the basis of impossibility if it does not possess the technology to produce a good that it agreed to produce.

Dills v. Town of Enfield (1989) MS

Facts: The Town of Enfield wished to have a private developer construct an industrial park on town property. Dills contracted to purchase the land to be developed, putting $100,000 down toward the purchase price. Because Dills was unable to obtain necessary mortgage financing, he was unable to submit final construction plans as required by the contract. Enfield voted to terminate the agreement, as permitted by the contract, and kept the deposit as liquidated damages. Dills claimed that his duty to provide the plans was excused on the grounds of impracticability.

Issue: Does the failure to obtain financing excuse performance of a construction contract as impracticable?

Rule: In order for financial burdens to warrant the discharge of a contract on the grounds of impracticability, the burdens must be highly exceptional and unforeseen at the time of the contract. Failure to obtain financing for a business venture is far less exceptional than other situations in which duties have not been excused (e.g., unexpected war), and is also a highly foreseeable event that was within the contemplation of the parties at the time of contracting.

Louisiana Power & Light v. Allegheny Ludlum Indus. (1981) MS

Facts: Allegheny stopped delivery of steel tubing because of an increase in the cost of performance which would have deprived it of anticipated profit.

Issue: Is the fact that performance under a contract will cause a party losses sufficient to show commercial impracticability?

Rule: A party seeking to excuse his duties by reason of a cost increase must show both that he can perform only at a loss and that the loss will be especially severe and unreasonable.
Note: This case was appealed on the issue of summary judgment and was therefore remanded for a factual application.

Kaiser-Francis Oil Co. v. Producer's Gas Co. (1989) MS

Facts: Kaiser-Francis and Producer's Gas had a contract under which Producer's Gas was required to pay for certain minimum quantities of gas from Kaiser-Francis' wells. The contract also contained a provision relieving the parties of liability if their failure to perform is due to *force majeure*. Producer's Gas claimed that this provision relieved it of the duty to take or buy when market demand resulted in a resale price below the contract price.
Issue: Does a *force majeure* clause relieve a take-or-pay vendee of its obligation to take or pay when market forces make the contract unprofitable?
Rule: A *force majeure* provision does not relieve a buyer from a take-or-pay provision when market changes make the contract unprofitable because this would unfairly reallocate bargained-for risks to the seller.

Washington State Hop Producers, Inc. v. Goschie Farms, Inc. (1989) MS

Facts: Washington State Hop Producers rented hop allotments, which were scarce farming commodities created by the Department of Agriculture (USDA). Goschie Farms submitted bids and was awarded a contract to purchase hop allotments from the plaintiff. Shortly after the contract was formed, the USDA unexpectedly made hop allotments much easier to purchase, reducing the rental value of some allotments by over 90 percent and rendering other allotments worthless. Goschie Farms and other buyers refused to perform and claimed frustration of purpose as a defense.
Issue: Can a party be excused from performance on the basis of frustration of purpose caused by unforeseen economic changes?
Rule: Unforeseeability and decline in market price are not grounds for rescission of a contract, but they are often evidence that the purpose of the contract was substantially frustrated.

Opera Co. of Boston, Inc. v. Wolf Trap Found. for the Performing Arts (1987) CPB

Facts: The Opera Company contracted to perform four operas in the Wolf Trap National Park. Wolf Trap canceled the last performance claiming that an electrical storm had terminated power to the pavilion rendering performance impossible.

Issue: When does the doctrine of impossibility excuse a party from performance?

Rule: A party may rely on a defense of impossibility of performance when there is an unexpected occurrence of an intervening act, such occurrence is of a character that its nonoccurrence is a basic assumption of the agreement, and it makes performance impracticable.

Note: The court accepted § 265 of the Restatement (Second) as the proper statement of the doctrine of impossibility.

Northern Corp. v. Chugach Electric Assoc. (1974) CPB

Facts: Northern was under contract to transport rock across a frozen river in order to repair a dam. Two half-filled trucks crashed through the ice, killing the drivers, before Northern terminated the contract for impossibility.

Issue: Does the doctrine of impossibility excuse performance if the contract could be completed using means other than those specified in the contract?

Rule: A party is discharged from its contractual obligations, even if it is technically possible to perform them, if the cost of performance would be so disproportionate to that reasonably contemplated by the parties as to make the contract commercially impracticable.

Eastern Airlines, Inc. v. McDonnell Douglas Corp. (1976) CPB, KC, R

Facts: McDonnell Douglas breached a series of contracts to build planes for Eastern by delivering late. It blamed these delays on informal government requests to give priority to military orders needed for Vietnam but was not allowed to introduce evidence that these requests were the cause of the delay. The informal requests contained an implied threat of formal sanctions to compel placing priority on military orders. The contract contained an excusable delay clause which included, but was not limited to, delay due to government priorities.

Issue 1: Does UCC § 2-615 prohibit parties from contracting to expand or limit the excuses available to a promisor for nonperformance?

Rule 1: Parties may contract to narrow or broaden excuses available to a promisor.

Issue 2: Does UCC § 2-615, which excuses delay when agreed upon performances have been rendered commercially "impracticable," require that an event be unforeseeable at the time the agreement was executed?

Rule 2: Section 2-615 may apply even when the superseding event is foreseeable if the circumstances causing the breach have made performance so different from what was anticipated that the contract cannot reasonably govern.

Downing v. Stiles (1981) CPB

Facts: Downing sold a half-interest in a restaurant to Stiles for $25,000 payable in monthly installments. The restaurant was located in the basement of a building and received most of its business from a bar located above. The bar went out of business, greatly affecting the restaurant. Stiles stopped making payments to Downing several months later.

Issue: When does the doctrine of commercial frustration apply to excuse a party from performance?

Rule: Commercial frustration applies only if all of the following conditions are met: the contract is at least partially executory, a supervening event occurred after it was made, the nonoccurrence of this event was a basic assumption on which the agreement was made, the occurrence substantially frustrated the party's principal purpose and the party did not agree to perform in spite of the occurrence of the event.

Note: The principal purpose of the contract was to continue the restaurant business; the bar's failure did not affect this purpose.

407 East 61st Garage Inc. v. Savoy Fifth Avenue Corp.
(1968) CPB

Facts: The Savoy Hilton Hotel had a five-year contract with a local garage in which it referred its guests to the garage for car services and in return received 10 percent of the parking revenues derived from these guests. The hotel closed prior to the expiration of the contract.

Issue: May a party be excused from performance under the impossibility doctrine because of financial difficulty?

Rule: A party may not unilaterally abrogate a contract merely because it would be financially disadvantageous to perform.

J.J. Brooksbank Co. v. Budget Rent-A-Car Corp. (1983) R
Facts: For nearly ten years, Budget provided Brooksbank, pursuant to their franchise agreement, with one-third of its reservations for cars free of charge. Technological advancements allowed Budget to centralize the system. Following these advances, Budget attempted to charge Brooksbank for all reservations.
Issue: May a party be excused from performance on the basis of impracticability due to technological change if such was not expressly accounted for in the contract?
Rule: If a substantial change occurs in a relationship, the agreement may be adapted to the new realities of their arrangement consistent with the original contract, but a party will not be excused from its obligations as a result of technological change.
Note: The court ruled that Budget is obligated to continue to provide Brooksbank with a discount of one-third off reservation costs.

Karl Wendt Farm Equipment Co. v. International Harvester Co. (1991) KC
Facts: International Harvester entered into a franchise agreement with Wendt. Due to a dramatic downturn in the farm equipment market, International Harvester sold its farm equipment division, and Wendt lost his franchise. Wendt claimed breach of the franchise contract. International Harvester claimed that it could not perform the contract because of economic hardship.
Issue: Do the doctrines of impracticability or frustration excuse failure of performance because of economic loss or hardship?
Rule: Economic loss or hardship caused by a dramatic downturn in a market does not excuse performance under the doctrines of impracticability or frustration.

International Mineral and Chemical Corp. v. Llano, Inc. (1985) KC
Facts: Llano sold natural gas to IMC under a contract requiring IMC to purchase a minimum amount of gas each month. A government regulation caused IMC to shut down its operation which used most of the natural gas purchased from Llano. IMC claimed that the regulation made it pointless to purchase the minimum amount of gas under the contract.
Issue: Is a buyer excused from performance if a government regulation makes performance impracticable?

Rule: A buyer is excused from performance if compliance with a government regulation makes performance impracticable, even if the buyer voluntarily complies with the regulation. Performance is impracticable if the regulation creates an unanticipated circumstance that renders performance fundamentally different from what reasonably should have been within the contemplation of both parties when they entered into the contract, or if the regulation makes performance unreasonably costly.

Chapter 8

CONDITIONS

A condition is an *event*, not certain to occur, which must occur, unless its nonoccurrence is excused, before performance under a contract becomes due (Rest. 2d. § 224). Failure to perform a condition discharges the other party's duty to perform. Example: B promises to pay A on the condition that A delivers the goods by a certain date. B does not have to pay if A does not make delivery in time: the condition fails.

I.   CATEGORIZATION OF CONDITIONS ACCORDING TO TIME

A.   Condition Concurrent
The parties are bound to perform at the same time so that the performance of each one is dependent on the simultaneous performance of the other. Example: B hands cash to C with one hand and takes goods with the other.

B.   Condition Precedent
An event, other than a lapse of time, must occur before the other party has an absolute duty of performance. Example: A must deliver the goods before B has a duty to pay.

C.   Condition Subsequent
An event discharges an already existing absolute duty of performance (very rare).

D.   Precedent v. Subsequent

1. No Substantive Difference

2. Procedural Difference

   a. The party to whom the duty is owed must prove that a condition precedent has occurred.

   b. The party who owes the duty must prove that the condition subsequent has occurred.

3. The Restatement (Second) does not distinguish between conditions subsequent and precedent.

II.   EXPRESS CONDITIONS

Parties can expressly agree that some event must occur before a party's duty to perform arises. Usually, all of the requirements of the express condition must be met before a duty to render the dependent performance arises. For example, if a contract for the sale of a car requires that a down payment be made by a specific date as a condition of delivery, late payment discharges the duty to deliver.

A.   Courts try to avoid forfeiture and may excuse the nonoccurrence of a condition if it is not a material part of the exchange. (Rest. 2d. § 229.)

B.   Courts may not strictly enforce a condition if substantial performance can be proved.

C.   To determine whether a contract contains an express condition, court looks at:

1. Language
   Words such as "provided that," "when," "as soon as," and "after" all suggest that a condition exists.

2. Intent of the Parties
   Intent of the parties is determined by looking at the contract, circumstances surrounding its formation, and the parties' conduct subsequent to its formation.

3. Control
   If occurrence of the event is within the control of one of the parties, it is more likely to be a condition.

D.   Conditions of Satisfaction
   An agreement can make a party's performance conditional upon his satisfaction with the other party's performance.

1. Objective standard of reasonableness is used where the condition calls for satisfaction as to commercial value or quality, operative fitness, or mechanical utility.

2. Subjective satisfaction is required where the condition involves fancy, taste, or judgment (dissatisfaction can be unreasonable as long as it is in good faith).

3. Satisfaction of an Independent Party

   a. Example: A party's duty to pay can be conditioned upon an architect's subjective approval of the builder's performance.

   b. Majority Rule
      To suspend a third party's approval as a condition, it must be demonstrated that the refusal was made in bad faith, not that approval was unreasonably or unfairly withheld.

   c. Minority Rule
      An unreasonable refusal is sufficient to excuse a third party's approval as a condition to payment.

III. CONSTRUCTIVE CONDITIONS

In the interest of fairness a court will sometimes imply certain events (performances) to be conditions that must be fulfilled prior to the rendering of future performance. That is the case, for example, when the parties have agreed to what duties are expected of each other but have not provided a sequence of performance for those duties. Example: A agrees to pay B and B agrees to build A's house, but there is no payment schedule.

A. A party's performance is a constructive condition to the performance of the other party's stated subsequent duties.

B. Order of Performance Not Agreed Upon:

   1. If exchange of performances can be rendered simultaneously, then courts view the performances as constructive concurrent

conditions, i.e., conditions precedent to each other, and both must be performed simultaneously. (Rest. 2d. § 234(1).)

2. If the performance of one party requires a longer period of time, his performance is usually due first and is a constructive condition precedent to the other's performance. (Rest. 2d. § 234(2).)

3. Where a contract is made to perform work and no agreement is made as to time of payment, the work must be substantially performed before payment can be demanded.

C.   Bilateral Contracts
The modern rule is that there is a presumption that mutual promises in a contract are dependent and are to be so regarded whenever possible.

IV.   EXCUSE OF A CONDITION

If a condition to a party's performance has not been satisfied, that party is discharged from having to perform, unless the nonoccurrence is legally excused.

A.   Nonmaterial Breach
The constructive condition that full performance must be rendered before the other party is required to perform is excused where the party rendering incomplete performance has only committed a nonmaterial breach. Example: A paid B $499. The contract price was $500. The "injured" party has to perform, but can recover any damages caused by the breach.

B.   Material Breach
If there is a material breach, the breaching party has failed to fulfill the constructive condition of full performance. The "injured" party's

duties do not arise, and he is discharged from having to perform. He has the option to repudiate the contract.

1. Factors Determining Materiality of Breach (Rest. 2d. § 241)

   a. The extent to which the injured party will be deprived of benefit expected.

   b. The adequacy of damages.

   c. The extent to which the breaching party would suffer forfeiture.

   d. Likelihood failure will be cured.

   e. Whether the breaching party's behavior comported with good faith and fair dealing.

2. If a party repudiates a contract, claiming failure of a condition which is later excused, he will have materially breached.

   a. As a caution, an injured party can request an assurance of due performance if there are reasonable grounds for insecurity. (UCC § 2-609; Rest. 2d. § 251.)

   b. Although a party has no right to refuse performance of one contract because the other party has breached a separate contract between them, such a situation may give rise to reasonable grounds for insecurity.

C. Doctrine of Substantial Performance
    Primarily applied to building contracts, this excuses the condition of complete performance if the work is substantially performed.

1. The test is whether the breach was material or not (see above for factors).

2. If a breach was minor, and there was substantial performance, the injured party has a claim for damages but must perform its obligations.

3. The rule prevents forfeiture where a breach is minor.

4. It is applied mostly to constructive conditions.

5. UCC § 2-601

Under the UCC, if the goods in a sale-of-goods contract are defective "in any respect," the buyer is entitled to reject the entire shipment, reject only the defective goods, or accept the whole. Courts have often applied the doctrine of substantial performance to limit a buyer's right to rejection.

a. The parties can "otherwise agree," i.e., provide an arrangement other than rejection for defective goods.

b. The buyer cannot reject goods under an installment contract unless the flaw substantially impairs the value of that installment or of the whole contract. (UCC § 2-612.)

c. Rejection by the buyer must take place "within a reasonable time." (UCC § 2-602(1).)

d. After the buyer has accepted under UCC § 2-606:

   i. There is no right of rejection.

   ii. Revocation of the acceptance is valid only if the nonconformity substantially impairs the value of the goods to him and takes place within a reasonable time. (UCC § 2-608.)

e. If the goods were rejected, and the time for performance has not expired, the seller may cure the defect. (UCC § 2-508.)

D.   Promise v. Condition

1. The performance of a party can be construed as either a condition, which must be fulfilled before the other has to perform, or as an absolute obligation (promise), which is not a condition to future performance. Due to the harshness of forfeiture, courts sometimes interpret express conditions to be promises in cases where a nonmaterial deviation from the required performance occurs. Example: B contracts to design C's home and to secure the city's approval of the plans. B does the work, but the city does not grant approval. To avoid forfeiture, courts may rule that B's obligation to secure the city's approval was a promise and not a condition for payment. Of course, C is entitled to damages for breach.

2. Courts look to the intent of the parties to determine if the contract language is a promise or a condition.

3. The language of the contract will be interpreted as a promise to avoid forfeiture in some cases. (See *Jacob & Young v. Kent.*)

4. Conditions with an Implied Promise
    A contract term may be both a condition and a promise for one party.

    a. A condition within control of the party may carry an implied promise of "best efforts" to perform the condition. Example: B promises to buy C's home, if he can obtain financing. B must make "best efforts" to obtain financing. Where a conditional promise is not performed, the other party is entitled to suspend performance and sue for damages.

    b. Order of Preferences
        The order of preference in interpreting nonperformance is first as a promise, then as a condition, and if the other two are not possible, as a promissory condition. (Rest. 2d. § 227.)

E. Divisible Contracts
It is not a condition precedent to the other party's performance that all segments of a divisible contract be performed.

1. If the part to be performed by one party consists of several distinct items, and the price to be paid by the other is apportioned to each item to be performed, such contract will generally be held to be divisible.

2. If a party performs a segment of a divisible contract, he is entitled to the other party's equivalent performance for the completed segment. (Rest. 2d. § 240.)

F. Anticipatory Repudiation
An anticipatory repudiation occurs when a party clearly indicates that it will not render future performance when it becomes due. Example: A contracts to sell wheat to B in November. In July, A informs B that he will not deliver the wheat. There is a requirement that the threatened future breach be total or material for the nonrepudiating party to be excused from rendering performance.

1. The nonrepudiating party is, therefore, excused from performing the constructive condition of manifesting a prospective ability and willingness to perform.

2. The nonrepudiating party is entitled not only to suspend his performance, but to cancel the contract and immediately sue for damages. (Rest. 2d. § 253; UCC § 2-610.)

3. The doctrine of anticipatory breach has not ordinarily been extended to unilateral contracts. Even if the party repudiates an installment contract, each delinquent installment must be sued upon after it becomes due.

4. Repudiation may be retracted prior to any material change of position by the other party in reliance on the repudiation. (Rest. 2d. § 256(1); UCC § 2-611.)

5. If a party's conduct indicates an inability to perform, the nonrepudiating party may suspend performance and request an adequate assurance of performance. Failure to give assurance within thirty days (UCC) or within a reasonable time may be treated as a repudiation. (Rest. 2d. § 251; UCC § 2-609(1).)

6. UCC Damages for Seller's Repudiation:

   a. UCC § 2-713(1) states that damages are measured from the time the buyer learns of breach by the seller.

   b. This section is modified by § 2-610(a), which states that the nonrepudiating party may await performance for a commercially reasonable time.

G. Prevention of Performance
   The nonoccurrence of a condition will be excused if the conduct of the party benefitting from the condition prevents the occurrence of the condition.

   1. The test is whether the party being prevented from performing the condition assumed the risk of the preventing party's conduct.

   2. Making performance more difficult, but not impossible, will not necessarily excuse the condition.

   3. In every contract, there is a constructive condition of cooperation. (Rest. 2d. § 205.)

H. Waiver of a Condition

   1. Which Conditions May Be Waived

      a. A party may waive performance of a condition inserted for his benefit.

      b. A party cannot, by waiver of a condition precedent to his own liability, create an obligation where none previously existed, unless consideration is given for the waiver.

c. Material conditions cannot be waived.

2. Types of Waiver

a. Estoppel Waiver
Estoppel Waiver is binding if manifestation of waiver of a condition, before it was to happen, is materially relied upon by the other party. However, a waiver can be retracted if no reliance occurred.

b. Election Waiver
Election Waiver is binding if a party decides to continue under the contract after a condition has not been performed.

3. After waiving a condition, a party still has a right to damages.

CASE CLIPS

Howard v. Fed. Crop Ins. Corp. (1976) DHH, FE, R

Facts: Howard, a farmer, informed Fed. Crop Insurance that his tobacco crop was damaged. Howard replanted the field before an adjuster could inspect the damage. Fed. Crop Insurance claimed the inspection was a condition precedent to payment of the claim and refused to pay.

Issue: Are words that are ambiguous as to whether they create a promise or a condition construed as creating a condition precedent?

Rule: The provisions of a contract will not be construed as conditions precedent in the absence of language plainly requiring such conditions.

Gray v. Gardner (1821) DHH

Facts: Gray sold Gardner a certain amount of whale oil, for which Gardner agreed to pay $5,198.87. The contract specified that if a greater quantity of oil arrived this year than last, the agreement was void.

Issue: Which party has the burden of proving the occurrence of a condition subsequent?

Rule: The party that wishes to avoid its obligation under a contract has the burden of proving the occurrence of a condition subsequent.

Parsons v. Bristol Dev. Co. (1965) DHH

Facts: Parsons' construction contract provided that he be paid 25 percent of the money at the start of work and that Bristol would be obligated to pay the rest only on condition of obtaining a loan, which it failed to do. Parsons sued for the value of the work done. The trial court ruled that Bristol was not obligated to pay because the condition was not met.

Issue: Is an appellate court compelled to accept any reasonable interpretation of a written instrument adopted by a trial court?

Rule: Where there is no conflict in the evidence, or a determination has been made upon incompetent evidence, an appellate court is not bound by a construction of the contract based solely upon the terms of the written instrument without the aid of extrinsic evidence.

Mascioni v. I.B. Miller, Inc. (1933) DHH, CPB

Facts: I.B. Miller, a contractor, was to make payments to his subcontractor Mascioni "as received from the owner." Mascioni brought suit to recover payments even though the owner had not paid I.B. Miller. I.B. Miller introduced extrinsic evidence to show that payment by the owner was a condition to payment to the subcontractor.

Issue: Can extrinsic evidence be introduced to interpret an ambiguous provision as a condition?

Rule: Extrinsic evidence of the intentions of the parties may demonstrate that an ambiguous express promise to pay a debt upon the happening of a certain condition includes an implication that the debt shall not be paid until the condition is satisfied.

Thomas J. Dyer Co. v. Bishop Int'l Engineering Co. (1962) FE, CPB

Facts: Dyer, a subcontractor, worked for Bishop, a general contractor under a contract that provided that Dyer would be paid five days after the owner paid Bishop. The owner paid Bishop a partial amount of the total due, and Bishop likewise reduced payment to Dyer.

Issue: Can a contractor shift the risk of nonpayment by the owner onto the subcontractor by making payment by the owner a condition to payment to the subcontractor?

Rule: If not clearly stated in the contract, payment by the owner will not act as a condition precedent to receipt of payment by the subcontractor. The contractor must pay, regardless of whether he is paid, unless there is a clear and definite contractual provision to the contrary.

Royal-Globe Ins. Co. v. Craven (1992) DHH

Facts: Craven was involved in a hit and run accident and was taken to the hospital where she remained in intensive care for 23 days. Craven's insurance policy required her to notify Royal-Globe of the accident within 24 hours of its occurrence as a condition to coverage. Craven waited for more than three months after her release from the hospital before notifying Royal-Globe of her accident. Royal-Globe sought a declaratory judgment on its potential liability.

Issue: May a disability serve to excuse performance of an express condition?

Rule: A disability may only serve to delay performance of an express condition until the disability is removed. The obligation is reinstated once the party burdened by the condition is able to fulfill its requirements.

Gilbert v. Globe & Rutgers Fire Ins. Co. (1919) DHH

Facts: Gilbert did not file a claim within 12 months after his cottage burned down, because the insurance company's adjuster promised he would be paid anyway. A year later the insurance company informed Gilbert that it would contest the claim, but he still waited close to three years before suing for damages.

Issue: Is an insurer, previously estopped from asserting that a condition was not met, allowed to make such an assertion if the reason for not bringing suit is no longer applicable and the insured is notified?

Rule: An insurer's promise that induces an insured party to not bring suit within the time limitation estops the insurer from pleading that the contractual condition has not been met. If the reason for not bringing suit is no longer effective, and the insured is notified, the insured must commence his action within a reasonable time.

Porter v. Harrington (1928) DHH

Facts: A contract provided that if payment default continued for a period of 31 days, the agreement would become void without notice, and all previous payments would be kept by the defendant as liquidated damages. After constantly accepting overdue payments for years, Harrington sought to cancel the contract without notifying Porter. The contract also provided that waiver of a breach was not a waiver of a subsequent breach of the same condition.

Issue: After constantly waiving a condition, can a party insist upon strict performance of a contract provision without notice if it would lead to a forfeiture by the other party?

Rule: When a party, without objection, has constantly waived a condition, an order of business has been established that supersedes the strict terms of the agreement. A party cannot then insist on strict compliance without giving notice, if doing so would cause forfeiture to the other party.

Clark v. West (1908) DHH, MS, FE

Facts: West, a publisher of law books, promised to pay Clark $6.00 per page for an acceptable manuscript if Clark did not drink and $2.00 per page if he did. West discovered that Clark was drinking alcohol during the term of the contract but told Clark not to worry. When the book was finished, West offered to pay only $2 per page. Clark claimed that the alcohol provision was a condition to the contract, which was expressly waived by West. West claimed abstinence was consideration for the contract.

Issue: May a condition to a contract be waived?

Rule: While a condition to a contract can be expressly waived, merely accepting a party's performance (West took the finished book) does not constitute waiver.

Inman v. Clyde Hall Drilling Co. (1962) DHH, FE, KC, MS, CPB

Facts: Inman's employment contract provided that, in case of any claim against the company, Inman had to send written notice within 30 days after the claim arose and bring suit six months after giving notice and not later than one year thereafter. Inman sued 12 days after being wrongfully discharged, without giving notice.

Issue: Must a party fulfill an express notice of claim requirement before filing a suit for breach of contract?

Rule: A notice of claim requirement which was made an express condition precedent to recovery on the contract must be fulfilled before suit is filed for breach of contract.

Grenier v. Compratt Constr. Co. (1983) DHH

Facts: Grenier contracted to perform various construction work for Compratt, agreeing to provisions conditioning payment upon the acquisition and delivery of a letter from the city engineer, warranting that a certificate of occupancy could be obtained by Compratt for any of its lots upon which Grenier worked. Although Grenier substantially completed its work within the required time, it was unable to promptly procure the letter because the City Engineer did not ordinarily write such letters. More than a week later, Grenier acquired a comparable letter from the assistant city attorney.

Issue: If satisfaction of a condition is impracticable, may the condition be excused?

Rule: Enforcement of a condition is subject to the principles of impracticability. If the occurrence of a condition is not a material part of the exchange, the condition may be excused, provided it was not in the contemplation of the parties when they entered into the contract that the condition would be impracticable and a forfeiture would result from its enforcement.

Nolan v. Whitney (1882) DHH, R

Facts: Nolan had substantially completed work due under the contract but was unable to secure the architect's certificate, which was required for payment of the last installment, because of minor defects.

Issue: If a party has substantially complied with the terms of the contract, may an architect refuse approval necessary for payment, if the performance involves only trivial defects?

Rule: Refusal to give an architect's certificate, because of trivial defects, to a party who has substantially performed his contractual duties is unreasonable, and dispenses with the approval requirement.

Fursmidt v. Hotel Abbey Holding Corp. (1960) DHH, R

Facts: Fursmidt's employment at Hotel Abbey was subject to the hotel's satisfaction with Fursmidt's performance. Hotel Abbey dismissed Fursmidt, claiming dissatisfaction.

Issue: What standard is used to determine if a party properly exercised its right to accept or reject a party's performance?

Rule: In contracts containing satisfaction clauses, the jury must look to see if the party is honestly dissatisfied before that party may terminate the contract. There is no requirement of reasonableness.

Nichols v. Raynbred (1615) DHH, KGK, R

Facts: Nichols promised to deliver a cow, while Raynbred promised to pay him 50 shillings.

Issue: Must a party assert that he performed his part of a bilateral contract in order to bring suit against the other party?

Rule: In a bilateral contract, a party may bring a lawsuit without asserting that he performed his part of the bargain.

Note: This case illustrates the older view that promises were independent of each other and that they were not constructive conditions for each other.

Kingston v. Preston (1773) DHH, KGK, MS

Facts: Preston promised to sell his business to Kingston, and Kingston promised to post a bond as security guaranteeing his payment. When he did not give security, Preston refused to sell. Kingston sued for breach, claiming that his promise was not a condition to the defendant's duty to sell.

Issue: When each party to a contract makes an interdependent promise to the other, may a party sue for breach without having substantially performed on its promise?

Rule: When parties exchange promises which are not independent, each party's substantial performance of its promise is a constructive condition to the other party's performance of any subsequent duties.

Price v. Van Lint (1941) DHH

Facts: Van Lint agreed to lend Price money to build a house. The contract required Price to take out a mortgage to secure Van Lint's loan, but both parties realized that due to some difficulties the mortgage would only be taken out after the loan was made. Van Lint was unable to make the loan on time and claimed he was excused from doing so because Price could not meet the condition precedent to making the loan.

Issue: Are mutual promises independent if the parties were aware that the performance of one promise may arrive sooner than the other?

Rule: Where a contract contains mutual promises to pay money or perform some other act, and the time for performance by one party does, or may, arrive before the time for performance by the other, the latter's promise is an independent obligation. Therefore, although the party that is required to perform first is entitled to sue for breach, he must still render performance or else be sued for breach himself.

Rubin v. Fuchs (1969) DHH

Facts: Fuchs' contract to sell land to Rubin required Rubin to place a $30,000 deposit in escrow and to make another $20,000 deposit after the property was subdivided and recorded. Fuchs asked Rubin to make the second deposit before the conditions were met and sold the land to another party when he refused.

Issue: Will the provisions of a bilateral contract be construed as conditions precedent if one performance is "subject to" and necessarily dependent upon another performance?

Rule: Generally, courts will construe promises in a bilateral contract as mutually dependent and concurrent; however, the provisions of a contract will be construed as conditions precedent if the language plainly requires such construction.

Ziehen v. Smith (1896) DHH

Facts: The defendant contracted to sell property to the plaintiff, who was unaware that the property was encumbered by an outstanding mortgage placed by the previous owner. An action to foreclose the mortgage was brought before the date on which the defendant was to transfer the property to the plaintiff, and a sale to a third party resulted. The plaintiff sued to recover his deposit and other expenses.

Issue: Is a formal tender of performance by the vendee necessary to maintain an action if performance by the vendor is impossible?

Rule: If the vendor of real estate under an executory contract is unable to perform on his part, a formal tender by the vendee is not required to maintain an action to recover the money paid on the contract or for damages.

Note: "Tender of performance" means that the party demanded performance by the other.

Cohen v. Kranz (1963) DHH, CPB

Facts: Cohen refused to buy Kranz's land after he discovered that the fence extended beyond the property, there was no certificate for use of the pool, and use of the land was restricted (by a covenant that could be removed). Cohen sued for his deposit.

Issue: Is a vendee required to tender performance and demand title in order to place a vendor with curable title defects in default?

Rule: Although a vendor with incurable title defects is automatically in default, a vendor with curable title defects must be placed in default by a vendee's tender of performance and demand for a good title deed.

Beecher v. Conradt (1855) DHH

Facts: Conradt promised to pay the purchase price in five installments. Beecher did not sue Conradt for the amount of each installment as they came due but sought to recover the entire amount after the last payment came due.

Issue: Is a party prevented from bringing suit against a party for independent installments if he did not bring suit for the independent installments as they became due?

Rule: A party's omission to insist upon the other party's strict performance of independent obligations, at the times when they are required, bars the party from suing on the independent obligations.

Osborne v. Bullins (1989) DHH

Facts: Bullins contracted to sell his land to Osborne for $85,000. The contract provided for payment to be made within 60 days of delivery of the deed and title. Osborne refused to close the deal after the 60 day period had passed, claiming inability to obtain the proper financing. Bullins sued for specific performance. The lower court directed Bullins to convey the property to Osborne, and deposit the deed with the court clerk, to be released when Osborne was able to pay the purchase price. Further, Bullins was granted a vendor's lien on the property.

Issue: May a court go beyond traditional legal remedies in fashioning a judgment to suit a particular controversy?

Rule: Courts are not bound by traditional damage measures in cases where they do not adequately protect the expectation interests of the non-breaching party. In such a case, the court is free to use judicial discretion in creating a remedy which suits the fact of a case, and sufficiently preserves the interest of the non-breaching party.

Note: The traditional legal remedy in this case would require Bullins to market the property to someone else, and limit the money judgment against Osborne to the price difference, if any.

Stewart v. Newbury (1917) DHH, FE, MS, CPB

Facts: Although a contract for excavation work did not specify the terms and conditions regarding time or manner of payment, Stewart alleged that payment was to be made in "the usual manner" (85 percent every 30 days). After Newbury refused to pay, Stewart asserted he was excused from completely performing the contract.

Issue: May a party discontinue performance and demand payment without having substantially performed?

Rule: Where a contract is made to perform work, and no agreement is made as to time of payment, the work must be substantially performed before payment can be demanded.

Tipton v. Feitner (1859) DHH

Facts: In one contract, Tipton agreed to sell Feitner an amount of dressed hogs for a certain price and an amount of live hogs for a different price on different delivery dates. The dressed hogs were delivered but not paid for, and the live hogs were never delivered. Feitner claimed that delivery of the live hogs was a condition precedent to payment of both contracts.

Issue: Is a contract severable if it includes two transactions that differ in subject matter, price, and delivery date?

Rule: A contract may be severable if it includes two transactions that differ in subject matter, price, and delivery date. Performance of either transaction cannot act as a condition precedent for the other independent transaction. In each individual transaction, however, delivery and payment are each conditions of the other, and neither party can sue for breach without having offered performance on his part.

Oshinsky v. Lorraine Mfg. Co. (1911) DHH

Facts: The defendant refused to accept the balance of "shirtings" because the plaintiff delivered them after the time specified in the contract.

Issue: Must a purchaser accept and pay for goods delivered after the day specified in the contract?

Rule: When time is of the essence, the purchaser is not required to accept and pay for goods unless they are delivered or tendered on the day specified in the contract.

Prescott & Co. v. Powles & Co. (1920) DHH

Facts: Prescott contracted to deliver 300 crates of onions, but was only able to ship 240 crates because shipping space had been restricted due to the war. Powles refused to accept the shipment. Prescott sold the onions elsewhere and sued for its loss from the contract price.

Issue: May a party sue for contract damages if it fails to fulfill an express condition for payment due to the interference of a third party?

Rule: An action on the contract is barred if full performance of contractual duties cannot be shown. Partial performance is adequate only when an act of the other party renders performance impossible, performance is waived, or a relevant excuse is provided for in the contract. (The parties were aware of the war and thus assumed the risk of its effects.)

Bartus v. Riccardi (1967) DHH, CPB

Facts: Bartus supplied Riccardi with a Model A-665 hearing aid, an updated version of the Model A-660 that Riccardi had ordered. When Riccardi, who was dissatisfied, returned the hearing aid, Bartus immediately informed him that he would either replace the model that had been delivered or would obtain the Model A-660 for him. Riccardi refused the offer.

Issue: May a seller cure a nonconforming tender?

Rule: Where the buyer rejects a nonconforming tender that the seller had reasonable grounds to believe would be acceptable, the seller is given a reasonable period of time in which to make a conforming tender if he gives the buyer seasonable notice. (UCC § 2-508(2).)

Plante v. Jacobs (1960) DHH, FE

Facts: Plante contracted to build a home for Jacobs who later refused to continue payment because of defects in the construction. Plante did not complete the house and sued for the unpaid balance. Jacobs claimed that Plante failed to substantially perform. The market value of the house was not significantly affected by the defects.

Issue: Is a contractor liable for failure to substantially perform if there are construction defects that do not significantly affect market value?

Rule: The test for substantial performance is whether the performance meets the essential purpose of the contract. As applied to construction of a house, substantial performance does not mean that every detail must be in strict compliance with the specifications and the plans. Contract recovery will be determined by the *cost of replacement rule* for small defects or by the *diminished value rule* to avoid unreasonable economic waste for defects, correction of which is expensive but adds little or nothing to the value.

Worcester Heritage Society, Inc. v. Trussell (1991) DHH

Facts: Worcester sold an historically significant building to Trussell. Under the agreement, Trussell was to perform a complete historic restoration of the property. The exterior portion of the restoration was to be completed within one year. If Trussel failed to complete the restoration within the year, Worcester could hire its own workers, at Trussell's expense, to complete the restoration. Although Trussell attempted to complete the project, work went much slower than expected, and five years later the exterior was only 75 percent complete. Worcester brought suit for rescission of the contract.

Issue: Is a court required to grant rescission for breach of a contract term?

Rule: In the absence of an express agreement to the contrary, a court has discretion to refuse to grant rescission as a remedy for breach, if the non-performance of the contract term is not material enough to go to the "essence" of the contract and other legal remedies are available.

Turner Concrete Steel Co. v.
Chester Constr. & Contracting Co. (1921) DHH

Facts: Chester, the contractor, paid Turner, a subcontractor, a substantial amount which Chester stated was the entire balance owed. Without giving notice, Turner stopped work because it felt it was not fully paid for its work. Turner refused to submit its claim for verification after Chester promised to pay outstanding charges six days later. Turner sued to recover its claim.

Issue: May a subcontractor abandon a project if full payment was delayed as a result of a bona fide dispute over the amount owed?

Rule: Although in large construction contracts where the work is spread over a considerable period of time the covenant to perform is normally dependent upon the covenant to pay, a contractor (subcontractor) is not entitled to abandon a contract because there is a dispute of reasonable delay as to payment unless there has been some wrongful act or default on the part of the owner (contractor).

K & G Construction Co. v. Harris
(1960) DHH, FE, CPB

Facts: K & G Construction, a contractor, hired Harris, a subcontractor, pursuant to a contract that required Harris to perform in a "workmanlike manner." Harris breached this requirement by negligently demolishing a wall, and the company refused to pay him. K & G Construction sued for its loss after it had to pay another subcontractor an additional sum to finish the work.

Issue: Are mutual promises dependent or independent promises?

Rule: Covenants are construed as dependent or independent according to the intention of the parties and the good sense of the case. The failure of a contractor (subcontractor) to perform in a workmanlike manner may justify an owner's (contractor's) refusal to make a progress payment.

Note: The modern rule holds there is a presumption that mutual promises in a contract are dependent and are to be so regarded, whenever possible.

Hathaway v. Sabin (1891) DHH, FE

Facts: The defendant hired the plaintiff to perform a concert. Defendant was required to rent a hall and to pay the plaintiff's salary but decided not to rent the hall when a snowstorm made it almost impossible for the musicians to come from a nearby town.

Issue: Will a reasonable belief that the other party will not be able to perform his part of the bargain excuse a party's failure to perform his own contractual obligations?

Rule: A party's reasonable belief that the other party will be prevented from performing does not excuse a failure on his part to perform his contractual duties.

Cherwell-Ralli, Inc. v. Rytman Grain Co., Inc. (1980) DHH, R

Facts: Despite an assurance from Cherwell-Ralli's president that deliveries would continue, Rytman Grain stopped payment on its check after it was told by a truck driver that the deliveries would soon end. Subsequently, Cherwell-Ralli demanded payment and Rytman Grain demanded adequate assurance of due performance.

Issue: Can a buyer demand assurance of due performance if the cause of its insecurity is an unreliable rumor?

Rule: The right to assurance of due performance is premised on having reasonable grounds for insecurity.

Greguhn v. Mutual of Omaha Ins. Co. (1969) DHH

Facts: Greguhn was covered for his permanent disability under an insurance policy that his two insurance companies, the defendants, repudiated. The trial court awarded Greguhn a lump-sum judgment for all future payments.

Issue: Does repudiation of an installment due under a unilateral contract amount to an anticipatory breach of the rest of the installments not yet due?

Rule: The doctrine of anticipatory breach has not ordinarily been extended to unilateral contracts. Even if the party repudiates the installment contract, each delinquent installment must be sued upon separately after it becomes due.

Reigart v. Fisher (1925) DHH

Facts: Although the buyer, Reigart, did not care how many acres he received, he refused further payment because the acreage of the property he purchased was less than represented in the contract's terms. The sellers, the

Fishers, sued for specific performance as the shortage in acreage was less than 6 percent of the purchase price.

Issue: If a misrepresentation does not materially affect the subject matter of a transaction, can the misrepresenting party sue for specific performance?

Rule: Specific performance is allowed if the misrepresentation of the estate is not substantial and does not so affect the subject matter of the contract that, but for such a misdescription, the contract would never have been made. When the sale can be enforced, the buyer shall have what the seller can give with an abatement for so much as the quantity falls short of the representation.

Ide v. Joe Miller & Co. (1984) DHH

Facts: One of the key reasons the Ides agreed to buy the Joe Miller & Co.'s farm was their belief that a well on the property could pump 350 gallons per minute. The well's true capacity was 113 gallons per minute.

Issue: Will a contract provision that was of great concern to one of the parties be considered a condition to be met before that party becomes obligated to perform?

Rule: A provision that goes to the root of the contract will be interpreted as a condition. Upon failure of a condition, the party not in default can opt for either termination of the contract with refund of monies paid, or specific performance and damages.

Pordage v. Cole (1669) KGK

Facts: Cole contracted to buy a house and land from Pordage, but failed to pay Pordage the balance of the purchase price. Pordage sought "debt upon the specialty" (or bond) without alleging that he conveyed the premises.

Issue: May a seller of land recover on a bond without alleging a tender of conveyance?

Rule: A seller could recover on the bond without alleging conveyance of the land. Likewise, if the seller has not conveyed the land, the buyer could compel a conveyance in an action of covenant.

Boone v. Eyre (1777) KGK

Facts: The plaintiff promised that he had good title to the plantation and the slaves which he conveyed to the defendant. The defendant pleaded that he failed to pay the agreed upon annuity because the plaintiff did not legally possess all the slaves and therefore did not have good title to convey.

Issue: Will a party's covenant be precedent to the other party's performance if the covenant only goes to a part of the consideration of the agreement?

Rule: When mutual covenants go to the whole of the consideration on both sides, they are mutual conditions, the one precedent to the other; when they only go to a part, they are independent covenants where a breach may be paid for in damages.

Norrington v. Wright (1885) KGK, R

Facts: Norrington agreed to sell Wright 5,000 tons of iron rails in shipments of about 1,000 tons a month. Norrington shipped the rails in quantities that varied both above and below the 1,000-ton agreement. Wright rescinded the contract after the third such shipment. Norrington claimed that as long as 5,000 were shipped, the size of each particular shipment was not important.

Issue: Does a seller have a right to vary shipment size from the stipulated quantity in the contract?

Rule: When goods are to be shipped under a contract in certain proportions monthly, the seller's failure to ship the required quantity in the first month gives the buyer the right to rescind the whole contract and bars a seller's action for damages for the nonfulfillment of the agreement.

Miron v. Yonkers Raceway, Inc. (1968) KGK

Facts: Finkelstein bought a horse that the seller, the plaintiff, represented as a great racer. Despite the trade custom to examine a racehorse's legs, Finkelstein did not examine the horse. Finkelstein attempted to reject the sale when he found that one of the horse's legs was lame but failed to conclusively establish the date of the fracture.

Issue: Does a buyer bear the burden of proving a breach of warranty if he fails to reject goods within a reasonable time?

Rule: A party accepts goods by failing to reject them within a reasonable time (UCC § 2-602(1)) and thus bears the burden of proving any breach of warranty. (UCC § 2-607(4).)

Maurice O'Meara Co. v. Nat'l Park Bank of New York (1925) KGK

Facts: The National Park Bank issued O'Meara's assignor a letter of credit for the purpose of shipment of newsprint paper. The letter was payable upon presentation of a sight draft and documents indicating the amount and quality of the newsprint paper. The bank refused to pay a sight draft when it realized the shipment consisted of inferior paper.

Issue: Must a bank perform its obligation to pay sight drafts under a letter of credit even if it knew the goods purchased are not of the quality stipulated in the contract?

Rule: If sight drafts, when presented, are accompanied by the proper documents, then a bank is absolutely bound to make payment under a letter of credit, irrespective of whether it knew or had reason to believe that the goods purchased under the letter are not of the quality stipulated in the contract.

Britton v. Turner (1834) KGK, MS, FE

Facts: Britton breached a 12-month employment contact without reason after completing 9 ½ months.

Issue: Is a party who voluntarily breaches an employment contract entitled to recover anything for the labor actually performed?

Rule: Although not entitled to recover on the contract itself, a defaulting plaintiff may receive the reasonable value of his services less the damages incurred by the other party. In determining the reasonable value of services, the contract price cannot be exceeded.

Smith v. Brady (1858) KGK

Facts: The plaintiff made many deviations from contract specifications to build the defendant's buildings. The defendant refused to make the final payment, although he took possession of the property.

Issue: May a party recover payments due only on the condition of performance by him if he cannot demonstrate the required performance or establish that the condition has been waived?

Rule: A party cannot recover payments that are due only on condition of performance by him, unless he can prove performance or waiver. The question of waiver is one of intention to be determined from all the circumstances. Mere use and occupation of defective premises does not constitute a waiver of the condition of full and proper performance.

Jacob & Youngs v. Kent (1921) KGK, KC, MS, CPB

Facts: Jacob & Youngs, a contractor hired to build a home for Kent, inadvertently installed a different brand of pipes than that specified in the contract. The pipes used were of comparable price and quality to those specified. Kent refused to pay Jacob & Youngs unless the pipes were replaced.

Issue: When will the inadvertent breach of a condition invoke damages rather than forfeiture?

Rule: When a party inadvertently breaches a contract in a nonmaterial manner the measure of damages will be the difference in value between the specified and the actual performances rather than the cost to correct.

Brown-Marx Associates, Ltd. v. Emigrant Sav. Bank
(1983) FE

Facts: Brown-Marx secured a loan commitment from the Emigrant Savings Bank, but the bank backed out of the agreement, stating that Brown-Marx failed to satisfy a minimum rental requirement.

Issue: Is failure to satisfy a minimum rental requirement in a loan agreement grounds for refusing the loan?

Rule: Because a specific minimum rental requirement is a precise requirement, a party will not have substantially fulfilled its obligation if it does not fulfill that requirement.

In Re Carter's Claim (1957) FE, MS

Facts: The plaintiff's contract to buy the defendant's business included a warranty that the financial condition of the company had not materially changed since the inception of negotiations and a condition that the plaintiff could refuse to buy if the company's financial condition was less favorable than at the time of negotiations. The plaintiff bought the company but later claimed breach of warranty because the financial condition was not as favorable.

Issue: May the failure of an express condition precedent be handled as a breach of warranty action for damages?

Rule: A failure of an express condition precedent may not be handled as a breach of warranty. If the condition is not fulfilled, the injured party has the right to refuse consummation of the sale or can waive the condition by completing the transaction (which the plaintiff did in this case).

Note: This case revolves around the interpretation of a provision: i.e., is it a condition or warranty/promise?

Vanadium Corp. v. Fidelity & Deposit Co. (1947) FE

Facts: Vanadium Corp. acquired Redington's interest in two leases for $13,000, subject to approval by the Secretary of the Interior. After being denied, Vanadium made no further efforts to secure approval and actually urged the Secretary not to reconsider his position. Redington had obtained a bond from Fidelity binding himself and the surety to return all of the money in the event of the Secretary's disapproval.

Issue: If both parties are required to make a good faith effort to secure a contract condition, can one act to hinder its occurrence?

Rule: Wherever the cooperation of the promisee is necessary for the performance of the promise, there is a condition implied in fact that cooperation and a good faith effort will be given.

E.I. Du Pont De Nemours Powder Co. v. Schlottman (1914) FE

Facts: Du Pont agreed to pay Grub, Schlottman's assignor, an additional $25,000 if, among other things, the property purchased was worth $175,000 to Du Pont after one year passed. Du Pont sold the property after six months.

Issue: Can a buyer violate a contractually provided for test to determine additional compensation for the seller?

Rule: If there is a contractually provided for test to determine additional compensation for the seller to be executed one year from the making of their contract, there is an implied promise that the buyer will operate the property for one year.

Morin Building Prod. Co. v. Baystone Constr., Inc.
(1983) FE, KC

Facts: Baystone contracted to construct an addition to a building for General Motors. Baystone subcontracted some of the work to Morin. The contract between Baystone and GM stated that the work would be subject to approval by GM's agent and that GM could make decisions based on artistic effect. GM did not approve of some of the walls, and Baystone refused to pay Morin for its work on the walls.

Issue: Must a satisfaction clause in a commercial contract be bound by objective criteria?

Rule: Because the contract was ambiguous as to whether the work had to satisfy the personal whim of the agent, and because the construction was for a factory and not an object of beauty, the contract should be read to be constrained by objective standards.

Mattei v. Hopper (1958) FE

Facts: Mattei agreed to buy Hopper's shopping center. The agreement called for a $1,000 down payment and the balance to be paid within 120 days subject to Mattei obtaining satisfactory leases. Hopper refused to complete the sale, claiming Mattei's promise was illusory because he was not actually bound: Hopper was obligated to sell, but Mattei only had to buy if he was satisfied with the leases.

Issue: Does a contract lack consideration if the assent of one party to the agreement is conditioned by a satisfaction clause?

Rule: An agreement that contains a satisfaction clause is not illusory (lacking consideration or mutuality of obligation) if performance of the condition can be judged by a reasonable person standard or the party subject to the satisfaction clause acts in good faith.

Thomas J. Dyer Co. v. Bishop Int'l Engineering Co.
(1962) FE, CPB

Facts: Dyer, a subcontractor, worked for Bishop, a general contractor under a contract that provided that Dyer would be paid five days after the owner paid Bishop. The owner paid Bishop a partial amount of the total due, and Bishop likewise reduced payment to Dyer.

Issue: Can a contractor shift the risk of nonpayment by the owner onto the subcontractor by making payment by the owner a condition to payment to the subcontractor?

Rule: If not clearly stated in the contract, payment by the owner will not act as a condition precedent to receipt of payment by the subcontractor. The contractor must pay, regardless of whether he is paid, unless there is a clear and definite contractual provision to the contrary.

J.N.A. Realty Corp. v. Cross Bay Chelsea, Inc.
(1977) FE, KC

Facts: Cross Bay Chelsea, through inadvertence, did not renew its lease with J.N.A. Realty within the time allotted. J.N.A. Realty sought to recover possession of the premises, and Cross Bay Chelsea asked the court to relieve it from a forfeiture.

Issue: Does a tenant suffer forfeiture when, through its own negligence, it forgets to renew its lease within the allotted time, and the landlord wishes to recover possession of the property?

Rule: An option to renew does not itself create any interest in property, and thus its loss is not a forfeiture, unless the tenant has invested substantially in improving the property for its use. Also, the court cannot rule, without a careful examination of the facts, whether negligence should be cause for the denial of equitable relief.

Mutual Life Ins. Co. of New York v. Johnson
(1934) FE

Facts: Cooksey's insurance policy provided benefits upon proof of total disability. Due to mental disability after suffering an accident, Cooksey was unable to give the contractually required notice of disability to Mutual Life.
Issue: Is mental incapacity a valid excuse for the failure to fulfill a procedural requirement of a contract?
Rule: To avoid harsh and unreasonable consequences, failure to perform a procedural contractual requirement may be excused if it is the result of mental disability.

Wisconsin Knife Works v. National Metal Crafters
(1986) FE, R

Facts: Wisconsin's purchase order included a provision that stated that the contract could not be modified without its agents written assent. When National missed the delivery deadlines, Wisconsin accepted the late shipments and issued a new set of orders. Wisconsin later terminated the contract after National missed more deadlines. National claimed Wisconsin "waived" the written modification requirement by acceptance of late shipments.
Issue: When does conduct implying assent to modification "operate as a waiver" (UCC § 2-209(4)) despite a clause voiding modifications not in writing?
Rule: Implied acceptance of a modification of a contract containing a clause forbidding anything but a written modification is effective as a waiver only when it is reasonably relied upon by the party seeking to enforce the modification.

Vidal v. Transcontinental & Western Air (1941) FE

Facts: The plaintiffs purchased four used planes from the defendant, payment to be made upon delivery. On the date set for delivery, the plaintiffs did not request the planes, and the defendant did not offer to deliver. The plaintiffs sued for damages.
Issue: May a party maintain an action if it was ready and willing to perform its obligations but did not actually request performance?

Rule: Where payment and delivery are concurrent conditions, a party must not only be ready and willing to perform its contractual obligations but must have made some offer of performance to maintain an action against the other party.

Kanavos v. Hancock Bank & Trust Co. (1985) FE

Facts: Kanavos contracted to acquire the right of first refusal to buy stock from Hancock Bank. The bank later sold the stock to a third party without giving Kanavos an opportunity to exercise his right.

Issue: In a contract which calls for concurrent performances, when is a repudiating party liable for its breach?

Rule: For a repudiating party to be liable for breach of a contract that calls for concurrent performances, the nonrepudiating party must prove that it had the capability to satisfy its contractual obligations.

Walker & Co. v. Harrison (1957) FE, CPB, R

Facts: Harrison rented a neon sign from Walker. The contract provided that Walker was to maintain the sign. Harrison repudiated the agreement after the company failed to clean graffiti and tomatoes from it.

Issue: May a party repudiate his contractual duties if the other party has committed only a minor breach of his obligations?

Rule: A party must prove that the other party committed a material breach of the contract before the contract can be repudiated. Repudiation is "fraught with peril," for should the court not find that the other party materially breached the contract, the repudiator himself will have been guilty of material breach.

Hochster v. De La Tour (1853) FE, MS, CPB

Facts: De La Tour repudiated an employment contract before the contract was to commence. Hochster, the employee, immediately brought suit for breach of contract.

Issue: May a repudiating party be sued before his performance is due under the contract?

Rule: Renunciation of a contract to do a future act may be treated as a breach of contract, and the repudiating party can be sued before his performance is due under the contract.

Taylor v. Johnston (1975) FE, MS

Facts: Taylor contracted to use the Johnston's stallion as a breeding stud for Taylor's mares. The contract provided that if the encounter was unsuccessful, Taylor would be entitled to another chance the following year. The Johnstons sold their stallion and informed Taylor that the contract was canceled, but agreed to let Taylor's mares breed, upon threat of suit. The stallion was constantly "booked" by its new owners and unavailable for Taylor's mares. Taylor bred his mares with another stud before the year was up, but had to abort the foals. (Taylor sued for breach, but the court decided that only an anticipatory breach could have occurred, because the year was not over.)

Issue: What are the remedies available to a party who disregards a repudiation which is later retracted prior to the time of performance?

Rule: Anticipatory breach occurs when a party to a bilateral contract expressly or impliedly repudiates the contract prior to the time set for performance. If the second party disregards the repudiation, and it is later retracted prior to the time of performance, then the repudiation is nullified, and the injured party is left with his remedies, if any, invocable at the time of performance.

Oloffson v. Coomer (1973) FE, R

Facts: Oloffson refused to accept Coomer's repudiation of a contract to buy corn. Although "cover" was immediately and easily available, Oloffson covered at high prices on the date when the corn should have been delivered.

Issue: If "cover" is immediately available, may a buyer refuse to accept a seller's anticipatory repudiation until the date when the goods should have been delivered?

Rule: If cover is immediately and easily accessible to the buyer, it is not "commercially reasonable" to await performance by the repudiating seller (UCC § 2-610(a)) as the buyer should "cover … without unreasonable delay" (UCC § 2-712(1)) or sue for damages at the time he learned of repudiation. (UCC § 2-713(1).)

Minor v. Minor (1960) FE

Facts: After her divorce, the plaintiff entered into a settlement agreement with her ex-husband by which he would pay her $10,000 in monthly installments in exchange for waiver of her alimony rights. After the plaintiff signed the waiver, her ex-husband constantly delayed payments and only sent the checks upon threat of legal action. The plaintiff finally decided to sue for the entire sum, even though there was no acceleration clause in the agreement.

Issue: Can unilateral contracts be anticipatorily breached?

Rule: The doctrine of anticipatory repudiation does not apply to a contract that has become unilateral because of one party's full performance. The injured party has to bring suit for each installment as it becomes due.

Nevins v. Ward (1946) FE

Facts: Nevins, the builder, refused to perform unless Ward advanced him money, in excess of the contract price, to meet his payroll obligations. Ward sent notice to Nevins directing him to cease work and then employed another contractor to finish the job.

Issue: If a party manifests an unwillingness or incapacity to perform his promise, may the other party change his position in a material way so that he is discharged from his contractual obligations?

Rule: If one party manifests that he cannot or will not substantially perform his promise, the other party is justified in changing his position; and is discharged from the duty of performing his promise. Substantial performance is a requirement for recovery in *quantum meruit*.

Pittsburgh-Des Moines Steel Co. v. Brookhaven Manor Water Co. (1976) FE, KC

Facts: Pittsburgh-Des Moines Steel (PDM) contracted to build a water tank for Brookhaven. Although Brookhaven was not required to pay until the work was completed, PDM requested that the money be placed in escrow or that its president would personally guarantee the payment, after it heard incorrect rumors that Brookhaven was in financial difficulties. When Brookhaven refused to do either, PDM sued for anticipatory breach.

Issue: Are rumors of financial difficulties sufficient grounds for insecurity with respect to the other party's ability to perform its obligations?

Rule: UCC § 2-609 allows a party to ask for adequate assurance of due performance and suspend its own performance until it receives such assurance only when reasonable grounds for insecurity arise with respect to the other party's performance. Rumors do not constitute reasonable grounds for insecurity.

AMF, Inc. v. McDonald's Corp. (1976) FE, MS

Facts: AMF contracted to sell 22 computerized cash registers to McDonald's. McDonald's canceled the contract after AMF's prototype performed unsatisfactorily, projected delivery of the units was delayed, AMF's plant was incapable of assembling the units, and AMF failed to provide adequate performance standards.

Issue: Can a party repudiate a contract if it has "reasonable grounds for insecurity?"

Rule: A contract can be repudiated if a party has reasonable grounds to believe the other party will not perform and no adequate assurances of performance are given. (UCC § 2-610.)

Kreyer v. Driscoll (1968) FE, R

Facts: Kreyer contracted to build a home for the Driscolls. Although Kreyer did not do defective work, it failed to complete much of the required construction; i.e., half of electrical, plumbing, heating and tile work was unfinished. The Driscolls refused to pay the balance owed, and Kreyer sued, claiming substantial performance. The trial court ruled that since the Driscolls did not rescind the contract, they had accepted the incomplete performance.

Issue: Can a builder claim substantial performance if his performance was not defective, but incomplete?

Rule: Substantial performance applies to work that is incomplete only when the incompleteness is minimal and not the contractor's fault. However, a contractor who partially performs can recover *quantum meruit* if the incompleteness is readily remedied, and the owner has assented to the part performance or accepted the benefit of it. The contractor is entitled to the unpaid contract price less the cost of completion and other additional harm to the owner, except that it must not exceed the benefit actually conferred upon the owner.

Continental Forest Products, Inc. v. White Lumber Sales, Inc. (1970) FE, R

Facts: Continental contracted to supply 20 installments of plywood to White Lumber. The quality of the wood in the first shipment deviated from contract specifications, and White Lumber notified Continental. The plaintiff promised to cure the problem in the future and did so. White Lumber refused to accept later deliveries.

Issue: Is an installment contract breached if the first shipment does not conform to specifications, but the seller's later shipments conform to specifications?

Rule: A curable nonconformity that only impairs the value of one installment is not a breach of the entire contract (UCC § 2-612), because the value of future conforming deliveries was not impaired.

T.W. Oil, Inc. v. Consolidated Edison Co. (1982) FE

Facts: T.W. Oil tendered defective merchandise to Con Ed, which properly refused it.

Issue: If a seller, acting in good faith and without knowledge of any defect, tenders nonconforming goods to a buyer who properly rejects them, does the seller have a right to cure?

Rule: If the seller meets commercial standards of fair dealing such that he acted in good faith when tendering the nonconforming goods, he has the right to cure.

Patterson v. Meyerhofer (1912) FE, MS

Facts: Patterson agreed to sell four houses to Meyerhofer. Both were aware that Patterson did not own the homes but intended to buy them at a foreclosure sale. Before the foreclosure occurred, Meyerhofer repudiated the contract and outbid Patterson for each house during the sale. Meyerhofer also bought a fifth house which both parties had orally agreed Patterson would keep. In defense of Patterson's suit for damages, Meyerhofer claimed Patterson breached the contract because he never conveyed the properties to her.

Issue: Can a party who causes the other party not to perform their contract raise such nonperformance as a defense to damages?

Rule: Every contract contains an implied promise by each party not to intentionally and purposely prevent the other party from carrying out the agreement. One who causes the breach of an agreement is precluded from recovering damages for nonperformance or from interposing it as a defense to an action on the contract.

Iron Trade Products Co. v. Wilkoff Co. (1922) FE

Facts: Wilkoff Co. was to supply Iron Trade Products with rails. Since there were only a few rail suppliers, Iron Trade Products' substantial purchases from parties with whom Wilkoff had been negotiating reduced the supply and drove up the price which caused it to refuse to perform.

Issue: May a party refuse to perform if the performance of his contractual obligations has been made more difficult by the actions of the other party?

Rule: Mere difficulty of performance will not excuse a breach of contract. A seller's duty to supply goods is not excused if the buyer's additional purchases of the goods elsewhere makes them scarce and difficult to obtain.

Parev Products Co. v. I. Rokeach & Sons (1941) FE, R

Facts: In exchange for the exclusive right to produce Parev's cooking oil, Rokeach promised to pay Parev royalties. Rokeach also promised not to market products that would compete with Parev's (and thus reduce Parev's royalties). Rokeach was forced to introduce a new, cheaper cooking oil because of increasing competition.

Issue: Does an exclusive right to sell a product imply a covenant not to compete?

Rule: Although a party who acquires an exclusive right to sell is entitled to sell a competing product, it must compensate the product's owner for loss of sales caused by the sale of the second product.

Wood v. Lucy, Lady Duff-Gordon (1917) FE, KC, R

Facts: Lady Duff-Gordon, a famous designer, gave Wood exclusive agency to place her endorsements on clothing designs, to place her designs on sale and to license others to market them. In exchange, Wood promised to keep the books and to split the profits evenly with Duff-Gordon. Duff-Gordon breached by endorsing designs herself and keeping the profits. In defense, she claimed that Wood's promise was illusory, as she had granted him exclusive agency, but he was not obligated to find designs or to sell her labels.

Issue: Is a contract void for lack of mutuality because one party did not promise to use reasonable efforts to perform his duties?

Rule: A promise to use reasonable efforts can be implied from a contract and, therefore, a contract does not fail for lack of mutuality because it does not contain explicit clauses requiring good faith efforts. (UCC § 2-306(2).)

Feld v. Henry S. Levy & Sons, Inc. (1975) MS, R

Facts: The defendant agreed to sell to the plaintiff the entire output of bread crumbs from its factory for a one-year period. Each party had the right to cancel upon six months notice. The defendant stopped production because its obsolete equipment was uneconomical, and offered to resume production at a higher price.

Issue: Must a seller who signs an output contract continue to produce goods for the term of the contract?

Rule: A party to an output contract is obligated to act in good faith and may cease production as long as it is acting in good faith. Whether a party acted in good faith is a jury question. (The case was remanded for further proceedings.)

Bloor v. Falstaff Brewing Corp. (1979) FE, CPB

Facts: Falstaff bought Bloor's brewing labels, trademarks, etc., for a set price plus a royalty for each barrel of Ballantine beer sold. Falstaff allowed sales of Ballantine beer to fall in the interest of increasing profits. A clause in their contract required Falstaff to use its "best efforts to promote and maintain a high volume of sales under Bloor's rights."

Issue: Is a "high volume of sales clause" breached by an emphasis on profits without regard to the effect on sales volume?

Rule: Although a party is not required to spend itself into bankruptcy, a clause requiring "best efforts to maintain a high volume of sales" for a specified product is violated by a philosophy that emphasizes profit without fair consideration of the effect on the sales volume.

Fortune v. National Cash Register Co. (1977) FE

Facts: National Cash Register fired Fortune, an at-will employee, in bad faith to avoid paying him a commission on sales.

Issue: Is there an implied requirement of good faith in at-will employment contracts that are terminable without cause?

Rule: An employment contract terminable at will contains an implied covenant of good faith and fair dealing, and a termination not made in good faith constitutes a breach of the contract.

Grouse v. Group Health Plan, Inc. (1981) FE

Facts: Grouse resigned from his job because he received an employment offer from Group Health. The offer was later revoked.

Issue: Are damages resulting from revocation of an at-will employment offer recoverable?

Rule: Under the doctrine of promissory estoppel, a promise that the promisor should reasonably expect to induce action or forbearance on the part of the promisee, and which does induce such action, is binding if nonenforcement would result in injustice.

Pine River State Bank v. Mettille (1983) FE

Facts: Pine River fired Mettille, an at-will employee. The bank had given Mettille an employee handbook that contained disciplinary procedures.

Issue: Can job-security provisions in an employee handbook, distributed after employment begins, become part of an employee's contract of employment?

Rule: Where an employment contract is for an indefinite duration, such indefiniteness does not preclude handbook provisions on job security from being enforceable.

Dove v. Rose Acre Farms, Inc. (1982) MS

Facts: Rose Acre offered Dove a bonus if certain construction work was completed, provided that Dove worked five days a week for ten weeks. Dove missed two days in the last week because he had strep throat, and he refused to make up the work on the weekend. Dove sued for the bonus although he was fully aware of the strict policies concerning absenteeism.

Issue: Is a party entitled to recovery on a contract if it does not perform all of the conditions of the contract?

Rule: A party must perform all conditions knowingly assented to before performance by the other party is due.

Wal-Noon Corp. v. Hill (1975) MS

Facts: The lessees, Wal-Noon, replaced their roof without notifying the lessors, and then sued the lessors for the cost of replacing the roof in accordance with the lessors' express covenant to repair and maintain the roof.

Issue: Is the lessor's performance under an express covenant to repair conditional upon notice from the lessee even if not expressly required by the contract?

Rule: Unless explicitly excluded therein, notice from the lessee is a condition precedent to the lessor's performance under an express covenant to repair.

Internatio-Rotterdam, Inc. v. River Brand Rice Mills, Inc. (1958) MS

Facts: A contract for the sale of rice required shipment by the end of December with at least two weeks notice to the shipper, River Brand Rice. The shipper canceled the contract after Internatio-Rotterdam failed to give notice by December 17. The buyer's letters of credit only guaranteed payment for a December delivery.

Issue: May a party cancel a contract upon the nonoccurrence of a condition precedent in a sale of goods contract?

Rule: If a provision "goes to the essence" of a sale of goods contract, it can serve as a condition precedent to delivery, the nonoccurrence of which entitles the seller to rescind the contract even if the buyer later performs.

North American Graphite Corp. v. Allan (1950) MS

Facts: North American Graphite hired Allan, an engineer, to design plans for the rehabilitation of a mine. The contract provided that $4,000 of his salary would be paid "as soon as the plant is in successful operation." North American Graphite later abandoned the project and wrongfully discharged Allan, but claimed it was not liable for paying the money because the condition precedent to payment, i.e., successful operation, had not occurred.

Issue: Will the courts make payment of a debt contingent upon the occurrence of a condition if the parties have neglected to expressly provide for such an arrangement?

Rule: Courts will imply a condition precedent to payment of a debt if it is consistent with the intentions of the parties as gathered from the language used, the situation of the parties and the subject matter of the contract as presented by the evidence.

Universal Builders, Inc. v. Moon Motor Lodge, Inc.
(1968) MS

Facts: Universal Builders' construction contract with Moon provided in part that all requests for building modifications had to be written and signed by Moon or its architect. Moon's agent orally requested modifications and promised to pay. Although the agent watched the work being done, Moon refused to pay.

Issue: Is an unwritten contract modification that was agreed upon by both parties valid if a contract requires that modifications must be in writing?

Rule: The effectiveness of a non-written modification, in spite of a contract condition that modifications must be in writing, depends upon whether enforcement of the condition is or is not barred by equitable considerations. When one party materially changes its position in reliance on the other party's waiver of a contract condition that modifications must be in writing, the condition will not be enforced.

Aetna Casualty and Surety Co. v. Murphy (1988) MS

Facts: Murphy allegedly damaged a building that Aetna insured. When Aetna sued Murphy, Murphy impleaded his insurer, Chubb, as a third-party defendant. The insurance contract between Murphy and Chubb stated that: "If claim is made or suit is brought against the insured, the insured shall immediately forward to [Chubb] every demand, notice, summons, or other process. ..." Chubb denied coverage because Murphy did not notify it of the suit for two years.

Issue: When is a party entitled to relief from disproportionate forfeiture due to breach of an express condition of an adhesion contract?

Rule: A party may be excused from the consequences of failing to comply with a contract condition if he can demonstrate that the noncompliance did not materially prejudice the other party.

Note: In the instant case, Chubb was allowed to deny coverage because Murphy did not show that his failure to comply with the notice requirement was not detrimental to Chubb's legitimate purpose of guaranteeing itself an opportunity to investigate accidents.

Goodison v. Nunn (1792) MS

Facts: The plaintiff never tendered the estate he agreed to convey but sued for breach of contract when the defendant did not pay the purchase money.

Issue: If a party has not tendered performance of his contractual duties, is the other party in breach if it does not perform?

Rule: A party is not guilty of breach of contract for nonperformance if the other party has not tendered performance of his reciprocal contract duties.

Palmer v. Fox (1936) MS

Facts: The plaintiff's assignor, Louis G. Palmer & Company, contracted to sell a parcel of land to the defendant on an installment plan. As part of the contract, Palmer & Company was to make improvements on the land, such as install a sewer system, water pipes, etc. Palmer & Company was to convey the land when full payment was made. Fox ceased payment after the plaintiff failed to make an improvement, and the plaintiff sued for damages, claiming that Fox's duty to pay was not dependent on the plaintiff's performance.

Issue: Will a party's nonperformance be excused if the other party materially breached a dependent covenant?

Rule: A party's material breach of a dependent covenant excuses the other party's counterperformance. Covenants are to be construed to be independent or dependent according to the "intentions of the parties and the good sense of the case." Given that both performances were to run concurrently, that the contract does not expressly state that the covenants are independent and that the agreed consideration was to be paid when the improvements were completed, it is reasonable to imply that the covenants are dependent.

O.W. Grun Roofing and Constr. Co. v. Cope (1975) MS

Facts: The plaintiff, Cope, hired Grun Roofing, a contractor, to install a new roof of uniform color. The roof installed had "streaky" shingles on three sides, but was durable.

Issue: Has a contractor substantially performed if his work was defective in a material way and cannot be remedied short of completely replacing the roof?

Rule: Substantial performance permits only such deviations as are inadvertent and unintentional, not caused by bad faith, do not impair the structure as a whole, and are remediable without doing material damage to other parts of the building in tearing down and reconstruction. In the matter of homes, an owner's taste or fancy may be controlling so that variations that would otherwise be considered trifling may bar a finding of substantial performance.

Foundation Dev. Corp. v. Loehmann's, Inc. (1990) MS, R

Facts: Loehmann's leased space in a shopping center from Foundation. The lease provided that time was of the essence and that Foundation could terminate the lease if Loehmann's did not pay outstanding charges within ten days after receiving a notice of default. Three months after a disputed bill was due, Foundation sent a notice of default. It was mailed on April 10, but because it was addressed improperly, Loehmann's did not disburse a check until April 25 and Foundation did not receive it until April 29. On April 28, Foundation brought suit to evict Loehmann's.

Issue 1: What is the standard for determining whether a breach is trivial or immaterial in the landlord-tenant context?

Rule 1: Whether a breach is material in the landlord-tenant context is determined by the extent to which the injured party will be deprived of a reasonably expected benefit and can be adequately compensated for the lost benefit, the extent to which the nonperforming party will suffer forfeiture, the likelihood the nonperforming party will cure his failure, and the extent to which the behavior of the nonperforming party comports with standards of good faith and fair dealing.

Note: Applying these factors to the instant case, the court found that the breach was immaterial because the only detriment Foundation suffered was the loss of the use of the funds for a few days, which is trivial when compared to the total value of the contract, and because Loehmann's behavior comports with standards of good faith and fair dealing.

Issue 2: What is the effect of a "time is of the essence" clause?

Rule 2: A "time is of the essence" clause elevates the importance of late performances as a factor in determining if a breach is material. It does not make late performance a material breach per se, especially if enforcement of the provision will cause unjust forfeiture or excessive penalty.

Lowy v. United Pacific Ins. Co. (1967) MS

Facts: Wolpin, a contractor, was hired to do excavating and grading of a street together with street improvement work. Payment for each type of work was listed separately, and Wolpin gave a different surety bond for each phase of the work. Wolpin performed 98 percent of the grading work before a dispute arose and he stopped performance. The plaintiffs hired another contractor to do the paving work. The plaintiffs claimed Wolpin should not be paid because performance of both phases was a condition to payment.

Issue: Can a contractor recover if it has substantially performed one phase of a severable contract and was prevented from completing the other phase by the other party's hiring of another contractor?

Rule: A contractor may recover under a contract for work it has completed if it has substantially performed one phase of a severable contract and was prevented from completing the other phase by the other party. (Rest. 2d § 240.)

Maxton Builders, Inc. v. Lo Galbo (1986) MS

Facts: Maxton Builders contracted to sell a house to the Lo Galbos, who tendered a check for 10 percent of the price as a down payment. The Lo Galbos canceled the contract and stopped payment on the check.

Issue: May a vendor on a real estate contract retain a down payment when a purchaser willfully defaults, or must a factual determination first be made as to whether loss of the down payment constitutes a penalty (i.e., treat the forfeiture as a liquidated-damages clause)?

Rule: Because courts should not depart from precedent in the absence of the most compelling reasons, especially where contract rights are at issue, the traditional rule that real estate down payments approximating 10 percent of the contract price do not have to be returned by the seller if the purchaser defaults will be retained.

Note: The Restatement takes the alternative view.

Centronics Corp. v. Genicom Corp. (1989) MS

Facts: Genicom had agreed to purchase business assets from Centronics. The contract provided that any dispute about the value of property transferred would go to arbitration. An escrow account was set up to provide compensation if a party was overpaid or underpaid. The contract provided that the "only way funds can be released is upon final determination of the purchase price." A dispute over the purchase price arose and release of the funds was withheld, pending resolution. Centronics asserted that Genicom's refusal to release funds was meant to pressure the plaintiff into conceding the disputed item.

Issue: May a contract provision be modified on the grounds that it is being utilized in bad faith?

Rule: A claim for relief from a violation of the implied covenant of good faith only applies where there is a promise that allows a party such a degree of discretion that its practical benefit can be withheld. Since the defendant in this case had no control over the amount of time that funds would be withheld, and whether the funds would be withheld was a bargained-for provision available to both parties, summary judgment was granted in favor of Genicom.

Omni Group, Inc. v. Seattle-First Nat'l Bank (1982) MS

Facts: Omni contracted to buy land from the Clarks subject to the requirement that Omni would be satisfied with a feasibility report made by its engineers and architects. The Clarks refused to sell, claiming lack of consideration because Omni's promise was illusory.

Issue: Does a condition precedent involving the satisfaction of a party render the said party's promise to perform illusory?

Rule: A condition precedent that requires a party's subjective satisfaction does not render a contract unenforceable, because it imposes a duty of good faith upon the said party in exercising good judgment.

Neumiller Farms, Inc. v. Cornett (1979) MS

Facts: A contractual provision permitted Neumiller Farms, a vegetable broker, to refuse to accept delivery of Cornett's potatoes, if it was not satisfied with them. After market prices fell, Neumiller Farms claimed it was not satisfied with subsequent shipments which experts later found to be suitable.

Issue: Must a rejection of goods based on a claim of dissatisfaction be made in good faith?

Rule: A claim of dissatisfaction by a merchant or buyer must be made in good faith, meaning both "honesty in fact and the observance of reasonable commercial standards of fair dealing in the trade." A rejection in bad faith is ineffectual and constitutes breach of contract.

Reid v. Key Bank of S. Maine, Inc. (1987) MS

Facts: Key Bank's predecessor extended $25,000 credit to the Reids, interest payable quarterly, principal callable "on demand." Documents provided various conditions that would render the obligation payable on demand and a series of events that would signify that the Reids were in default. For no apparent reason, the Reids' credit was shut off, which caused them to lose their business and home.

Issue: Are lenders subject to a good faith requirement for calling loans that are payable on demand?

Rule: When notes become payable on demand only after enumerated events, "on demand" is a relative and qualified provision that is subject to a good faith requirement.

Note: In the instant case, the court upheld a jury finding of bad faith because the notes were called without notice and for no apparent reason (the Reids' position had not changed since the credit was extended).

Orange & Rockland v. Amerada Hess Corp. (1977) MS

Facts: Amerada Hess had a requirements contract with Orange & Rockland to supply fuel oil. As the price of oil began to rise rapidly, O & R's demand surpassed their requirements contract estimate by 40 percent. Amerada Hess refused to meet O & R's demands for fuel oil.

Issue: Must a seller satisfy a buyer's needs which were incurred in bad faith and are unreasonably disproportionate to contract estimates?

Rule: A term that measures the quantity to be supplied by a seller to a buyer of goods by the requirements of the buyer means such actual requirements as may occur in good faith, except that no quantity unreasonably disproportionate to any stated estimate can be demanded. (UCC § 2-306(1).)

James I. Barnes Constr. Co. v. Washington Township (1962) MS

Facts: Barnes was hired by Washington Township to build a school, with final payment on the contract conditioned on the receipt of an engineer's certificate of substantial completion. Zechiel, an engineer, issued the certificate, but the Township refused to pay the final installment to Barnes because of the poor quality of the building.

Issue: When contract payment is conditioned on the satisfaction of an engineer or architect, is the professed satisfaction reviewable by the court?

Rule: An engineer or architect's decision concerning the satisfactory completion of contracted work is not conclusive; it can be reviewed by a court. The issuance of a certificate establishes a prima facie case that can be overcome by a showing of fraud or mistake.

Bolton Corp. v. T. A. Loving Co. (1989) MS

Facts: The State hired Loving to be the "project expediter" for a construction job. Loving's responsibilities included scheduling the work of all prime contractors and maintaining that schedule. Loving also had the authority to allocate responsibility for any delays. Bolton contracted directly with the State to do the heating and ventilation work. Bolton brought suit as a third-party beneficiary, claiming that the defendant breached its contract with the State by causing Bolton "undue delay" that prevented it from timely performance of its contract.

Issue: Where responsibility for making decisions on claims between contractors on a construction project is delegated to a party, what weight must be given to such decisions?

Rule: In construction contracts where judgment of the quality of prime contractor's performance is contractually delegated, such determinations are *prima facie* correct, and the burden is upon the other parties to show fraud or mistake.

Michael-Curry Co. v. Knutson Shareholders (1989) MS

Facts: A contract contained a clause that provided "any controversy arising out of or relating to ... the making [of this agreement] shall be settled by arbitration."

Issue: Is an arbitration clause applicable to controversies concerning allegations of fraud?

Rule: Whether issues of fraud are subject to arbitration depends on the intent of the parties, as manifested by the language of the arbitration clause. Issues of fraud are subject to arbitration if the language specifically shows that the parties intended to arbitrate fraud, or is sufficiently broad to comprehend that the issue of fraudulent inducement be arbitrated.

Container Technology Corp. v. J. Gadsden Pty., Ltd
(1989) MS

Facts: Container Technology and Gadsden submitted a contract dispute to arbitration. The arbitrators found for Gadsden. Container Technology appealed to have the award set aside on grounds that the arbitrators failed to follow the terms of the contract and gave undue weight to hearsay evidence. Container Technology also sought to depose the arbitrators.

Issue: Is an arbitration award subject to judicial review?

Rule: An arbitration award is not open to review on the merits, which include determinations of factual issues, the credibility of witnesses and weight given to their testimony and the arbitrators' interpretation of the contract. Similarly, arbitrators may not be deposed for the purpose of evaluating their thought processes.

McCloskey & Co. v. Minweld Steel Co. (1955) CPB

Facts: Minweld Steel contracted to supply and erect steel for the construction of hospitals. Due to the outbreak of the Korean War, Minweld Steel was unable to obtain the steel and asked for assistance from McCloskey & Co, the plaintiffs. Although Minweld Steel stated that they "were anxious ... that there be no delay in the final completion of the buildings," McCloskey sued for anticipatory breach.

Issue: Does a request for help in fulfilling contractual obligations amount to an anticipatory breach absent a positive statement of unwillingness to perform?

Rule: To give rise to a renunciation amounting to a breach of contract, there must be an absolute and unequivocal refusal to perform or a distinct and positive statement of an inability to do so. The court also stated that failure to take preparatory action before the time for performance is not an anticipatory breach.

Audette v. L'Union St. Joseph (1901) CPB

Facts: The decedent, Audette, received medical attention from a doctor who refused to give him a sworn certificate necessary in order to receive benefits from L'Union St. Joseph. His administratrix sued to compel the defendant to pay for Audette's medical care.

Issue: Is the refusal of a third party to aid compliance with the terms of a contract grounds for excusing a party from complying with those terms?
Rule: A party to a contract is not excused from the performance of some term by the uninfluenced refusal of a third party to aid in its fulfillment.

General Credit Corp. v.
Imperial Casualty and Indemnity Co. (1959) CPB

Facts: General Credit financed the leasing of two cars to Service Trucking which had the cars insured by Imperial. The insurance agreement stated that General Credit's interest in the cars was covered under the policy "provided, also, that in case the
Lessee ... shall neglect to pay any premium due under such policy the Lienholder [General Credit] shall, on demand, pay the same." After the lessee fell behind on insurance payments and crashed both cars, General Credit brought this action against Imperial for $1839.20 in damages to the cars. Imperial counterclaimed that General Credit was responsible for $1786.86 in insurance premiums owed by the lessee.
Issue: Do clauses in a unilateral contract act on a promisee as conditions or promises?
Rule: While unilateral contracts bind promisors to their promises, they impose only conditions on promisees.
Note: Insurance policies are typical of unilateral contracts in which only one party makes a promise. Only the insurance company is bound to its promises upon the condition of premium payment by the beneficiary. As a matter of construction, these agreements will be read to operate most strongly against the interests of the authoring party.

Charles Ilfeld Co. v. Taylor (1964) CPB, R

Facts: A tri-partite contract between Charles Ilfield Co., a financing and accounting company, the Allens, purchasers of a grocery, and the Taylors, the sellers, provided that the Company would supply $7,000 to the Allens for the down payment. It further provided that the debt owed to the Company was to be satisfied before the Taylors were to be paid, and that the Company would keep the books and prepare an inventory of the store every two months. The Taylors failed to subordinate their obligation to the Company's, and the Company failed to complete the books and inventories as stipulated.
Issue: When is a clause in a bilateral or multilateral contract a promise rather than a condition?

Rule: The intention of the parties controls; however, if the intent is unclear, the courts lean toward an interpretation of the clause as a promise. A supplemental term will be read as a promise, while a material and essential one will be read as a condition.

Note: As the Company had fulfilled the material conditions of the contract by financing the sale, the Taylors were bound to subordinate their debt, regardless of the Company's failure to fulfill their promise to keep the books.

Hicks v. Bush (1962) CPB

Facts: Hicks and Bush contracted to combine their business interests to effect a more efficient operation. Hicks performed his obligations, but Bush did not. Bush sought to introduce evidence that the parties had made a contemporaneous oral agreement stipulating that the contract would only be binding if they obtained financing, which was not forthcoming. The writing was silent on this issue.

Issue: Is parol testimony admissible to prove the existence of a condition precedent to a written agreement?

Rule: Parol testimony is admissible to prove a condition precedent to the legal effectiveness of a written agreement if the condition does not contradict the express terms of such written agreement "in a real sense."

Edmund J. Flynn Co. v. Schlosser (1970) CPB

Facts: A cooperative apartment purchaser, Schlosser, together with the building's agent, Edmund J. Flynn, had submitted Schlosser's candidacy for occupancy to the coop board for approval. Board approval was a condition precedent to the sale of the apartment. Schlosser attempted to revoke her offer to purchase before board approval had been given.

Issue: Is a condition precedent a prerequisite to the existence of a contract, or is it a prerequisite to an obligation of both parties to immediately perform the contract?

Rule: The contract exists prior to the condition's satisfaction if mutual assent is present, and satisfaction of the condition precedent then binds both parties to performance of the contract.

Monroe Street Properties, Inc. v. Carpenter (1969) CPB

Facts: Western Equities, Inc., represented by Carpenter, offered to buy ten insured first mortgages and notes with $1,000,000 of Western stock from Monroe Street Properties. Monroe promptly accepted the offer complete with Western's condition that the stock would not be redistributed but held as an investment for three years. Monroe then deposited ten uninsured, heavily encumbered mortgages in the escrow account that had been created and demanded that Western deliver the stock. Seeing that the mortgages did not meet the contract specifications, Western did not comply.

Issue: What constitutes an adequate tender of performance?

Rule: Tender of performance means the ability and willingness to execute performance concurrently with the other party, plus notice of that ability.

Note: A party must tender its own performance before declaring the other party in breach. In this case, Monroe never made an adequate tender because the mortgages were unfit for the transaction.

Hadden v. Consolidated Edison Co. (1974) CPB

Facts: Upon learning of Hadden's participation in a meeting to bribe a public official, his superior told Hadden he must retire from Con Ed or he would be discharged. By his testimony in a criminal trial after his retirement, Con Ed learned of a number of incidents during which Hadden accepted over $30,000 in bribes and gifts from contractors. The board of directors of Con Ed discontinued his pension payments even though no clause in the plan stipulated honesty and loyalty as requirements. The only requirements were age, service, and lack of discharge.

Issue: Under what circumstances will violation of constructive conditions, terms imposed by law in the interest of justice and the absence of contractual provisions, excuse performance of a contract?

Rule: Violation of constructive conditions by a party will not excuse another's performance if the violating party has substantially performed its obligation.

Note: The court found that Hadden's thirty-seven years of service outweighed a few years of misconduct.

Hadden v. Consolidated Edison Co. (1978) CPB

Facts: See facts above. Before his retirement, Hadden denied and concealed the receipt of any gifts or bribes, claiming that the bribe-approach was his only incident of misconduct. On the basis of this affirmative misrepresentation, Con Ed allowed him to retire rather than be discharged.

Issue: When can an option or right that has been waived be recovered?

Rule: The waiver of an option or right that has been induced by fraudulent misrepresentation is invalid.

A.B. Parker v. Bell Ford, Inc. (1973) CPB

Facts: Parker purchased a Ford truck from Bell Ford with defective wheel casements. Parker complained to Bell Ford that the defects caused excessive tire wear, prompting an unsuccessful attempt by the dealer to repair the vehicle. Without further contact with Bell Ford or any contact with Ford Motor Co., Parker sued on warranty and contract theories.

Issue: What is a buyer's obligation upon learning of a defect in goods before action for recovery may be brought?

Rule: UCC § 2-607(3)(a) provides that a buyer must provide notice to the seller of any breach in order to open the way for negotiation, settlement and remedy without the need for litigation.

Martin v. Schoenberger (1845) CPB

Facts: Not stated.

Issue: Is recovery available to a party who has only partially performed?

Rule: No recovery is permitted for a party who has failed to perform the entire agreement.

Note: This is the common law rule based on the idea that a party should not benefit from its own wrong. This has been modified in favor of the rule adopted in the Restatement (Second) of Contracts which allows limited restitution in order to prevent the non-breaching party from obtaining a windfall.

Lancellotti v. Thomas (1985) CPB, KC

Facts: Thomas agreed to sell his business to Lancellotti for $25,000 and to lease the land it occupied with the stipulations that only Lancellotti would own and operate the business and that he would erect an additional building within a year. After a dispute arose over the additional building, Lancellotti breached and sued to recover the $25,000.

Issue: Can a breaching party recover for any loss incurred in the attempt to perform?

Rule: The Restatement (Second) of Contracts § 374 provides that a party in breach is entitled to restitution for any benefit conferred upon the other party in excess of the loss caused by the breach.

Carrig v. Gilbert-Varker Corp. (1943) CPB

Facts: Carrig contracted with Gilbert-Varker Corp., a contractor, to have thirty-five houses built on a plot of land. Each unit had an individual mortgage, and the contractor was paid as any given units advanced past certain stages of construction. Carrig brought an action against the contractor for failing to erect fifteen houses and failing to erect the other twenty to specification. Gilbert-Varker brought an action for payments outstanding on the twenty finished houses.

Issue 1: What is the remedy for partial performance?

Rule 1: The remedy for partial performance is the cost of completion in excess of the contracted price.

Note: In this case, the owner recovered the excess cost of building the fifteen houses himself.

Issue 2: How does the characterization of a contract as entire or divisible affect the remedy available to the party in default?

Rule 2: A party in default will not recover if the contract is entire because entire performance is a condition of payment. If the contract is divisible, the party in default can recover on all completed units.

Note: In this case, the contractor recovered for the money still owed on the twenty finished houses.

Keystone Bus Lines, Inc. v. ARA Services, Inc. (1983) CPB

Facts: ARA bought bus facilities and contracts from Keystone. ARA agreed to pay Keystone $50,000 each year for the next two years if ARA gross revenues exceeded certain amounts. Keystone claimed that ARA misallocated resources to intentionally keep revenues below the specified amounts.

Issue: When may a condition precedent be excused?

Rule: If a condition precedent to a promise which would otherwise occur is prevented or hindered by a promisor, the condition is excused, and the promisor is liable for fulfillment of the promise.

Note: Since the court found that ARA acted in good faith and did not attempt to reduce revenues, it was not responsible for the failure of the condition to occur.

Swartz v. War Memorial Commission of Rochester (1966) CPB

Facts: A contract which gave the exclusive concession for the sale of food, beverages and souvenirs to Swartz provided that Swartz obtain all necessary licenses and share a certain percentage of the profits with the War Memorial Commission. When the prohibition on the sale of alcoholic beverages at the War Memorial was lifted, Swartz refused to apply for the necessary license. The Commission terminated his concession, and he brought this action.

Issue: What duty is imposed upon a party to a contract with regard to the goal of the agreement?

Rule: A party to a contract is required to use reasonable efforts to carry out the mutual intent of the agreement. Here, the mutual intent was to earn a profit, and Swartz's failure to attempt to obtain the license constituted a default on his obligation.

Stop & Shop, Inc. v. Ganem (1964) CPB

Facts: Stop & Shop, Inc. leased a lot with a supermarket to Ganem for a substantial rent with the provision that the lessors would also receive a percentage of gross sales over a certain amount. Ganem operated the space as a market for several years, opened two competing markets and decided to close down the lot in question.

Issue: When a contract provides for contingency payments, is there an implied covenant that the party to pay will attempt to operate so as to produce those payments?

Rule: Covenants will not be found by implication unless the implication is clear and undoubted according to justice, common sense and the probable intention of the parties.

Note: In this case, the substantiality of the rent being paid weighed against an inference that the percentage rent clause included a covenant to continue operations.

Schenectady Steel Co. v. Bruno Trimpoli General Constr. Co. (1974) CPB

Facts: Bruno Trimpoli contracted with Schenectady for the procurement and erection of steel for a bridge. The contract stated that "time is of the essence" and that the work must be completed by the end of 1968. In early 1969, after several delays, Schenectady was unable to provide a schedule to Bruno Trimpoli on demand, but was allowed to continue work on the steel for several more weeks. Dissatisfied with the progress, Bruno Trimpoli terminated the contract.

Issue: Does the UCC apply to contracts involving both goods and services?

Rule: The UCC applies to contracts in which the provision of goods is the primary purpose of the contract. The UCC does not apply to a contract for work, labor and materials (i.e., construction) as the primary purpose is service.

Schenectady Steel Co. v.
Bruno Trimpoli General Constr. Co. (1974) CPB

Facts: See facts above. The issue of whether the "time is of the essence" obligation was reimposed after Bruno Trimpoli's waiver was appealed.

Issue: What effect does an express or implied waiver of the "time is of the essence" clause have on the obligations of a promisor?

Rule: Waiver of the "time is of the essence" clause leaves a lesser obligation to perform within a reasonable time. The timeliness obligation can be expressly reimposed upon the promisor.

Note: In this case, the court found that although the timeliness duty was waived, Schenectady did not even satisfy the lesser duty of performance within a reasonable time, thereby justifying termination.

Sharp v. Holthusen (1980) CPB

Facts: The Sharps entered into a contract for the sale of land to the Holthusens which stipulated that the Holthusens would make monthly payments to the Sharps, assume the Sharps' outstanding loan, and satisfy both in full within a year. Three months after the due date for the entire payoff, the Holthusens attempted to tender payment but were stalled by the need to correct a water supply problem. Shortly thereafter, full tender including attorney fees incurred by the delay was made to the Sharps. The Sharps rejected the tender and brought this action for forfeiture.

Issue: Is there any relief from forfeiture for a party in default?

Rule: The court provides relief from forfeiture to parties who make full compensation to the other party within a reasonable time period and who have made good faith efforts to avoid default.

Burger King Corp. v. Family Dining, Inc. (1977) CPB

Facts: Burger King granted Family Dining Buck and Montgomery Counties in Pennsylvania as their "exclusive territory" subject to the condition subsequent that one Burger King restaurant be opened and maintained each year for the first ten years and that these ten be maintained for the remaining eighty years of the agreement. When Family Dining fell behind on the fourth and fifth restaurant, Burger King allowed it an extension. When it fell behind on the ninth and tenth, Burger King terminated the "exclusive territory" agreement.

Issue: When may a condition subsequent be excused?

Rule: The Restatement of Contracts § 302 provides that a condition may be excused if its requirement will impose extreme forfeiture and its occurrence forms no essential part of the exchange.
Note: Here, Burger King had previously waived the condition and provided no notice that it had been reimposed as an essential element of the contract.

Xanthakey v. Hayes (1928) CPB

Facts: Long-term tenants of a commercial property failed to give notice of renewal of the lease sixty days in advance of expiration. They were three days late for this deadline. The landlord sought to evict them.
Issue: Will principles of equity excuse a party from the express condition of timely acceptance of an option contract?
Rule: When an option is an element of consideration for a contract, and unconscionable hardship would result from withdrawal of the option, equitable principles will excuse the promisee for failure to notify of intent to exercise the option in a timely manner.

C & J Fertilizer, Inc. v. Allied Mutual Ins. Co. (1975) CPB, KC

Facts: C & J bought an insurance policy from an agent of Allied to cover their loss in case of burglary. The policy was purchased before it was produced for C & J to read. During negotiation, C & J was led to believe that the only exception to the coverage was a burglary by an "insider" of the corporation. In fact, the burglary definition required that there be visible damage to the exterior of the building. When approximately $10,000 in chemicals were stolen, C & J was denied coverage because the evidence of force was on the interior of the building.
Issue: On what bases will a court refuse to enforce an adhesion contract?
Rule: A contract containing a few negotiated terms and a number of obscure ones will be read to comport with the reasonable expectations of the promisee, to satisfy an implied warranty of fitness for the purpose intended, and to avoid any outcomes which reflect an absence of assent on the part of the promisee, unfair surprise, failure of notice, disparity of bargaining power or substantive unfairness.

Western Hills, Oregon, Ltd. v. Pfau (1973) CPB

Facts: Pfau and his partner contracted to buy a tract of land from Western Hills, subject to the condition that a development plan satisfactory to both parties was approved by the city planning commission. The commission's reaction to the initial plans was favorable. Pfau tried to back out of the contract, having pursued approval no further on the ground that the city sewer arrangements were unsatisfactory. Pfau was aware of the sewer arrangements at the time of contracting.

Issue 1: May a party rely on the absence of a condition to withdraw from a contract if the party itself failed to pursue that condition?

Rule 1: Where a contract contains a provision for a condition to be met by a party, that party must make a reasonable effort to meet the condition.

Issue 2: When may a party to a contract with a condition of satisfaction not use personal dissatisfaction to escape obligations imposed by the contract?

Rule 2: If a party anticipates or is aware of circumstances before contracting, it cannot claim dissatisfaction with such circumstances to avoid its obligations under the contract. Any such claim must be made in good faith.

Van Iderstine Co., Inc. v. Barnet Leather Co., Inc.
(1926) CPB

Facts: The sales by Van Iderstine to Barnet of 15,000 veal skins in August and 6,000 in September were subject to the approval of the quality of the skins by an impartial expert, Jules Star. Jules Star rejected 3,500 of the first batch and all 6,000 of the second as inferior. When Van Iderstine later tendered completion of the first order, Barnet refused to purchase the skins regardless of approval by Jules Star.

Issue: What constitutes a waiver as a matter of law of a condition precedent to an exchange?

Rule: If a party refuses to accept a tender of performance regardless of whether the condition was satisfied or interferes in bad faith with the fulfillment of a condition, that party has waived the condition as a matter of law.

Note: Barnet breached by failing to accept the remainder of the first order regardless of approval, but was justified in refusing tender of the inferior second order which was rejected by Jules Star.

Terminal Constr. Corp. v. Bergen Co.
Hackensack Riv. San. Sewer Dist. Auth. (1955) CPB

Facts: The Bergen County Sewer Authority appointed an engineer to "determine ... the amount, quality, acceptability, and fitness of the several kinds of work [completed by Terminal] which are to be paid for." In his role as arbitrator, he found that Terminal was not entitled to payment for certain portions of its work on a sewage treatment plant.

Issue: Under what conditions will the findings of an arbitrator appointed by contracting parties be set aside?

Rule: When the findings of an arbitrator are shown to have been arbitrary or in bad faith, such findings amount to constructive fraud and will be set aside.

Daniels v. Newton (1874) CPB

Facts: The defendants had 60 days to perform their agreement to purchase land but breached the agreement before the end of the 60 days.

Issue: Can suit be brought against a party who renounced a contract before the time for performance has arrived?

Rule: One can only recover for actual injuries. Therefore, a party cannot recover for anticipated injuries when the other party announces his intention not to render a future performance. Suit can only be brought after the time for performance has passed.

Diamond v. University of Southern California (1970) CPB, R

Facts: Diamond, an attorney and representative of 600 others similarly situated, was promised the option to purchase a ticket to the Rose Bowl if he purchased "economy" season tickets. When the team won the right to advance to the Rose Bowl, the University discovered that it was unable to furnish ticket applications to Diamond's class. Diamond commenced this action. Soon after, the University issued ticket applications to Diamond's class.

Issue: Can a promisor in a unilateral contract repudiate that contract before the arrival of its date for performance?

Rule: A promisor in a unilateral contract cannot breach before the date for performance has arrived.

Note: Diamond's claim was premature; the University satisfied its promise before the date for performance had arrived.

Jones Associates, Inc. v. Eastside Properties, Inc. (1985) KC

Facts: Jones, an engineering and surveying firm, contracted with Eastside to supply a number of studies and maps concerning Eastside's 180 acre land parcel. A contract term provided that Jones was "responsible for obtaining King County approval for all platting." Jones was unable to obtain the county plat approval. Eastside withheld payment, claiming that Jones' inability to obtain the approval was a failure of a condition precedent to payment, and thus excused performance.

Issue: How should a court decide whether or not a contract provision is a condition precedent, failure of which would excuse performance, or a mere promise, failure of which leads to damage liability?

Rule: A contract provision will be construed to create a condition precedent if, after examining the contract in light of the surrounding circumstances, the court finds the parties clearly intended to create a condition precedent. If the intent of the parties is unclear, the provision will be interpreted as promise, since the law disfavors forfeitures.

United States Fid. & Guar. Co. v. Bimco Iron & Metal Corp. (1971) KC

Facts: Burglars broke into plaintiff Bimco's warehouse, removing high voltage wire and transformers, which had been part of the building, and causing damage to the front door. Plaintiff's insurance policy, held by defendant United States Fiduciary, was ambiguous as to coverage for theft of property resulting from burglary. After the time for filing proof of loss had expired, an agent for the defendant told the plaintiff that the insurance company would only pay for the damage to the door. Defendant denied liability for the stolen wire and transformers on two grounds: that the loss was excluded under the terms of the policy, and that the plaintiff had failed to file a timely proof of loss. Plaintiff sued to recover the money it believed was due under the policy, and asserted that the defendant had, through its actions, waived their right to prompt notice of loss.

Issue 1: How should a court interpret an ambiguous clause in an insurance contract?

Rule 1: An ambiguous clause found in an insurance policy should be liberally construed in favor of the insured and strictly construed against the insurer, as long as the interpretation is not unreasonable.

Issue 2: May a condition precedent be waived by actions which occur after expiration of the time of performance of the condition?

Rule 2: A waiver of a condition precedent may be established by conduct occurring after the time for performance of the condition has expired, because a waiver need not be supported by consideration or detrimental reliance to be valid.

Sackett v. Spindler (1967) KC

Facts: Spindler owned and operated a newspaper. Sackett agreed to pay $85,000 in a series of three installments in exchange for 6,316 shares of stock in the newspaper. Sackett paid the first two installments on time. Sackett paid Spindler the final installment by check, but the bank returned the check for insufficient funds. Spindler granted Sackett a number of extensions in the payment deadline, but after two months, Spindler informed Sackett that Sackett had breached the contract and that Spindler would not sell Sackett the stock.

Issue: When does a failure to perform by one party constitute a breach such that the other party's duty to perform is discharged?

Rule: Whether a party's duty to perform under a contract is discharged depends upon whether the failing party's performance constitutes a material breach. Factors considered in determining the materiality of a failure include: whether the injured party will subtantially obtain the benefits of the contract, whether damages will adequately compensate the injured party, partial performance by the failing party, the hardship on the failing party if the contract is terminated, the failing party's willfullness, negligence, or innocence, and the certainty or uncertainty of completed performance by the failing party.

Harrell v. Sea Colony, Inc. (1977) KC

Facts: Harrell entered into a written contract with Sea Colony for the purchase of a condominium that required a deposit of $5000. Harrell requested a release from the contract, contingent on Sea Colony's agreement to return his deposit. Sea Colony proceeded to sell the condominium to a third party. Harrell was notified that while his cancellation request was granted, the request constituted an anticipatory breach for which his deposit would be kept as damages.

Issue: When may the actions of a party to a contract be construed as an anticipatory repudiation?

Rule: Anticipatory repudiation occurs when there is a "definite and unequivocal manifestation of intention" of a party to discontinue performance as promised under the terms of the contract. A mere request for cancellation does not itself rise to the level of a repudiation.

Note: Anticipatory repudiation by one party serves to release the non-breaching party from further obligations under the contract.

Doubleday & Co. v. Curtis (1985) R

Facts: The actor Tony Curtis made a two-novel contract with Doubleday. When his second novel encountered unfavorable reviews with his Doubleday editor, he refused to incorporate changes, accept editing help or send the novel to a "novel doctor." Doubleday terminated the contract pursuant to the condition that the novel must be "satisfactory to Publisher. ..."

Issue: If a contract contains a condition of satisfaction and implies that the producer will help the creator to meet this condition, what are the limitations on the producer's right to terminate for dissatisfaction?

Rule: A producer may, in its discretion, terminate a production contract, provided that the termination is made in good faith and the failure of the creator to submit a satisfactory product was not caused by the bad faith of the producer.

Merritt Hill Vineyards Inc. v. Windy Heights Vineyard, Inc. (1984) R

Facts: Merritt Hill agreed to purchase a majority stock interest in one of Windy Heights' vineyards and tendered a $15,000 deposit. The agreement provided "conditions precedent" to be satisfied before the deal went through. Merritt refused to close when it learned that Windy Heights failed to satisfy a condition.

Issue: What is the difference between a promise and a condition?

Rule: A promise is a manifestation of an intention to act or not act in a manner specified so as to ensure a commitment to the other party (Rest. 2d § 2). A condition is an event that must take place, unless excused, before a contractual obligation is to take effect (Rest. 2d § 224).

Margolin v. Franklin (1971) R

Facts: Franklin entered into an installment contract for the purchase of a car. Franklin asked Margolin if the payment schedule could be modified, and Margolin orally agreed. Franklin paid the monthly installments pursuant to the new schedule, but the car was repossessed.

Issue: May a seller declare a forfeiture after he has orally modified the buyer's written installment payment schedule?

Rule: Forfeiture may occur where a payment clause has been waived, only if the vendor gives the purchaser reasonable, definite, and specific notice as to a change of intention to waive.

Oneal v. Colton Consolidated School District No. 306 (1976) R

Facts: Oneal, a teacher suffering from failing eyesight, tendered his resignation to the school board conditioned upon his receipt of sick-leave benefits. The school board denied his request for sick-leave benefits and discharged him. Oneal claimed that the school board breached the contract by denying him sick-leave benefits. The school board argued that it could not have breached its contract, because Oneal's failing eyesight made it impossible for him to perform the contract.

Issue: Does a party breach a contract when the contract is impossible to perform?

Rule: Where performance is impossible, a party cannot be charged with breach of contract, because the contractual duty is discharged by law.

Handicapped Children's Education Board of Sheboygan County v. Lukaszewski (1983) KC, R

Facts: The Board hired Lukaszewski to serve as a speech and language therapist. Lukaszewski breached her contract by accepting another job, but returned after being threatened with legal action. Lukaszewski then visited her doctor, who diagnosed her as having high blood pressure induced by her job. Lukaszewski resigned and a new therapist was hired.

Issue: Under what circumstances may health problems justify a breach of contract?

Rule: A health danger will excuse nonperformance when the danger is not caused by the breaching party, or if the danger is not foreseeable when the party enters into the contract.

Whitman v. Anglum (1918) R

Facts: Whitman contracted to purchase 175 quarts of milk each day for a year from Anglum. Anglum's cows were quarantined, and eventually killed. Anglum claimed he was excused from performance by reason of the quarantine, which made it illegal for him to deliver milk.

Issue: Is a supplier excused from performance when the supplier's source of product is destroyed, but the contract does not specify that the product must come from a particular source?

Rule: When a supplier's source of products need not come from any particular source, the performance of the contract is not excused for impossibility if the supplier's source is destroyed.

Aluminum Company of America v. Essex Group, Inc. (1980) R

Facts: ALCOA agreed to produce aluminum for Essex. The contract tied the price of the aluminum to the Wholesale Price Index-Industrial Commodities (WPI-IC). ALCOA claimed that both parties had intended this formula to serve as an objective measure of increases in ALCOA's non-labor costs of producing the aluminum. However, the WPI-IC formula failed to track the actual cost of production, causing ALCOA to face more than $75 million in losses. ALCOA sued to have the contract modified on the ground of mutual mistake.

Issue: What are the circumstances under which a party may obtain judicial relief through mutual mistake?

Rule: Where both parties make a mistake of fact that relates to a basic assumption of the contract, the law of mutual mistake allows for judicial relief where the lack of equivalence between the parties is severe, so long as the party negatively affected has not assumed the risk. The doctrines of impracticability and frustration of purpose also discharge an obligor from his duty to perform a contract where a failure of a basic assumption of the parties produces an extremely inequitable relationship.

Hope's Architectural Products, Inc. v. Lundy's Construction, Inc. (1991) R

Facts: Hope's, a custom window manufacturer, contracted to sell windows to Lundy's. Lundy's allegedly threatened to withhold payment after a delayed delivery by Hope's. Hope's then demanded that Lundy's pay before delivery. Lundy's did not pay and Hope's did not deliver. Lundy's then terminated the contract and obtained an alternate supplier.

Issue: Is a party who suspends performance after demanding assurances and not receiving them entitled to damages if the other party terminates the contract?

Rule: If one party asks for assurances of performance and the other party fails to give them, the party requesting assurance is entitled to suspend performance and may recover damages if the other party subsequently terminates the contract.

National Knitting Co. v. Bouton & Germain Co. (1909) R

Facts: Bouton ordered a quantity of gloves from National, a large portion of which was delivered. National, however, failed to deliver the remainder. Bouton did not pay, and National sued to recover for the goods actually delivered.

Issue: How do courts determine whether a contract is severable?

Rule: If a contract is naturally severable (e.g., goods are measured in units and a per-unit price is provided), courts are inclined to hold a contract severable and grant recovery for the goods that were actually delivered. If, however, the express or implied intent of the parties is to condition payment upon delivery of all items, then the court will consider the contract to be non-severable.

Graulich Caterer Inc. v. Hans Holterbosch, Inc. (1968) R

Facts: Holterbosch operated a pavilion at the World's Fair and needed food. It arranged to obtain food from Graulich. Graulich's first delivery did not compare favorably with the original samples and was rejected. The second installment was similarly unacceptable.

Issue: May a party cancel a contract when its supplier makes multiple deliveries of nonconforming goods?

Rule: When nonconformity substantially impairs the value of a delivered installment and the nonconformity cannot be cured, a party may reject the installment. When the nonconformity substantially impairs the value of the contract, a buyer may cancel the whole contract. (UCC § 2-612.)

Manitowoc Steam Boiler Works v. Manitowoc Glue Co. (1903) R

Facts: Plaintiff constructed and connected a steam boiler for Manitowoc Glue. When operated, the boiler failed to meet the specifications of the contract. Both parties tried to increase the efficiency of the boiler, but were unable to do so. When the defendant refused to pay, the plaintiff sued to recover the contract price.

Issue: May a party recover on a contract when his performance does not meet contract specifications?

Rule: A party who makes a contract cannot recover payment until he performs the contract entirely and according to its terms. However, recovery may be allowed when a party, unintentionally and in good faith, completes a structure that substantially accomplishes the purposes for which it was built, and when the cost of bringing the structure up to contract specifications is easily ascertained.

Plante v. Jacobs (1960) R

Facts: Plante contracted to build a home for Jacobs who later refused to continue payment because of defects in the construction. Plante did not complete the house and sued for the unpaid balance. Jacobs claimed that

Plante failed to substantially perform. The market value of the house was not significantly affected by the defects.

Issue: Is a contractor liable for failure to substantially perform if there are construction defects that do not significantly affect market value?

Rule: The test for substantial performance is whether the performance meets the essential purpose of the contract. As applied to construction of a house, substantial performance does not mean that every detail must be in strict compliance with the specifications and the plans. Contract recovery will be diminished by the *cost of replacement rule* for small defects, and by the *diminished value rule* to avoid unreasonable economic waste, in cases of defects whose correction is expensive but adds little or nothing to the value.

Jacob and Youngs v. Kent (1921) R

Facts: Jacob & Youngs, a contractor hired to build a home for Kent, inadvertently installed a different brand of pipes than that specified in the contract. The pipes used were of comparable price and quality to those specified, but Kent refused to pay Jacob & Youngs unless the pipes were replaced.

Issue: Is a party who inadvertently breaches a contract in a nonmaterial and insignificant manner liable for breach?

Rule: Considerations of both justice and the intentions of the parties will allow the court to characterize some promises as merely independent and insignificant promises allowing only nominal damages as opposed to treating such promises as conditions of the contract.

Hochster v. De La Tour (1853) R

Facts: After De La Tour repudiated an employment contract before the contract was to commence, Hochster, the employee, brought suit for breach of contract.

Issue: May a repudiating party be sued before his performance is due under the contract?

Rule: Renunciation of a contract to do a future act may be treated as a breach of contract, and the repudiating party can be sued before his performance is due under the contract.

Oak Ridge Construction Co. v. Tolley (1985) R

Facts: Oak Ridge contracted to construct a house and drill a water-supply well for the Tolleys. The contract specified that the well should be 150 feet in depth, but provided a formula for calculating an extra charge if a deeper well was required. The completed well was 800 feet deep. Tolley disputed the extra charge for the well. Oak Ridge then claimed breach of contract, terminated the contract, and ceased performance.

Issue 1: When may a party terminate a contract based on the anticipatory breach of the other party?

Rule 1: A party may terminate a contract based on anticipatory breach when the other party acts or uses language in such a way as to constitute a "definite and unconditional repudiation" (UCC § 2-610, Comment 2). Mere expression of doubt as to a party's willingness or ability to perform is not enough to constitute repudiation.

Issue 2: How do courts determine whether a failure to perform is a material breach?

Rule 2: In determining whether a failure to perform is a material breach, the courts will consider whether the injured party was deprived of the expected benefits of the contract, whether injured party can be adequately compensated for deprivation of the benefit, whether forfeiture could occur, the likelihood that the nonperforming party will cure its failure, and whether the nonperforming party comported with good faith and fair dealing practices.

Pittsburgh-Des Moines Steel Co. v. Brookhaven Manor Water Co.
(1976) R

Facts: Pittsburgh-Des Moines Steel (PDM) contracted to build a water tank for Brookhaven. Although Brookhaven was not required to pay until the work was completed, PDM requested that the money be placed in escrow or that its president would personally guarantee the payment, after it heard incorrect rumors that Brookhaven was in financial difficulties. When Brookhaven refused to do either, PDM sued for anticipatory breach.

Issue: Are rumors of financial difficulties sufficient grounds for insecurity with respect to the other party's ability to perform its obligations?

Rule: UCC § 2-609 allows a party to ask for adequate assurance of due performance and suspend its own performance until it receives such assurance only when reasonable grounds for insecurity arise with respect to the other party's performance. Here, there were no reasonable grounds for PDM to invoke this section.

Model Vending, Inc. v. Stanisci (1962) R

Facts: Model, a lessor of vending machines, entered into an agreement giving it the exclusive privilege of selling merchandise from its machines in Stanisci's bowling alley. One year into a five-year agreement, Stanisci closed down the machines. During the third year, a fire destroyed the premises. Model claimed damages for the loss of profits over the full five-year period.

Issue: If a party breaches a contract, but performance would have been subsequently excused because events occurring after the breach made performance impossible, is the nonbreaching party entitled to damages for the full term of the contract?

Rule: Where performance is excused for impossibility, damages for breach of contract by the promisor are limited to those damages recoverable prior to the occurrence of the impossibility.

International Environmental Corp. v. International Telephone and Telegraph (1975) R

Facts: International Environmental(IE) and International Telephone and Telegraph (ITT) entered into a contract stating that ITT "may order from time to time" air handling and coil fan products. ITT never ordered any products. IE claimed the contract was a requirements contract and sued for damages.

Issue: How should the court interpret disputed language in a contract?

Rule: A court must interpret ambiguous words in a contract within the context of the whole agreement, the circumstances surrounding the negotiations, and the intent of the parties. However, express language in a contract may not be contradicted by extrinsic evidence.

Printing Center of Texas, Inc. v. Supermind Publishing Co., Inc. (1984) R

Facts: Supermind paid Printing Center to print books. Upon delivery, Supermind found the books to be nonconforming and rejected the delivery. Supermind sued for a refund.

Issue: May a buyer reject goods which fail to conform to a contract?

Rule: A buyer may reject goods in good faith if the evidence establishes nonconformity with the contract.

Moore v. Fellner (1958) R

Facts: Moore, an attorney, represented the Fellners at trial on the basis of a contingency fee agreement. When the case was appealed, Moore sent a letter asking for $2000 plus costs to further represent them. The Fellners obtained substitute counsel to handle the appeal. The trial court's decision was affirmed and Moore sought to recover his contingency fee.

Issue: Does an attorney breach his contract and forfeit his right to recovery of a contingency fee when he asks his client for an additional fee to continue representation on appeal?

Rule: Where a contract is deemed divisible, an attorney has the right to recover reasonable compensation for his services during the duration of the attorney-client relationship, less the expenses incurred by the client in obtaining other counsel.

Koehler v. Buhl (1893) R

Facts: Buhl hired Koehler under a contract that required Koehler to perform to Buhl's satisfaction. Koehler was discharged for unsatisfactory performance. Koehler claimed his work was objectively satisfactory and sued for the full amount due under the contract.

Issue: What is the standard by which an employee must complete his work "to the satisfaction of his employer"?

Rule: When an individual contracts to do work to the satisfaction of his employer, the employer's subjective judgment is conclusive and is not subject to a reasonableness requirement.

Ericson v. Playgirl, Inc. (1977) R

Facts: Playgirl offered to include pictures of Ericson, an aspiring actor, in the *Best of Playgirl*. Ericson accepted the offer on the condition that his picture appear on the cover of the magazine. Ericson's photo was mistakenly left off the cover. Ericson sued for the lost publicity he would have received had the condition been fulfilled.

Issue: Does a plaintiff have a right to compensation where his complaint is based on a loss of general publicity bearing no relation to the practice of his art?

Rule: For publicity to be of value to an artist's career, it must be related to the performance of his art, such that a breach of contract resulting in lost publicity directly affects his earning power. Damages from loss of general publicity alone are speculative and conjectural, and a claim for such damages will be rejected.

Glen Cove Marina, Inc. v. Vessel Little Jennie (1967) R

Facts: Donohue, a charter yacht owner and operator, contracted with Glen Cove to have his yacht, Little Jennie, stored for the winter and repaired. No date was set for completion of the required repairs, but by early April, Donohue feared that the repairs might not be completed by May 1, the beginning of the charter season. Donohue pressed Glen Cove for completion, but the repairs were not completed until May 9. Glen Cove sought to recover payment under the contract, but Donohue argued that Glen Cove had breached the contract by failing to perform by May 1.

Issue 1: Is "time of the essence" when a contract does not specify a date for completed performance?

Rule 1: Where parties to a contract fail to specify a date for performance, performance must be tendered within a reasonable time. What constitutes a "reasonable time" depends on the relationship between the parties, the subject matter of the contract, and the time required for an individual of ordinary diligence to perform under similar conditions. In this case, the court found a "reasonable time" to be May 1.

Issue 2: When a contract for work, labor or services is to be completed within a reasonable time, may a party rescind the contract due to a delay in performance by the performing party?

Rule 2: When a contract for work, labor or services is to be completed within a reasonable time, a party may rescind a contract due to a delay in performance by the performing party after giving the performing party reasonable notice of his intention to rescind and a reasonable time in which to tender the promised performance. If a party with the privilege to rescind allows the performing party to go on performing, making improvements, or otherwise changing his position without some warning that the contract is at an end, the party desiring rescission will continue to be bound under the contract. In this case, the court found that Donohue had failed to notify Glen Cove of his intention to rescind and that Glen Cove could therefore recover on the contract.

Fablok Mills, Inc. v. Cocker Machine & Foundry Co. (1973) R

Facts: Fablok ordered ten knitting machines from Cocker. The delivered machines were defective, but Fablok accepted delivery. Cocker attempted to remedy the problems but was unable to do so. Fablok, after two years, revoked its acceptance and sought rescission and damages for breach of warranty after Cocker refused to further remedy the situation.

Issue 1: What factors determine whether a buyer revokes acceptance within a reasonable time?

Rule 1: Factors to consider in determining whether a buyer has revoked his acceptance in a reasonable time are the nature, purpose and circumstances of such action. The fact finder determines whether revocation occurs within a reasonable time.

Issue 2: Is rescission barred when a buyer continues to use the goods after revoking acceptance of them?

Rule 2: A buyer's continued use of goods after notice of rescission will often bar a claim of revocation. The trier of fact may, however, determine that the continued use of goods will not bar a claim, such as where the buyer is unable to purchase a suitable substitute for the goods at issue.

Nees v. Weaver (1936) R

Facts: The Weavers sought to recover for services rendered in constructing a garage roof for the defendant. The defendant alleged that the work was unsatisfactory and that the contract had not been substantially performed.

Issue: May a party recover for services performed where his work has not fully conformed to the contract?

Rule: A party may recover the contract price, less the cost of completing the work, if he has made a good faith effort and has substantially performed the contract. Where a party fails to substantially perform, he may not recover under quantum meruit unless a use amounting to an acceptance by the owner can be shown.

Gibson v. Cranage (1878)

Facts: Gibson expressly agreed to the condition that Cranage must be personally satisfied with his portrait of Cranage's deceased daughter before being required to pay. Cranage was dissatisfied and refused to pay.

Issue: Is a contract term requiring personal satisfaction an enforceable condition?

Rule: If a contract's express terms provide that a party is to be personally satisfied before having to perform his part of the contract, that party may insist upon his right as given him by the contract. However, the dissatisfaction must be in good faith.

Williams v. Hirshorn (1918) R

Facts: Plaintiff sued to receive the $50 owed to him on a contract to waterproof the walls of defendant's cellar. The contract stated that the payment would be rendered after "a satisfactory test" had been performed. A test was performed, and the defendant claimed the work was unsatisfactory and refused to pay.

Issue: When may a promisor find a performing party's work to be unsatisfactory and thereby escape liability?

Rule: A promisor's dissatisfaction must be actual and genuine, not feigned, before he may escape liability.

Haymore v. Levinson (1958) R

Facts: Haymore constructed a house which was purchased by the Levinsons, who placed $3000 of the contract price in escrow until "satisfactory completion of the work." When the money was requested, the Levinsons claimed that they were not fully satisfied.

Issue: What standard should be applied when a contract requires "satisfactory completion of the work"?

Rule: Building contracts generally fall within an objective standard which requires that work be completed in a reasonably skillful and workmanlike manner, such that it would meet the approval of reasonable and prudent persons.

Gerisch v. Herold (1912) R

Facts: Plaintiff, Herold, agreed to construct a house in a workmanlike manner under the direction of an architect, and to find good, proper, and sufficient materials for completing the job. The contract provided that final payment would only be made after the architect had certified Herold's work and after the owner or his agent had expressed satisfaction with the work. Herold brought this suit to collect the final payment, claiming that defendant wrongfully withheld his satisfaction and that the architect's certification showed the work to be satisfactory.

Issue: When a contract requires the receiving party's approval of completed work before payment is tendered, what standard of satisfaction should be applied when deciding whether the receiving party has wrongfully withheld his approval?

Rule: If a contract requires the receiving party's satisfaction before payment is tendered, the receiving party must be subjectively satisfied with the performing party's work before payment is due. Objective standards, such as the certification of a third party, do not apply to the satisfaction requirement, unless provided for in the contract. In this case, the contract only called for third party certification with respect to the quality of the workmanship and materials; completion of the entire contract was contingent on the receiving party's satisfaction with the house.

Chapter 9

THIRD-PARTY BENEFICIARIES

Generally, contracts between two parties only confer benefits on the parties. Sometimes, two parties may make a contract for the benefit of a third party. The overriding issue in these cases is who is entitled to sue in case of breach. Example: A pays C to sing for B. If C does not sing, can B, the third-party beneficiary, sue C? Can A sue C?

I.   INTENDED V. INCIDENTAL BENEFICIARIES

Only an intended third-party beneficiary is entitled to sue if the contract made for his benefit is breached.

A.   Intended Beneficiary
To conclude that a third party was intended to be a beneficiary, courts must determine that this would effectuate the intentions of the parties, and either

1. The obligee was to pay money to the beneficiary, or

2. Circumstances indicate that the promisee intended to give the beneficiary the benefit of the promised performance, as indicated by:

   a. Whether the beneficiary is named in the contract.

   b. Whether performance was to be made directly to the beneficiary.

   c. Whether the beneficiary can change the terms of the performance.

   d. Whether the beneficiary could have reasonably relied on the contract.

B.   Incidental Beneficiary
Although an incidental beneficiary receives the benefits of a contract made between other parties, he is not entitled to sue if that contract is

breached because it was not intended that he receive any benefits. A party is an incidental beneficiary if he does not satisfy the standards of an intended beneficiary. Example: A contracts with State to build a new exit for the highway. B owns a gas station near the site of the new exit. The new exit will be beneficial to B's business, but he is only an incidental beneficiary of the contract.

II.   TYPES OF BENEFICIARIES

Traditionally, there were two types of beneficiaries.

A.   Creditor Beneficiary
If a party contracts with a second party to repay the first party's debt to a third party, the third party is called a creditor beneficiary. Example: A owes B $100. C owes A $100. To satisfy his debt with A, C promises A that he will pay B (the creditor beneficiary) $100. Note: The creditor (B) always retains the right to sue the original debtor (A).

B.   Donee Beneficiary
If a party contracts with a second party to confer a benefit on a third party, the third party is called a donee beneficiary. Example: B promises A to give C $1,000 from A's estate at A's death. Note: The donee beneficiary (C) does not have a right to sue the promisee (A), but may sue the promisor in case of breach.

C.   Restatement (Second) § 302
The traditional "creditor" and "donee" categories have been eliminated. All beneficiaries are classified as intended or incidental.

III.   LAWSUITS IN BENEFICIARY CUSTOMS

Lawsuits arise when the promisor fails to confer the agreed upon benefit to the intended beneficiary.

A. Intended Beneficiary v. Promisor

    1. The promisor's defenses include any defenses which could have been raised if the promisor were sued by the promisee (no mutual assent, failure of consideration, etc.).

    2. The promisor cannot raise any claims that the beneficiary and the promisee may have against each other because the promisor's rights and obligations stem only from the contract with the promisee.

    3. Exception: If the promise was qualified, such that the promisor agreed to make payment "only if the promisee was indebted to the beneficiary," then the promisor may prove that there was no debt.

B. Intended Beneficiary v. Promisee

    1. If the benefit is not conferred onto the beneficiary, that party cannot bring suit against the promisee because they are not involved in a contractual relationship.

    2. Exception: A creditor beneficiary may sue the promisee directly on the original contract lending to the promisee.

C. Promisee v. Promisor
A promisee may bring suit against a promisor to enforce a promise that would benefit a third-party beneficiary.

IV. MODIFICATION OF A BENEFICIARY'S RIGHTS

A. After a contract has been made for the benefit of a third party, the contracting parties may usually modify or rescind the contract, denying the benefit to the intended third party, unless:

    1. The contract expressly states that it cannot be modified, or

    2. The contract is silent on the issue of modification, and the third party has materially relied on it, brought suit to enforce it or manifested assent to it.

B. The beneficiary is entitled to any consideration the promisee gets from the promisor for an ineffective attempt to modify the contract.

CASE CLIPS

Lawrence v. Fox (1859) DHH, KGK, FE, MS, CPB

Facts: Holly owed Lawrence $300. Holly loaned Fox $300 on condition that he repay the $300 to Lawrence, in satisfaction of Holly's debt. Fox did not pay.

Issue: Can a third party creditor-beneficiary sue to enforce a contract between two other parties that was made for the benefit of the third party?

Rule: A third party can sue to enforce an agreement between two other parties which was made for the benefit of the third party even though there is no privity with the third party.

Seaver v. Ransom (1918) DHH, KGK, FE

Facts: Beman was about to die and wanted to change her will to provide for her niece, Seaver. Because Beman was afraid she would die before a new will could be written, her husband promised that he would provide for their niece at his death if the will was left unchanged. At his death, her husband left nothing to Seaver, who sued his administrator.

Issue: May third party donee-beneficiary enforce a promise made between two others for its benefit?

Rule: A party may enforce a contract made for its benefit by two other parties. Third-party beneficiaries are an exception to the requirement of privity between contracting parties.

Vikingstad v. Baggott (1955) DHH

Facts: Baggott, a real estate broker, took a $1,000 earnest money deposit from Vikingstad as part of an agreement to buy real estate. Vikingstad later changed his mind, and Baggott agreed to refund the $1,000 if he found another buyer. Baggott sold the property to Mr. Lang, who bought it on the condition that the money be refunded to Vikingstad, so as to extinguish any claim he might have to the property. Baggott never returned the money, and Vikingstad sued as a third-party beneficiary of Baggott's contract with Lang.

Issue: Does the reason for conferring the benefit on the third party affect that party's right to enforce the contract?

Rule: If the terms of the contract necessarily require the promisor to confer a benefit upon a third person, the third party has standing to enforce it. It is irrelevant that the actual motive or purpose of the parties was to protect their own interests.

F.O. Bailey Co. v. Ledgewood, Inc. (1992) DHH

Facts: Plaintiff owned a building and occupied a portion of it for the purposes of operating an antique business. A third party eventually obtained property rights to the unoccupied portion of the building, and subsequently entered into a series of contracts with the defendant for the renovation of the building. Some of the work benefitted the plaintiff exclusively, while other parts benefitted the entire building. Upon completion of the renovation, the plaintiff sued for breach, claiming that the work done under the contract was faulty and incomplete.

Issue: When may a court allow a plaintiff who benefits from a contract to which it is not a party, to bring suit for breach of the contract?

Rule: In order to bring a successful third party beneficiary contract claim, a plaintiff must prove a clear and definite intention on the part of the contracting parties to give the plaintiff the benefit of their performance. Otherwise, the plaintiff is merely an incidental beneficiary and may not sue to enforce the contract.

H.R. Moch Co. v. Rensselaer Water Co. (1928) DHH, KGK, CPB

Facts: Rensselaer contracted with the city to provide it with water. A fire burned down Moch's warehouse because of inadequate water pressure in the city's hydrants, caused by Rensselaer's negligence. Moch sued for damages, claiming to be the third-party beneficiary of Rensselaer's contract with the city.

Issue: Can a member of the general public sue for improper performance of a government contract made on the public's behalf?

Rule: One who indirectly benefits from a contract made between two other parties cannot sue to enforce the contract. To have standing the party must prove an intention to make the defendant liable to the general public.

Heyer v. Flaig (1969) DHH

Facts: Flaig, an attorney, drew up a will for his client, who wished to leave her entire estate to her daughters, the plaintiffs. Flaig neglected to exclude his client's second husband from the will, and the plaintiffs' inheritance was reduced by $50,000 as a result.

Issue: Is an attorney who erred in drafting a will liable to a person named in the instrument?
Rule: A client's intended beneficiaries can sue an attorney for malpractice if he negligently failed to fulfill the testamentary instructions of the client.

Robson v. Robson (1981) DHH

Facts: The defendant and his son signed a contract that provided that the son's wife, the plaintiff would receive $500 per month for life if the son died. The plaintiff divorced the son before he died and sued to enforce the clause.
Issue: May contracting parties revoke a benefit promised to a third party, prior to the vesting of the beneficiary's rights?
Rule: Contracting parties can discharge, rescind or revoke benefits promised to a third party before the rights vest, provided that the beneficiary did not detrimentally rely on the right prior to its vesting.

Rouse v. United States (1954) DHH, KGK, FE, CPB

Facts: Winston signed a promissory note for construction of a heating system in her house. The U.S. eventually took assignment of the note. Rouse bought Winston's house agreeing to assume Winston's debt, but failed to make payments. The U.S. sued to enforce the contract, claiming it was a third-party beneficiary. Rouse defended that Winston fraudulently misrepresented the condition of the heating plant and that it had not been properly installed and, thus, the U.S. did not deserve to be paid.
Issue: What defenses can be raised against a third-party beneficiary?
Rule: A party which promises to make a payment to another party's creditor can assert any defense against the creditor that it could have asserted had it been sued by the promisee. If a promisor's agreement is to be interpreted as a promise to discharge whatever liability the promisee is under, the promisor is allowed to show that the promisee was not actually liable (because of improper performance by the third party). However, when the promise was to pay a certain amount of money to the promisee's creditor, it is immaterial to challenge whether the promisee is actually indebted.

Vrooman v. Turner (1877) KGK, CPB

Facts: Evans mortgaged his property to Vrooman, the plaintiff. Evans later conveyed the property to Mitchell, who conveyed it to Sanborn. Neither Mitchell nor Sanborn agreed to assume the mortgage as part of the conveyance. Sanborn conveyed to Turner, the defendant, who agreed to assume the duty to pay the mortgage. Vrooman sued to foreclose the mortgage.

Issue: Is a purchaser of property, who agrees to assume the mortgage on it, obligated to repay the mortgage if the seller did not have such an obligation?

Rule: A purchaser of property who agrees to assume a mortgage on it is not liable to the mortgagee if the property is purchased from one who was not liable to the mortgagee.

Note: Evans cannot enforce the Sanborn-Turner agreement as a third-party creditor-beneficiary because Sanborn had no obligation to Evans. Vrooman can only sue Evans.

Socony-Vacuum Oil Co., Inc. v. Continental Casualty Co. (1955) KGK

Facts: A general contractor provided performance and payment bonds to ensure all of its subcontractors and materialmen, as was required by law (for government projects). The prime contractor also required one of its subcontractors to furnish a surety bond to pay the subcontractor's debts for "all labor and material" should the subcontractor default. Socony-Vacuum, a materialman, was not paid by the subcontractor and sued Continental, the surety company, claiming to be a third-party beneficiary of the subcontractors agreement with the prime contractor. (The statute of limitations prevented Socony-Vacuum from recovering under the prime contractor's payment bond.)

Issue: May a third party recover from a surety if his loss falls within the bond's classification?

Rule: A direct third-party beneficiary can recover under a bond that contains language that suggests the party is covered by the bond.

Lucas v. Hamm (1961) KGK, CPB

Facts: Hamm, an attorney, prepared a will for his client. After the will was probated, a provision was declared invalid because of an error made by Hamm. The plaintiffs sued Hamm because they received $75,000 less than they would have received had the provision been valid.

Issue: May an intended beneficiary of a will sue an attorney for improperly drawing the will?

Rule: When the main purpose and intent of a testator in making his agreement with an attorney is to benefit a third party named in the will, as a matter of policy the intended beneficiaries may recover as third-party beneficiaries in the event of the attorney's breach.

Isbrandtsen Co., Inc. v. Local 1291 of Int'l Longshoremen's Assn. (1953) KGK

Facts: A ship's cargo was spoiled when longshoremen stopped work, despite an agreement not to strike made between their union and a Marine Trade Association. The contract stated that it was made expressly for the benefit of members of the trade association who employed longshoremen. Isbrandtsen, the original charterer of the ship, sued to recover damages.

Issue: May one enforce a contract to which he is neither a party nor an intended beneficiary?

Rule: One who is neither a party nor an intended beneficiary, but nevertheless would benefit from performance of the contract, is an incidental beneficiary and cannot enforce the contract.

Moch Co. v. Rensselaer Water Co. (1928) DHH, KGK, CPB

Facts: Rensselaer contracted with the city to provide it with water. A fire burned down Moch's warehouse because of inadequate water pressure in the city's hydrants, caused by Rensselaer's negligence. Moch sued for damages, claiming to be the third-party beneficiary of Rensselaer's contract with the city.

Issue: Can a member of the general public sue for improper performance of a government contract made on the public's behalf?

Rule: One who indirectly benefits from a contract made between two other parties cannot sue to enforce the contract. To have standing the party must prove an intention to make the defendant liable to the general public.

Martinez v. Socoma Companies, Inc. (1974) KGK, FE, MS

Facts: Socoma was paid by the government to retrain "hard-core unemployed" persons. Socoma breached the contract and the plaintiffs, unemployed persons, sued, claiming to be third-party beneficiaries. The contract provided that in case of breach, Socoma would return the money it received to the government.

Issue: May a member of the public sue to enforce a government contract if he lost benefits as a result of its breach?

Rule: Merely being a potential recipient of benefits from a government contract does not by itself confer upon a party the right to enforce the contract. It must be shown that a clear intention existed to benefit the specific party and that, in appropriate cases, a private right of action was created as remedy in case of breach.

Holbrook v. Pitt (1981) KGK

Facts: The government enacted a program to provide housing assistance to low-income families by paying subsidies to landlords (defendants). Tenants were only eligible for assistance after being certified by the landlord, and they were not automatically given "retroactive certification" (i.e., subsidies accruing between the time that a family is eligible for assistance and the time of certification). Tenants (plaintiffs) sued to demand, as third-party beneficiaries, retroactive certification and that unreasonable delays in granting certification be declared a breach. The legislative history, the method used to calculate subsidies, and the language of the act suggested that protection of tenants was its primary goal. The program was also intended to minimize claims on housing insurance funds.

Issue: Must a governmental contract for the protection of third parties have that goal as its sole purpose in order to allow the third parties to claim rights as beneficiaries?

Rule: Where a government program is designed for the specific protection of a class, as evidenced by the legislative history, the purpose of the program, the method used to calculate subsidies, and express language in the contracts embodying the program, members of that class have standing to enforce it in case of breach. The existence of other subsidiary purposes does not defeat the parties' status as protected beneficiaries.

Ford v. Mutual Life Ins. Co. of New York (1936) KGK

Facts: Ford took out a life insurance policy, naming his wife as the beneficiary. The policy allowed Ford to redeem its cash value after 20 years. Ford sued to recover the cash value of the policy.

Issue: Is it necessary to have the consent of a beneficiary in order to change the beneficiary's rights/interests in an insurance policy?

Rule: When a beneficiary has a vested interest in an insurance policy, the policy cannot be surrendered to recover its cash value without the beneficiary's permission.

Copeland v. Beard (1928) KGK, FE

Facts: Beard bought land from Copeland's debtor, agreeing to pay the debtor's obligation to Copeland. Before Copeland could agree to the assignment of the debt, Beard resold the property to another party who promised to repay the debt. Copeland sued Beard when he was not paid by the second buyer.

Issue: Does a creditor-beneficiary have a cause of action against a promisor who was discharged of the duty to repay the debt before the beneficiary agreed to the assignment?

Rule: When a debtor contracts with another, for a valuable consideration, to assume and pay his debt, the creditor has an option to accept or reject the new party as his debtor. The promisor and promisee, however, can rescind or discharge their duties at any time before the election is made.

Lewis v. Benedict Coal Corp. (1960) KGK

Facts: As part of a collective-bargaining agreement with a union, Benedict Coal was required to pay royalties for each ton of coal produced into a welfare fund for miners. Benedict Coal withheld payments equal to the amount of damages caused by a subsequent strike, which breached the agreement. The plaintiffs, the trustees of the fund, sued as third-party beneficiaries to recover the money.

Issue: Is a promisor entitled to reduce the amount of benefits to a third-party beneficiary to reflect damages it incurred because of the promisee's breach?

Rule: Absent an express contract provision, a set-off cannot be used to recover a debt owed by a contracting party at the expense of a third-party beneficiary.

Hale v. Groce (1987) FE, R

Facts: Groce was to draw up a will and trust for a client who wanted a certain gift left to Hale. After the client died, Hale discovered that Groce had failed to put in a provision declaring Hale a beneficiary.

Issue: May a third-party beneficiary of a contract recover for negligent acts of the parties to the contract?

Rule: A third party may recover for the negligent performance of a party to a contract.

Jacobs Associates v. Argonaut Insurance Co. (1978) FE

Facts: Jacobs Associates was a subcontractor of Target on a construction job. In accordance with the terms of the general contract, Target secured a bond from the defendant, Argonaut Insurance. Target was later adjudicated bankrupt and Jacobs Associates sued the insurance company, claiming it was a third-party beneficiary of the bond agreement.

Issue: May a third party maintain an action against a promisor surety if there was an express promise to pay the third party?

Rule: When a promisor agrees with the promisee to pay the promisee's debt to a third party, the third-party beneficiary can enforce the contract against the promisor.

Salesky v. Hat Corp. of America (1963) FE

Facts: Salesky was granted a pension in case of her husband's death, as part of her husband's employment contract. The contract allowed the husband to make modifications and he did, by later making his sister his beneficiary instead of his wife. At her husband's death, Salesky sued for the pension.

Issue: Are benefits granted to a third-party beneficiary revocable if the contract reserved such power?

Rule: Benefits may be rescinded or revoked without permission from a third-party beneficiary if her rights arose under a contract that specifically provided that the benefits were revocable, so long as they have not yet vested.

Dutton v. Poole (1677) MS, CPB

Facts: Poole promised his father that he would pay his sister, Dutton's wife, £1,000, if the father would not sell some land. Poole never paid his sister the money.

Issue: Can a beneficiary of a contract, who was not in privity to its making, sue to enforce the contract?

Rule: A beneficiary to a contract between two other parties may enforce the contract if one of the makers was a close relative of the beneficiary.

Johnson v. Holmes Tuttle Lincoln-Mercury, Inc.
(1958) MS

Facts: Holmes Tuttle, a car dealer, sold Caldera a car, promising that full insurance coverage would be provided. Although Holmes Tuttle added the cost of premiums to Caldera's monthly payments, it failed to take out a policy. Caldera got into an accident with Johnson, the plaintiff. Johnson sued Holmes Tuttle claiming that it was a third-party beneficiary of the promise to take out insurance.

Issue: May a third-party beneficiary enforce a contract if he was a member of a class that was to obtain a benefit under the contract?

Rule: A third-party beneficiary may enforce a contract made by two other parties, even if he was not identified as an individual, as long as he is a member of the class for whose benefit the contract was made.

Lonsdale v. Chesterfield (1983) MS

Facts: Chesterfield subdivided and sold parcels of land. Each sales contract contained a clause stating that Chesterfield would install a water system, which was to be paid for by the owners of the parcel. Chesterfield sold its interest to Sansaria. A clause in their contract provided that Sansaria would install the water system, but it did not. Purchasers of the subdivisions sued to enforce the agreement between Sansaria and Chesterfield.

Issue 1: May a party enforce a contract between two other parties if it is to benefit from the contract?

Rule 1: Third parties who benefit from a contract between two others may enforce the contract, provided the parties to the contract intended that one party assume a direct obligation to the third party.

Issue 2: May one avoid liability by delegating duties?

Rule 2: Liability cannot be avoided by delegating a duty. The delegator remains secondarily liable.

Fourth Ocean Putnam Corp. v. Interstate Wrecking Co., Inc. (1985) MS

Facts: Fourth Ocean owned a hotel that had been destroyed by fire. Believing that the structure was a public nuisance and a fire hazard, the Village hired Interstate Wrecking to tear down the building, to remove all walls and foundations one foot below grade level, and to crush and remove the slab. The Village later recovered the costs from Fourth Ocean. A few years later, Fourth Ocean began new construction on the site and discovered that the walls and foundations had not been removed, and the slab had not been crushed.

Issue: Where two parties contract to satisfy the obligation of a third party, does the third party have rights as a third-party beneficiary?

Rule: Where two parties contract to satisfy the obligation of a third party, the third party does not have rights as a third-party beneficiary if the parties performed the contract for the purpose of satisfying some other party (i.e., the third party's obligee).

Note: Thus, the court found that the contract between Interstate Wrecking and the Village was intended to benefit the villagers by satisfying Fourth Ocean's obligation to remove the hazard.

Visintine v. New York, Chicago & St. Louis Ry. Co.
(1959) MS

Facts: The state of Ohio contracted with the defendants to demolish a railroad grade crossing. The state later entered into a separate contract with Visintine to do another part of the demolition work. Visintine sued to enforce the contract between the defendants and the state, claiming damages caused by the defendants' delay in its performance. The contracts reflected specifications and work schedules that required all contractors to cooperate and coordinate their efforts.

Issue: Does a contractual provision requiring separate contractors working on the same project to cooperate and coordinate their work, make each contractor a third-party beneficiary of the other's contract with the owner?

Rule: A party is a creditor-beneficiary if the performance of a contract between two other parties will satisfy an actual, supposed, or asserted duty owed by the promise to the beneficiary. There is no valid reason for restricting the meaning of "duty" to those involving a monetary debt only. Thus, if the promisor takes on the duty to perform a service on behalf of the promisee, the third party is also a creditor-beneficiary.

Note: In this instance, the defendants assumed Ohio's duty to provide Visintine with a site on which it could do its work in performance of the contract. The emphasis on cooperation and coordination in the contracts suggests that the performance of each contractor's duty was dependent on that of the others.

Zigas v. Superior Court of California (1981) KC, MS

Facts: In a class action suit, a group of tenants sought damages for landlords' violations of a financing agreement with the federal government that limited the amount of rent landlords could charge tenants.

Issue: Is state law applicable in determining whether tenants have standing to maintain a third-party cause of action to enforce provisions of a financing agreement where the federal government is a party?

Rule: State law is applicable to determine whether tenants have standing to sue as third-party beneficiaries to enforce provisions of a financing agreement between private parties and the federal government, provided the controversy raises no questions regarding liability of the United States.

Alexander H. Revell & Co. v. C.H. Morgan
Grocery Co. (1919) MS, CPB

Facts: C.H. Morgan contracted to have Lidke install new fixtures in its store. Lidke did a poor job, and the parties made a second contract whereby C.H. Morgan agreed to pay for the materials if Lidke finished the work properly. Lidke did not do the work, and C.H. Morgan refused to pay Alexander H. Revell, a materialman, for supplies.

Issue: Are the rights of a third-party beneficiary dependent on proper performance of the obligations of the contracting parties?

Rule: When a contract is entered into by two parties for the benefit of a third, the third party's rights are subject to the "equities" between the original parties. Any defense that can be asserted against one of the contracting parties can also be asserted against the third party.

Tweeddale v. Tweeddale (1903) MS

Facts: In exchange for consideration, Daniel Tweeddale gave his mother a bond (promise) that he would give her and his brother Edwin Tweeddale a share of the money Daniel would receive from the sale of land. To secure the bond, Daniel gave his mother a mortgage on the property. Daniel later sold the land and settled with his mother (who discharged the mortgage) and revoked his promise to his banker. Edwin only became aware of Daniel's promise after it was rescinded. Edwin sued as a third-party beneficiary of Daniel's contract with their mother.

Issue: May a third party's rights be rescinded before he is aware of them?

Rule: When two parties contract to pay money to a third party in exchange for consideration, the law establishes privity between the promisor and the third person, and the liability is binding, regardless of whether the beneficiary has knowledge of the transaction.

Morstain v. Kircher (1933) MS

Facts: The Browns gave Morstain a mortgage on their property to secure a promissory note they had given to her. The Browns later conveyed the property to Kircher, who promised to pay the mortgage. Kircher later reconveyed the land and the mortgage to the Browns, who defaulted on the note. Morstain sued Kircher for the value of the note.

Issue: Can a promisor be discharged from a debt owed to a third-party creditor-beneficiary?

Rule: Discharge of a promisor by a promisee in a contract is effective against a creditor-beneficiary if the beneficiary does not bring suit upon the promise or otherwise materially change his position in reliance on the promise before he knows of the discharge or variation.

Detroit Bank & Trust Co. v.
Chicago Flame Hardening Co., Inc. (1982) CPB

Facts: Three partners made a contract to provide a cash stipend to their spouses in case of their death. The agreement was later rescinded, but one of the spouses challenged the rescission after her husband died.

Issue: May a contract be modified or rescinded to the detriment of a third-party beneficiary?

Rule: A contract may be modified or rescinded to the detriment of a third-party beneficiary at any time before the contract is accepted, adopted or acted upon by the third-party beneficiary.

Western Waterproofing Co. v.
Springfield Housing Authority (1987) CPB

Facts: Western Waterproofing was a subcontractor to Bildoc, which had a waterproofing and weatherization contract with Springfield Housing Authority (SHA). The contract required SHA to procure a payment bond from Bildoc, which it did not do. Western contributed labor and materials toward completion of the project but never received its payment of $129,000. After failing to collect on its default judgment against Bildoc, Western resumed proceedings against SHA as a third-party beneficiary.

Issue: May a third-party beneficiary sue a public entity when such entity has failed to secure a surety bond as required by the contract?

Rule: If an element of a contract is intended for the direct benefit of a third party, such third party may sue for breach. Payment bonds, by definition, exist for the protection and direct benefit of third parties.

Erickson v. Grande Ronde Lumber Co. (1939) CPB

Facts: Erickson was a creditor of Grande Ronde. The Stoddard Company assumed the debts of Grande Ronde. Erickson sought judgment against both companies.

Issue: Is a creditor entitled to judgment against both a debtor and the promisor who has assumed its debts?

Rule: Both promisor and debtor are liable for a debt to the credit beneficiary though there can be only one satisfaction of the debt.

Drewen v. Bank of Manhattan Co. (1959) CPB

Facts: As part of a divorce agreement between husband and wife, the husband promised to never reduce their children's interest in his estate as set forth in a will executed on the day of the agreement. Later, after his ex-wife had died, the husband executed a new will which altered the arrangements for the children. The suit was brought by the administrator of the ex-wife's estate against the executor and trustee of husband's will.

Issue: Does a promisee of a contract for the benefit of a third party have a right to sue for damages?

Rule: A promisee of a contract for the benefit of a third party has sufficient interest in the enforcement of the promise to sue for damages.

Note: The ex-wife's right to enforce the contract passed to her estate with her death.

Guy v. Liederbach (1983) KC

Facts: Liederbach, an attorney, was retained by Kent to draft a will naming Guy as beneficiary and executrix. At the direction of Liederbach, the will was signed by Kent, and witnessed by Liederbach and Guy. Upon Kent's death, a New Jersey court invalidated the legacy to Guy, pursuant to a statute which prohibited attesting witnesses from being beneficiaries to the will. Guy brought a third party beneficiary suit against Liederbach.

Issue: May a named beneficiary of a will bring a suit against an attorney whose actions encroach upon the beneficiary's entitlement?

Rule: A named legatee may bring a suit as an intended third party beneficiary of the contract between an attorney and testator for the drafting of a will which names the legatee as beneficiary. Although there is no privity between the parties (e.g., attorney-client), the Restatement (Second) § 302 allows third party actions where the intent to benefit is clear and the promisee is unable to enforce the contract.

Note: A majority of states follow the traditional rule that an attorney-client relationship is necessary to bring a malpractice suit against an attorney.

Biggins v. Shore (1989) KC

Facts: Mr. Biggins sold his share of a business to Shore, reserving the right to certain payments to be made during his life, and continuing to be paid to his wife if she survived him. Mr. Biggins subsequently drafted a memo that gave Shore the power to change the beneficiary of the payments upon Mr. Biggins' death. After Shore exercised the option, Mrs. Biggins sued to be reinstated as the beneficiary of the payments, claiming that the modification was ineffective.

Issue: May a promise which benefits a third party be modified or revoked before the benefits accrue?

Rule: In the absence of express language reserving the right to modification, a promise intended to benefit a third party becomes indefeasible when created, regardless of whether detrimental reliance by the beneficiary occurs.

Note: This rule is codified by Restatement (Second) § 142.

Lawrence v. Fox (1859) R

Facts: Mr. Holly owed Lawrence $300. Holly loaned Fox $300 on condition that he repay the $300 to Lawrence, in satisfaction of Holly's debt. Fox did not pay.

Issue: Can a third party creditor-beneficiary sue to enforce a contract between two other parties that was made for the benefit of the third party?

Rule: A third party can sue to enforce an agreement between two other parties which was made for the benefit of the third party even though there is no privity with the third party.

Pierce Associates, Inc. v. The Nemours Foundation (1988) R

Facts: Nemours hired a general contractor to complete the interior of its hospital. The general contractor hired Pierce, as subcontractor, to complete the mechanical work on the project. The entire hospital project was plagued by delays and disputes that prompted Nemours to withhold payments due to Gilbane under the general contract. In response, Pierce suspended performance of its subcontract. Nemours hired a new contractor to complete Pierce's work and sued Pierce for damages.

Issue: When is a nonparty considered a third-party beneficiary of a contract?

Rule: A nonparty is considered to be a third party beneficiary to a contract when the language of the contract expresses an intent to confer third party beneficiary status to that party.

Chapter 10

ASSIGNMENT OF RIGHTS AND DELEGATION
OF DUTIES

Assignment and delegation involve the transfer of contractual rights or duties to a third party. The issues that usually arise involve questions of which rights/duties are transferable, what are the consequences of such transfers for the original parties, and what is the extent of the third party's obligations.

I.   DEFINITIONS

A.   Assignment
     A party to a contract (assignor) transfers contractual rights to a third person (assignee).

B.   Delegation
     A party to a contract (obligor/promisor) transfers contractual duties to a third person (delegatee).

C.   Assignment and Delegation v. Third-Party Beneficiary v. Novation

     1. Assignment and delegation occur after a contract is executed. There is no requirement that both parties agree to it.

     2. Third-party beneficiaries are created at the time the contract is made.

     3. Novations occur when both parties agree that a third party substitute for one party.

II. ASSIGNMENT

A.   An assignment is a present transfer of contractual rights. A promise to transfer contractual rights at a future date is not an assignment. UCC Article 9 covers many assignments.

B. Rights That May Be Assigned
Generally, all contractual rights are assignable, with the following exceptions:

Mnemonic: **POP FRED**

1. **P**rohibited by law
2. **OP**tion to enter a bilateral contract that is accompanied by an impermissible delegation of duties
3. **F**uture rights
4. **R**isks to obligor are substantially altered
5. **E**xpress agreement prohibiting assignment
6. **D**uty of obligor would be altered

1. **P**rohibited by Law
A right cannot be assigned if a statute or public policy prohibits the assignment of that type of right. The most common examples are rights to future alimony payments, torts claims that are assigned to lawyers, and rights to wages.

2. **Op**tions

a. Unilateral options may be assigned. Example: Joe tells Moe, "If you give me $250,000 within 30 days, I will sell you my house." Moe can assign the option to Bo.

b. Options for bilateral contracts can only be assigned if unaccompanied by an impermissible delegation. Example: Joe tells Moe, "I will give you 30 days to promise me that you will buy my house for $250,000 and also play tuba at my wedding as part of the deal." Moe can assign his right (option) to Bo, but Bo's acceptance is only valid if Moe, not Bo, plays the tuba (a duty) at Joe's wedding. Note: See "Delegation" for more on impermissible delegations.

3. **F**uture Rights
Rights that are expected to arise in the future are not assignable. An attempt to make a present assignment of future rights has the effect of a promise to assign the rights when they do arise. If the

assignment is based on an existing contract, however, it is enforceable. Example: B, a buyer, assigns the rights to future deliveries he will receive from S, a seller, under their present contract. The assignment would be shaky if B promises to assign future deliveries from a contract he hopes/expects to make with S in a few months.

4. Risk to Obligor Substantially Altered
   Assignment is not permitted if the obligor's risk will be materially changed as a result. Risks do not have to be increased, just altered. Example: S sells a plane to B and attempts to assign the insurance policy on it. The assignment is ineffective because the policy is based on the age, experience, etc., of the pilot which varies from person to person.

5. Express Contractual Clause Not to Assign
   A general clause prohibiting assignment will not usually invalidate an assignment of rights under the contract. Although the assignment is effective, the assignor is held to have breached the contract. The Rest. 2d. § 322 and UCC § 2-210 provide that an express contractual clause prohibiting assignment is valid and that subsequent assignments are breaches of the contract. The Restatement provides the following exceptions (rights assignable regardless of contrary clauses):

   a. The right to sue for breach of contract by the other party.

   b. The right to return performance where the assignor has fully performed his obligations.

   c. An anti-assignment clause is waivable by the party for whose benefit it was made.

   d. An agreement not to "assign the contract" is construed to bar delegation of duties only, not assignment of rights. However, language that clearly bars assignment will be upheld as barring assignment of rights also (see *Allhusen v. Caristo Construction Corp.*). Note: Under UCC Article 9, which covers commercial financing, any anti-assignment term in a contract that comes within the scope of Article 9 is ineffective.

6. **D**uty of Obligor Altered
Assignments that materially change an obligor's duties are prohibited.

   a. Personal Service Contracts
   Employers cannot assign rights to receive services if the services are unique or based on a special relationship.

   b. Output Contracts
   At common law, such contracts were not assignable. The UCC allows assignment of output contracts if the output of the assignee will not be unreasonably disproportionate to the assignor's expected production under the original contract.

III. REQUIREMENTS OF AN EFFECTIVE ASSIGNMENT

A. Present transfer

B. Adequate description of the right to be assigned

C. Does not have to be in writing, except for the following:

   1. Interest in land

   2. Sale of goods over $500

   3. Chose in action worth more than $5,000

   4. Security interests under UCC Article 9

   5. Wage assignments

D. Consideration is not required. However, a gratuitous assignment is revocable.

    1. Automatic revocation occurs upon:

        a. Death of assignor.

        b. Bankruptcy of assignor.

        c. Subsequent reassignment of the right by assignor to another person.

        d. Notice is given by assignor to assignee that the assignment has been revoked.

    2. Gratuitous assignments can be made irrevocable by:

        a. Delivery to the assignor of a document symbolizing the right that was assigned (stock certificate, bankbook, insurance policy, etc.).

        b. A writing, made by the assignor, providing that the assignment will not be revoked.

        c. Detrimental reliance by the assignee on the assignment.

        d. Obligor rendering the assigned performance.

        e. Giving consideration for the assignment.

IV. RIGHTS OF THE PARTIES AFTER AN ASSIGNMENT

A. Privity of contract is established between the obligor and assignee and erased between obligor and assignor.

B. Rights of the Assignee
The assignee "steps into the shoes" of the assignor and thus can directly enforce the contract.

C.   Rights of the Obligor
The obligor may assert any defense against the assignee that would have been available to assert against the assignor. For example, if the assignor did not give consideration or misrepresented a material fact, this defense can be raised against the assignee's right.

D.   Rights of Assignee Against Assignor
If the assignee is unable to recover from the obligor, that party may try to recover from the assignor.

   1.   Gratuitous Assignment
   Assignee will not recover unless detrimental reliance is shown.

   2.   Assignment for Value
   An assignment that is given for consideration contains the following implied warranties:

      a.   Assignor will not impair enforcement of the right.

      b.   The right assigned is valid and all encumbrances have been disclosed.

      c.   Any documents that evidence the transferred right are valid.

      d.   The assignor does not warrant the credit-worthiness of the obligor unless the assignor expressly agrees to guarantee it.

E.   Rights of Sub-assignees
If an assignee assigns the right to yet another party, all of the implied warranties of the original assignor are not automatically transferred unless the original assignor makes an express agreement. However, the sub-assignee is responsible for the transferred duties.

V.   MODIFICATION BY THE OBLIGOR AND ASSIGNOR

An obligor and assignor may attempt to modify their agreement in a way that will affect the assignee's rights. The effect of such modification depends on the extent of the obligor's awareness of the assignee:

A. Modification Before Obligor Receives Notice of the Assignment
The obligor and assignor can modify in good faith. (Rest. 2d § 318.)

B. Modification After Obligor Receives Notice of the Assignment
The assignor and obligor can only make a "good faith" modification if the assignor has not fully performed all duties under the contract.

VI. DELEGATION OF DUTIES

Delegation involves the transfer of contractual duties. Unlike an assignor, whose rights to benefits terminates, a delegator remains liable under the contract should the delegatee improperly perform his duties.

A. Types of Nondelegable Duties

1. Contracts involving performance requiring special skills. A contract is delegable, despite a personal preference of the obligee that the original obligor perform, if the services do not require a special skill.

2. "Special trust" relationships (e.g., doctor-patient).

3. Contract provision expressly prohibiting delegation.

B. Rights and Duties After Delegation

1. Obligee must accept services that were lawfully delegated.

2. The delegator remains liable for performance after delegation unless the obligee specifically consented to the delegation, thus forming a novation.

3. The Delegatee

   a. Delegation
   Delegatee may perform the duties at his option.

   b. Assumption
   Delegatee must perform because he agreed to do so in exchange for consideration. The obligor becomes a third-party beneficiary to delegatee's agreement to perform.

   c. Novation
   Under a novation, all parties must agree to the new arrangement. Delegation and assumption do not have to be approved by the obligee to be valid.

CASE CLIPS

Langel v. Betz (1928) DHH, FE, MS, KGK, CPB

Facts: Langel contracted to sell property to Hurwitz and Hollander (vendees). The vendees assigned the contract to Benedict, who assigned it to Betz. The assignment did not contain a delegation of duties. Betz refused to perform any duties.

Issue: Does the assignment of rights under a contract burden the assignee with liabilities under the contract?

Rule: Absent reason to believe otherwise, acceptance of rights under a bilateral contract by an assignee will not imply acceptance of duties under the same contract.

Cook v. Lum (1893) DHH, MS

Facts: Green obtained a piece of paper listing her deposits. Before she died she gave the paper to Cook, who tried to collect from Green's executor, Lum, claiming that a gratuitous assignment of the right to Green's money had been made.

Issue: Is a gratuitous assignment irrevocable?

Rule: Transfer of a legal document symbolizing the assigned rights is considered an irrevocable assignment only if the transaction will deprive the donor of all control over the property. Since Green could withdraw the money without showing the paper, she did not relinquish control.

Cochran v. Taylor (1937) DHH

Facts: Taylor gave an option for the purchase of land to the Cochran's assignor for $1 consideration. The option was executed under seal.
Issue: May an option founded upon valid consideration be revoked at will by the offeror?
Rule: A valid option cannot be withdrawn, revoked or rescinded at will by the offeror within the time provided for acceptance.

Macke Co. v. Pizza of Gaithersburg, Inc. (1970) DHH, FE, CPB, R

Facts: Pizza of Gaithersburg contracted to have vending machines installed by Virginia Coffee Co. The defendant sought to terminate the contract when Virginia Coffee's assets were purchased by Macke, which assumed Pizza of Gaithersburg's contract as a result.
Issue: Are rights and duties that arise out of an executory bilateral contract assignable?
Rule: Rights are assignable under an executory bilateral contract. A duty is delegable when the services are not of a personal or unique character.

Allhusen v. Caristo Constr. Corp. (1952) DHH, MS

Facts: Caristo Construction contracted with a subcontractor to paint. The subcontractor assigned his right to payment to a third party, who assigned it to Allhusen. A contract clause prohibited assignment of "monies due or to become due" without written permission from Caristo.
Issue: What is the legal effect of a contractual provision prohibiting assignment?
Rule: When clear language is used, parties may limit the freedom of alienation of rights and prohibit an assignment.

Ford Motor Credit Co. v. Morgan (1989) DHH

Facts: Morgan purchased a car at a car dealership, from a salesman who gave assurances of the economy and reliability of the car. Morgan financed the acquisition through Ford Motor Credit. Over the next 18 months, Morgan experienced multiple problems with the car, and finally decided to discontinue payments to Ford. Ford took action to recover and sell the vehicle, but found that the car had been vandalized beyond repair. Subsequently, Ford sued to recover the outstanding balance owed by

Lehman was ineffective because it involved payment of future proceeds that were not in actual existence at the time of the assignment.

Issue: May rights that have not accrued because the assignor has not completed his performance be assigned?

Rule: Future contractual proceeds may be effectively assigned if the contract is already in existence.

In Re City of New York v. Bedford Bar & Grill, Inc. (1957) KGK

Facts: To secure a loan, Bedford Bar & Grill assigned the rights to a possible refund it would get if its liquor license was revoked to a bank. The license was revoked, and the bank claimed the refund because Bedford defaulted on the loan. New York City, the plaintiff, claimed the refund because the defendant owed taxes.

Issue: Are the rights of an assignee of monies yet to come into existence subordinate to the lien of a judgment creditor?

Rule: A judgment creditor's lien prevails over the equitable lien of an assignee of property yet to be acquired at the time of assignment.

Speelman v. Pascal (1961) KGK, CPB

Facts: Pascal gratuitously assigned, in writing, a percentage of his profits from a musical to Speelman, his secretary. After Pascal's death, the musical was produced and was a big hit (*My Fair Lady*). Speelman sued Pascal's estate for her promised share of the profits.

Issue: Does the delivery of a letter constitute a valid and complete assignment?

Rule: A signed and delivered writing is an irrevocable and valid assignment, even if the assignment was gratuitous.

Boston Ice Co. v. Potter (1877) KGK

Facts: Citizen's Ice Co. contracted to supply Potter with ice. The Boston Ice Co. bought Citizen's and continued to supply ice to Potter, although it did not inform him of the change in ownership. Potter refused to pay when he discovered the change a year later. Potter had previously contracted with Boston Ice directly and was extremely dissatisfied with services provided under that contract.

Issue: Does performance by a party who was assigned a contract impose liability on the other party?

Rule: Acceptance of an assignment may not be presumed from the acceptance of goods. Therefore, privity of contract only exists when the purchaser of the goods has been notified of and accepted the assignment.

The British Waggon Co. and the Parkgate Waggon Co.
v. Lea & Co. (1880) KGK

Facts: Parkgate Waggon leased some wagons to Lea & Co. It was also obligated to repair and maintain the wagons. Parkgate delegated its duties to British. Lea & Co. refused to pay, claiming that the delegation was invalid.

Issue: Are duties that are not personal delegable?

Rule: Contractual duties are delegable, absent a clause prohibiting such delegation, if the delegator was not selected with reference to his individual skill, competency, or other personal qualifications.

Arkansas Valley Smelting Co. v. Belden Mining Co.
(1888) KGK

Facts: Belden agreed to sell ten thousand tons of lead to Billings. Billings conveyed the contract to Arkansas Valley, providing notice to Belden, which refused to perform.

Issue: Is an assignment valid if it is made without the consent of the obligor?

Rule: Assignment of a contract is effective despite objections by the obligor, but only if the assignor has completed all of his obligations under the contract. Otherwise, the obligor might be exposed to greater uncertainty of receiving the return performance than it contracted for (i.e., Belden relied on Billings' skills, solvency, etc., in making the contract, not on Arkansas Valley's).

Cuban Atlantic Sugar Sales Corp. v.
The Marine Midland Trust Co. of New York (1962) KGK

Facts: Cuban Atlantic contracted to have Ocean Trading transport its sugar. Ocean assigned its contract to Marine Midland in order to obtain funds. Cuban Atlantic made prepayments on freight charges to Marine Midland in expectation of Ocean's performance. Due to difficulties, Ocean was unable to perform, and Cuban Atlantic sued Marine Midland to recover the prepaid monies.

Issue: Does the assignor's failure to perform allow an obligor to recover prepaid fees from the assignee?

Rule: An assignee must return monies received from an obligor when the assignor fails to perform his contractual commitment.

Commercial Credit Corp. v.
Orange County Machine Works (1950) KGK

Facts: Ermac Co. contracted to buy a press for Orange County Machine Works. As part of the deal, Orange County Machine gave Ermac a promissory note payable upon delivery of the press. Ermac gave the note to Commercial Credit Corp., in exchange for money to buy the press. Commercial Credit was fully aware of Ermac's contract with the defendant at the time it advanced the money. Ermac was unable to buy the press, and the note was unpaid. Commercial Credit sued Orange County Machines for the advanced money, claiming to be a holder in due course of the defendant's note.

Issue: May a finance company that actively participated in an assignment be a holder in due course?

Rule: When a finance company actively participates in a transaction from its inception, such as by counseling and aiding the future vendee-payee, it is not regarded as a holder in due course of the note given in the transaction. The defense of failure of consideration may properly be maintained.

Note: A holder in due course is one who takes a negotiable instrument for value and in good faith, without notice of any defense or claim against it by any other party.

Babson v. Village of Ulysses (1952) KGK

Facts: An electric utility signed a long-term contract with Ulysses, whereby Ulysses was required to pay a fixed fee of $100 a month and an additional fee depending on the amount of electricity used. The utility assigned the fixed fee to Babson. The remainder of the contract, including the duty to provide electricity, was assigned and delegated to another company, which convinced Ulysses to build its own power plant. Ulysses stopped paying Babson.

Issue: May an assignee prevent termination or modification of an agreement?

Rule: A contract may be revoked or modified without the permission of an assignee if the assignee did not assume the assignor's performance obligations.

Dearle v. Hall (1828) KGK

Facts: Brown assigned his rights to yearly payment from his father's estate to Dearle in exchange for a lump sum. Brown repeated the transaction with Sherring. Brown also sold his right to the annuity to Hall. None of the assignees knew of each other.

Issue: Who will prevail when the same property is assigned to several assignees who did not have notice of the other assignments?

Rule: An earlier assignment is effective against later assignment only if actual delivery of the property has been completed and notice has been given.

Note: In the instant case, Hall was allowed to keep the annuity because he had no notice of Dearle and because payment of the annuity had never actually been made to Dearle.

State Factors Corp. v. Sales Factors Corp. (1939) KGK

Facts: Lerner assigned its accounts receivable to Sales Factors Corp. Lerner then assigned the same accounts to State Factors, who was unaware of the earlier assignment. State Factors chose not to notify the creditors of the assignment, and payments were thus made to Sales Factors. State Factors sued for the value of the accounts.

Issue: When two assignees give value for an assignment, who will prevail?

Rule: A subsequent purchaser of legal accounts who paid consideration and was unaware of an infirmity has legal title superior to that of an earlier assignee.

Note: The Restatement's "Four Horsemen Rule" provides that a subsequent good-faith purchaser for value, without notice of the first assignment, prevails if he either obtains payment or satisfaction of the obligor's duty, obtains judgment against the obligor, makes a novation or obtains delivery of a tangible token or writing that has to be surrendered by the terms of the obligor's contract. A later assignee also prevails if the first assignment is revocable or voidable.

Evening News Ass'n. v. Peterson (1979) FE, R

Facts: Peterson, a newscaster at a TV station, contested the assignment of his employment contract when the station was sold.

Issue: May an employment contract be assigned?

Rule: An employment contract is assignable if it was not based on a personal relationship, and the employment was not materially changed by the assignment.

Larese v. Creamland Dairies, Inc. (1985) FE, R

Facts: Larese, a franchisee, agreed that it would not sell or lease its interests in the franchise without Creamland Dairies' consent.

Issue: Does a franchisor have an absolute right to refuse to consent to the sale of a franchisee's interest to another prospective franchisee?

Rule: If the franchisor does not specifically bargain for an absolute right of refusal, the right of refusal will be limited to only reasonable refusals.

United California Bank v. Eastern Mountain Sports, Inc. (1982) FE

Facts: Snow Lion assigned its accounts receivable to United California Bank. Eastern Mountain Sports refused to make full payment, requesting a set-off for defective goods that were sent to it by Snow Lion.

Issue: May an obligor reduce his payments to an assignee in the amount of the reduced value of the assignor's performance?

Rule: If an assignor does not properly perform his obligations to an obligor, the obligor can reduce his payments to the assignee by the damages attributable to the assignor's breach.

Madden Engineering Corp. v. Major Tube Corp. (1978) FE

Facts: Major Tube Corp. entered into a requirements contract to supply all of Archer's paper cores needs. Major Tube was also allowed to sublease a part of Archer's building. Major Tube then assigned the proceeds from the contract to Madden Engineering as security for a loan. Because of Major Tube's financial difficulties, the contract was later modified to allow Archer to purchase paper cores elsewhere and to actually buy the cores for Major Tube and then deduct the cost from the invoice. Archer requested a set-off for these costs and for garnishments and attachments it had to pay.

Issue: Is an obligor's and assignor's good faith modification of their agreement effective against the assignee, when performed after the assignment and without the assignee's consent?

Rule: Under UCC § 9-318, a good faith modification between an obligor and assignor is effective against an assignee when the assignor's payment has not been earned by full performance, even if the assignment was complete, and the assignee did not consent after notification. The set-off is only permitted as to items that arose out of the contract, i.e., garnishments and attachments that were not computed as part of the set-off.

Fitzroy v. Cave (1905) MS

Facts: Five creditors assigned to Fitzroy debts owed them by Cave. Fitzroy attempted to force Cave into bankruptcy so that he would be dismissed from his position as a director of Fitzroy's corporation.

Issue: May an otherwise proper assignment be challenged because of the improper motives of the assignee?

Rule: A valid assignment is not affected by the assignee's motive.

Crane Ice Cream Co. v. Terminal Freezing & Heating Co. (1925) MS

Facts: Mr. Fredrick, an ice cream plant owner, made a requirements contract to buy ice from Terminal. Terminal renewed the contract because he was satisfied with Fredrick's adherence to the contract terms, which included exclusivity, timely payment and good faith efforts to maintain a sufficient volume of purchases. Terminal refused to honor Fredrick's assignment of the contract to Crane Ice Cream.

Issue: Is an assignment invalid if the contract was induced by personal factors?

Rule: A contract may not be assigned if part of its inducement was based on personal factors. A person has the right to the benefit accruing from the character, credit and substance of the other party to the contract.

Note: The court was motivated largely by the fact that because this was a requirements contract, Terminal was in a vulnerable position.

Robert S. Pinzur, Ltd. v. The Hartford (1987) MS

Facts: When Patka was admitted to a hospital for treatment, she assigned her health insurance payments directly to the hospital and physicians. The insurance company, The Hartford, did not pay on the claims, and the various creditors who had rendered medical services billed Patka. Patka hired Robert Pinzur to secure the benefits, for which he was to receive a 33 percent contingency fee. Robert Pinzur secured the benefits, but The Hartford paid them entirely to the creditors, claiming that Pinzur's lien was not effective because Patka had assigned all of her rights.

Issue: Is an assignment of direct insurance payments an assignment of all rights under the policy?

Rule: Where no consideration is given, and the assignor still remains liable for the debts, an assignment of direct insurance payments is not an assignment at all, but is a mere authorization to facilitate payment.

Burrows v. Burrows (1922) MS

Facts: Burrows' mother gave her a check and her checkbook, just hours before her final departure. Burrows's father, the plaintiff, the administrator of his wife's estate, claimed that the gift was revoked by the mother's death. Burrows claimed part of the account (represented by the check) was assigned to her.

Issue: Does a check given by a deceased constitute an enforceable assignment of the issuer's rights to her bank account?

Rule: The death of a drawer before a check is presented acts as a revocation of the order and, therefore, writing the check is not a valid assignment.

Gardner v. Hoeg (1836) MS

Facts: Hoeg, a sailor, borrowed some money and made an arrangement for the support of his family in exchange for assigning his wages from an upcoming sea voyage. Gardner, Hoeg's creditor, sued for the money under the theory that the assignment violated public policy.

Issue: May future wages be assigned?

Rule: Future wages may be assigned if not contrary to public policy.

Taylor v. Barton-Child Co. (1917) MS

Facts: As security for a loan, Barton-Child assigned present and future accounts receivables to Taylor's assignor. Barton-Child later went into bankruptcy, and its trustee claimed that the assignment of future accounts was invalid.

Issue: May the assignment of accounts receivable be enforced in equity against a trustee in bankruptcy?

Rule: Future rights that have yet to accrue may not be assigned. Such an assignment is only valid if the assignor reaffirms it after acquiring possession.

Continental Purchasing Co., Inc. v. Van Raalte Co., Inc. (1937) MS, CPB

Facts: Potter assigned all of her wages to Continental Purchasing as security for an account. Van Raalte, Potter's employer, continued to pay Potter's wages to her, despite notification of the assignment.

Issue: Is one liable for paying his indebtedness to an assignor rather than an assignee?

Rule: If a debtor who has been given notice of an assignment pays an assignor any money that, under the assignment, belongs to the assignee, or if he does anything prejudicial to the rights of the assignee, the debtor is liable to the assignee for any resulting damages.

Lonsdale v. Chesterfield (1983) MS

Facts: Chesterfield subdivided and sold parcels of land. Each sales contract contained a clause stating that Chesterfield would install a water system, which was to be paid for by the owners of the parcel. Chesterfield sold its interest to Sansaria. A clause in their contract provided that Sansaria would install the water system, but it did not. Purchasers of the subdivisions sued to enforce the agreement between Sansaria and Chesterfield.

Issue 1:   May a party enforce a contract between two other parties if it is to benefit from the contract?

Rule 1:   Third parties who benefit from a contract between two others may enforce the contract, provided the parties to the contract intended that one party assume a direct obligation to the third party.

Issue 2:   May one avoid liability by delegating duties?

Rule 2:   Liability cannot be avoided by delegating a duty. The delegator remains secondarily liable.

Arnold Prod. Inc. v. Favorite Films Corp. (1962) MS

Facts: Arnold Productions, owner of two movies, contracted to give Favorite Films exclusive distribution rights. The agreement contained a clause stating the rights were personal and could not be assigned. Favorite Film assigned TV rights to the movies to Nationwide, over whom it exercised supervisory control.

Issue: Is a partial assignment of rights and duties valid if expressly forbidden in the contract?

Rule: An assignor who assigns some, but not all, of his rights under a contract has not breached a contractual clause prohibiting assignment of the contract if the assignor exercises supervisory control over the assignee.

Sally Beauty Co. v. Nexxus Prods. Co., Inc. (1986) KC, MS

Facts: Nexxus had entered into a contract under which Best Barber would be the exclusive distributor of Nexxus haircare products throughout most of Texas. Best Barber was acquired and merged into Sally Beauty, which was the subsidiary of another manufacturer of haircare products and a direct competitor of Nexxus. The defendant canceled the contract, claiming that it was not assignable in such a situation.

Issue: May a "best efforts" contract be assigned to a marketplace competitor of the obligee?

Rule: A "best efforts" contract may not be assigned to a marketplace competitor of the obligee without the obligee's approval, because it is reasonable to expect that the performance the obligee will receive will be substantially different from that for which he bargained.

Dissent: Such a contract may be assigned because in businesses, unlike the legal-services industry, there is no fiduciary duty that makes it impossible to sell competing lines of merchandise. In the absence of monopolistic situations, there is no reason to assume that a distributor would unfairly favor its parent's products over other lines, because such action would not be consistent with the main objective of maximizing profit in a competitive market.

Donovan v. Middlebrook (1904) CPB

Facts: Middlebrook employed Toch to sell his real estate in New York City and agreed to give him a commission if he was successful. Toch procured a purchaser with the assistance of Horowitz. In exchange for his help, Toch agreed to pay Horowitz one half of his the commission. Horowitz further gave his claim to Donovan who sought to recover from Middlebrook.

Issue: Does the agreement to pay a debt out of a designated fund constitute a valid assignment?

Rule: The agreement to pay a debt out of a designated fund does not operate as an assignment since the assignor retains control over the subject matter.

Cooper v. Gidden (1987) CPB

Facts: Cooper sold the Blackwell Sand Company to Stewart under an agreement which included a covenant by Cooper not to compete. Stewart later assigned his interest in the sand company to Gidden. Cooper then prepared to re-enter the sand and gravel business. Gidden filed for an injunction claiming that all rights under the agreement between Cooper and Stewart, including the covenant not to compete, had been assigned to him.

Issue: Is a covenant not to compete against a business assignable to a new party?

Rule: All contractual rights received by the original purchaser, including a covenant not to compete, are validly assignable as long as there were no words of restriction in the covenant that make it personal in nature.

Seale v. Bates (1961) CPB

Facts: The Seales contracted for 300 hours of dance lessons with Bates Dance Studios. Bates then assigned the contract to Dance Studio of Denver. The Seales continued to take lessons but were very dissatisfied and sought rescission.

Issue: If a party assents to the assignment of a contract, may it later claim that the contract is non-assignable?

Rule: When a party implicitly consents to an assignment, it is in effect a waiver of this possible breach.

Western Oil Sales Corp. v. Bliss & Wetherbee (1927) CPB

Facts: McCamey, Sheerin & Dumis contracted with Western to sell and deliver oil. The contract contained a provision allowing assignment. Western renounced all liability under the contract after assigning all the benefits and obligations to American Oil. Because Western would not recognize its continued liability, McCamey, Sheerin & Dumis refused to continue performance and treated the contract as terminated. They subsequently conveyed all their rights and claims under the contract to Bliss & Wetherbee.

Issue: May a party release itself, by assigning its obligation to another, from liability under a contract without the consent of the other party to the contract?

Rule: When a contract is assignable, a party may assign the benefits and delegate the obligations under the contract, but it remains liable for the proper performance of those obligations unless the other party to the contract consents to the assignment.

Note: By repudiating all liability, Western committed an anticipatory breach enabling the sellers to terminate the contract.

Franklin v. Jordan (1968) CPB

Facts: Ackerman assigned to Franklin an option contract for the exclusive right to purchase a tract of land from Jordan. The contract required that Ackerman sign a note personally promising to pay the balance of the purchase price, due after the initial payment. Franklin sued for specific performance after submitting a promissory note signed only by himself.

Issue: May an option holder assign his obligation to sign a promissory note?

Rule: An option holder in a bilateral contract may assign his rights to receive benefits but not his obligation to make promises when the terms of the agreement prohibit such a delegation.

John Ludwick, Assignee of Jacob Bollinger
v. Michael Croll (1799) CPB

Facts: Bollinger claimed the right to 1,152,000 acres of land in Kentucky based upon a pretended survey. He sold the land to the Croll and four others and then assigned his right to receive payments to John Ludwick. After realizing he had been swindled, Croll refused to pay John Ludwick.

Issue: May the assignee of a bond collect payment when the obligor, who is responsible for payment, was swindled by the assignor?

Rule: The assignee of a bond takes it at his own peril, subject to every defense, which may be used by the obligor against the assignor.

Federal Deposit Insurance Corp. v. Registry Hotel Corp.
(1986) CPB

Facts: A bank made a series of loans to Frownfelter Construction. In consideration for the loans, Frownfelter assigned the bank a security interest in a construction contract it had with Registry. Registry accepted the bank as an assignee of the contract. Registry later terminated the contract with Frownfelter which defaulted on its loans. Registry contracted with another company to do the work which then subcontracted with Frownfelter. After the bank went into receivership, the FDIC sued Registry.

Issue: Does an assignee of a contract acquire corresponding rights in new contracts which do not closely correspond to the original agreement?

Rule: If the original parties to an assigned contract are not in privity to new contracts made after the breach, the assignee of the original agreement does not acquire corresponding rights in any new contracts undertaken if done so in good faith and in accordance with commercial reasonableness.

Fall River Trust Co. v. B.G. Browdy, Inc. (1964) CPB

Facts: Fall River Trust had an arrangement with a bankrupt company to take assignments of its accounts receivable as security for money advanced. Fall River claimed that Browdy owed it $7,596.93 because of its outstanding account with the bankrupt company. As a defense, Browdy claimed the company owed it at least that amount because of goods the bankrupt company had received from Browdy but never returned.

Issue: If a party has a claim or defense under a contract which has been assigned, may this claim or defense be raised against the assignee?

Rule: A party to the original contract may claim a defense to the rights of an assignee when its claim arises from the contract between itself and the assignor.

<h3 style="text-align:center">First American Commerce Co. v.
Washington Mutual Savings Bank (1987) CPB</h3>

Facts: First American received a loan from First Security Realty Services, which then assigned its proceeds to Washington Mutual. A portion of the loan was held back pending completion of tenant improvements on a commercial building. Upon completing the improvements, First American requested the release of the withheld funds and was refused by First Security, claiming that its duties under the loan terminated with the assignment to Washington Mutual.

Issue: Does an assignment of benefits by a contracting party also discharge that party's duties under the contract?

Rule: A party retains its duties under a contract unless it substitutes an assignee for itself with a novation. A novation is not created by inference; it must be clear that the parties to the original contract intended to pass responsibility to another by either novation or clear, express language to the same effect.

<h3 style="text-align:center">Old West Enterprises, Inc. v. Reno Escrow Co. (1970) CPB</h3>

Facts: Old West received legal services from an attorney. The attorney assigned his rights to payment for the services to Reno in the form of an "account stated" agreement with Old West. Old West disputed the sum it owed to Reno, claiming that the amount stated was excessive.

Issue 1: What is an account stated?

Rule 1: An account stated is an agreement, based upon prior transactions between parties, where the parties agree to a certain sum due from the transactions and a promise is made to pay that sum. Before the sum is agreed upon by both parties, the agreement is an account rendered.

Issue 2: May a parties' silence as to objections to the terms of an account rendered serve to create an account stated?

Rule 2: Failure to object to the terms of an account rendered raises only a rebuttable inference that the debtor consents to the account.

Herzog v. Irace (1991) KC

Facts: Jones told Irace, his attorney, that he was assigning a portion of his proceeds from a pending lawsuit to Dr. Herzog in exchange for medical treatment. Jones directed Irace to pay Herzog directly from the proceeds upon conclusion of the suit. After the lawsuit was settled, Jones told Irace that he had changed his mind and that he would pay Herzog himself. Irace sent the funds to Jones. Jones sent Herzog a check, but Jones' check was returned for insufficient funds. Herzog sued Irace.

Issue: May an assignee enforce an assignment against an obligor who has been charged by the assignor with forwarding the assigned fund?

Rule: If the assignor notifies an obligor that he is irrevocably assigning his rights in a fund to a third party and directs the obligor to pay that fund directly to the assignee, the obligor thereafter holds the assigned fund in trust for the assignee. If the obligor pays the assigned fund to any party other than the assignee, the assignee may enforce his obligations against the obligor directly.

Julian v. Christopher (1990) KC

Facts: Julian owned a tavern and restaurant business which was located in a building he rented from Christopher. The lease contained a term prohibiting the tenant from subletting or assigning the property without the consent of the landlord. Julian asked the landlord for permission to sublet an apartment located atop the tavern, but the landlord refused to consent unless the tenants paid additional rent. Nevertheless, Julian sublet the apartment without Christopher's permission. Christopher then sued for repossession of the building.

Issue: Does a clause in a lease stating that the landlord can withhold consent to a sublease or assignment give the landlord the right to withhold consent arbitrarily and unreasonably?

Rule: A landlord cannot withhold his consent arbitrarily or unreasonably if a lease contains a clause providing that the tenant must obtain the landlord's consent in order to assign or sublease.

Note: A landlord may reserve the right to arbitrarily and unreasonably prevent a sublease or assignment by a freely negotiated provision in the lease clearly spelling out his intent.

Herzog v. Irace (1991) R, KC

Facts: Jones was injured and went to Herzog, a doctor, who recommended surgery. Jones had no money, so Jones wrote a letter to Irace, his lawyer, assigning his right to proceeds from a pending settlement to Herzog. When the settlement was received, however, Irace sent the money directly to Jones. Herzog sued the lawyer based on Herzog's rights as assignee.

Issue: May a party validly transfer his right to proceeds from pending litigation?

Rule: The transfer of a future right to proceeds from pending litigation is a valid and enforceable assignment. The entire future right need not be transferred; a partial assignment is valid.

Klinkoosten v. Mundt (1916) R

Facts: Klinkoosten sued Mundt to recover on a $25 promissory note Mundt had given in partial payment for printing machinery. Before the note matured, Mundt had transferred the machinery to a third party who had agreed to execute new notes for the unpaid balance on the machinery. The new notes, however, were never executed.

Issue: What is required to create a valid novation?

Rule: A valid novation requires (1) an express or implied agreement on the part of the creditor to substitute the new debtor in place of the original debtor and (2) an express or implied agreement to release or discharge the original debtor.

Smith, Bell & Hauck, Inc. v. Cullins (1962) R

Facts: Plaintiff purchased an insurance agency operated by Cullins' former employer. Plaintiff sought to enforce a prior covenant between Cullins and the former employer that prohibited Cullins from engaging in the insurance business for three years following termination of his employment.

Issue: Is an employee's agreement not to compete assignable?

Rule: A restrictive covenant signed by an employee governs only the relationship between the employee and the employer with whom the covenant was made. Thus, an agreement not to compete with an employer is personal, and is not assignable without the consent of the employee.

Note: Other jurisdictions hold that an employee's covenant not to compete is not personal, but marketable, along with other assets of an employer's business.

Mitchell v. Aldrich (1990) R

Facts: Mitchell contracted to buy Comette's herd of cows, but because many of Comette's assets (including the cows) served as security for a mortgage, the approval of Comette's bank was required. The bank sent Aldrich to appraise Comette's cows. Aldrich brought Drew with him. Aldrich told Comette that the bank would never approve Comette's contract with Mitchell and suggested that Comette sell the cows to Drew instead. Comette, believing that Aldrich was acting as the bank's agent, agreed, and sold the cows to Drew. Mitchell sued Aldrich for wrongful interference with contractual relations.

Issue: When may a party be held liable for wrongful interference with contractual relations?

Rule: An interfering party is liable to another party when it knowingly and intentionally intrudes in a contractual relationship with the purpose of disrupting that relationship.

Adler, Barish, Daniels, Levin and Creskoff v. Epstein (1978) R

Facts: Adler sought to enjoin former associates of its firm from interfering with existing contractual relationships between Adler and its clients.

Issue: May former associates at law firms be enjoined from intentionally interfering with the existing contractual relations between their former employer and its clients?

Rule: While terminated employees may pursue their own business interests, they may be enjoined from seeking to represent their former law firms' clients who have pending legal matters. Permitting such attempts would pose a risk to the rational decision-making abilities of clients, and may unfairly prejudice the former employer.

Chapter 11

STATUTE OF FRAUDS

The general rule in contracts is that most oral agreements are valid and enforceable. However, under the Statute of Frauds, which originated in England, certain types of contracts are only enforceable if they are in writing. The main purpose of the Statute is to prevent fraudulent claims by requiring that written evidence of the claims be shown. The Statute of Frauds is only a screening device; a party that has written proof of an agreement does not automatically prevail. Rather, the party must then proceed to prove its case on the merits (i.e., was there a breach? consideration? duress?). Thus, to say that a contract "falls within" the Statute simply means that it will only be enforced if it is in writing, and the plaintiff prevails on the merits. Conversely, a contract that "falls outside" the Statute is one that can be enforced without written documentation if the plaintiff wins on the merits. Moreover, oral contracts that fall within the Statute are enforced on grounds of equity (fairness) in some circumstances.

I.   CONTRACTS WITHIN THE STATUTE OF FRAUDS:

The following types of contracts fall within the Statute of Frauds:

Mnemonic: **MAD GLO**

A.   **M**arriage was consideration for promise.
B.   **A**dministrator or Executor.
C.   **D**ebt of another (suretyship).

D.   **G**oods which sell for more than $500. (under common law, or UCC applies to contracts between merchants)
E.   **L**and Sales.
F.   **O**ne year provision.

These provisions are not mutually exclusive and are detailed below.

A.   Contracts Made in Consideration of **M**arriage (Rest. 2d. § 124)
       A promise to give or pay property in exchange for marriage is unenforceable unless written. If no property is involved (e.g., A

promises to marry B "in exchange for" B promising to marry A), there is no writing requirement.

B.   Administrator or Executor (Rest. 2d. § 111)
A promise by an administrator or executor of an estate to *personally* pay the debts of the estate must be in writing to be enforceable.

C.   Debt of Another/Suretyship (Rest. 2d. § 110)
A promise to pay the debts or defaults of another (suretyship agreement) is enforceable only if written. To fall within the Statute a suretyship must have the following elements:

1.   Secondary Liability
The promisor/guarantor must be only secondarily liable for another's debt. Example: B tells C to deliver a boat to A. If B intends to pay for the boat in the case that A defaults, then the agreement is a surety and has to be in writing. But if B tells C to charge the purchase price to his account, then there is no suretyship, and an oral promise is enforceable.

2.   Promisee's Awareness
The promisee-creditor must be aware or have reason to know that a suretyship relationship existed between the parties, and the promise must be made to the creditor directly. If the creditor does not know that a suretyship existed, the promises are enforceable, even if they are oral. The reason for this rule is to protect a creditor from being tricked into relying on a party's oral promise, which is actually a surety that requires writing to be enforceable.

3.   Novation
A novation is a promise to pay the debt of a third party which is given in exchange for a promise that the third party will no longer be liable. Novations are outside the Statute of Frauds and valid if oral.

4.   Main-Purpose Rule (Rest. 2d. § 116)
In order for a promise of suretyship to fall within the Statute of Frauds, the main purpose of the promisor must have been to benefit the third party whose debts he guarantees. If a promisor

acts to further his own interests, such a promise is enforceable even if oral. Usually, the issue of who benefits from the promisor's guarantee can be determined by looking at the consideration that is given in return for it.

D.   Sale of **G**oods for More than $500 (UCC § 2-201(a))
Any contract for the sale of goods (including securities) which are for $500 or more, must be in writing. Exceptions: There are sale of goods contracts for $500 or more that are enforceable if unwritten:

Mnemonic: **SAG**

1. **S**pecifically Manufactured Goods not Suitable for Others
An oral agreement/promise involving unique goods which are specially manufactured is enforceable. (UCC § 2-201(3)(a).) Rationale: A seller would not produce these goods if there was no agreement, because there is no market for them.

2. **A**dmission by Party Against Whom Enforcement is Sought
If a party admits that an agreement existed, no written memorandum is required. However, the contract is limited to those terms (i.e., quantity) that are admitted. (UCC § 2-201(3).)

3. **G**oods Accepted or Paid for by the Buyer
No written evidence is needed with respect to goods that have been paid for or have been received and accepted. (UCC § 2-201(3)(c).)

E.   Interest in **L**and (Rest. 2d. § 125)
A contract for the sale or purchase of an interest in land must be in writing to be enforceable.

1. Types of interests:

   Mnemonic: **MELT**

   a. **M**ortgages
   A promise to give a mortgage as security for a loan must be in writing. However, assigning rights of a mortgage is valid if orally done.

   b. **E**asements

   c. **L**eases
   Some states allow oral leases of less than one year duration.

   d. **T**imber
   Contracts for sale of timber must be written if buyer will cut wood after title to the land passes to him. Contracts involving minerals, oil, etc., must be in writing if minerals are to be removed.

2. A contract that incidentally involves land (e.g., to build a house or to lend money to buy land) does not fall under this provision.

3. Part Performance
   An initially unenforceable oral land contract may become binding if the parties act in reliance upon it.

   a. A vendor who conveys land under an oral contract can recover the contract price.

   b. A vendee who acts in reliance upon an oral land contract (e.g., improves the land, takes possession, or pays taxes on the land) can have the contract enforced.

F.   Performance Takes Longer than **O**ne Year (Rest. 2d. § 130)
A contract that, by its terms, cannot be performed within one year is unenforceable if it is not written.

1. The one-year period begins to run from the date the contract is formed, not the date set for beginning performance.

2. One-Year Duration
   For a contract to fall under this provision of the Statute of Frauds, performance in less than a year must be impossible. This requires more than an expectation that it is highly unlikely that a contract will actually be performed within a year. The basic issue is whether, theoretically, the agreed performance could occur within a year, even if the contract expressly provides a longer duration.

   a. Performance v. Discharge
      The fact that a contract could be discharged within a year (by impossibility of performance, death of one of the parties, etc.) does not mean that the contract is taken out of the one-year provision.

      i. If the contract is prematurely terminated by some event, and its principal purpose has been fulfilled, the performance requirement is met. Example: A promises to hire B for the duration of B's life. B could die within a year, so the contract is outside the Statute of Frauds because the main purpose, to hire B for life, has been achieved.

      ii. A premature death will satisfy the performance requirement if the death of a party will not mean that full performance was not rendered. Example: A promises to support B, a minor, until B is 18 years old. If B died within a year, A would still be considered to have met his obligation, so the contract is outside the Statute. However, if A hires B to sing in a club for five years, and B dies within a year, his obligation was not met and the contract still falls within the Statute.

   b. Termination

      i. A contract that may not be completed within a year but could be terminated within that time is covered by the Statute and must be written.

ii. The courts are split as to whether contracts that cannot be performed in one year, but allow either party the right to terminate (so that it could theoretically end within a year), are covered by the Statute of Frauds.

II. ELEMENTS REQUIRED TO SATISFY THE STATUTE OF FRAUDS

A. A written contract or memorandum must contain the following elements to satisfy the Statute of Frauds (Rest. 2d. § 131):

1. Purpose of the contract.

2. Terms and conditions of the agreement (essential terms).

3. Parties to the contract.

4. Consideration.

5. Signature of the party to be charged. A party's initials or stamped or typed name may also suffice.

A written memorandum that contains the above elements will satisfy the Statute even if it was not created for that purpose.

B. UCC § 2-201 Requirements

1. Under the UCC, which applies to sale-of-goods contracts, the requirements of a written memorandum are satisfied if a writing is;

a. Sufficient to indicate that a contract for sale has been made between the parties, *and*

b. Signed by the party against whom enforcement is sought.

2. A writing that omits or erroneously states a term is still valid, but the agreement is only enforceable as to the quantity of goods stated in the memorandum.

3. A memorandum that omits a price term may be enforceable if the parties can introduce collateral evidence as to the agreed upon price or if the court will imply such a term. (UCC § 2-305.)

4. An unsigned, written *confirmation* of an oral agreement that is sent *between merchants* will satisfy the Statute if it is received, the party receiving it knows or should know of its contents, and the party does not object to it within ten days. (UCC § 2-201(2).)

III. CONTRACTS THAT VIOLATE THE STATUTE OF FRAUDS

A contract that does not satisfy the requirements of the Statute will be either voidable, at the option of the parties, or void, depending on the jurisdiction.

A. If only part of the contract is within the Statute, the entire contract is unenforceable if that part does not satisfy the Statute. This rule does not hold, however, if the portion within the Statute has already been fully performed.

B. Full Performance
As a general rule, any oral contract that has been fully performed will be enforced. Example: A orally promises to work for B for 2 years and has completed performance. The contract is enforceable. Contracts for the sale of goods are enforceable for the amount of goods that have been accepted or paid for.

C. Alternative Promises
A party that promises to perform any of several alternative performances, some of which violate the Statute of Frauds, can be bound to perform those that do not.

IV. MODIFICATION AND RESCISSION

A written agreement can be orally rescinded. However, modification of an existing contract will be effective only if it satisfies the requirements of the contract (i.e., if this is a type of contract that has to be written, then the modification must also be written). An invalid oral modification of a contract leaves the original contract in effect without the changes. However, material reliance on an oral modification may make it enforceable to avoid injustice. (Rest. 2d. § 150.)

V. REMEDIES

A party that has partly performed under a contract that is later invalidated by the Statute of Frauds is entitled to certain remedies.

A.   Unjust Enrichment
A party that confers benefits upon another is entitled to restitution for those benefits if the contract is later voided. A plaintiff can recover the market value (as opposed to contract price) of his performance if he can prove it. If the defendant is willing to perform, then there are no restitution damages. Additionally, a party can sometimes recover the value of acts done in reliance upon the contract. Example: A moves to New York to fulfill his oral agreement with B. A may be able to recover his moving expenses.

B.   Promissory Estoppel
A court will sometimes enforce an "invalid" oral contract on its terms if it was foreseeable that the defendant's conduct would cause the plaintiff to change his position in reliance on the oral contract. Usually, if a defendant has willfully lied by saying that the contract was not subject to the Statute of Frauds or that he would not raise the Statute as an objection, a court will enforce the oral contract. In some cases, if a plaintiff performs his obligations without any fraudulent inducement, a court may enforce the promise so as to avoid injustice. (Rest. 2d. § 139.)

CASE CLIPS

Boone v. Coe (1913) DHH, KGK
Facts: Coe agreed to provide a dwelling for the plaintiffs on the condition that they would move from Kentucky to Texas and cultivate his farm for one year. The agreement violated the Statute of Frauds because it could not be

performed within one year from the date of its inception. The plaintiffs sued to recover their traveling expenses.

Issue: Can a party recover the value of expenses incurred in reliance on a contract that is unenforceable under the Statute of Frauds?

Rule: Damages may not be awarded for violation of a contract that is unenforceable under the Statute of Frauds.

Note: Today, such reliance damages would probably be awarded to avoid injustice.

Lawrence v. Anderson (1936) KGK, CPB

Facts: After her father was injured in an accident, Anderson orally promised to pay the plaintiff, a doctor who provided emergency care for her father. After the father died, the plaintiff tried unsuccessfully to collect from his estate. He then tried to sue Anderson.

Issue: Is an oral promise to pay for services provided to another enforceable under the Statute of Frauds?

Rule: A promise to pay for services to be provided to a third party, makes the promisor a surety. Such an agreement is subject to the Statute of Frauds if it is apparent that the promisee (who provided the services) intended the third party to be the primary debtor and the promisor to be only secondarily liable.

Eastwood v. Kenyon (1840) KGK

Facts: The defendant, for consideration, orally promised to pay the plaintiff's debt to a third party. The defendant refused to pay, claiming the agreement was void as against the Statute of Frauds.

Issue: Does the Statute of Frauds void an oral agreement between a debtor and a party that promised to assume the debtor's debts?

Rule: Promises to pay the debt of a third person are within the Statute of Frauds only if they were made to a creditor. An oral promise made to a debtor, however, is outside the Statute.

Taylor v. Lee (1924) KGK

Facts: Lee orally promised to pay for supplies plaintiff would furnish to a third party during the course of a year (suretyship agreement).

Issue: Does the Statute of Frauds void an oral promise to pay for future goods that will be delivered to a third party?

Rule: The Statute of Frauds does not void an agreement to pay for goods supplied to a third party when credit was granted because of the agreement.

Witschard v. A. Brody & Sons, Inc. (1932) KGK

Facts: Brody orally promised the plaintiff that it would guarantee payment for supplies delivered to a third party if the party defaulted. The plaintiff extended credit to the third party who eventually defaulted. Brody refused to pay, claiming the oral agreement violated the Statute of Frauds.

Issue: Must a promise to pay for the debts of another be written to be enforceable?

Rule: A promise to pay the debts of another must be in writing if the original debtor remains primarily liable (i.e., the promisor only pays in case of default by original debtor).

Colpitts v. L.C. Fisher Co. (1935) KGK

Facts: Fisher, a corporation, was in debt to its creditors and employees, the plaintiffs. It decided to reorganize itself by assigning its assets to its creditors (to prepay that debt). Fisher also orally agreed with its workers that if they forbore from collecting their debt against the old corporation, the reorganized company would employ them and repay the debts of the former corporation to them. Fisher later claimed that its promise to repay the debt of a third party (the former corporation) was void because it was unwritten. The plaintiffs answered that Fisher's main purpose in assuming the debt of the old corporation was to benefit itself by keeping its employees, and thus under the "Main-Purpose" rule, the oral promise was enforceable.

Issue: Is an oral assumption of another's debt enforceable if the promisor's main purpose in making the promise is to further his own interests?

Rule: Under the Main-Purpose rule, a promisor who orally assumes the debt of another for the primary purpose of furthering his own interests is bound to his oral promise, and the Statute of Frauds will not apply.

Note: In this case, the promisor, Fisher, did not act for its own benefit.

Bader v. Hiscox (1919) KGK

Facts: Hiscox's son seduced and impregnated the plaintiff, who brought a civil action for damages and initiated criminal charges against him. Hiscox orally promised to give the plaintiff a tract of land if she dropped the civil action and married his son (a marriage would cause the dismissal of the criminal action). The plaintiff agreed but Hiscox refused to convey the land, claiming that oral promises involving conveyance of land, marriage and assumption of another's debt all violated the Statute of Frauds.

Issue: Can an oral promise, made in consideration of marriage, be enforced if marriage was only incidental to the true purpose of the contract?

Rule: An oral promise given in consideration of marriage does not fall within the Statute of Frauds if the main purpose was not marriage but to escape criminal liability. Furthermore, since the plaintiff had fully performed, Hiscox was estopped from claiming that an oral promise to convey land is void. Finally, Hiscox's obligation was primary and upon his own credit when he acted to dismiss his son's liability for damages from a civil suit.

Doyle v. Dixon (1867) KGK, MS

Facts: The defendant sold his store to the plaintiff and orally promised to refrain from opening another one for five years. The defendant later opened a new store and claimed his promise violated the Statute of Frauds because it could not be performed within one year.

Issue: Is a promise to refrain from competition for five years within the Statute of Frauds?

Rule: An agreement regarding personal services falls outside the Statute of Frauds if it is possible that the agreement would be fully performed if a party died within a year of making the contract.

Note: In the instant case, the promisor's death would not defeat the purpose of the contract, which was to avoid competition.

Harvey v. J.P. Morgan & Co. (1937) KGK

Facts: J.P. Morgan orally promised Harvey a lifetime pension after she sustained injuries while working. J.P. Morgan later reneged, claiming the promise violated the one-year provision of the Statute of Frauds.

Issue: Must a promise of a lifetime pension be in writing to be enforceable?

Rule: A promise of a lifetime pension is outside the Statute of Frauds because the contract could theoretically be completed within a year if the promisee died.

Montuori v. Bailen (1935) KGK

Facts: The defendant held an outstanding mortgage on the plaintiff's property. After the plaintiff breached the mortgage agreement, the plaintiff's agent signed a document in which the defendant agreed not to foreclose the property if the plaintiff accounted for all the rents. Later, the defendant orally promised not to foreclose on the mortgage if the plaintiff repaired and maintained the property. The plaintiff complied, but the defendant foreclosed.

Issue: Is an oral agreement regarding possession of land within the Statute of Frauds?

Rule: The right to possession of land is an interest in it, and a contract to surrender possession or to forbear for a time from exercising a right to take and retain possession is within the Statute of Frauds and void if unwritten.

Amsinck v. American Ins. Co. (1880) KGK

Facts: The plaintiffs made an oral contract to buy a ship, which they immediately sought to insure with American Insurance. A claim arose before the sales contract was reduced to a writing. The insurance company claimed that the plaintiffs did not own the ship (and could not collect insurance) because the purchase, which was for an amount over $500, violated the Statute of Frauds.

Issue: Can a third party challenge the validity of a contract that violates the Statute of Frauds?

Rule: A contract that does not satisfy the Statute of Frauds is voidable only by the parties to the contract. It cannot be challenged by a third party.

Crabtree v. Elizabeth Arden Sales Corp.
(1953) KGK, KC, MS, CPB

Facts: Crabtree was hired to work for the Elizabeth Arden cosmetics company. His employment was to last for two years with prearranged pay raises. Although a formal contract was never executed, the terms were listed in several informal writings—welcome memos, payroll change cards and secretary's notes—some of which were signed by Elizabeth Arden.

Issue: Can several writings be used to construct a memorandum that satisfies the Statute of Frauds?

Rule: Several writings can be joined to form a memorandum that satisfies the Statute of Frauds if they all refer to the same transaction or subject matter, are properly signed and describe the terms of the agreement.

Hughes v. Payne (1908) KGK

Facts: Hughes received a written receipt, signed by Payne, which acknowledged Hughes' part payment of $300 on a land sale agreement and further promised to make a conveyance upon full payment. The receipt did not mention when full payment was to be made or how much money was still owed. Hughes sought to introduce oral evidence on these issues, but Payne claimed that the Statute of Frauds would bar the action.

Issue: What is the legal effect of a contract that lacks terms required by the Statute of Frauds?

Rule: A court can reform and enforce a contract that has missing terms by use of extrinsic oral evidence if it is satisfied that the terms were omitted due to mistake, oversight or fraud.

Baldridge v. Centgraf (1910) KGK

Facts: Baldridge orally promised to sell his land to Centgraf and agreed to allow Centgraf to occupy the land until the sale was executed. Baldridge later claimed that the oral promise violated the Statute of Frauds and sued to eject Centgraf.

Issue: Does possession of real property make an oral contract valid on the theory of partial performance?

Rule: Mere possession of real property does not constitute partial performance of an oral contract and will not remove the requirements of the Statute of Frauds.

Harry Rubin & Sons v. Consolidated Pipe Co.
(1959) KGK

Facts: Rubin claimed he made three oral contracts, each in excess of $500, ordering plastic hoops from the defendant, a manufacturer. Rubin introduced three writings in court. The first was the order form for the first shipment, the second was a letter that stated, in part, "that upon completion of the [first] order," Consolidated will produce the second order. Finally, Rubin sent a confirmation of the last order, which included the size, quantity and price of the items desired.

Issue: Does a written memorandum confirming an oral agreement satisfy the requirements of the Statute of Frauds?

Rule: A writing that affords a basis for believing that the offered oral evidence rests on a real transaction satisfies the Statute of Frauds. Under UCC § 2-201(2), an unsigned written confirmation of an oral agreement is satisfactory if it is between merchants, sent within a reasonable time after the oral agreement was made, sufficient to bind the sender, received, there is no reply and no objection is made within ten days of its receipt, although the recipient had reason to know of its contents.

Imperator Realty Co., Inc. v. Tull (1920) KGK

Facts: Imperator and Tull entered into a written contract to exchange property. They made a subsequent oral modification of the contract, whereby housing-code violations did not have to be repaired if the owner tendered the monetary value of repairs. Tull refused to accept Imperator's building, which had code violations, although Imperator had tendered the requisite cash amount. Tull claimed the contract had to stand on its terms because the oral modification violated the Statute of Frauds.

Issue: What is the effect of an oral modification of a written contract to transfer land?

Rule: The general rule that a modification of a contract must be in the same form as that required for the original contract is excused where a party acts in reasonable reliance on an oral modification that is minor in character.

Alaska Airlines, Inc. v. Stephenson (1954) KGK

Facts: Stephenson relocated his family after he was promised a written employment contract by Alaska Airlines.

Issue: Can an oral agreement, which is otherwise invalid under the Statute of Frauds, be binding on the theory of estoppel?

Rule: An oral contract that is ordinarily within the Statute of Frauds is valid on the theory of estoppel if the additional factor of a promise to reduce the contract to a writing is present.

State Automobile Ins. Co. v. Wilson (1955) MS

Facts: A third party was injured in an accident with a driver insured by State Automobile. Afraid of future liability, State Automobile orally promised to pay two doctors, Claude and Foster Wilson, if they cared for the third party. The driver insured by State Automobile was later found not liable for the third party's injuries. The insurance company claimed its promise to the Wilsons to pay for the debt of another (the driver) violated the Statute of Frauds.

Issue: Do all promises to pay for debts of another have to be written?

Rule: A promise to pay the debt of another does not fall within the Statute of Frauds if the promise was made for the promisor's benefit.

North Shore Bottling Co. v. C. Schmidt & Sons, Inc. (1968) MS

Facts: North Shore orally contracted to be the exclusive distributor of Schmidt's beer in New York "for as long as Schmidt sold beer in the New York metropolitan area." Schmidt later contracted with another distributor and claimed its oral promise was unenforceable because it could not be performed within a year.

Issue: Does an oral contract of indefinite duration violate the Statute of Frauds?

Rule: An agreement that could theoretically terminate within a year does not violate the one-year provision of the Statute of Frauds, even if the parties contemplated a longer duration.

Note: The court reasoned that Schmidt could stop doing business in New York within a year.

Mason v. Anderson (1985) MS

Facts: By oral agreement, Mason loaned $5,000 to Anderson's decedent, to be repaid in monthly installments of $200. Only $1,100 had been repaid when the borrower died. Mason sued for the remaining amount. Anderson claimed that the loan could not be enforced under the Statue of Frauds because it would have taken over a year to repay.

Issue: Does the Statute of Frauds apply to an agreement that cannot be performed within one year where one party has fully performed?

Rule: Where one party fully performs under an agreement and thereby incurs a detrimental change of position, the one year provision of the Statute of Frauds does not prevent that party from proving the existence of a contract by parol evidence.

National Historic Shrines Foundation v. Dali (1967) MS

Facts: Dali, an artist, orally agreed to paint a picture of the Statue of Liberty during a televised fund raiser and to donate the picture to the Foundation so that it could sell it.

Issue: Is an oral promise to paint and donate a picture worth more than $500 within the Statute of Frauds?

Rule: Painting and donating a picture is not a "sale of goods" and is therefore outside the Statute of Frauds.

Drury v. Young (1882) MS

Facts: Young orally contracted to buy tomatoes from Drury. Drury later reneged, claiming his promise violated the Statute of Frauds. Young seized Drury's records, in which there was a written memorandum detailing their agreement. The memo was kept in Drury's safe.

Issue: Must a writing that is required by the Statute of Frauds be delivered?

Rule: Delivery is not essential to the validity of a note or memorandum of sale, as long as it is signed by the party to be charged, and other evidence suggests that the party knew of the agreement.

Clark v. Larkin (1952) MS

Facts: Pursuant to an oral contract, Larkin made a down payment on land he bought from Clark. He wrote the essential terms of the agreement on the back of the check. Larkin later tried to renege, asserting the Statute of Frauds.

Issue: Is the Statute of Frauds satisfied by written notations on the back of a check?

Rule: A check fulfills the writing requirement of the Statute of Frauds if the names of the parties, the terms and conditions of the contract and a description of the property sufficient to render it capable of identification are written on the back.

Azevedo v. Minister (1970) MS, CPB

Facts: Minister orally contracted to sell hay to Azevedo. Minister sent periodic accountings to Azevedo as the hay was delivered which mentioned the quantity of hay bought, among other terms. Azevedo later refused to accept more hay.

Issue: Do periodic accountings that are sent subsequent to an oral agreement to which they refer satisfy the writing requirement of the Statute of Frauds?

Rule: An accounting satisfies the requirement of a writing if the party receiving the accounting of the oral agreement does not object within a reasonable amount of time. (UCC § 2-201.)

DF Activities Corp. v. Brown (1988) MS

Facts: DF asserted and Brown denied that the latter agreed by phone to sell a chair to DF. DF sent a letter of confirmation and a $30,000 check, but Brown returned the letter and the check and wrote that the chair was no longer available. The UCC Statute of Frauds barred the court from hearing the case, unless Brown were to admit in her pleading, testimony or otherwise in court that a contract for sale was made. Brown denied under oath that a contract had been made. DF argued that if it could have deposed Brown, she would have admitted otherwise.

Issue: Is a plaintiff entitled to discovery where a sworn denial by the defendant serves to dismiss the suit under the Statute of Frauds?

Rule: A party in a suit on a contract within the Statute of Frauds may not resist a motion to dismiss, backed by an affidavit that the other party denies the contract was made, by arguing that discovery may prove otherwise. The high unlikelihood that the other party will blurt out an admission in a deposition, since doing so may be an admission of perjury, does not warrant the additional judicial proceedings.

Ozier v. Haines (1952) MS

Facts: Relying on trade custom, the plaintiffs orally contracted to buy grain from Haines. The plaintiffs immediately resold the grain to a third party in Haines' presence. Haines later refused to perform, asserting the $500 sale of goods provision of the Statute of Frauds.

Issue: Can one be estopped from asserting the Statute of Frauds as a defense?

Rule: Promissory estoppel acts as a bar to a Statute of Frauds defense only if misrepresentation or concealment of material facts by the party asserting the defense induced the other party to act.

R.S. Bennett & Co. v. Economy Mechanical Indus., Inc. (1979) MS

Facts: Bennett, a pump supplier, orally reduced the price on its pumps on the condition that if the contractor, Economy, was awarded the job it would buy from Bennett. Economy lowered its bid, using Bennett's lower price and was awarded the job. Economy then bought pumps elsewhere, despite its oral promise.

Issue: Does asserting the Statute of Frauds as a defense preclude recovery on a promissory estoppel theory?

Rule: A successful defense based on the Statute of Frauds does not preclude recovery under promissory estoppel because of the requirement that relief is granted to avoid injustice.

Thompson v. Stuckey (1983) CPB

Facts: Thompson was orally promised by Stuckey, the agent of Witcher Creek Coal Co., a bonus of $100,000 in addition to his salary upon the sale of the coal mine he was to prepare for use. Witcher sold the mine but never paid Thompson his bonus.

Issue: Does the statute of frauds bar enforcement of oral contracts which are only capable of being (but not actually nor intended to be) performed within one year?

Rule: The statute of frauds permits enforcement of oral contracts which are intended to be, capable of being or actually performed within one year.
Note: When the contract in dispute was not actually performed within one year, the court must find clear and convincing evidence that the contract exists before submitting the question of capability to the jury.

Hopper v. Lennen & Mitchell, Inc. (1944) CPB

Facts: Hopper entered into an oral contract to advertise the products of Lennen & Mitchell for a minimum of twenty-six weeks and a maximum of five years. The five years consisted of ten equal periods; before the end of each, Lennen & Mitchell had the option to cancel. Lennen & Mitchell repudiated the contract.
Issue: Does the statue of frauds bar enforcement of a contract which may be terminated within one year but which extends for more than one year?
Rule: A contract which may be completed and legally terminated within one year is not rendered unenforceable by the statute of frauds.

McIntosh v. Murphy (1970) CPB, KC, R

Facts: While living in Los Angeles, McIntosh accepted a one-year oral employment contract to be an assistant sales manager at Murphy's car dealership in Hawaii. Two months after accepting the job and relocating, he was fired.
Issue: Is there a remedy for a party who detrimentally relies on an oral contract in violation of the one year provision of the statute of frauds?
Rule: Principles of equity allow a party in detrimental reliance on a promise within the statute of frauds to enforce the promise if injustice can be avoided only by enforcement. The court adopted § 139 of the Restatement (Second) of Contracts.
Note: A contract falls within the statute of frauds if the time from the date of contracting to completion is expected to be greater than one year.

Cohn v. Fisher (1972) CPB, KC

Facts: Fisher wrote a check as a deposit on Cohn's boat stating on the memorandum "Deposit on aux. sloop, D'Arc Wind, full amount $4,650." Unable to have the boat inspected in time, Fisher attempted to postpone the closing date. Cohn refused, sold the boat to someone else at a lower price and sued to recover the difference.
Issue: In order to satisfy the statute of frauds, what function must be performed by written evidence of an oral contract for the sale of goods?

Rule: The writing need only afford a basis for believing that the offered oral evidence rests on a real transaction. The writing should state the object of the contract and the quantity term and should be signed by the party to be bound.

Note: Fisher's check satisfied the requirement of a writing. The statute of frauds can also be satisfied by the admission a party bound to the contract or by tender and acceptance of partial payment.

Potter v. Hatter Farms, Inc. (1982) CPB

Facts: After orally contracting with Hatter Farms for the sale of young turkeys, Potter turned down offers from other buyers. Hatter repudiated the contract.

Issue: Is promissory estoppel an exception to the statute of frauds?

Rule: If all the elements of promissory estoppel are proven (actual reliance, substantial change in position by the promisee and foreseeability to the promisor), the doctrine bars the assertion of the statute of frauds as a defense.

Yarbro v. Neil B. McGinnis Equipment Co. (1966) CPB

Facts: Yarbro made oral promises to pay delinquent payments on a tractor that Russell had purchased from McGinnis. Yarbro had wanted to buy the tractor himself and used it repeatedly after Russell bought it.

Issue: When can oral promises to pay the debt of another (ie., suretyship) be enforced despite the statute of frauds?

Rule: When the "leading object" of the promisor in paying the debt of another is to secure a benefit to himself, his oral promises to pay can be enforced despite the statute of frauds requirement of a writing.

Dienst v. Dienst (1913) CPB

Facts: The husband in a divorce proceeding claimed that his wife made an oral promise to execute a will leaving her estate to him if he should survive her, in exchange for his leaving his employment and moving to her town to marry her.

Issue: Is an oral promise in exchange for agreement to marry enforceable?

Rule: The statute of frauds renders void any oral promise made upon consideration of marriage, except the mutual promise to marry.

Shaughnessy v. Eidsmo (1946) CPB

Facts: The Shaughnessys leased a house from Eidsmo for a year with the option to buy it afterwards. At the end of the year, they expressed their intention to buy to which Eidsmo responded positively, stating that he did not have time to execute a contract but that his word was good. One year later they still did not possess the deed, prompting this action for specific performance.

Issue: In order to enforce an oral contract for specific performance of a real property exchange, will partial performance by possession and payments suffice to remove the contract from the statute of frauds?

Rule: The acts of taking possession and of making part payment, when they are performed in reliance upon an oral contract so as to be unequivocally referable to a vendor-vendee relationship, are sufficient to remove the contract from the statute of frauds without proof of irreparable injury through fraud.

Winternitz v. Summit Hills Joint Venture (1988) KC

Facts: Winternitz operated a pharmacy under a six-year lease with Summit Hills. Near the end of the lease, Winternitz told Summit Hills that he would like to renew his lease. He also mentioned that he might sell his pharmacy and asked if he would be able to assign the renewed lease. Summit Hills orally agreed to renew the lease and said Winternitz could assign the lease if the new tenant was financially sound. Winternitz found a financially sound tenant who wanted to buy the pharmacy, but Summit Hills refused to renew Winternitz's lease. Summits Hills said it wanted to negotiate a new lease with the buyer on its own.

Issue: Is an oral agreement to renew a lease enforceable under the statute of frauds?

Rule: An oral agreement to renew a lease is unenforceable under the statute of frauds because a lease conveys an interest in land.

Note: An oral agreement to renew a lease may, however, serve as a basis for a malicious interference with contractual relations claim with respect to a third party.

Bazak International Corp. v. Mast Industries, Inc. (1989) KC

Facts: Mast offered to sell Bazak certain textiles that Mast was closing out. Bazak agreed to buy the textiles after orally negotiating the terms of the sale. At Mast's request, Bazak faxed five purchase orders outlining the terms of the agreement. None of the purchase orders contained explicit words of confirmation and each of the purchase order forms contained pre-printed language identifying it as "only an offer." Mast received the purchase orders and expressed no objection to any of the terms. However, Mast refused to deliver the textiles.

Issue: Must a writing contain explicit words of confirmation or express references to a prior agreement to satisfy the requirements for confirmatory writings between merchants under UCC § 2-201(2)?

Rule: A writing need not contain express references to a prior agreement or explicit words of confirmation to satisfy UCC § 2-201(2). A writing satisfies the requirements of the UCC for confirmatory writings between merchants if it affords a basis for believing that it reflects a real transaction between the parties.

PRACTICE ESSAY QUESTIONS
Excerpted from Blond's Contracts Essay Questions
$19.95 Available from your bookstore or call 1-800-366-7086

QUESTION 1

Art and Betty owned adjoining farms in County, an area where all agriculture requires irrigation. Art bought a well-drilling rig and drilled a 400-foot well from which he drew drinking water. Betty needed no additional irrigation water, but in January 1985, she asked Art on what terms he would drill a well near her house to supply better tasting drinking water than the County water she had been using for years. Art said that because he had never before drilled a well for hire, he would charge Betty only $10 per foot, about $1 more than his expected cost. Art said that he would drill to a maximum depth of 600 feet, which is the deepest his rig could reach. Betty said, "OK, if you guarantee June 1 completion." Art agreed and asked for $3,500 in advance, with any additional further payment or refund to be made on completion. Betty said, "OK," and paid Art $3,500.

Art started drilling on May 1. He had reached a depth of 200 feet on May 10 when his drill struck rock and broke, plugging the hole. The accident was unavoidable. It had cost Art $12 per foot to drill this 200 feet. Art said he would not charge Betty for drilling the useless hole, but he would have to start a new well close by, and could not promise its completion before July 1.

Betty, annoyed by Art's failure, refused to let Art start another well and, on June 1, she contracted with Carlos to drill a well. Carlos agreed to drill to a maximum depth of 350 feet for $4,500, which Betty also paid in advance, but Carlos could not start drilling until October 1. He completed drilling and struck water at 300 feet on October 30.

In July, Betty sued Art seeking to recover her $3,500, plus the $4,500 paid to Carlos.

On August 1, County's dam failed, thus reducing the amount of water available for irrigation. Betty lost her apple crop worth $15,000. The loss could have been avoided by pumping from Betty's well if it had been operational by August 1. Betty amended her complaint to add the $15,000 loss.

In her suit against Art, what are Betty's rights and what damages, if any, will she recover? Discuss.

ISSUE/FACT LADDER

Issue	Facts
Paragraph 1 Statute of Frauds	The contract was an oral one, but capable of being completed within one year.
Paragraph 1 Offer	Betty added a June 1 deadline to Art's proposal to drill to a maximum depth of 600 feet at $10 per foot.
Paragraph 1 Counteroffer	Art's request for payment in advance was a counteroffer.
Paragraph 1 Acceptance	Betty accepted Art's counteroffer when she agreed to advance him $3,500.
Paragraph 1 Consideration	Art received $3,500 in consideration for his drilling of the well.
Paragraph 1 Materiality of Date of Completion	It is likely that Betty's insistence on a guaranteed date of completion made this a contract where "time is of the essence."
Paragraph 2 Anticipatory Repudiation	On May 10 Art told Betty that he could not promise the completion of the well by July 1.
Paragraph 2 Art's Possible Defenses - (1) Impossibility (2) Commercial Impracticability (3) Mutual Mistake	(1) Art's drill hit rock at 200 feet. He could not render performance in the designated time. (2) Art already spent $2,400 on the drilling, all of which he would have had to absorb as a loss. (3) Neither party appeared to know, at the time of contract formation, that rock was present below the surface.
Paragraph 2 Availability of Restitution for Art	Art expended $2,400 on the drilling operation and was then forced by Betty to discontinue work. However, no benefit was conferred upon Betty by these expenditures.

Paragraph 3 Did Betty Breach?	Betty did not let Art start another well.
Paragraph 3 Impact of the Betty-Carlos Contract on the Materiality of the Completion Date of the Betty-Art Contract	Carlos said that he would not be able to start drilling until October 1. Therefore, the expected date for the well's completion was almost 5 months after the agreed upon date in the Betty-Art contract.
Paragraph 4 Measure of Damages	Betty sought to recover $8,000 from Art in expectation damages.
Paragraph 5 Consequential Damages	Betty suffered crop loss in the amount of $15,000 due to the fact that she had no well from which to draw water to irrigate.

ISSUE OUTLINE

I.   Contract Formation

     A. Statute of Frauds

     B. Offer

     C. Acceptance

     D. Consideration

II.   Art's Breach

     A. Anticipatory Repudiation

     B. Materiality of Date for Performance

     C. Defenses

III.   Remedies

     A. Restitution

     B. Expectation Damages

     C. Consequential Damages

IV.   Betty's Breach

V.   Remedies

SUBSTANTIVE ANSWER

I.   Contract Formation

The statute of frauds requires that certain types of contracts be in writing in order to be enforceable. The following five categories of contracts fall within the statute of frauds: land, marriage, executor-administrator, suretyship, and contracts that cannot be performed within one year from their formation. The contract between Art and Betty, although oral, does not fit within any of these categories and is therefore enforceable.

In order for a contract to be enforceable there must be a valid offer, an acceptance, and consideration. A valid offer must be an objective manifestation of an intent to create a contract, creating in the offeree the power to bind the offeror through acceptance. An offer must contain all of the essential elements of the agreement in order to be valid. The four essential elements are (1) the subject matter, (2) the parties, (3) the time for performance, (4) and the price. Art's proposal to drill a well for Betty to a maximum depth of 600 feet and at a price of $10/foot appears to be too indefinite to create a power of acceptance in Betty due to the lack of a time for completion of performance. However, Betty's request for a guaranteed time of completion supplied the last essential term of the agreement, and is therefore a valid offer.

Like the offer, the acceptance must be an objective manifestation of an intent to enter into a binding contract. Therefore, Art's request for $3,500 in advance constituted a counteroffer because he was clearly negotiating rather than attempting to accept the offer and bind Betty. Betty's acquiescence to Art's modification constituted the acceptance and bound him to the agreement, creating an enforceable contract.

A contract is supported by consideration when the obligations of the respective parties arise as a result of a bargained-for exchange. Art and Betty's contract required Art to drill a well to a certain depth and within a specified period of time. In consideration for Art's work, Betty agreed to pay him $10 for every foot that he drilled beneath the surface. Therefore, both parties' performance was supported by consideration.

It therefore appears that Art and Betty had a binding contract. The next step in the analysis is to determine which party breached, and whether the breaching party can assert any defenses.

II.   Art's Breach

On May 10, when Art's drill broke after hitting undetected rock, he explained to Betty that he would not be able to finish the job by June 1. In fact, he could not even promise that the well would be drilled by July 1. By making such an admission Art may have anticipatorily repudiated the contract. Anticipatory repudiation occurs when one party informs the other, prior to the date for performance, that the first party will not or cannot perform. This repudiation may be stated, or it may be gleaned from the conduct of the repudiating party. In the case of a promisor's statement, the statement will constitute a repudiation if it is made to the promisee, and the promisee reasonably interprets the statement to mean that the promisor will not perform. Betty reasonably interpreted Art's statement to mean that he will not render performance on June 1 because he could not even guarantee performance on July 1.

Where the promisor repudiates the contract prior to the date for performance, and the repudiation is a breach of a material term, the promisee may bring suit for damages as soon as he learns of the repudiation and may cancel his own performance. However, if the repudiation does not involve a material term in the contract, then the promisee is not relieved from his own duty to perform, even though he may still sue for damages immediately. Therefore, in the case of Art and Betty's contract, it is first necessary to determine whether or not the date of completion of the well was a material term of the contract, or, in other words, whether the June 1 guarantee made this a contract where time was "of the essence." If the June 1 deadline was a material term then Art repudiated the entire contract, thereby relieving Betty from her duty to perform. If it was not a material term then Betty had a duty to render performance and was therefore in breach when she refused to do so.

Although there is a presumption in most contracts that time is not "of the essence," Betty expressly contracted for completion of the well by June 1. Art agreed to this condition. Therefore, it is likely that a court will find the June 1 deadline to be a material term of the contract. Since Art repudiated a material term he was in breach, and Betty's performance was relieved. Unless Art can assert defenses to his breach, he is liable for damages.

Art can try to assert several defenses to his breach. One of the possible defenses is mutual mistake. The defense of mutual mistake requires that both parties to the contract make an erroneous assumption regarding an existing fact that goes to the essence of the contract. The mistake must also materially affect the agreed exchange of performances, and the party trying to assert the defense cannot be the party who was to bear the risk of the mistake.

Art and Betty did not know about the underlying rock, and this mistake certainly had a material effect on the agreed exchange of performances, making the bargain a losing proposition for Art. However, in a contract such as this, where the parties do not expressly allocate the risk, a court will place the risk on the party reasonably expected to bear it. And, since Art has undertaken to drill a well for a profit, a court would probably find it reasonable to place the burden of risk on him. Therefore, the defense of mutual mistake would probably be unsuccessful.

Another defense that is available to Art is that of impossibility. The defense of impossibility may be asserted when some event occurs after contract formation and before performance is due that makes one party's performance impossible. Art would have to claim that the subject matter of the contract had been destroyed, thereby excusing him from performing. However, a court would probably not allow this defense because the drill was not the sole and exclusive mode of performing the contract, i.e., Art could have purchased another drill.

A defense related to impossibility is that of commercial impracticability. Commercial impracticability allows a party to avoid performing his duty under the contract when some unforeseen event intervenes between the time of contract formation and the time when performance is due. The intervening event must be such that it makes the cost so extreme that performance, while not strictly impossible, is extremely impracticable. The promisor must also not bear the risk of the impracticability. This defense is more likely to excuse Art's performance than the impossibility defense, but a court could determine that Art bore the risk for the same reasons as discussed above under the mistake defense.

III.   Remedies

If a court allows any of the above defenses, the contract would be rescinded and Betty could obtain a refund of her $3,500 as restitution. Art would not be able to recover any portion of the sum he expended in drilling to a depth of 200 feet because he had conferred no benefit upon Betty.

If none of the above defenses are recognized Art will be liable to Betty for expectation damages. Since the aim of expectation damages is to place the nonbreaching party in the same position as if the contract had been performed, Art would have to pay Betty $4,500. This would constitute a refund of Betty's $3,500 advance, plus an additional $1,000 to make up the difference. Betty would not be able to obtain both a refund of her $3,500 and $4,500 paid to Carlos. Such an award of damages would constitute unjust enrichment.

Betty would also be unable to recover the $15,000 she lost as a result of her crop loss. These damages are referred to as consequential damages because they follow, not as an immediate result of the breach, but as a remote consequence. Such remote damages are only recoverable when the breaching party either had actual notice of the possibility of such consequences, or should have reasonably foreseen that such damages would result.

It is highly unlikely that a court would consider the destruction of the County dam a foreseeable event, and Betty did not expressly tell Art that she needed the well for irrigation purposes. On the contrary, she expressed a desire to have the dam built for drinking water purposes.

IV.   Betty's Breach

There is a possibility that a court will find that the July 1 deadline was not a material part of the contract. It could look upon Betty's contract with Carlos as evidence that time was in fact not material, and that Betty was merely requesting that Art complete the well by a specified date. The absence of direct damages as a result of Art's nonperformance and the fact that the parties did not truly bargain for the June 1 deadline is some indication that the deadline was not a condition of the contract, the breach of which would relieve Betty of her duty to perform. If Art's repudiation did not go to a material part of the contract, then Betty only had a right to sue for damages immediately, but not to cancel her own performance. She was under a duty to allow Art to complete the work. Therefore, when she dismissed Art she placed herself in breach.

V.   Remedies

Art is entitled to expectation damages if Betty breached. His expected profit on the well would have to be calculated. Considering that the well turned out to be 300 feet deep, and Art's profit would have been $1/foot, his damage award should be $300.

QUESTION 2

Bilder operated a building company specializing in custom-built houses. In order to maintain his high standards of construction, Bilder kept his company small and never had more than two projects going at one time.

Homer owned a lot in Suburban Estates on which he wanted to build a house. After hearing of Bilder's reputation for doing superior work, Homer decided that he would have his house built by Bilder. On April 15, Homer and Bilder entered into a valid written contract for the construction of the house. According to the contract, construction was to be completed no later than November 30, and the contract price, $300,000, was to be paid upon completion.

Bilder estimated that the work would take about four months and, knowing that he was obligated to begin work on two other houses on December 1, determined that if he started construction on Homer's residence on July 1, he would finish by about the end of October. This left a one-month period, which Bilder considered adequate to accommodate unanticipated delays.

Bilder started construction on Homer's house as scheduled. By the end of August, the work was one-half completed at a cost to Bilder of $120,000.

On September 1, the developer of Suburban Estates obtained a temporary injunction against both Homer and Bilder restraining further construction of Homer's house on the ground that the house violated the subdivision's minimum set-back requirement. Upon receiving notice of the injunction, Bilder stopped work.

Six months later, the injunction was dissolved and the lawsuit was dismissed as without merit. By that time, Bilder, already at work on other projects, refused to resume performance for Homer, and demanded payment of one-half the contract price.

Because of increased construction costs, it appeared certain that it would cost Homer $200,000 to have another contractor finish the house.

Homer sued Bilder for breach of contract and specific performance. Bilder counterclaimed, seeking to recover $150,000.

What are the respective rights and liabilities of Homer and Bilder against each other, and what remedies can each obtain against the other? Discuss.

ISSUE/FACT LADDER

Issue	Facts
Paragraph 2 Terms and conditions	Construction of the house was to be completed by November 30. Contract price was to be paid upon completion.
Paragraph 2 Time of the Essence	The house was to be completed by November 30.
Paragraph 2 Condition Precedent	Contract price was to be paid upon completion.
Paragraph 5 Breach by Bilder	When Bilder received the temporary restraining order he stopped work.
Paragraph 5 Temporary Impossibility Defense	Bilder was prohibited under the court order from working.
Paragraph 6 Temporary Impossibility Ceased	The restraining order was lifted six months later.
Paragraph 6 Breach by Bilder	Bilder refused to continue work.
Paragraph 6 Commercial Impracticability Defense	Bilder had a tight schedule. Bilder had a small company.
Paragraph 7 Substantial Performance	It would cost Homer $200,000 to have another contractor finish the house.
Paragraph 7 Expectation Damages	It would cost Homer $200,000 to have another contractor finish the house.
Paragraph 8 Specific Performance	The contract is for real estate.

ISSUE OUTLINE

I.   Terms of the Contract

II.   Effects of the Court Order

A. Bilder Breached

B. Temporary Impossibility

III. Effects of Lifting the Court Order

A. Duty to Build Resumed

B. Bilder Breached

IV.   Bilder's Defenses

V.   Homer's Remedies

VI.   Bilder's Remedies

SUBSTANTIVE ANSWER

I.   Terms of the Contract

The contract between Bilder and Homer is valid. It stipulates that the house must be completed by November 30, and that payment is to be made upon completion. The stated deadline will most likely be construed as a condition precedent to payment of the contract price. A condition precedent is an event which must occur before a party's contractual obligation is due. It must be determined whether the deadline stated is a material part of the contract, and thereby whether time is of the essence. If so, then Homer's obligation to pay the contract price depends upon the performance of the condition precedent — completion by November 30.

II.   Effects of the Court Order

A.   Bilder Breached

Bilder failed to finish the house by the date agreed upon — November 30. If the deadline was a material part of the contract, Bilder's failure to complete the house by this date constituted a breach of the contract.

B.   Temporary Impossibility

Bilder can employ the doctrine of temporary impossibility to contend that his performance should be excused. Where unexpected events occur after the creation of the contract and render performance impossible, then one party's failure to perform its duty may be excused. The injunction made it impossible for Bilder to work on the house for six months.

III.   Effects of Lifting the Court Order

A.   Duty to Build Resumed

Bilder's reliance on the doctrine of temporary impossibility will not free him completely of his contractual duties. If the contingency which renders performance impossible lasts only temporarily, then the party's duty to perform will normally resume after the performance becomes possible again.

B.   Bilder Breached

If the court determines that Bilder was obligated to complete the house after the restraining order was lifted, then Bilder's final refusal constituted a breach of the contract.

IV.   Bilder's Defenses

Bilder may present several defenses. Bilder can argue that the contract should be rescinded, and his duty discharged, because the hardship to him is too great. If performance of an obligation is rendered temporarily impossible by certain conditions, and the obligation is substantially more burdensome when those conditions end than it was initially, the contract may be voided. Bilder's business is small, and he had a full schedule at the time the restraining order was lifted, making the obligation more burdensome for him.

Bilder can further argue that he should be excused from performance on the grounds of commercial impracticability. If unexpected, intervening events caused performance to be extremely costly and inefficient from a commercial standpoint, performance may be excused. Bilder may argue that the court order was unexpected and has disrupted his schedule. Requiring him to perform would be costly for him, resulting in great inefficiency. Courts are very reluctant, however, to excuse performance on this theory.

V.   Homer's Remedies

If Bilder was in breach, then Homer can recover damages at law or request specific performance. The normal measure of damages at law is expectation damages. Homer could recover the difference between the market price and the unpaid contract price, i.e., the cost to him of hiring another contractor to finish the house and the unpaid contract price. If Homer pays the full contract price, then the unpaid amount is zero, and this difference would be $200,000. Therefore he gets $200,000 back from the contract price. This is correct, since it would require $200,000 to complete the house.

Specific performance will be awarded when certain conditions are present. There must be a valid contract, whose terms are definite and certain. The normal legal remedy must be inadequate. Specific performance is often granted when the contract involves a product which is unique in some way. Homer should argue that Bilder's homes represent a unique variety of high-quality residences, and that Homer cannot acquire such a product elsewhere.

Homer is not assured of obtaining this remedy. Specific performance will not be granted if ordinary legal remedies are adequate. Bilder must therefore argue that these damages do compensate Homer adequately. Moreover, specific performance will only be awarded where enforcement of the decree will be feasible for the court. Complex construction contracts are normally considered difficult to enforce. The court may very well refuse this remedy for this reason. Likewise, specific performance will not be granted in contracts for personal services. If the court views Bilder's performance as a personal service, then specific performance will be denied.

VI.   Bilder's Remedies

If the court finds that Bilder is in breach, he cannot recover on the contract. However, he can recover in restitution, or quantum meruit. This measure awards the plaintiff an amount equal to the benefit conferred on the other party. Here, that amount is $100,000, since from Homer's point of view, the half-completed house has a value of $100,000.

If Bilder is excused from performance, then the court may give either restitution, or perhaps reliance damages. These would be calculated according to the cost to Bilder of the unfinished work, $120,000. Courts will normally not award reliance damages if the contract has been rescinded.

TABLE OF AUTHORITIES

Uniform Commercial Code

Restatement (Second) of Contracts

TABLE OF CASES

THE BEST WAY TO LAND A LEGAL JOB:
AN INTERNSHIP

The Experienced Hand

A Student Manual for Making the Most of an Internship

by
Timothy Stanton
Kamil Ali

Sponsored by The National Society for Experiential Education

ernships are the hottest way to get job experience, learn about the legal ofession, and showcase your talents before potential employers. *The Experienced and* is a wonderful guide that will show you how to find an internship and do your st while there. The book contains worksheets to help you evaluate and complish your goals, advice on how to enlist faculty support for academic credit your internship, a sample learning contract, a sample evaluation form, actual se histories, journals, sample letters and resumes. *The Experienced Hand* is a luable resource if you are considering work experience as part of your legal ucation.

EXPERIENCED HAND: A Student Manual for Making the Most of an Internship by Timothy Stanton and Kamil Ali, $11.99

24 Hours!

BLOND'S® LAW GUIDES

PRECISELY WHAT YOU NEED TO KNOW

- **Hanau Charts** Flow charts for organization
- **Case Clips** Facts, issue, and rule for every case
- **Outlines** Concise arrangement of the law
- **Mnemonics** Memory aids and devices

$14.99 per copy, keyed to the following texts:

Administrative Law
Code: 1AL1-AC
Bonfield
Breyer
Gellhorn
Cass
Schwartz
Mashaw

Procedure
Code: 1CP1-AC
Cound
Field
Rosenberg
Hazard

Procedure
Code: 1CP2-AC
Yeazell

Commercial Law
Code: 1CL1-AC
Whaley
Jordan
Farnsworth

Commercial Paper
Code: 1CL1-AC
Whaley
Speidel
Jordan
Farnsworth

Constitutional Law
Code: 1CO1-AC
Brest
Cohen
Ducat
Gunther
Lockhart
Rotunda
Stone

Contracts
Order Code: 1CT1-AC
Dawson
Kessler
Fuller
Murphy
Calamari
Rossett

Contracts
Order Code: 1CT2-AC
Farnsworth 4th Ed.

Contracts
Order Code: 1CT3-AC
Farnsworth 5th Ed.

Corporations
Order Code: 1CP1-AC
Cary
Choper
Hamilton
Henn
Jennings
Solomon
Vagts

Criminal Law
Order Code: 1CR1-AC
Kadish
LaFave
Kaplan
Weinreb
Dix
Johnson
Moenssens

Criminal Procedure
Order Code: 1CP1-AC
Kamisar
Saltzburg
Weinreb/Crim. Proc.
Weinreb/Crim. Just.
Miller

Domestic Relations
Order Code: 1FL1-AC
Areen
Foote
Krause
Wadlington

Evidence
Order Code: 1EV1-AC
McCormick
Green
Weinstein
Kaplan
Cleary

Family Law
Order Code: 1FL1-AC
Areen
Foote
Krause
Wadlington

Income Tax/Corporate
Order Code: 1TC1-AC
Lind
Kahn
Wolfman
Surrey

Income Tax/Personal
Order Code: 1TP1-AC
Klein
Andrews
Surrey
Kragen
Freeland
Graetz

International Law
Order Code: 1IL1-AC
Sweeney
Henkin

Property
Order Code: 1PR1-AC
Browder
Casner
Cribbet

Property
Order Code: 1PR2-AC
Dukeminier

Sales and Secured Transactions
Order Code: 1CL1-AC
Whaley
Speidel
Jordan
Honnold
Farnsworth

Torts
Order Code: 1TR1-AC
Epstein
Keeton
Franklin

Torts
Order Code: 1TR2-AC
Henderson

Torts
Order Code: 1TR3-AC
Wade

ORDER TODAY Books Shipped Within 24 Hours!

SULZBURGER & GRAHAM PUBLISHING
505 Eighth Avenue
New York, NY 10018

800-366-7086

ORDER FORM

Name: _____ Phone: _____

Shipping address: _____ Law School: _____
(No PO Boxes)
_____ Graduation: _____

City/State/Zip: _____

Credit Card #: _____ Expiration: _____

Signature: _____

BLOND'S LAW GUIDES $15.99

___ Torts
___ Torts, Prosser Ed.
___ Torts, Henderson Ed.
___ Property
___ Property, Dukeminier Ed.
___ Evidence
___ Contracts
___ Contracts, Farnsworth Ed.
___ Family Law
___ Income Tax
___ Corporations
___ Criminal Law
___ Civil Procedure
___ Civil Procedure, Yeazell Ed.

___ International Law
___ Constitutional Law
___ Administrative Law
___ Commercial Law
___ Criminal Procedure

BLOND'S ESSAY SERIES $21.99

___ Torts
___ Contracts

BLOND'S MULTIPLE CHOICE $29.99

___ Multistate Questions

BAR EXAM ESSAY $24.99

___ Scoring High On Bar Exam Essays

Shipping Information

)UPS Ground: $3.00 per order
)
)Second Day Air (3 day if ordered late):
)$7.00 first book, $1.00 each additional book

)Next Day Air:
)$10.00 first two books, $3.00 each
)additional book
)Saturday delivery an additional $10.00

Delivery time will vary, based on distance from New York City. Washington/Boston corridor can expect delivery 2 working days after shipment. West Coast should allow 6 working days, unless Second Day or Next Day Air is specified when ordering.

PLEASE MAKE CHECKS AND MONEY ORDERS PAYABLE TO: **SULZBURGER & GRAHAM PUBLISHING**